The Life of a Movement Lawyer

The Life of
a Movement
Lawyer

Lewis Pitts and the Struggle
for Democracy, Equality, and Justice

Jason Langberg

THE UNIVERSITY OF
SOUTH CAROLINA PRESS

© 2024 University of South Carolina

Published by the University of South Carolina Press
Columbia, South Carolina 29208

uscpress.com

Printed in the United States of America

Library of Congress Cataloging-in-Publication Data can be found
at https://lccn.loc.gov/2023057830

ISBN: 978-1-64336-481-0 (hardcover)
ISBN: 978-1-64336-482-7 (ebook)

*To unsung social justice lawyers,
rebellious lawyers, revolutionary lawyers,
radical lawyers, and movement lawyers—
past, present, and future*

It pains me to say it, but justice is a counter-cultural value in our legal profession. Because of that, you cannot be afraid to be different than others in law school or the profession—for unless you are, you cannot be a social justice lawyer.

—William P. Quigley, "Letter to a Law Student Interested in Social Justice" (2007)

There are enough lawyers in this world defending the way things are. Plenty of lawyers protect unjust people and institutions in our social, economic and political systems. Plenty of lawyers work for structures that perpetuate and increase the racism, militarism and materialism in our world. These lawyers are plentiful and well-compensated. True structural and fundamental change will not come by aiming at small revisions or reforms. If we are going to transform our world, we need lawyers willing to work with others toward a radical revolution of our world. We need no more lawyers defending the status quo. We need revolutionaries.

—William P. Quigley, "Revolutionary Lawyering: Addressing the Root Causes of Poverty and Wealth" (2006)

Contents

Preface

I entered The Green Bean, a coffee shop in downtown Greensboro, North Carolina, and sat nervously at an empty table. After ten minutes or so, in walked a five-foot, eight-inch tall, 130-pound, fit, tan, sixty-year-old man sporting a short-sleeved, button-down print shirt, khaki shorts, sandals, a neatly trimmed beard, glasses, and an earring. As he walked toward me, he pointed in my direction and asked with a smile, "Jason?" As soon as I stood to shake his hand, he threw his arms around me and pulled me in for a hug. He enthusiastically said, in a thick, scratchy southern accent, "Hey buddy!" while tightly squeezing me with one arm and firmly slapping my back with the other.

I was a rising second-year law student and aspiring civil rights lawyer for children and youth; he was the managing attorney at Advocates for Children's Services (ACS), a statewide project of Legal Aid of North Carolina (LANC). I was interested in practicing in my home state of North Carolina after graduation and had asked Lewis Pitts to meet me for coffee in his hometown.

My nervousness melted away as Lewis quickly made me feel like we'd been lifelong friends. We talked for hours. His genuine attentiveness, smile, and energy were infectious. He spoke passionately about pressing issues for vulnerable children, connecting those issues to interspersed rants about neoliberalism and capitalism. For the first time since starting law school, I felt inspired and thought perhaps becoming a lawyer wasn't such a terrible decision after all.

In the fall of 2007, I volunteered to write a model appellate brief for Lewis and ACS arguing for a state constitutional right to counsel at public expense for economically disadvantaged public school students facing long-term suspension or expulsion. The following year, Lewis offered me one of LANC's community lawyering postgraduate fellowships to work at ACS. I gladly accepted in early 2009.

Nine months later, I returned to North Carolina, passed the bar exam, and started working with Lewis and ACS's four other staff members. For the next four years, Lewis and I worked side by side on a variety of issues, including funding for public education, individualized services for students with disabilities, and the school-to-prison pipeline.

Lewis treated ACS staff like family—inquiring often about our well-being and loved ones, allowing us into his personal life and home, and joining us for special occasions outside of work. Even though he was decades older and more experienced and accomplished than we were, Lewis welcomed our feedback, valued our opinions, gave us autonomy, and shared leadership opportunities with us. He lacked the territorialism, ego, and braggadocio often exhibited by managers, lawyers, and white men in positions of power.

During our years working together, Lewis and I cocounseled cases, attended conferences and community events, ranted and schemed over meals or drinks, and got to know each other's families. He taught me, and continues to teach me, about the importance of empathy and hope, being driven by love and a personal and professional ethic, work–life balance, the root causes of poverty and inequality, thinking outside the box, movement lawyering, speaking truth to power, acting boldly, and so much more.

When Lewis retired from LANC in January 2014, I stepped into his huge shoes as the head of ACS. However, work wasn't the same without him. Eighteen months later, I moved on as well. Lewis continues to live in Greensboro and advocate for justice; I'm now in Colorado. Despite no longer working together and the physical distance between us, Lewis and I have remained close. We visit each other occasionally and regularly talk by phone, text, and email.

One of the many lessons Lewis instilled in me is the importance of remaining vigilant against what he calls "the virus of despair and pessimism." As immunization against "the virus," he prescribes an abundance of "spiritual Gatorade"—those activities that renew one's hope, recharge one's soul, and energize one's spirit. After the 2016 presidential election, I needed a quadruple dose of spiritual Gatorade and knew others would similarly need help to "stay sane in an insane world," as Lewis likes to say. So, in December 2016, I approached Lewis about writing his biography.

Always humble, quick to deflect praise and credit others, and aware of his privileges, Lewis was reluctant to be the subject of a book. However, he warmed to the idea as we discussed how the book wouldn't be his story alone, but also the stories of his comrades and clients. Lewis describes his career as a pearl necklace, with himself as a string winding through the lives of people— beautiful and unique pearls—who he struggled alongside. This book is intended to highlight the tireless, self-sacrificing struggle that Lewis and many others engaged in against social and economic injustice for more than four decades.

Lewis and I also talked about how the book could be instructive spiritual Gatorade for people fighting injustices similar to those he tackled throughout his career, including right-wing extremist judges, environmental degradation caused by greed and under-regulation, voter suppression, employment discrimination, mental health crises among children, and corrupt and racist policing. I reminded Lewis of what he wrote to me in 2013, when I was extremely anxious about my son being born into a world that can be so cruel:

> No doubt the picture is bleak, and the pain and suffering are rampant. No doubt the change process is shamefully slow, even as the stark injustices are causing most people to rethink their worldviews. But hope is not based on an assessment of the world; it is an orientation of the heart and mind. And shaping that orientation is one of the few things we have control over. We retain, even during the dark hours, the freedom to choose our response to injustice. Given your values, you certainly will not exercise your freedom to become indifferent to the injustice and opportunities to fight back. You will resist; you will retain your dreams, vision, and aspirations.

Eventually, Lewis agreed to the book, writing, "If the stories can keep hope alive, I'm in 100%. All efforts to inspire and pump up activist lawyers and non-lawyer activists are desperately needed during this period of madness." "I hope we help grow empathy and courage, like they were tulips or tomatoes in a greenhouse," he added.

Given my love and admiration for Lewis, and the alignment of our political views, this biography isn't intended to be neutral or objective. However, the stories also aren't fictionalized or dramatized. Every detail is supported by firsthand accounts and other research. Plenty of existing books exaggerate details and sensationalize the lives of famous activists. Among the many reasons why sharing Lewis's story is worthwhile is precisely because he doesn't come from a family of activists or a tragic past; he didn't attend Ivy League schools; he hasn't clerked for a federal or appellate judge, argued cases at the US Supreme Court, or run well-known national organizations; and he hasn't cruised into retirement as a professor or politician. Nevertheless, Lewis has positively impacted thousands upon thousands of lives through hope, empathy, compassion, love, and profound faith in people. If he could do it, so can we.

Abbreviations and Initialisms

ABA	American Bar Association
ACLU	American Civil Liberties Union
ACS	Advocates for Children's Services
ADHD	attention-deficit/hyperactivity disorder
AG	attorney general
ALJ	administrative law judge
ARC	alcohol rehabilitation center
ASFA	Adoption and Safe Families Act
ASLB	Atomic Safety and Licensing Board
BATF	Bureau of Alcohol, Tobacco, and Firearms
BCC	Beloved Community Center
BEST	Best Educational Support Team
CASE	Citizens' Action for Safe Energy
CCI	Central Correctional Institution
CEO	chief executive officer
CIA	Central Intelligence Agency
CIS	Christic Institute South
CLA	Carolina Legal Assistance
CP&L	Carolina Power & Light
CUNY	City University of New York
CWP	Communist Workers Party
DA	district attorney
DFS	Division of Family Services
DHS	Department of Human Services
DOJ	US Department of Justice
DSS	Department of Social Services
EEOC	Equal Employment Opportunity Commission
EPSDT	Early and Periodic Screening, Diagnostic, and Treatment
FBI	Federal Bureau of Investigation
GAL	guardian ad litem

GCRF	Greensboro Civil Rights Fund
GJF	Greensboro Justice Fund
GOP	Grand Old Party
GPD	Greensboro Police Department
GROW	Grassroots Organizing Workshop
GTRC	Greensboro Truth and Reconciliation Commission
GTCRP	Greensboro Truth and Community Reconciliation Project
HEAL	Health, Education, and Advocacy Link
HB	House Bill
IRS	Internal Revenue Service
KCC	Keysville Concerned Citizens
KKK	Ku Klux Klan
LANC	Legal Aid of North Carolina
LAP	Legal Action Project
LME	local management entity
LSC	Legal Services Corporation
LSNC	Legal Services of North Carolina
MHU	mental health unit
NAACP	National Association for the Advancement of Colored People
NC WARN	North Carolina Waste Awareness and Reduction Network
NCRA	National Child Rights Alliance
NCRC	National Committee for the Rights of the Child
NLG	National Lawyers Guild
NOW	National Organization for Women
NRC	US Nuclear Regulatory Commission
NSC	National Security Council
NVRI	National Voting Rights Institute
PACA	People Allied for Child Advocacy
PATH	People Are Treated Human
PRTF	psychiatric residential treatment facility
PSO	Public Service Company of Oklahoma
PTSD	posttraumatic stress disorder
RICO	Racketeer Influenced and Corrupt Organizations
ROTC	Reserve Officers' Training Corps
SAC	State Advisory Council
SBI	State Bureau of Investigation
SCHIP	State Children's Health Insurance Program
SCLC	Southern Christian Leadership Conference

SJI	Southern Justice Institute
SMART	Selma Movement against Racial Tracking
SRS	Savannah River Site
TMI	Three Mile Island
TRO	temporary restraining order
UMWA	United Mine Workers of America
UN	United Nations
UNCG	University of North Carolina at Greensboro
US	United States
USC	University of South Carolina
WVO	Workers Viewpoint Organization

Chronology

1947–1957	Clinton, South Carolina
1957–1966	Bethune, South Carolina
1966–1970	Wofford College
1970–1973	University of South Carolina School of Law
1973–1976	Richland County Public Defender's Office
1976–1978	The Law Offices of Warren and Pitts
1978–1980	Antinuclear Movement
1980–1985	Christic Institute
1985–1992	Christic Institute South
1992–1994	Southern Justice Institute; and Legal Action Project (National Committee for the Rights of the Child)
1994–1996	Carolina Legal Assistance
1996–2000	Mental Health Unit (Legal Services North Carolina)
2000–2014	Advocates for Children's Services (Legal Aid of North Carolina)
2014–Retirement	

Introduction

Lewis Pitts has been, at his core, a social justice movement lawyer since 1978—albeit not always by more refined and rigorous current definitions. After spending the first five years of his career as a public defender and partner in a two-person law firm, he spent the next sixteen years embedded in multiple movements: the antinuclear movement, movements for racial justice, and a movement to protect abused and neglected children. Even after external forces pushed him into working in legal aid offices, with limitations that accompany federal funding, for the last two decades of his career, Lewis remained determined to infuse movement lawyering into his work. Now, even in retirement and after having publicly resigned from the North Carolina State Bar, he continues to engage in movement work. Throughout it all, he has had a deep understanding of and a keen sense of how to use the flaws and limitations of the law and legal system for social change; a burning desire for lasting, systemic, radical change; and a profound love for and sense of solidarity with marginalized and oppressed communities. He's among the precious few lawyers who truly view their own liberation as bound with the liberation of those most impacted by injustice.

At the time Lewis evolved into a "movement lawyer," the term was nebulous, uncommon, or unheard of to most, including to Lewis and his comrades. In fact, he never recalled hearing the phrase until the latter half of his career. He didn't have access to the movement lawyering literature, courses, training, and mentoring that exist today. Movement lawyering is an increasingly popular concept among public interest attorneys and legal scholars. Compared to a decade or two ago, movement lawyering is more often part of organizations' mission statements or articulated strategies, the focus of law school courses and clinics, and the subject of law review articles.

Movement lawyering is simple in aims and complex in means. It supports and advances social movements that are led by those most directly impacted, focuses on building and exercising collective power, and aims at achieving systemic change. The approach is based on principles of autonomy, self-determination, solidarity, and liberation, and a recognition that lasting social change is the result of social movements, not litigation. Thus, communities, not movement lawyers, identify grievances, demands, strategies, tactics, and solutions.

Movement lawyers are Swiss Army knives for communities, not hammers looking for nails. They see themselves as partners, not dictators; comrades, not elites. They work alongside impacted communities, both with respect to legal tactics and other movement work, including, for example, leadership development, community education and outreach, strategic communications, campaign development, investigations and research, drafting and advocating for legislation or policies, and infrastructure and institution building.

Movement lawyers approach communities with respect, politeness, persistence, humility, hope, joy, and love. They listen and learn and develop an understanding of a community's cultures, values, concerns, beliefs, and ideas. They are aware of and examine their own privileges, cultural views, stereotypes, and overgeneralizations. They are comfortable with uncertainty, conflict, chaos, criticism, and being uncomfortable. They are flexible, creative, innovative, and accountable to communities.

Additionally, movement lawyers recognize the limitations of the legal system, understand that the law is a tool and not a solution, and are committed to justice, not the law. However, they also understand that litigation can be a useful tactic because of its potential to raise public consciousness, provoke public debate, build confidence among nonlawyer advocates, energize movements, and create coercive disruption, costs, and negative publicity for adversaries. For movement lawyers, litigation is an organizing opportunity, courtrooms are political venues, legal processes are just as important as legal outcomes, and the ultimate goal isn't to win a lawsuit but rather to achieve organizing objectives and build power.

The Life of a Movement Lawyer follows one lawyer's unlikely and unconventional path to becoming a movement lawyer, the successes and challenges he experienced as a movement lawyer, and his determination to continue movement lawyering as a legal aid attorney and retired nonlawyer.

Part I of this book describes how Lewis went from being raised in a white, middle-class, Christian bubble in rural South Carolina, surrounded by and involved in racism and ignorant of civil rights movements across the country, to being interested in public service and a career in law at the end of college, to being a law school graduate who was committed to public interest law. Part I then details the first five years of his legal career—three as a public defender and two as a partner in a two-person law firm.

Part II chronicles the sixteen years Lewis spent as a movement lawyer, first for the antinuclear movement, then for racial justice movements, and finally for a children's rights movement. It also includes a chapter about Lewis's detour to work on a Racketeer Influenced and Corrupt Organizations (RICO) Act lawsuit against retired military and Central Intelligence Agency (CIA) leaders, drug kingpins, arms dealers, mercenaries, and other anti-communist extremists allegedly responsible for a bombing in Nicaragua, among other crimes. Part II concludes with how legal, political, and financial pressures pushed Lewis out of full-time movement lawyering.

Part III discusses Lewis's return to a more traditional, and often less radical, practice setting—this time, legal aid. It traces his two decades spent advocating for services for people with mental health needs and for children, while trying to infuse movement lawyering concepts into his work. Part III also recounts how Lewis was drawn back into movement lawyering, including pro bono work on an election finance reform movement and an antiwar movement. Finally, it details Lewis's retirement and resignation from the North Carolina State Bar.

The Life of a Movement Lawyer is based on extensive research, including interviews and correspondence with more than a hundred individuals who have been part of Lewis's life; his diary, correspondence, yearbooks, academic transcripts, military and state bar records, and other personal materials; contents in special collections at various universities and libraries; oral histories; thousands of newsletter, newspaper, magazine, and journal articles; case files, trial transcripts, and court opinions; extensive organizational records; and other sources, including books, videos, maps, speeches, websites, press releases, government records, and photographs.

This book is a tribute to Lewis Pitts and his career. It's also meant to be spiritual Gatorade for readers. However, the principal goal of the pages that follow is to inspire the next generation of social justice movement lawyers.

PART I

The Making of a Movement Lawyer

(1947–1978)

CHAPTER I

Childhood and College

From the time of his birth on December 12, 1947, until he graduated college in 1970, Pascal Lewis Pitts Jr., "Lewis," had a clear path to a relatively easy, prosperous life. The white son of loving, college-educated, Christian, middle-class parents, he had the privilege, social capital, and opportunities to become a prominent community member, carrying on family and southern traditions.

Lewis's mother, Martha Arlevia Wood Pitts, came from a long line of preachers and grew up in Methodist parsonages throughout South Carolina. In 1943, she graduated from Columbia College, a Methodist liberal arts college for women, and moved to Clinton, South Carolina. She taught "Bible" in Clinton Public Schools and Sunday school at Broad Street Methodist Church. She was also president of the Woman's Society of Christian Service at the church, recording secretary of the Clinton Music Club, a member of the Clinton Garden Club, and active in the Parent-Teacher Association at Florida Street Elementary School. She was an avid reader and enjoyed cooking and sewing.

Lewis's father, Pascal Lewis Pitts Sr., earned a degree in textile chemistry from Clemson University and then returned to his hometown of Clinton. Lewis Sr.'s mother was a homemaker and raised her seven children; his father had various occupations, including farmer and small-business owner. Lewis Sr. owned and operated Pitts Meat Market. In his free time, he rode his motorcycle, played golf, and volunteered at church. "Momma" and "Daddy," as Lewis called them, married in June 1946.

The Pittses called Clinton—then a mill town of approximately seven thousand residents—home for the first decade of Lewis's life. For the first three years, they occupied the first floor of a two-story boarding house. Lewis's autobiography, self-published in elementary school, read, "The people who lived upstairs in our apartment like me very much. They would come and play with me and they taught me to walk and eat beans."

In 1950, soon after the birth of Lewis's brother, Paul, the family moved onto family-owned land on the edge of town. Daddy and two of his brothers, Billy and Fred, built adjacent brick homes atop a hill. Upon that hill, Lewis learned the value of a close-knit, loving community.

Billy, his wife, Louise, and their two children, "Billy Boy" and Dianne, lived on one side of Lewis and his family. Billy ran the town's tractor store. Lewis swears that Uncle Billy made Billy Boy and Dianne swig castor oil at the end of every summer in order to "clear their systems" and "tune them up" before the new school year.

Fred, his wife, Katrine, and their daughter, Eleanor, lived on the other side of Lewis and his family. Fred worked at the Texaco service station and was a rowdy, cigar-smoking heavy drinker who died of liver disease.

Lewis recalled, "It was pretty neat—three brothers and their wives and children, all on a hill, sharing meals and a farming-type orientation. Cool breezes would blow at night. The red clay would be a mess when it rained. The cows would bellow."

Two of Daddy's other brothers and his sister also lived in Clinton. Earl ran Pitts Vegetable Market. Charles owned and operated Pitts Service Station and Coal Company. Fay was a teacher who'd serve on the Clinton City Council. Daddy's fifth brother, Harold, was an electrical engineer in Greensboro, North Carolina.

Momma's only sibling, Paul Wood, lived in Camden, South Carolina, just ninety-five miles away. He practiced obstetrics and gynecology for thirty-five years, reportedly delivering 6,840 babies.

Soon after Momma and Daddy had their third child, Margaret, in 1952, Martha's mother, Bessie Reasonover Wood, "Gram," moved in with the Pittses. Gram helped with childcare and cooking. She baked "some mighty fine sweet, doughy, biscuit-type things called 'stickies,'" Lewis recollected.

Daddy's mother, Lydie Eron Simpson Pitts, "MaMa," lived in a large house beside Lewis's elementary school. Lewis reminisced about Chic Ray's, a tiny corner store near MaMa's house: "This store, as I recall, existed for the sole purpose of selling candies and goodies to the school children passing by daily. For a nickel you could buy an unbelievable amount of candy. If having your grandma's house and a candy store right beside the school you attend every day isn't a piece of heaven, I don't know what is."

Large family gatherings took place at MaMa's house, with southern cooking and ice-cold sweet tea aplenty. Her Black maid, Henrietta, worked wonders in the kitchen. After the gluttony, Daddy and his brothers retired to couches and an easy chair in the living room. Their cacophony of snoring would eventually drown out the ticking of the pendulum clock on the mantel.

Lewis had an idyllic childhood on the family land, which included pastures, woods, creeks, farm animals, and a barn. He and Paul spent most of their time pretending to be cowboys. They wrote to Santa Claus, "We are two fine little boys, ages two and five. Please bring each of us a gun and holster, a cowboy suit and hat, and whatever surprises you can." Nearly every Saturday morning, after watching *Howdy Doody*, they joined Billy Boy to ride the families' horses, Blackie and Dick. They played "cowboys and Indians," leaping over ditches, sprinting through meadows, and hiding behind trees as they pursued or evaded one another.

Lewis, Paul, and Billy Boy treated the families' two-story barn as their clubhouse. There, they played tag and hide-and-seek and mimicked Tarzan, swinging down from the loft. During storms, they'd lay atop hay bales, a piece of straw in their mouths, talking and listening to the sweet music that rain played on the tin roof. Lewis shared, "The sensations and memories of these experiences can't be conveyed adequately by words. It's more like feelings, music, and poetry, flowing 'ever gentle on my mind,' as Glen Campbell's song put it."

The rambunctious boys also enjoyed chasing farm animals, including the cows and pigs Daddy raised and slaughtered to sell at his market. Lewis wrote, "While we were repeatedly instructed not to chase the cattle because it'd make their meat tough, we did it anyway. Just like a rodeo. What thrills and fun!" He reflected on helping Daddy round up cows: "I was about as big as a minute. I'd stake off my turf, hold my hands out, and prevent cows from passing by waving my arms and loudly shouting cowboy-like phrases, such as 'get back now,' 'hey now, cow,' and 'get 'em up.'" Lewis believes the cow wrangling prepared him to play linebacker in high school, despite weighing 130 pounds.

Lewis tagged along with Daddy and Daddy's friend Tan Ray to animal auctions. While returning home with cows and pigs in the truck bed, Tan Ray would playfully squeeze Lewis's leg, just above the knee, until Lewis, unable to withstand the pain any longer, shouted the magic words—"calf rope!"

Lewis's sixth-grade autobiography provides other highlights from life in Clinton:

> When I played, I had two imaginary friends, Ken and Bubba. We had a very good time playing.

Every week, a garbage truck would come and get trash. It would make a lot of noise. So, I decided I would be a garbage man. . . .

I went to kindergarten for a year. We would have an activity period and Tommy Johnson would always want to wrestle with me. He would win most of the time. . . .

In the second grade my teacher was Mrs. Young. We started having science. I liked it and wanted to be a scientist or a doctor. . . . I would ask questions she didn't know the answer to. She would get very mad at me.

Miss Gary was my third-grade teacher. She was an old lady, but very sweet.

In July 1957, Lewis and his immediate family moved 110 miles east to Bethune, South Carolina, because Daddy had accepted a job there as a foreperson at the Kendall Company's new textile finishing plant. Lewis said Bethune was "a town of about 600, including indoor pets." He was sad to leave Billy Boy and the family land in Clinton, but still visited often.

In Bethune, the Pittses rented a small home until Lewis's other sister, Helen, was born in 1959. Then, Daddy borrowed money from the family's doctor back in Clinton to build a house. Momma and Daddy didn't want or need much material wealth. Helen wrote, "Momma said the bank would call, on occasion, to say that they were about to be overdrawn." Greg Brown's song, "Cheapest Kind," comes to mind when Lewis thinks of his parents.

In addition to working at the plant, Daddy was president of the local Lions Club. Momma taught in the Kershaw County schools, tutored adults who were learning to read, was a member of the Woman's Club of Bethune, and served on the Kershaw County Library Board. Together, they volunteered through their new church, Bethel United Methodist.

In 1960, Lewis graduated from Bethune Elementary School as class president. He then attended Bethune Middle/High School, where he earned As and Bs, had perfect attendance most years, and rarely misbehaved. An "agonizing moral issue" for Lewis was whether to allow friends to copy his answers on tests. A demerit for talking in study hall was an "emotional crisis." Lewis's teachers were Momma's coworkers and church friends in their small town; so, in his words, "getting caught would've been a personal and family disaster."

Lewis participated in Future Farmers of America, Beta Club, and student council. He also played football as quarterback, safety, and linebacker; baseball as first baseman; and basketball as a five-foot, eight-inch center. Lewis's

classmates voted him "Most Athletic" and coaches selected him as "the most valuable senior boy in athletics." Lewis's sisters described him as a "little big fish in a small pond." His graduating class had twenty-four students, some of whom drove the school buses. His friend and teammate Doug Mays, "Skipper," described Lewis as a leader and motivator, with "a heart that was a lot bigger than his physical body." Mays remembered Lewis's work ethic and hustle, saying that he "always gave one hundred percent," "was like a little water bug all over the place," and "would be going crazy, like his pants were on fire." Mays chuckled as he recalled Lewis, "already jacked up" at 5:45 A.M., picking him up in the Pitts's old Plymouth sedan for two-a-day football practices. When the team ran laps, Lewis always finished first, despite being the only player who never cut corners. Teammates jokingly reminded Lewis that he didn't "always have to be a hero," Mays recollected.

During summers, Lewis played sports, rode bicycles, went on an annual family vacation to the beach, attended church camp, and frequented lakes, swimming holes, and public pools. At the Big Springs community pool, he was enamored with Duane Eddy, a country music singer whose twangy songs blared from the jukebox.

Lewis was also a boy scout outside of school, literally and figuratively. He achieved the second-highest Boy Scouts of America rank attainable—Life. He didn't curse, drink, use drugs, or fight. He wouldn't even consume carbonated drinks because "they'd mess up your wind for sports," he explained. He attended church with his family on Wednesdays and twice on Sundays. He had only one girlfriend, Jessica Davis, who was voted "Miss Bethune High School." His childhood friend Bennie Copeland said Lewis was "straight as an arrow but fun loving."

At a young age, Lewis's friends and family recognized many of the traits that Momma and Daddy instilled in him and that'd make him an effective advocate in adulthood. Mays described Lewis as "one of the good guys" who'd "put you ahead of himself," and as never negative, whiny, or angry. Helen remembered that Lewis was especially kind to Bobby Kelly, a fellow teenager with special needs who was the manager for the football and basketball teams. Helen wrote, "I adored [Lewis]. He was and is a loving and kind big brother. . . . He's compassionate and truly one of the kindest people I know. Always fighting for the underdog. Big into family. Sentimental, soft-hearted. He has always been gentle and kind. . . . Give you the shirt off his back kinda guy." Lewis's brother shared similar sentiments: "He was and has always been . . . loving, caring, sharing, supporting." Paul added, "Lewis is always on the lookout for any rose-colored glasses he can find. He then buys every pair and hands them out as needed."

Momma and Daddy weren't activists or very politically active; however, they provided Lewis the foundation on which he built a life dedicated to public service. They taught him, through words and deeds, the importance of hard work, dependability, community engagement and service, and a strong moral compass. Perhaps more important, Momma and Daddy modeled goodness and gentleness. They loved their children dearly and often told them so. Lewis wrote, "I was so damn lucky to have had them both fully in my life. They gave me the foundational values of caring and loving others, empathy, and 'an injury to one is an injury to all.'"

Racism

As much of the country was in the midst of civil rights movements and social revolution, Clinton and Bethune remained free of marches, sit-ins, and boycotts and firmly entrenched in the Jim Crow status quo. Martin, Malcolm, and Medgar; Huey, Bobby, and Stokely; Rosa, Ella, and Fannie Lou—they were all strangers to Lewis. A profile of Lewis in the *Robeson County Leader*, in 1989, read, "There was a time when [Lewis] was not too aware of social injustice. Growing up in the rural calm of Bethune, South Carolina in the 1950s and 1960s, a child of the Southern middle class, he . . . never spent much time wondering why the black maid always rode in the back seat of the family car when his mother returned her to the other side of town."

In fact, Lewis didn't know, until recently, that his ancestors bought and sold enslaved people. Likewise, he only recently learned that, in 1933, male relatives of his father were involved in, if not the leaders of, a mob that kidnapped, badly beat, and lynched Norris Dendy after he argued with and struck a white man. Dendy was part of Clinton's most prominent Black family at the time. He worked as a businessman and truck driver, and his wife ran a grocery store. Together, they had five children, the youngest of which was five months old at the time Dendy was murdered.

Lewis at least recalls being exposed, as a child, to racism and white supremacy, even if he didn't fully understand or find it offensive at the time. The Ku Klux Klan (KKK) was active in areas where he grew up. In fact, a KKK headquarters was located in Laurens, South Carolina, just nine miles west of Clinton. In October 1957, when Lewis was nine years old, the Klan held two meetings, including cross burnings, in Clinton that drew more than four hundred attendees. He also remembered witnessing a roadside KKK cross burning while traveling with his family.

As a student, Lewis was aware that his public schools were completely segregated. Despite living in areas with significant Black populations, Lewis didn't have a Black classmate until the start of his senior year in 1965—more than a decade after *Brown v. Board of Education* was decided. Moreover, his high school newspaper was the *Dixie Cat*—a combination of Dixiecrat and wildcat, the school's mascot. Lewis's classmates and teachers hung a Confederate flag along the side of their bus during a field trip to Washington, DC, where they excitedly posed for photographs with their US senator and infamous bigot, Strom Thurmond. Next to Lewis in his senior class photo are two students holding a Confederate flag; the caption reads, "LEST WE FORGET." The one Black student in the senior class, John Mungo, whose family was responsible for integrating the school, speculated that he was purposely excluded from the photo.

Lewis also engaged in two racist acts that he can recall—both of which felt harmless to him at the time but caused him to feel tremendous shame and regret as an adult. First, Lewis and the other football team tri-captains, during their senior year, painted "KKK" on part of a bedsheet, which they hung from Bethune's water tower, and "Ku Klux Klan Rides Again" on the other part of the bedsheet, which they strung across the main street, from Piggly Wiggly to Western Auto. One of the tri-captains recalled that, unbeknownst to the boys at the time, the KKK was having a big rally about fifteen miles away during that same weekend. Afterward, Lewis drove down Main Street to admire their work; however, a police officer was already removing the sheet. The officer lifted the sheet so Lewis could nervously travel underneath. The officer recognized the car and alerted Momma and Daddy. Upon arriving home, Lewis immediately confessed to his parents. The next day, Daddy and Bethune's mayor, who attended the same church as the Pittses, ordered the boys to climb the water tower to remove the remaining sheet. Lewis's friend Sonny Garner, whose father ran Bethune's grocery store, told Lewis that the prank caused Black residents to stock up on groceries in order to avoid being out later when the Klan arrived.

The second incident occurred in 1966, during the summer after Lewis graduated high school, when he was working construction at Daddy's plant. For $1.25 an hour, Lewis moved tile, poured concrete, and shoveled dirt in extreme heat. He said the experience was "a nightmare of drudgery and exploitation," and wrote:

I got to listen to the mostly African American labor crew tell their stories of women, wine, and living on job sites. I learned about hard physical labor, injury, finding your work boots on Monday morning, and other stuff of blues and country songs.

I remember one very old, small, African American man on our crew. We were forced to wear hardhats. But, one day, when the old man wasn't wearing his, a cement block fell and hit him on the head. . . . The site boss man—a short, white man with a big belly—yelled at the old man for not wearing a hardhat and being injured. It broke my heart. As limited as my perspective was, I still had a sense that the old man's life had been a struggle. I learned about worker "alienation," to use Marx's term I learned later.

One day, a young, white plumber's assistant approached Lewis about buying a raffle ticket for a Ford Mustang. Lewis bought a ticket, even though he knew all proceeds were going to benefit the KKK.

Lewis doesn't believe that he inherited bigotry from his parents or recall ever feeling animosity toward Black people. So, he believes the sheets prank and raffle ticket purchase were the products of unconscious bias, ignorance, adolescence, and the infectious culture of racism and white supremacy in rural South Carolina. Lewis reflected, "Holy shit, what an ideological cesspool; so glad I emerged from it."

Wofford College

In September 1966, Lewis matriculated at Wofford College, a private, Methodist institution in Spartanburg, South Carolina. Wofford was, in Lewis's words, "an all-male school for white guys who wanted to just be mid-level establishment people." Indeed, the college admitted its first Black student just two years earlier. Wofford gave Lewis a "King Teen Scholarship," which was awarded to "South Carolina male high school seniors who [were] nominated by their classmates as possessing outstanding qualities of character, scholarship and leadership." Lewis didn't consider applying to other colleges because attending Wofford "was just what you did if you were a respectable young man in South Carolina," he explained.

Lewis began college aspiring to become a doctor like his uncle Paul, who had attended Wofford. As a kid, when his sister Helen had a minor injury, Lewis would put on his toy stethoscope and announce, "I'm Dr. Pitts and am here to make it better." However, at Wofford, he didn't study much; instead, he focused on sports, drinking, women, and road trips with the "Space Cowboys"—the name, adapted from a Steve Miller Band song, that he and his friends gave themselves. So, after just one semester, Lewis changed his major to English.

Bennie Copeland said Lewis "broke loose" in college and would get "drunk as a skunk" and in "bar room brawls." Lewis recalls two fights, both of which involved him being "pretty pickled" at "beer joints." The first involved a Marine making fun of Lewis's facial hair and calling him a "hippy." The second involved Lewis rudely demanding a beer from a bartender, and then promptly being whacked on the head with a slap jack and encircled by guys who kicked and pounded him. Lewis joked that after the latter incident, he chose to redirect his fighting toward injustice.

During the school year, Lewis also played intramural sports and worked part-time leading youth activities at the YMCA and loading trucks at a warehouse. He spent his first and third summer breaks working as a laborer for construction companies in Camden and Florence, respectively. During the summer of 1968, he assisted mechanics who repaired looms in a textile mill. He handed them tools and materials as they weaved through loud machines and cotton dust. He also scrubbed looms in the oppressive summer heat. On breaks, Lewis and the mechanics sat in a bathroom, which they referred to as "the shithouse," smoking cigarettes. He wrote about these summer jobs, "They taught me the value and hardship of blue-collar work, and about 'payday nights and painted women,' as the Jerry Lee Lewis song goes. I learned respect for working people and their hardships—Monday morning blues, being hot as hell and dirty, short lunches, and getting up early."

Paul joined his brother at Wofford in 1968. They hitchhiked back and forth between Bethune and Spartanburg, until Lewis bought a beat-up Volkswagen Beetle with thirty-five horsepower, a pillowcase for a gas cap, and a belt holding down the hood.

The most significant development during Lewis's time at Wofford was his burgeoning open-mindedness, freethinking, and progressiveness, which he attributes to "thinking friends" from bigger cities, beginning to smoke marijuana, and reading the works of philosophers Bertrand Russell and Will Durant. Lewis was, as he likes to say, "born, raised, and miseducated in South Carolina." He reflected, "I didn't think in high school or the first two years of college. What a wasted opportunity. Will Durant taught me, 'The only permanent happiness is the pursuit of knowledge and the joy of understanding.'"

"Wofford was the place and time that really opened Lewis's eyes to life beyond small town South Carolina," Paul shared. Helen recalled, "At Wofford, Lewis grew his hair long and that bothered Daddy. Daddy told him, 'Don't come home 'til you cut our hair!' But Momma took up for Lewis and made Daddy rescind his command." Steve Swearingen, Lewis's closest friend among the Space Cowboys, wrote, "I think Lewis really started developing his passion for fairness and justice in his last years at Wofford."

Wofford required students to attend church twice a week; otherwise, Lewis stopped voluntarily going to church. Two decades later, a *Robeson County Leader* article read, "Religion was an indispensable key to the process of [Lewis's] development, although Pitts, the grandson of a Methodist minister, admits to rebelling against the established church during his college days. 'But when you peel away the form and the hypocrisy of the church to the essence, which is to love all people, treat them fairly, and deal with their suffering—well, my mom and dad did a good job of giving me that message,' he said."

Surprisingly, at least in retrospect, Lewis participated in US Army Reserve Officers' Training Corps (ROTC) throughout college. He explained that joining ROTC was the norm for men who weren't on college varsity sports teams, and that ROTC paid participating upperclassmen. According to Lewis, ROTC at Wofford typically involved marching to "left, left, left, right, left" and to call and response songs; disassembling, cleaning, and reassembling rifles; instruction about military history and other topics; and once a week, wearing a buttoned-up uniform, tie, shiny dress shoes, and polished brass buttons and collar pins. The only aspect he enjoyed was the athletic activities, such as traversing monkey bars, throwing grenades, and running while wearing boots. The only useful takeaway from ROTC for Lewis, other than money, was the "Five Ps" mantra he learned—"proper planning prevents poor performance"—which he later applied to trial preparation.

Lewis's Vietnam War draft lottery number wasn't pulled during college. However, he signed a six-year military service commitment in fall 1968 and was on track to graduate as an Army Reserve second lieutenant in spring 1970. During summer 1969, he attended six weeks of mandatory basic training at Fort Bragg. The emphasis was on, in Lewis's words, "killing, and avoiding being killed by, 'gooks,'" a racial slur for east and southeast Asian people. The only upside of basic training, he said, was exposure to racial minorities. His closest friends in Fort Bragg were two Hispanic cadets. During their only day of leave, the three of them went to the beach and "drank all the beer they could," Lewis recalled. He also distinctly remembered getting lost on a compass training course with a Black cadet. Lewis wrote, "I ran out of water in my canteen, and he offered me a drink from his. I was a bit freaked out to drink after him—having never shared food or drink with an African American person—but did so out of need. He was the better man no doubt."

However, even before basic training, Lewis had begun rethinking his future. Deployment to Vietnam was a real possibility. Although he wasn't an antiwar activist yet, Lewis had a mushrooming disdain for violence and US foreign policy and wanted a way out of the Army.

Lewis was interested in law as a career path because, during his junior year, he enjoyed an internship with South Carolina Attorney General (AG) Daniel McLeod in which he conducted legal research, sat in on meetings, and prepared talking points for speeches. Additionally, Lewis believed that the law could be used for good and that pursuing a respectable profession, such as being a lawyer, would please Momma and Daddy. Heading into his final year of college, Lewis had narrowed his postgraduate plans to three options: immediately join the Army as a second lieutenant; reject a second lieutenant post and risk being drafted and deployed to Vietnam anyway; or pursue a deferment to attend law school.

CHAPTER 2

Law School and the
Public Defender's Office

Lewis applied to one law school—the University of South Carolina (USC)—because he was confident that he'd be admitted and it was affordable, near his parents, and where his first cousin once removed coached the freshman football team. He didn't consider applying to law schools that were more prestigious or well known for public interest law, mostly because his plans for law school and a career weren't well formulated and he knew little about schools outside of South Carolina.

After being accepted to USC, he secured an education deferment of active duty in exchange for agreeing to be an Army second lieutenant after law school. Having served two years in ROTC at Wofford after signing a six-year service commitment, he'd have four additional years in the military after graduating from USC.

In May 1970, Lewis moved to Cayce, a Columbia suburb. That summer before law school, he worked as a lifeguard and the youth director at Forest Lake Country Club, which, per its deed, remained all-white until 2017.

During law school, Lewis lived in a used mobile home that his parents had bought and loaned him. He planted the two-bedroom, ten-feet wide and forty-feet long trailer in a mobile home park six miles from the school. Lewis's bedroom had just enough space for a twin-size bed. Sonny Garner, Lewis's high school classmate, rented the larger bedroom for two years.

Their neighbors were mostly male USC undergraduates and other young men. David and Frank lived next door to Lewis and Garner. David was known as "Quack" on account of the way he moved his neck like a duck while chugging beer. Frank introduced Lewis to playing guitar and cooking beef heart and sold Lewis his Triumph Bonneville motorcycle for $200. Garner fondly remembered drinking cheap beer with Lewis and the neighbors, and "staying in hot water" with the property owner for being boisterous and blocking the street while playing basketball. Garner described Lewis as a serious student who "worked hard and played hard" and was "popular with the ladies" because, in part, they thought he "looked like Jesus Christ." Lewis wrote, "I was riding a motorcycle, drinking, dating lots, and having a blast."

Amidst the fun, Lewis began his forty-year journey as a public interest lawyer. During his first year of law school, he befriended Professor Jon Thames. Lewis participated in Thames's clinic, which was one of the first law school clinics in the country dedicated to representing youth in delinquency cases. Sporting long hair and a beard, Lewis rode his motorcycle into public housing and other low-income communities to meet with clients and their families. He said the motorcycle earned him "cool points" among the youths. Lewis met with clients in their homes to better understand them and their lives, which, in turn, enabled him to more effectively humanize them and contextualize their conduct for prosecutors and judges. The clinic was especially exciting for Lewis because his participation came on the heels of a series of US Supreme Court cases that strengthened due process for juveniles—specifically, *Kent* in 1966 (establishing minimum due process for youth waived to the adult criminal system), *Gault* in 1967 (establishing minimum due process for juvenile delinquency proceedings), and *Winship* in 1970 (establishing that juveniles have a due process right to "proof beyond a reasonable doubt" in delinquency and criminal proceedings).

As a law student, Lewis also helped form the Petigru Society, a public interest student organization. Lewis and his fellow members worked to increase enrollment of Black students in the law school and engaged in pro bono work (i.e., legal work donated for the public good), including for Hospital Workers' Union No. 1199, the American Civil Liberties Union (ACLU), and the National Welfare Rights Organization. Lewis's law school classmate Mark Tanenbaum remembered him as a "gentle soul" who "remained true" to his "leftie" values.

In February 1972, Lewis began clerking in the Richland County Public Defender's Office. The office was established in 1966, as a pilot project on the heels of the US Supreme Court decisions in *Gideon v. Wainwright* in 1963 (holding that criminal defendants who cannot pay for their own lawyer are entitled to a state-appointed attorney on their behalf) and *Miranda v. Arizona* in 1966 (holding that individuals subjected to a custodial interrogation must be told, among other rights, that they have the right to the presence of an attorney and that, if they cannot afford an attorney, one will be appointed for them). As a clerk, Lewis observed trials, handled preliminary hearings, and hung around seasoned defense attorneys. He zealously advocated for his clients, which some judges perceived as an affront to traditional decorum and their authority—a tendency that'd continue throughout Lewis's career. For example, he recalled:

> I fussed with the judge over some point of law—likely dealing with the constitutional rights of poor folks. The judge had me put in a holding cell until the end of probable cause hearings that day. . . . I was proud of doing what a lawyer is supposed to do—provide vigorous advocacy. I didn't act rudely or try to pick a fight, but I knew I was right. I wasn't in the cell for long, but there was that feeling of being physically subjected to the will and power of some "official" who could and did act arbitrarily. That's a frightening thought. It certainly can "chill" advocacy if there isn't a powerful counterforce upholding the legitimate adversarial nature of the proceedings.

After that experience, Lewis began stashing a toothbrush and handkerchief in his back pocket whenever he went to court—just in case he was jailed for contempt again. His mother taught him about the usefulness of handkerchiefs and that "to forget a handkerchief is as bad as forgetting to floss."

Susan Johnson

During his second year of law school, Lewis visited his cousin, an assistant state AG, at work. In the copy room, a twenty-year-old secretary caught Lewis's eye. Susan Johnson worked at a state program that administered federal grants to law enforcement agencies. Lewis struck up a conversation with her.

Not long after Lewis and Johnson began dating, Garner moved out of Lewis's trailer, and she moved in. Both were outgoing, joyful, and from small South Carolina towns. He found her to be genuine, caring, and attractive. Garner described Johnson as "a sweetheart; real friendly and bubbly." Lewis had a motorcycle; she had a sports car. They'd often take road trips to the mountains or beaches and occasionally to a nudist camp outside of Columbia. Once they strapped a tent to the handlebars of Lewis's motorcycle and rode fourteen hours roundtrip to the Grand Ole Opry in Nashville, which Lewis called the "Redneck Mecca." "He swept me off my feet and won my heart," Johnson recalled.

Conscientious Objector

As the end of law school neared, Lewis again sought to avoid military service. Three years after his deferment, he was even more opposed to war and US foreign policy. Nearly sixty thousand Americans had already died in Vietnam. Moreover, he had fallen in love with Johnson and didn't want to be away from her. So, he decided to apply for discharge as a conscientious objector.

Lewis gathered letters of support from his parents, Professor Thames, Bob Hallman (his friend from law school), local family court judge James Spigner, and Juanita Huffman (Spigner's secretary). Judge Spigner wrote about Lewis, "His effort here . . . has literally saved the lives of a lot of children who would otherwise continue on in their miserable status or fall into a career of crime. He is one of the most sincere and conscientious persons I have known." "He has so much compassion toward his fellow man that I do not feel that he could ever bear arms," Huffman's letter read. Professor Thames confirmed that Lewis's objection to the Vietnam War "reache[d] to the most fundamental religious and philosophical beliefs." Finally, Momma and Daddy shared, "We tried to teach him the dignity and worth of all human life, and . . . that violence and aggression are usually uncivilized responses to conflict. . . . [He] can best serve his country and the advancement of moral justice by continuing his involvement in legal aid to underprivileged persons and by voluntary service to the community."

On July 31, 1972, Lewis submitted his "Application for Discharge from the US Army on the Grounds of Conscientious Objection to War and Participation Therein in Any Form," in which he explained:

> The nature of my belief in opposition to all wars stems from my moral and ethical convictions about what is right and wrong. . . . My parents tried and succeeded in teaching me the sacredness of human life, not just in the abstract, but also in everyday relationships with people. . . . This parental guidance laid the foundation for the development and evolvement of my conscience. . . . Essentially, my "religion" is to treat all men justly. . . .
>
> Having as deep a feeling as I do for mankind and human life, I will not allow myself to become, directly or indirectly, a part of the armed forces whose main function is to prepare for and promote war. . . .

I now think I can contribute most through the law profession. . . . Through this type of work I hope to make some contribution to bettering the plight of mankind.

Lewis passed the mandatory mental exam for conscientious objector applicants and met with an Army chaplain in November 1972. The chaplain reported:

Lt. Pitts' basis for his present action is grounded in a very personalized humanistic, sociological approach to life and a highly structured ethical position. . . . I believe the man to be very sincere in his belief and to hold his convictions as most crucial. . . . I feel that this man has honestly developed in his thinking to the point where he is a full-blown humanist and sincerely dedicated to the service of mankind. . . . Lt. Pitts' tenets and beliefs are not grounded in emotion, but rather are based on intellectual enlightenment and social realism. I find no reason to doubt his sincerity and feel that he has arrived at a deep and mature position of conviction.

Despite Lewis's heartfelt application, letters of support, mental stability, and chaplain report, the investigating officer determined that Lewis failed to demonstrate "deeply held moral and ethical beliefs" and hadn't legitimately changed in his beliefs since 1970, when he agreed to be commissioned after law school. The officer recommended rejecting Lewis's application.

When Lewis graduated from law school in May 1973, he still hadn't received a final decision about his discharge application. He began contemplating whether, if the application was denied, he'd flee to Canada. Desperate, he wrote to his senator, Strom Thurmond, pleading with him to pressure the Army to issue its decision. Lewis doesn't know if Thurmond received or acted on the letter. Regardless, a couple months later, another hearing officer interviewed Lewis. Then, in September 1973, Lewis was honorably discharged as a conscientious objector and freed to pursue a public interest law career.

Discharge also meant Lewis could continue being with Johnson. In November 1973, after dating for a year, they wed in his parents' home in Bethune. The newlyweds and their dog, Prince, moved into a small house in Columbia. Lewis described Prince as "the child of a greyhound and a deer," and said that no matter how high they built their fence, Prince would inevitably jump over it, run away, and "return with shit all over his head."

Public Defender

Lewis accepted an assistant public defender job in the Richland County Public Defender's Office. His experiences as a clinical student and clerk with that office and a lecture by William Kunstler inspired Lewis to become a trial lawyer. Kunstler—"the country's most controversial and, perhaps, its best-known lawyer," according to the *New York Times*—defended members of the Catonsville Nine, Freedom Riders, Black Panther Party, Weather Underground, and American Indian Movement, as well as other high-profile clients. In October 1971, Kunstler spoke at USC about the Attica Prison uprising and other prisoner-led movements for penal reform. At the time, Lewis couldn't imagine that he'd work with Kunstler fifteen years later.

During the summer after graduation, Lewis studied for the South Carolina Bar exam and continued clerking at the public defender's office. After the exam, he traveled to Houston, Texas, the farthest he'd ever been from home, for the National Association of Criminal Defense Lawyers annual training. For three weeks, he lived in the University of Houston dorms and was trained on various aspects of trial practice. His favorite part of the experience—other than a concert featuring Willie Nelson, the Doobie Brothers, and ZZ Top—was experienced criminal defense attorneys regaling Lewis and the other neophytes with war stories from courtroom battlefields. They amused Lewis with sayings like, "The only thing you waive is the American Flag! And the only thing you stipulate is the innocence of your client!" They boasted of fighting like hell for clients and making life hell for prosecutors.

After passing the bar exam, and in November 1973, being sworn in to the South Carolina Bar, Lewis was immediately thrown into the deep end, handling all types of adult criminal trials and appeals. Lewis's supervisor was Costa Pleicones, a fellow Wofford and USC graduate who'd go on to serve as chief justice of the South Carolina Supreme Court. Lewis was aided by Charles Cannon and Lucious Anderson, the public defender office's pistol-toting, Black investigators. Pleicones wrote that Cannon was "slick" and "charmed people into cooperation," whereas Anderson was "physically imposing." Lewis, Cannon, and Anderson laughed hysterically while listening to recordings of Richard Pryor. In 1974, Gaston Fairey joined Lewis as a fellow assistant public defender. Fairey described meeting Lewis:

I believe, that first day, Lewis and I went to the jail to interview new clients. I, as the rookie, sat in with him and witnessed his easy manner of compassion and understanding when meeting and listening to the stories of the men and women who came into the interview room. I believe it was Lewis who first led me to the conclusion that there are no "bad" people, just people who sometimes do "bad" things. He had no fear of the clients and no compunction about placing an arm around a shoulder when the clients got up to leave the room.

As a public defender in South Carolina's largest city, Lewis handled interesting and challenging cases. His clients included defendants charged with crimes committed inside Central Correctional Institution (CCI), South Carolina's only maximum-security prison until 1975. CCI, which the *New York Times* designated the "prison from hell," held more than 1,300 men. Some bunks were five beds high; some cells were five-feet wide by six-feet long. CCI also housed the state's execution chamber where 243 men died on "Old Sparky," the electric chair. CCI closed in 1994, after a federal court mandated alleviation of overcrowding and the local government condemned a portion of the facility. When the prison was demolished in 1999, a former inmate commented, "If CCI's walls could talk, they would scream."

Fairey described one of his first hearings with Lewis: "We were representing two young men who had been in a shootout in a bar. It was just like in the cowboy movies—the two sides threw down tables and started shooting at each other. Lewis and I looked at each other as we walked out of the hearing and just laughed—what a world we had entered."

Lewis and others represented Henry Clay Moore, a man charged with raping a woman and then stabbing her and her four-year-old son to death in their home. Lewis argued that Moore was not guilty by reason of insanity. A jury found Moore guilty, and the judge gave him two consecutive life sentences.

Lewis and Pleicones represented Francis Franklin, who was charged with murdering Jarman Casey, a Catholic priest, chaplain at CCI, and member of a prominent local family. The state initially sought the death penalty; however, in 1972, the US Supreme Court issued its decision in *Furman v. Georgia*, effectively nullifying all existing death sentences and halting all executions for a four-year period. Franklin, a parolee and former inmate at CCI, had been staying at Casey's apartment and maintained that he had repelled sexual advances by Casey. Lewis and Pleicones were reluctant to introduce the priest's alleged sexual preferences; they didn't want to be seen as implying that it was okay to kill someone because he was gay. The prosecutor wouldn't discuss a plea deal because of the prominence of Casey's family. In a serendipitous turn of events, the state introduced the alleged motive in the trial. The jury ultimately convicted Franklin of manslaughter instead of murder.

Lewis also worked on a case involving the murder of Kershaw County Sheriff's Deputy Ernest Potter. However, Lewis's most memorable clients were James Worley and Claude Callahan.

James Worley

While working in the Richland County Prison Camp in June 1972, James Worley contracted severe poison ivy, causing him to experience swelling, rashes, and open, running sores. His three requests to see a physician were denied. In a desperate attempt to alleviate the excruciating pain, he poured bleach on his open sores. Unrelieved, Worley fled to Georgia, where a doctor successfully treated his condition. Two years later, he was arrested in Florida and extradited to South Carolina.

At Worley's trial for escape, Lewis argued the necessity defense—that is, Worley wasn't criminally liable because his conduct was necessary to prevent the greater harm of extreme physical pain and suffering. However, the judge refused to instruct the jury about the necessity defense. Worley was convicted and sentenced to an additional year in prison.

Lewis appealed Worley's case to the South Carolina Supreme Court. In 1975, the court held, in *State v. Worley*, "There possibly may be situations when a prisoner's dilemma is so serious an escape could be justified. If a prisoner is in need of emergency medical treatment to avoid death or immediate, serious permanent bodily injury, he may have a defense of necessity submitted to the jury." However, the court ultimately affirmed Worley's conviction because he "remained at large for two years instead of immediately surrendering to authorities after receiving medical treatment." The Associated Press covered the case with headlines such as "Prisoners Itching to Escape" and "Itchin' to Get Out." Nevertheless, Lewis had established new precedent that could help protect incarcerated individuals.

Claude Callahan

Lewis described Claude Callahan as a short, stocky Black man with a low
IQ and severe speech impediment. On Saturday, September 23, 1972, Callahan was arrested and charged with burglary. While Callahan was in custody,
Harry Snipes, the Columbia Police Department's captain of detectives, began
to suspect that Callahan was connected to an unrelated case involving the
rape and robbery of a young white woman. Lewis said Snipes was known as
"Hosepipe Harry" because of his reputation for using a hosepipe to beat confessions out of suspects. Callahan confessed to committing the crimes against
the woman. However, according to Lewis, Callahan falsely confessed, before
being Mirandized, once on Saturday and again on Sunday, because Snipes
told Callahan he'd be released on bond if he admitted to the crimes. Moreover, Callahan didn't match the woman's description of the suspect, Lewis
recalled. Pleicones believed that Callahan was just seeking the approval of,
and trying to please, law enforcement.

Judge Julius Ness, "Bubba,"—a former Republican state legislator—
presided over Callahan's trial. Lewis described Ness as a "mean, cruel, immoral,
corrupt asshole," "known for threatening lawyers who challenged him in any
way with jail time." When Lewis was a long-haired law clerk, Ness would
glare at him, grimace, and make scissoring motions with his fingers. Lewis
remembered Ness kicking a Black lawyer out of the courtroom because of the
design of his sportscoat. (Ness's grandson, Judge Julius Ness Richardson, is a
Trump appointee on the US Court of Appeals for the Fourth Circuit.) Ness
didn't like Lewis's beard or long hair; so, he demanded that Lewis be replaced
as Callahan's attorney. The public defender's office refused.

Lewis was terrified of failing Callahan. He wrote about the start of the
trial, "I remember not only feeling my heartbeat like a bass drum, but also
hearing the sucker beating. I thought I was going to choke to death."

During the trial, accounts of Callahan's confession differed dramatically,
including when he was Mirandized. Also, the opposing sides debated whether
Callahan possessed the capacity to voluntarily confess. Lewis called a psychiatrist to the stand, who testified that Callahan had an IQ of fifty-five to
sixty-five, "mental retardation," and limited ability to think and reason under
stress. Nevertheless, Ness ruled that Callahan's confessions were voluntarily
given after *Miranda* warnings, and thus, admissible. After three hours of deliberation, the jury found Callahan guilty of burglary, rape, and robbery.

Lewis appealed to the South Carolina Supreme Court. During the pendency of the appeal, Ness became a justice on that court. The court found that Ness failed to make a reliable determination regarding the voluntariness of Callahan's confession and remanded the case. The court's opinion ended, "If it is determined that the Sunday confession was not voluntary, an order reversing the conviction and granting a new trial shall be entered."

Callahan's conviction was ultimately affirmed, and he was given a thirty-year prison sentence, even though he barely grasped what was happening. Lewis was devastated.

Moving On

By fall 1976, Lewis had been with the public defender's office for four years—one as a clerk and three as an attorney. He had earned the respect of his colleagues. For example, Fairey wrote in 2017, "Lewis remained the most consistent liberal thinker I have ever known. . . . From the first day I met him, 45 years ago until now, I believe he hasn't for a day lost the drive and dedication that measures his life. . . . He has lived his life for others." Bob Hallman, Lewis's friend since law school, was in private practice and assigned cases by the public defender's office when it needed outside, conflict-free counsel. Hallman shared, "While Lewis' excellent grasp of both procedural and substantive aspects of the law were evident, it was his compassion for clients and passion for justice that gained him the praise and respect from other lawyers and attention from judges."

Lewis had also been with Susan Johnson for about four years. He loved her and being a public defender but felt like he was outgrowing and losing interest in both. His politics, beliefs, and aspirations were becoming increasingly distinct from Johnson's. Lewis felt as if their relationship had "lost energy" and he was "too young and restless to be married and settled down." He yearned to expand his horizons—personally and professionally.

Lewis was reading *Monthly Review* and *The Guardian* (the leftist, New York City–based newspaper), and the works of Karl Marx, Will Durant, and others. Lewis had also befriended Brett Bursey, a local activist and organizer who taught Lewis about the Weather Underground, dangers of nuclear power, and other causes of so-called radicals. Additionally, representing clients ensnared in the criminal justice system, Lewis said, "began to lift up the covers" for him to see "how much systemic racism and criminalization of poverty there is." For the first time he felt compelled to advocate for systemic change.

Meanwhile, Lewis's friend and law school classmate Bob Warren had invited Lewis to join his public interest law practice in Allendale, South Carolina. The offer excited Lewis because, in his words, Warren was "energetic, upbeat, and a delight to be around"; was a "fearless, scrappy fighter" who "knew how the power structure was rigged and mean as a snake"; and had "the fire in his belly for civil rights." Lewis had reservations about being in private practice and charging clients, even on a reasonable sliding scale. However, he believed Bob's top priority would unwaveringly be clients' interests and justice.

In September 1976, Lewis quit his job and separated from Johnson. He packed up the Chevrolet Chevelle sedan that he purchased from Fairey's uncle and left Columbia to join Warren in Allendale.

CHAPTER 3

The Law Offices
of Warren and Pitts

Lewis and Robert Wardlaw Warren, "Bob," were cut from the same cloth. Like Lewis, Warren grew up in a small South Carolina town, his father was an entrepreneur, his mother was a teacher, his family was active in church, he was an undersized star high school athlete, and he attended a private South Carolina college, where he participated in ROTC, moved left politically, and was an English major. After serving in the Army for a couple of years in Hawaii and Indianapolis, Warren matriculated in the JD/MBA dual degree program at USC.

Warren wrote, "Lewis and I met at the law school when he drove up on his motorcycle and I parked my bicycle next to him. We both had beards and ready smiles as we joked about our modes of transportation." They quickly became friends and together helped form the Petigru Society, volunteered for the South Carolina Public Interest Research Group, took civil rights seminars, and hung out with Professor Thames. Lewis affectionately called him "Lawyer Warren" throughout their nearly fifty-year friendship.

After graduating from USC in December 1972, Warren returned to his hometown of Allendale to open a solo law practice. Allendale is a small, high-poverty, predominantly Black town seventy-five miles south of Columbia. Warren lived with his wife, Caro, and their two daughters in a three-bedroom house on the edge of town. His offices were in a building on Main Street where his father's drugstore was on the first floor and his father's hotel had been on the second floor. Warren took over the mortgage from his father, boarded up most of the hotel rooms, and used the remainder of the second floor for his practice.

Warren represented low-income and Black clients and handled controversial cases. No other firm in the area was welcoming of Black clients, and there wasn't a local public defender or legal aid office. One of Warren's first organizational clients was the local National Association for the Advancement of Colored People (NAACP). The chapter asked him to investigate the death of Wallace Youmans, an eighteen-year-old Black man killed by white men in Allendale County. They reportedly shot Youmans in a random ambush as retaliation for the wounding of a white man a week earlier. Warren also assisted the local NAACP chapter with parade permits and voting rights issues.

Word of Warren's affordable, zealous advocacy for marginalized populations, and his willingness to confront the white, monied, good old boy power structure, quickly spread. His work, however, attracted hostility from white locals. He was blamed for Allendale closing, rather than racially integrating, the only public pool. Caro's bridge club friends quit en masse to protest his efforts. Tom Johnson, a lawyer and Warren's friend, said Warren "was perceived as a pinko communist trying to help Russia take over America." Warren shared that his uncle offered him $30,000 to leave town because he was causing too much trouble for their family.

The blowback, in addition to Warren working long hours for little money, caused friction between Caro and him. They separated a few years after moving to Allendale. Caro and their daughters moved out of the house around the same time that Lewis decided to leave Susan Johnson and the public defender's office.

In September 1976, Lewis moved in with Warren. Together, they jogged, competed in tennis, played the fiddle and dobro, took road trips, double-dated, and spent time with Warren's daughters. They also hung out at juke joints and social gatherings in the Black community to build relationships and better understand an "isolated Black community steeped in discrimination," Lewis said. Amazingly, according to Lewis and Warren, they never tired of one another or had major disagreements. "Ain't life rich!" became their motto and remained their maxim for decades.

Lewis continued reading leftist literature, motorcycling, and smoking pot. He became the South Carolina director of the National Organization for the Reform of Marijuana Laws and led the local chapter of Let Those Who Ride Decide, an organization opposed to mandatory motorcycle helmet laws.

They renamed the firm "The Law Offices of Warren and Pitts." The duo accepted almost any criminal or civil case that presented a worthy cause, irrespective of clients' ability to pay. They went up against law enforcement, prosecutors, landlords, employers, banks, and others in Allendale and the surrounding counties. They argued cases before South Carolina Supreme Court justices down to local magistrates, such as Ray Edenfield.

Edenfield held hearings in his office, which was next to his printing company. He carried a pistol and wheeled an oxygen tank behind him. During proceedings, Edenfield would remove his oxygen mask to take a drag from a cigarette. "Lewis and I were both scared he'd set the place on fire, but somehow, all of us escaped without incident," Warren wrote. After issuing warrants, Edenfield would occasionally get into his car, turn on a flashing blue light that he had installed, and accompany police officers to execute the warrant.

Lewis and Warren prided themselves on providing clients with zealous advocacy and "bad guys" with fearless opposition. The pair had a saying—"too many asses to bite"—because, according to Warren, they "were both bulldogs that'd bite anything unjust." Lewis told the *Black Mountain News* in January 2018, "One of the many things I learned from Bob was having the courage to speak truth to power. He was a person with bulldog tenacity . . . in fighting for what is right, and for the underdog." Lewis and Warren believed that if they, as white lawyers, didn't have the chutzpah to boldly stand up to the power structure, then they couldn't fairly expect their marginalized clients to fight. Warren shared:

> Lewis represented a client charged with heroin possession. There was no probable cause and Lewis made an impassioned motion to dismiss the charges before Circuit Court Judge Walter Bristow Jr., a highly respected attorney and former state legislator. The judge wavered before he ruled in favor of Lewis' motion.
>
> After court, we had breakfast with the judge and his wife. We talked about what we would've done if the judge hadn't dismissed the case against the client. We told him and his wife that if the judge, as smart and knowledgeable as he was, had been unable to follow the Constitution, then we would've been forced to abandon our law practice, go into the swamps, and lead a revolution to have our country be law-abiding.
>
> After that conversation, word got around that there were rebels in Allendale who were committed to taking extreme measures to enforce the Constitution.

Another example of "ass biting" occurred when State Supreme Court Justice Julius Ness and US District Court Judge Robert Hemphill were chosen to receive special honors at a South Carolina Trial Lawyers Association convention in Hilton Head, South Carolina. Ness, who Lewis had tussled with as a public defender, reminded Lewis of what Jesus said in the Gospel of Luke: "Woe to you lawyers as well! For you weigh men down with burdens hard to bear, while you yourselves will not even touch the burdens with one of your fingers." The Trial Lawyers Association and South Carolina bar mailed postcards to lawyers soliciting fifty-dollar contributions for a USC endowment in Hemphill's name and portraits of both men.

Lewis and Warren went to the convention with their own table and chairs and a sign with a quote from the Book of Mark: "Watch out for the teachers of the law. They like to walk around in flowing robes and be greeted with respect in the marketplaces, and have the most important seats in the synagogues and the places of honor at banquets. They devour widows' houses and for a show make lengthy prayers. These men will be punished most severely." Lewis and his law partner held a press conference and issued a statement expressing their opposition to honoring the judges:

> This system of justice by the rich, for the rich . . . victimizes poor and low-income working people, minorities and economically exploited women. That two of the most insensitive judges to these groups of exploited people would be selected for awards . . . should not be a surprise. The rich get richer while the unjust system rewards and perpetuates itself. Even though these judges are notoriously insensitive, anyone who has had contact with the legal system knows they don't stand alone in failing to give the people justice. . . .
>
> Lawyers at this convention would admit to us in private that they believe Judge Hemphill and Justice Ness to be extremely insensitive to individuals and their civil liberties. Yet these lawyers let their own financial interest take precedence over social justice and curry favor from these two powerful judges by bestowing honors upon them. By speaking out today we hope this action will encourage other lawyers to assume their duty under the Code of Professional Responsibility to improve the legal system.

The statement listed some of the judges' egregious actions, including unfairly fining Black civil rights lawyers; writing that women's liberation was "haunting the legislature"; referring to US Equal Employment Opportunity Commission (EEOC) staff as "ambulance chasers"; refusing to hold a bond hearing for two defendants while they were jailed for seventeen months; and referring to plaintiffs in a case about assistance from the Department of Social Services (DSS) as "parasites on society" who were "on the tit."

Associated Press coverage of their protest appeared in local newspapers and *The Transcript*, a South Carolina Bar publication, printed their statement. According to Lewis, several lawyers called him and Warren to praise the letter but still wouldn't speak up for fear of reprisal.

Palmetto Alliance Protest at Nuclear Plant Site in Barnwell

During his second year in Allendale, Lewis became keenly interested in the antinuclear movement, which was peaking in the United States. His attention was piqued by Brett Bursey, his friend and an environmental justice organizer. Additionally, in 1971, Allied-General Nuclear Services began building a four-hundred-acre commercial nuclear reprocessing plant in Barnwell, South Carolina, less than twenty miles north of Allendale.

The Palmetto Alliance, an antinuclear and consumer advocacy group coled by Bursey, established a twenty-acre tent city near Barnwell and planned a march and civil disobedience at the plant for spring 1978. Lewis and Warren assisted the alliance with planning. The experience was Lewis's first with large-scale organizing. He was fascinated by the complex discussions regarding logistics and tactics and the consensus-building process. Lewis and Warren both wanted to participate in the civil disobedience; however, one of them needed to be an observer and provide legal services to arrestees. They drew straws; Warren won.

Lewis and Warren notified law enforcement of the planned civil disobedience ahead of time in order to decrease the likelihood of a violent confrontation. State authorities responded by moving National Guard units that specialized in crowd control to the Barnwell Armory.

On April 30, 1978, an estimated 1,200 people—including Lewis and Warren—marched three miles along Highway 64, from the campsite to the plant and back. They sang "Monster Barnwell, Monster Barnwell, shut it down, shut it down!" to the tune of the French round "Frère Jacques."

The next day, May Day, approximately 280 protesters entered plant property and refused to leave for three hours, ignoring multiple demands from Allied-General representatives. Bursey announced to onlooking journalists that protesters, soaked by heavy rain, were presenting Allied-General with "a human petition" to close the plant. Officers arrested protesters for trespassing and loaded them onto awaiting Department of Corrections buses. Authorities provided hot dogs to the arrestees while they awaited arraignment. Most demonstrators were released on fifteen-dollar bond and transported back to the campsite; however, about twenty-five of them, including Warren, refused to pay as a form of continued protest and spent the night in the Barnwell County Detention Center.

Prosecution of the protesters who didn't pay a fine presented an opportunity for The Law Offices of Warren and Pitts to challenge a state criminal statute that'd often worked against their clients, especially Black defendants. A South Carolina law, codified in 1868, allowed magistrates to delegate to local sheriffs or other officials the power to select "respectable voters" for pools of prospective jurors in criminal cases—called venires.

Barnwell County Magistrate Harry Flowers presided over Warren's trial in May 1978. A Barnwell County sheriff's deputy used his delegated authority to select forty registered respectable voters for the venire. The county's registered voters were thirty-seven percent Black and fifty-three percent female; yet the pool had only two Black people and two females. Lewis, as counsel for his law partner, objected to the venire selection process, asserting that it precluded a representative cross section of the community and an impartial jury. In legal terms, he argued that allowing law enforcement officials to handpick prospective jurors violated the Fifth, Sixth, and Fourteenth Amendments to the US Constitution. Flowers overruled his objection.

During the trial, Flowers frequently told Lewis to argue the issue of trespassing, not nuclear power. On May 12, 1978, the jury convicted Warren of trespass after five minutes of deliberation. Flowers had given other Barnwell protesters a choice between fifteen days in jail or a one-hundred-dollar fine but immediately sentenced Warren to the former. However, after an emotional appeal from Lewis, Flowers changed Warren's penalty to a fine.

Lewis and Warren filed a motion for a new trial and a notice of appeal with the General Sessions Court. They argued that Flowers erred by refusing to quash the venire because "the small, rural county voter registration list allowed the Chief Deputy opportunity to select people known to him to be adverse to the cause espoused by Appellant or people obligated to the Sheriff's office for whatever reason."

Judge Rodney Peoples heard the case on June 1, 1978. Lewis and Warren were familiar with Peoples and certain he'd rule against them; so, they moved for the judge to recuse himself. At the hearing on the motion, Lewis accused Peoples of, in past cases, displaying "bias and lack of impartiality," becoming "a member of the prosecutorial team," catering to law enforcement, "utilizing gestures and mannerisms . . . to discredit the defendant or the defense attorney," intimidating and harassing defense attorneys, demonstrating "a lack of sensitivity" toward defendants, and being "condescending toward underprivileged and poor people in the courtroom." Warren accused Peoples of "open hostility" toward them, being "close-minded about sentencing alternatives," showing their clients "a consistent lack of compassion," and giving harsher sentences to defendants who seek a jury trial instead of pleading guilty. Peoples didn't recuse himself; instead he promptly upheld Warren's conviction.

With help from the ACLU, Lewis and Warren appealed to the South Carolina Supreme Court. In May 1979, the court's five justices—all white men, including Julius Ness—heard oral arguments. Lewis presented legal arguments against the venire statute; then, the fireworks started.

Standing before the justices, Lewis questioned "the integrity of the judicial process" in South Carolina. He disclosed that a former South Carolina Supreme Court law clerk told him that the justices disregard the law if they're convinced a defendant is guilty. "Tell me what charges you are making against this court so I'll know whether to get the security guard or let you continue with your argument," the chief justice snapped. Lewis fired back, "I'd rather talk candidly in front of the court than behind your backs."

After Lewis finished, Warren rose and stepped to the podium adorning a sport coat, without a tie. The chief justice promptly announced that Warren wouldn't be heard without a necktie, angrily admonishing, "Don't ever come into this court without a tie. Every attorney who appears before this court must wear a tie." The chief justice then seemingly remembered that rules regarding attire didn't apply to pro se appellants (i.e., those representing themselves) and told Warren, "If you're appearing for yourself, I'll hear you, but if you're appearing as an attorney, I won't." Warren said he was representing himself and doesn't wear neckties because they symbolize economic division. He explained, "We represent working people; people who are exploited by insurance companies, finance companies, agrichemical companies, and other corporate conglomerates, which unconstitutionally and unconscionably attempt to take advantage of their positions. Most of our clients do not wear ties." Warren felt comfortable not wearing a tie during oral argument because he was representing himself for a change and, therefore, didn't have to worry about the best interests of a client.

Two weeks later, the court issued its opinion in *State v. Robert Warren*, finding that the "unbridled authority" afforded to the delegated party per the venire statute had "abundant" "potential for abuse" and did "not tend to assure a cross-section of citizens fairly representative of the community." The court reversed Warren's conviction and remanded his case for a new trial, which never happened. The *Charlotte Observer* reported, "The 4–1 opinion, handed down Monday, sent shock waves through the state judicial system. Supreme Court officials said Friday they are receiving 100 inquiries about the decision every day. . . . In a follow-up order Wednesday, the court ordered the state's 331 magistrates to postpone all criminal trials until the General Assembly adopts legislation replacing the stricken law. . . . S.C. court officials expect a surge in requests for jury trials, and, eventually, a jump in motions to drop charges because the accused has not gotten a speedy trial. They also expect a boom in magisterial frustration."

Attorneys from other states who were interested in bringing a similar challenge to venire laws contacted The Law Offices of Warren and Pitts for guidance. Lewis and Warren were given the South Carolina ACLU's Cooperating Attorney Award for their efforts. However, most media coverage of the case focused on the necktie controversy. *The State* read, "A tieless lawyer and his denim clad law partner accused a visibly surprised South Carolina Supreme Court Monday of routinely dismissing criminal cases to avoid ruling on 'critical issues of criminal law.' Several conservatively dressed lawyers present in the courtroom called it a 'most unusual confrontation,' and one lawyer dubbed the exchange 'the hottest show in town Monday.'" The Associated Press reported that "Warren's tielessness" and Lewis's remarks "provoked the ire of the justices." Alan Pritchard, then editor of the *Sacramento Bee*, took a particular interest in Lewis and Warren, writing:

> I was beginning to worry that cravat dandies had downed the bare-necked proletariat until I heard about an Allendale, S.C. law firm that is fighting ties in court. And winning.
>
> To find two of them defending the right to appear before the bench with naked neck was gratifying, but then South Carolinians are no strangers to revolt.
>
> [Warren and Lewis] have been engaged in this sort of neckwear warfare for more than a year. It's not a frivolous whim. They strongly believe that wearing neckties is hazardous to relationships

with their clients and that a lawyer's right to appear in court shouldn't be determined by folds of cloth knotted at the neck.

Warren explained to Pritchard, "My clients don't wear ties and when my partner or I wear them it sets us apart from them and interferes with our representation of them. And we thought it very important to be able to relate to juries. . . . We don't think we are better than the general public."

Moving On

After only a couple of years in Allendale, Lewis was ready to leave. He loved Warren and found tremendous joy in living and working with him. However, the financial pressures of operating a small public interest law firm that served low-income clients in a rural area, a growing distaste for the legal system, and a vindictive power structure drove Lewis out of Allendale.

Lewis and Warren struggled to keep their firm financially afloat. They charged clients—those who could afford to pay anything—on a sliding scale. For example, for fifty dollars, Lewis spent dozens of hours working on a case involving a defective mobile home and malfeasance by a finance company. Clients who couldn't afford monetary payment sometimes exchanged services or goods for representation. Lewis and Warren were once given a bushel of peas for legal services rendered. Occasionally, they won attorney's fees or received financial assistance from Warren's father. They also borrowed money to cover basic expenses, including once after men showed up at their office to turn off the electricity for nonpayment. Lewis and Warren also tried fundraising but were typically rejected, including by Billy Graham, Jane Fonda, and Morris Dees, founder of the Southern Poverty Law Center.

Lewis didn't mind being broke, as long as he was having fun and pursuing justice. "We didn't have the proverbial pot to piss in, but we ate," he said. However, less than a year after joining Warren, Lewis began agonizing over tensions between, on one hand, earning a living and keeping the firm afloat and, on the other hand, charging poor clients or keeping attorney's fees. His journal entries, in August 1977, reflect his second thoughts about going into private practice, as well as his growing disdain for the legal system:

> I hate charging clients a fee; it defeats the good vibes of feeling like you helped somebody. The people around here that we represent

barely make ends meet and I know that feeling. If, on my budget, I had to go to a fucking lawyer and pay several hundred dollars for access to justice, I'd be shittin'. . . . Entire scheme of jurisprudence geared around fee generation. . . .

There should be free legal services for all people. Would it overload the system? My first response is, fuck it if it does—beef up the system. The whole legal framework purportedly in existence for people to seek redress of wrongs is structured so as to generate fees for fucking lawyers! . . . Very disgusting.

Seems I can't get away from the disquietude of having "work" necessitating an emphasis on getting money rather than serving and doing good. The "getting money" is certainly not stacking up riches and [we're] barely surviving, but the disquietude is there just the same. But for commitment made to Bob, I believe I'd be looking into another arrangement. It's not a dissatisfaction living in Allendale, but . . . it's that the whole legal system is geared toward fee generation. If I continue to do same daily tasks or type work, but on salary and never "feeing" clients, I think I'd feel fulfilled. . . .

Lewis's and Warren's financial hardships and job satisfaction were heavily influenced by their relationships with the local power structure. They had agitated prosecutors and judges with their zealousness, fearlessness, honesty, unconventional tactics, and political activities. The local prosecutor at the time—Randolph Murdaugh III, father of notorious murderer Alex Murdaugh—told *The State* decades later, "Warren was too zealous, at times, for his own good."

Eventually, Lewis and Warren had to advise prospective clients that their firm couldn't get a fair shake from judges. Lewis wrote, "We were pretty much on the shit-list of most establishment judges, and hence, a successful economic practice was nearly impossible given the discretion trial judges used against us, combined with the money we didn't have for appeals." In 2018, Warren told the *Black Mountain News*, "My former law partner, Lewis Pitts, and I tried to make the Constitution apply to all citizens, especially to those who never experienced equal rights under the law. And when we called out judges and pointed out the inequities in the system, the system quite naturally responded."

Five years into his legal career, Lewis decided that he didn't want to focus specifically on individual issues for individual clients, especially if he had to charge them; instead, he wanted to work for systemic change. He wrote in his journal, "I feel the need to 'serve' humanity more than I'm doing." He had also realized that the law and legal system alone don't effectuate lasting systemic change; and instead, they must be tools used to serve the needs of social movements. So, in fall 1978, without regrets about his time in Allendale, Lewis decided to leave The Law Offices of Warren and Pitts and become a full-time antinuclear movement lawyer, even though, at the time, the decision wasn't that clear cut in his mind and he didn't have the language to describe this new path.

Warren had a whirlwind couple of years following Lewis's departure. He dissolved their practice, unsuccessfully ran for South Carolina Senate (although he won Allendale County), worked for legal services in other cities, and briefly managed State Senator Tom Turnipseed's campaign for US Congress. In 1980, after he "had worn out his welcome in South Carolina," Warren wrote, he moved to Black Mountain, North Carolina. He worked at Pisgah Legal Services in nearby Asheville before opening a new public interest law practice focused on representing Native Americans and sick nuclear workers. For the next thirty-five years—until advanced Parkinson's disease forced his retirement in 2017—Warren continued championing equal justice for the oppressed and exploited.

Lewis and Warren were friends for nearly a half century. They visited each other and spoke on the phone often, spending countless hours reminiscing, giving each other advice, playing music, and laughing out loud. They also collaborated on other cases and campaigns. An article about Warren in *The State* shortly after his death in March 2020 read, "Pitts said . . . the needy 'have lost a friend and an advocate in the truest sense.'"

PART II

Movement Lawyering

(1978–1994)

CHAPTER 4

Antinuclear Movement

The antinuclear movement in the United States dates to the 1950s, after the atomic bombings of Hiroshima and Nagasaki, and as the government tested nuclear weapons amid escalating Cold War tensions. In the 1960s and early 1970s, antinuclear momentum slowed, at least in part because the United States signed treaties limiting nuclear testing and proliferation and other issues, such as the Vietnam War and civil rights, had come to the forefront. However, the antinuclear movement regained prominence and peaked in the late 1970s and early 1980s. Local groups organized to oppose construction of nuclear plants across the country. Coalitions of environmentalists, antiwar activists, public health officials, worker safety advocates, scientists, and others raised concerns about uranium mining, radiation, nuclear waste management, and government spending on nuclear weapons and energy. They succeeded in delaying or halting construction of some nuclear plants.

Lewis's involvement in the antinuclear movement began in April 1978, when he joined Palmetto Alliance organizing against nuclear plants and waste disposal in Barnwell, South Carolina. A *St. Louis Post-Dispatch* columnist wrote about Lewis, "He became active in the anti-nuke movement, he said, because his home state 'had been made the commode of the nuclear industry. We were receiving about 85 percent of the nation's nuclear waste.'" In Barnwell, Lewis met Tom Campbell, a former songwriter and talent coordinator for Disneyland who organized benefit concerts for environmental justice causes. He convinced Lewis to attend antinuclear events in Seabrook, New Hampshire, to meet Danny Sheehan and Sara Nelson and learn more about the Karen Silkwood case. In August 1978, Lewis traveled to New Hampshire where he met with Sheehan and Nelson and observed civil disobedience at the Seabrook Station Nuclear Power Plant.

Sheehan and Nelson are work and life partners. Sheehan is a devout Catholic from Upstate New York, with three degrees from Harvard. During his first few years out of law school, Sheehan worked at a Wall Street law firm, famed defense attorney F. Lee Bailey's law firm, and the ACLU. After attending an all-girls prep high school in Illinois, Cornell University, and the University of California, Berkeley, Nelson cofounded a documentary film production organization and was a television news reporter and anchor. When they met Lewis, Sheehan was chief counsel for the National Office of Social Ministries of the Jesuit Order and Nelson was the national labor secretary at the National Organization for Women (NOW). They were working on an antinuclear campaign centered on the suspicious death of Karen Silkwood, a nuclear plant worker in Oklahoma.

After two days with Lewis in New Hampshire, Sheehan and Nelson invited him to join the Silkwood campaign's legal team. The offer included free housing with a wealthy campaign supporter in Oklahoma City, but no salary or benefits. Lewis was a licensed attorney with five years of trial experience. He could've found a stable job with a good salary and benefits. Nevertheless, he found the prospect of an adventure in an unfamiliar place alluring. He was also attracted to Sheehan's larger-than-life personality and big picture thinking. Lewis said that Sheehan's "soft, goofy bear hugs" made him "think of warm milk and chocolate chip cookies." Most importantly, Lewis had an opportunity to become a full-time antinuclear movement lawyer. So, he accepted the invitation and, in September 1978, packed up his Chevrolet Chevelle again and headed west. He'd spend the next two years traversing the country embedded in antinuclear movements.

Silkwood Campaign in Oklahoma

Karen Silkwood was a chemical lab technician at Kerr-McGee Corporation's plutonium fuels production plant in Crescent, Oklahoma, and an active union member. In the early 1970s, she was gathering evidence to support her claim that Kerr-McGee, the country's largest uranium producer at the time, was negligent in maintaining worker safety.

After being exposed to plutonium at work and, suspiciously, in her home, Silkwood died in a car crash in November 1974. At the time of her death, she was en route to share secret documents about Kerr-McGee with a *New York Times* reporter. Evidence strongly suggested she was forced off the road by another driver. Nevertheless, Oklahoma Highway Patrol officials concluded she fell asleep at the wheel after taking sedatives. The US Department of Justice (DOJ), Federal Bureau of Investigation (FBI), US

Nuclear Regulatory Commission (NRC), and Congress all supposedly investigated the circumstances surrounding Silkwood's death and claimed to have found no criminal conduct.

Two years later, Silkwood's parents filed, on behalf of her three children, a federal lawsuit against Kerr-McGee officials and FBI agents. The lawsuit alleged negligence by Kerr-McGee in operating the plant, conspiracy by Kerr-McGee to violate Silkwood's constitutional rights, and conspiracy by the FBI to assist Kerr-McGee. The alleged conspiracies involved interfering with the exercise of First Amendment and due process rights by Silkwood and other union organizers and subjecting Silkwood and others to illegal surveillance, searches, wiretaps, firings, transfers, and other coercive tactics to hinder their union organizing. The Silkwood estate demanded $1.5 million in actual damages and $70 million in punitive damages.

The Karen Silkwood Fund formed, in March 1978, to unify the campaign's litigation with related investigation, public education, and fundraising efforts. Nelson headed the Fund; Sheehan was its principal attorney. Oklahoma attorneys, Arthur Angel and James Ikard, represented Silkwood's estate. Jerry Spence, a legendary plaintiffs' attorney, later joined the legal team for the trial.

In September 1978, US District Court Judge Frank Theis dismissed the conspiracy allegations because he found the defendants' alleged animus wasn't directed at a protected class, such as racial minorities or women, but rather it was aimed at employees organizing around working conditions. Lewis arrived in Oklahoma in time to assist with appealing the conspiracy dismissals to the US Court of Appeals for the Tenth Circuit.

Lewis quickly familiarized himself with the case and pored over deposition transcripts and discovery materials in search of evidence that Silkwood was targeted because she was a woman. Such evidence, however, was scant. In December 1980, the Tenth Circuit affirmed the dismissals, agreeing with Theis's reasoning that the alleged animus arose out of Silkwood's and her associates' union activities, not their sex. The US Supreme Court declined to hear the case. Consequently, only the negligence claim went to trial and Lewis's role in the Silkwood litigation largely ended.

The jury ultimately awarded the Silkwood estate more than $10 million. However, the defendants prevailed on appeal to the US Supreme Court and the case was remanded to the district court. The parties eventually settled in August 1986, with Kerr-McGee agreeing to pay $1.38 million. Silkwood posthumously became, according to media and advocates, an "anti-nuclear martyr."

Although Lewis had only a minor role in the Silkwood campaign, the experience significantly impacted him. It was his first foray into a national campaign that involved education, organizing, and litigation. The experience also deepened his understanding of the interconnectedness of corporations and government. Moreover, Lewis said he learned from Sara Nelson's "brilliant coalition-building" and "ability to lift up of intersectionalities" among women's rights, civil liberties, and environmental justice.

Nevertheless, his disillusionment with traditional lawyering that began in Allendale intensified. Lewis was frustrated by, as he wrote in his journal at the time, the "hierarchical team of elitist lawyers" working on the Silkwood case because they failed to adequately connect the legal case to grassroots movements and broader critiques of capitalism. He resolved to take a community lawyering approach to his continued antinuclear activism. Lewis wrote to Rob Hager, one of the more progressive attorneys who worked on the Silkwood case, "My energies and efforts more than ever must be in the 'streets.'"

Sunbelt Alliance Movement in Oklahoma

Lewis's work on antinuclear campaigns was primarily with nonlawyer activists and organizers, including Jim Garrison. Garrison knew Danny Sheehan from their time together at Harvard Divinity School and moved to Oklahoma to work on the Silkwood campaign. Garrison and Lewis became close friends. Lewis found him to be brilliant, with good energy and an impressive ability to make very complicated information about nuclear energy accessible and persuasive. Garrison was struck by Lewis's "overwhelming friendliness" and "graciousness." He described Lewis as "a pleasure to be around," "smart," and "completely committed."

Garrison introduced Lewis to the Sunbelt Alliance, a coalition of antinuclear affinity groups, including musicians, artists, Native Americans, and students and faculty from the University of Tulsa. The alliance focused on preventing construction of the Black Fox Nuclear Power Plant, thirty miles east of Tulsa, by the Public Service Company of Oklahoma (PSO). With the Kerr-McGee plant where Karen Silkwood worked and the proposed Black Fox plant only two hours apart, Garrison said of the region at the time, "It was hot, man; the center of the center; a two-front war." Only a couple of months after moving to Oklahoma, Lewis began spending most of his time on the Black Fox campaign. He and Garrison traveled together to community meetings in Tulsa, Norman, and other Oklahoma cities.

When in Tulsa, Lewis often stayed with Jim Primdahl, who was a carpenter and artist and part of the Foxhounds affinity group, one of the more radical Sunbelt Alliance groups. Primdahl described the group as "a ragtag consortium of Tulsa's finest thinking people." "Much of the discussions in some groups were 'terrorist' enough in nature to have rendered [them] jailbait," he added. Foxhounds members participated in civil disobedience trainings, protested, and aided jailed activists.

Lewis recalled a time that he and Primdahl received last minute word of an antinuclear organizing meeting in Gary, Indiana. They were dropped off near the interstate at about 2:00 A.M. and then hitchhiked in freezing temperatures to Gary. Lewis said, "We'd catch a ride just long enough for our mustaches, beards, and drooly noses to thaw out." In 2017, Primdahl wrote from his home, which he shares with a horse, in Costa Rica, "Lewis was never a center of attention; not his nature; soft spoken and sensible, never intending to influence other than through logic. . . . Lewis was my main man. He showed me a line in the sand is essential. . . . Not a day goes by that I don't proclaim, 'Ain't Life Rich,' with a chuckle of my own. . . . Not a day passes without at least a nanosecond of his energy passing thru me; voltage for the revolution we all were and remain committed to 'by any means necessary.' . . . Lewis is the most honorable person I have ever known!"

During the Black Fox campaign, Lewis also got to know Frank Thomas, a Native American medicine man. Thomas invited Lewis and other antinuclear activists to participate in sweat lodges. Lewis adopted Thomas's practice of always carrying on his person a copy of the US Constitution. To this day, a copy lives in Lewis's briefcase. He explained, "I see plenty wrong with the Constitution and the structure of government. . . . But as Anne Braden taught me, they let the genie out of the bottle with regard to noble ideals of equality, justice, and democracy by the People."

PROTEST ON OCTOBER 7, 1978

Lewis helped organize demonstrations at the Black Fox plant in October 1978. He negotiated ahead of time with the Rogers County Sheriff's Office, local prosecutor, and PSO to arrange for nonviolent protests, followed by peaceful arrests of demonstrators for trespassing and their release on-site. This gentle approach was designed to attract warier and more conservative activists to the direct action. Lewis told a *St. Louis Post-Dispatch* columnist, "We have to trespass to educate the people to the threat the nuclear process holds for everybody, whether they are John Birchers or hippie types."

Yet, tensions remained between protesters and those in the antinuclear movement who believed civil disobedience would alienate moderate supporters. For instance, Carrie Barefoot Dickerson—the founder and cochair of Citizens' Action for Safe Energy (CASE), one of the other local antinuclear groups advocating against the Black Fox plant—tried to convince Sunbelt Alliance members not to engage in civil disobedience. She wrote in her autobiography, *Aunt Carrie's War Against the Black Fox Nuclear Power Plant*, "'Oklahoma is a very conservative state,' I told them, 'and if you follow through on the occupation, we will all lose credibility with very many people.'" She acknowledged that the civil disobedience "attracted lots of attention and made more people aware that fellow citizens were deeply concerned about the dangers of nuclear power," but she also believed "it had an even greater negative impact"—specifically, "an immediate and devastating effect on CASE's ability to raise money for the legal intervention." Additionally, Dickerson wrote, "The civility and respect that CASE members had so carefully maintained was . . . destroyed."

On October 7, 1978, Sunbelt Alliance members played music and sang songs at their campground. Then, 348 protesters, led by Frank Thomas and activist turned actor Wes Studi, marched about a mile from the campground to the plant. Lewis and other demonstrators used homemade ramps to climb over the PSO's barbed-wire fences. They were arrested and then filed through a trailer to receive citations for trespassing.

In January 1979, Lewis requested a jury trial for 132 of the demonstrators—those who did not either forfeit their twenty-five-dollar bonds by failing to appear or plead guilty—so they could use the proceedings to educate local community members about the dangers of nuclear power; however, Rogers County District Court Judge David Allen Box denied his request. Regardless, a couple of months later, charges against the 132 protesters were thrown out after Box ruled that the state failed to prove trespassing in an enclosed area occurred. The assistant district attorney (DA) hadn't identified the Black Fox site as an enclosed area in the indictment and then didn't call a witness to establish that protesters went over a fence on October 7.

PROTEST ON OCTOBER 31, 1978

In the weeks after the October 7 protest, Lewis and thirteen other Sunbelt Alliance members, including Jim Garrison and Jim Primdahl, held secret meetings about using more guerilla warfare-type tactics to convey that pre-orchestrated civil disobedience wasn't the only feather in their activism caps. Then, in the early morning hours of October 31, 1978, the "Halloween Fourteen," as the Alliance members were known, gathered for a rally in a sweat lodge before Frank Thomas's lieutenants drove them to the plant. They scaled the perimeter fence, crawled across the plant grounds, and chained themselves to earth-moving equipment. At sunrise, they were discovered. Law enforcement and PSO workers used torches to cut them loose. The protesters were then arrested for trespassing and jailed.

At arraignment, the judge set bail at twenty-five dollars; however, on principle, the "Halloween Fourteen" refused to pay. Primdahl told the judge, "I will not pay the . . . bond and I will set myself in a situation in jail where you will have to take care of my withering body. I will not eat another bite until you release me and my brothers and sisters on personal recognizance." During their three days in jail, the Halloween Fourteen staged a hunger strike. They were joined, in a show of solidarity, by a group of immigrant detainees.

Judge Box again denied Lewis's request for a jury trial. On May 14, 1979, Box found all fourteen activists guilty of trespassing and ordered each of them to pay court costs of thirty-two dollars, although he called the defendants' actions "commendable." They didn't have to pay a fine because they had already served time in jail. The "Halloween Fourteen" demonstrators' convictions were overturned on appeal because Box had improperly denied them a jury trial.

LICENSING BOARD HEARINGS

A panel of the NRC's Atomic Safety and Licensing Board (ASLB) planned to conduct hearings about Black Fox in February 1979. The ASLB issued a protective order closing the portion of the hearings in which the "Reed Report" was going to be discussed. The report was General Electric Company's 1975 analysis of its own boiling water reactor for nuclear power plants, like the one proposed at Black Fox. The report contained numerous criticisms of the reactor's design. General Electric argued the Reed Report included trade secrets, and, therefore, should remain confidential.

On February 20, 1979, Lewis filed in a federal district court, on behalf of Sunbelt Alliance member Brian Hunt, a request for a temporary restraining order (TRO), preliminary injunction, and permanent injunction preventing the ASLB from excluding the public from the hearing. Hunt and fellow Sunbelt member Hal Rankin chained themselves to a swinging gate in the federal courthouse in Tulsa where the hearings were held. After ten to fifteen minutes, deputy US marshals used bolt cutters to free Hunt and Rankin, and then took them into custody.

Two days later, District Court Judge H. Dale Cook held a hearing on Lewis's motion for a TRO. Lewis argued that the Sunshine Act of 1976 required that the hearings be open to the public. The Sunshine Act mandated that all meetings conducted by federal agencies be open to the public unless a specific exemption applied. Lewis also argued that the ASLB had not made a determination regarding the public's interest in the hearing before issuing the protective order and that the public's interest in the safety information in the Reed Report outweighed any potential damage to General Electric's commercial interests. Cook denied the request for a TRO, but before ruling on an injunction, he ordered briefs from the parties, by February 27, about whether the Sunshine Act applied to the ASLB's Black Fox licensing hearings. He promised speedy action on the request for injunctive relief.

The parties submitted timely briefs; however, on Wednesday, February 28, before Cook ruled on the injunction, the Black Fox hearings concluded three days early. Thursday, Friday, and Saturday had been reserved for the ASLB to hear excerpts from the Reed Report. Instead, the report was discussed in a closed session on the prior Tuesday. Although excerpts from the report were entered into the public record, the transcript from the closed hearing was withheld.

After the hearings ended, Cook ordered the parties to show cause regarding why the injunction request should not be dismissed as moot. On April 19, 1979, Cook dismissed the action that Lewis filed, finding that the Sunshine Act did not apply to the ASLB in the context of the Black Fox hearings. The US Court of Appeals for the Tenth Circuit later affirmed the decision.

Meanwhile, on March 28, 1979, a federal magistrate fined Hunt and Rankin fifty dollars and gave them ten-day suspended jail sentences for a misdemeanor charge of "disrupting proceedings of government employees." They lost their appeals. Lewis advised Hunt and Rankin about their civil disobedience but did not represent them in their criminal case.

PROTEST ON JUNE 2, 1979

On June 2, 1979, approximately 339 activists, including Lewis, in driving rain, climbed a fence, walked nearly three miles while chanting "No more nukes" and "Save our children," and then occupied the muddy Black Fox construction site. They were arrested, photographed, cited, and released.

Lewis and Rob Hager, who was licensed in Oklahoma, represented themselves and about one hundred other protesters. They leveraged the prospect of each defendant requesting a separate trial, thereby overwhelming the small town's court, to pressure the DA into allowing expert testimony in a large joint trial.

The joint trial took place in September 1979. Lewis and Hager mounted a duress defense, which to be successful, generally requires a showing that the defendant faced an imminent threat of serious bodily injury or death, reasonably feared such harm would take place, and had no reasonable, noncriminal means of avoiding the threat. Their primary purpose in arguing duress wasn't to "win" in the traditional sense of an acquittal but rather to use the courtroom as a platform for exposing the threats posed by nuclear power.

The lone prosecution witness was a security coordinator at the Black Fox plant. Lewis and Hager called as witnesses a University of Tulsa Business School professor, ten representative defendants, two survivors from Hiroshima, a survivor from Nagasaki, and John Gofman. The business professor testified about the potential negative economic impacts of the plant. One of the Hiroshima survivors sobbed uncontrollably while testifying about a close friend who died of radiation poisoning. Gofman had a PhD and medical degree, was a professor of molecular and cellular biology at the University of California, Berkeley, helped develop the atom bomb during World War II, and chaired the Committee for Nuclear Responsibility. Gofman testified, "There is no so-called safe dose of radiation and saying that there is a safe and permissible dose is a fraud." He estimated that for every year Black Fox operated, approximately 450 nearby residents would eventually die from exposure. He said the plant was "a license to commit murder."

On September 20, 1979, the trial ended with a hung jury—three jurors voted to convict; three voted to acquit. Rather than retry the case, the prosecutor dismissed the charges. Charles Sackrey, an economics professor and one of the defendants, shared that Lewis was "widely known as brave, strong, and honest"; "an exceptionally talented, genuinely special person"; and always bringing "new and useful ideas to discussions about how to bring more joy and less fear into the world." The presiding judge, David Box, wrote to Lewis, "In many ways I feel privileged to have been part of [the trial], and I believe in the truth and correctness of the decisions made. . . . You have, I think, demonstrated the strength of non-violence in the courtroom." Hager reflected, "Lewis was very effective in putting Judge Box at his ease, setting the right friendly tone so that the judge was able to be fair-handed during the jury trial and so that the jury was, in turn, free to be fair-minded in their verdict."

In February 1982, the PSO formally canceled construction of Black Fox because of opposition, cost overruns, and rate increases that'd hurt business. Jim Primdahl reminisced about the Sunbelt Alliance, "The talent was so diverse, complete, and unwavering, we were truly unstoppable and unbreachable, and after four years, we delivered the head of PSO to the public."

KATIE GREENE

Another lasting outcome of the movement against Black Fox was Lewis's relationship with Katie Greene. Lewis first met Greene, ten years his junior, at a Foxhounds meeting in fall 1978, when she was a student at the University of Tulsa and a burgeoning activist. After her first Foxhounds meeting, Greene formally joined the group and began assisting with organizing efforts. In early 1979, she became one of three Sunbelt Alliance staff organizers. She and Lewis crossed paths at meetings, events, and the Sunbelt office. After getting arrested during the June 2 civil disobedience, they had their first date—dinner at a vegetarian restaurant and then a Sunbelt Alliance party.

Lewis was attracted to Greene's feistiness, intelligence, activism, and beauty. They had similar political orientations and mutual friends. He said the connection "seemed so natural." Greene reflected about what initially drew her to Lewis: "Like others, I saw in Lewis a man deeply concerned about environmental and social justice issues and passionate about devoting his time and talent to support the grassroots movements . . . and to redress injustices. He was a 'people's lawyer,' willing to get into the ring with the powers-that-be, 'to speak truth to power.' He spoke lovingly of his family and friends. He was at ease with people from all walks of life. He was sure-footed, confident."

During their first year of dating, Lewis stayed with Greene in Tulsa in between trips for antinuclear activities and ongoing cases with Bob Warren in South Carolina. Lewis and Greene also traveled together, including rendezvousing at an antinuclear event in Texas in summer 1979, demonstrating at the Pentagon in April 1980, and hitchhiking to an Equal Rights Amendment rally in Chicago in May 1980.

Comanche Peak Life Force Movement in Texas

In April 1979, the American Indian Environmental Council held a three-day antinuclear gathering at Mount Taylor, New Mexico. The event included workshops, cultural events, and music, including a concert featuring Bonnie Raitt, Jackson Browne, and others. Lewis took a break from the Black Fox campaign to attend. He volunteered to perform manual labor, such as hauling firewood. He also negotiated with the local National Guard installation to borrow a water tanker, which he drove to the campsite. He spent most of the weekend learning from Chicano and Native American activists, including John Trudell. Lewis shared his most vivid memory of the gathering: "There wasn't a shower; so, I'd just stick my head under a water pump. I was a smelly fucker by the third day. I didn't know blue jeans could get so dirty."

While in New Mexico, Lewis met Texas-based antinuclear activists, Mavis Belisle and Jim Schermbeck. Belisle was a former Peace Corps volunteer in Micronesia and then an editor at the *Texas Catholic* newspaper. Schermbeck was an undergraduate student at Austin College.

Belisle and Schermbeck were part of the Armadillo Coalition, an antinuclear organization in the Dallas-Fort Worth area focused on opposing Texas Utilities' Comanche Peak Nuclear Power Plant. The plant was in Glen Rose, about seventy-five miles southwest of Dallas. Construction of the $1.7 billion plant began in 1974, with operations scheduled to begin in 1981.

More radical Armadillo Coalition members, led by Belisle and Schermbeck, formed a new organization—the Comanche Peak Life Force—to escalate resistance to the plant. To prepare for civil disobedience, they turned to the Sunbelt Alliance for guidance. Jim Garrison and Brian Hunt traveled from Oklahoma to train Life Force's leaders, who, in turn, taught their members. The Life Force still needed a lawyer to represent members who'd be arrested.

Belisle and Schermbeck knew of Lewis through Garrison and Hunt and news of the Black Fox resistance. So, when they met Lewis at Mount Taylor, Belisle and Schermbeck asked him for help. Lewis wrote, "Mavis was a wonderfully kind and gentle woman, but with firmly held values and the courage to fight for them. . . . She was very level-headed, but fierce in her activism." He agreed to provide free legal advice and representation for Life Force members.

The Life Force planned to occupy Comanche Peak in June 1979. Lewis made multiple visits to the area, during which he stayed with Belisle, whose home was the Life Force's headquarters. Belisle recalled Lewis easing the anxiety of Life Force members and making protesting "feel natural." Jerry Palmer, a Life Force protester, said Lewis "just flowed with what was going on,'" "didn't try to take over or direct," "was always supportive of what they were doing," "always just said, 'Yea, we can do that,'" "was in the group" and not "on the outside," "built trust with people," and was "definitely a warrior." Palmer added, "He was a real force. It was a pleasure and an honor to be around someone who cares about life on the planet and country as much as Lewis did. His attitude helped generate a lot of positive feelings." Another protester said Lewis was "totally authentic" and "the real deal." Schermbeck shared his memories of Lewis with the Texas Legacy Project: "He stayed with us quite a while. And he went into town and talked to the sheriff, and the judge, and everybody, all the authority figures in town about what he called 'greasing the operation' . . . so it wouldn't be a surprise and so that by the time we got out there, it was a very choreographed action." "I realize now of course that he was really acting this whole time as an organizer who happened to have a handy law degree," Schermbeck wrote in 2023.

On June 9, 1979, Life Force members—joined by Lewis, Katie Greene, and others from the Sunbelt Alliance—camped along the banks of the Paluxy River. They played music and sang songs around a campfire. Belisle fondly remembered "a real innocence" about the evening.

The next morning, the group traveled ten minutes north to Comanche Peak. Forty-eight protesters climbed over the perimeter barbed-wire fence using makeshift ladders, walked further into the property, sat, and chanted. They ignored plant security's order to leave. Sixty supporters outside the fence chanted, "No nukes! No nukes!" News media observed the action. The sheriff announced that the protesters were under arrest and directed them to board two awaiting school busses. At the jail in Glen Rose, they were given citations for criminal trespass, fingerprinted, and released on personal recognizance. Their strategy was known as "sheep to slaughter" civil disobedience in antinuke circles. Jerry Palmer described the event as a "wonderfully choreographed, first-of-its-kind act of civil disobedience in Texas against nuclear power."

The Life Force sought a public trial. Lewis told the *Texas Observer*, "The purpose is not to win a legal case, but to get a forum for education. What we wanted was a head-on debate: is nuclear power so dangerous that it compels people to break the law?" Similarly, Lewis explained to the *Fort Worth Star-Telegram* that the trial would be a forum to discuss "the real issue"— nuclear power. Somervell County Judge Sam Freas, who presided over the trial, shared similar sentiments with the *Texas Observer*: "These trials are not a waste of money. They bring a certain amount of exposure and revelation as to the possible haphazardness of federal and state agencies, as well as the owners and operators of these plants."

Through contacts at the ACLU, Lewis recruited Thomas Mills, a Dallas-based attorney in private practice, to serve as pro bono cocounsel for the defendants. While working on the case in Glen Rose, Lewis and Mills spent nights sleeping on the floor of a church. Mills recalled Lewis reading aloud passages written by Karl Marx and then asking what he thought, even though they'd just met and Mills was comparatively more conservative. "He was a hero, very much admired and loved by a lot of people in the group," Mills shared. Mills also wrote, "[Lewis] was really lead counsel, and I loved his personality and easy way of dealing with people."

Later in June 1979, all forty-eight protesters were tried together over three days. Schermbeck described the scene: "The Glen Rose courthouse . . . d[id]n't even have inside bathrooms, it had an outhouse. And the courtroom itself was not air-conditioned. So, you had this 'Inherit the Wind' quality to it; everybody had fans in there; and . . . intermixed with the locals were people like me that had hair down to here and full beards and everything. It was quite a mix of folks."

The state rested its case after only twenty minutes and one witness—the county sheriff. Five or six defendants, including a pregnant mother and a nun, then testified that the dangers of nuclear energy compelled their civil disobedience. Lewis also called as expert witnesses Dr. Ernest Sternglass, a professor in the Department of Radiology at the University of Pittsburgh School of Medicine, and Rosalie Bertell, a nun, activist, author, epidemiologist, and research scientist at the Roswell Park Comprehensive Cancer Institute. To appeal to jurors and the broader public in the rural area, Sternglass and Bertell focused their testimony on the impacts of nuclear radiation and waste on humans, farm animals, and crops. A *Texas Observer* reporter wrote:

> For the past six months, the citizens of this small North Texas town have been witnessing a rather extraordinary kind of grassroots political protest. . . . The purpose of the protest is public

education. The issue is the people's right to know about the haz-
ards posed by a nuclear power plant. . . . More important than the
occupations, however, has been the series of trials which have followed. The trials have attracted scientists, lawyers, and grassroots
political organizers from all over the country. They are transforming the small county courtroom in Glen Rose into a focal point for
the debate on nuclear power—raising questions which are still too
rarely heard by the general public.

Lewis and Mills said during closing arguments that if the prosecutor "had
been the state's attorney in Massachusetts, then he would have prosecuted the
patriots of the Boston Tea Party." They ended their presentation with a quote
from Albert Einstein: "To the village square we must take the facts of atomic
energy; from there must come America's voice."

The trial ended in a hung jury. Four of the six jurors found in favor of the
defendants. Schermbeck wrote, "Jubilation creeped slowly across the benches
where 20 to 30 defendants had sat for the entire trial and then, pandemonium,
as their weariness faded and the reality of the jury's action sank in." Jerry
Palmer recalled, "Life Force members and our supporters burst into the town
square and spilled into the parking lot, singing and shouting 'No nuke around
here!'" A juror "came up and shook our hands, tears in his eyes, about what
he had found out; just an amazing sight," Schermbeck said. One juror shared
with reporters, "I don't approve of them, but I'm sort of for them. I think they
did some good—some people learned a lot they didn't know beforehand."
Another juror commented, "I thought all we had to worry about was it blow-
ing up. During the trial, the main thing that dawned on me was the radiation
it put out every day. I've told a bunch of people about that." A juror told the
defendants on the courthouse steps, "If I'd known what I know now on June
10, I'd have climbed that fence with you." One juror, who was a railroad me-
chanic and hog farmer, divulged, "I went up there thinking they were guilty
and thinking it would be dull. . . . But I sat up there three days and never did
get sleepy. It was interesting. The two professors they had up there definitely
changed my mind. What really stuck was what they said about the low-level
radiation and cancer rates. I figured if those people had read up on it the way
they seemed to and knew it was dangerous and cared that much about it, they
have a right to do it."

Belisle credited the victory to Lewis skillfully "handling the local people"
and being "compatible with jurors," especially the moonshiner. Palmer said

Lewis was "smooth talking," "down to earth," and a "pleasure to be around." He also recalled that Lewis could talk to jurors "just like they were his next-door neighbors." Schermbeck wrote, "Besides a natural charisma and good looks, Lewis is blessed with one of the sweetest Carolinian accents it's ever been my pleasure to hear. Using it he could make getting busted in rural Texas over a high-profile political fight as inconvenient as getting a traffic ticket. His self-possession was very convincing to us, the Judge, the Sheriff, and ultimately the jury."

Schermbeck told the Texas Legacy Project, "The trial was much more . . . lasting in terms of its impact than the occupation was even, for that town. . . . It was transforming for us and for them, as well. And that was probably the highlight of that whole chain of events down there in Glen Rose." He wrote that the trial created "a new air of cooperation between the Life Force and the other antinuclear groups who were keeping their distance before"; helped "in dispelling stereotypes" about the defendants; "put the issues of nuclear power on display as never before"; and "spurred a wave of new energy and enthusiasm towards grassroots organizing in the Glen Rose area." Finally, Schermbeck wrote, "The success we had in the first and only trial of nuclear power in Texas is directly attributable to Lewis's presence and guidance."

Christic Institute Formation

In fall 1979, Danny Sheehan convened a small group of friends and colleagues, most of whom worked on the Silkwood campaign, including Lewis. The meeting took place at Arupe House, an old Catholic convent in Washington, DC. Sheehan wrote in his autobiography, *The People's Advocate*, "It was at this meeting that we resolved to form a permanent organization. . . . We would become 'the people's advocates' for those who had long been denied justice. . . . We would serve as 'the people's Justice Department,' taking on cases that extended well beyond nuclear power and nuclear weapons issues. . . . We decided to call ourselves the Christic Institute. 'Christic' was the designation given by Pierre Teilhard de Chardin, a famous Jesuit theologian and philosopher, . . . to 'that binding force that binds every ultimately non-divisible integer of matter in the entire physical Universe together into one, single, harmonic whole.'" Sheehan explained that he invited Lewis to join the new organization because Lewis produced quality work for the Silkwood case; is loving, considerate, compassionate, caring, hopeful, "dedicated to justice," "the real deal," and a "complete and full human being"; and "has all of the attributes of a Saint."

Despite Lewis's antipathy toward the Silkwood legal team and growing disdain for the legal profession, he chose to be a founding staff and board member. First and foremost, Christic Institute's mission aligned with his values and interests, as well as with the liberation theology precepts he learned from his mother. Additionally, the other board members agreed to Lewis continuing to focus on grassroots antinuclear campaigns. He was also allured by the relative stability and income Christic could provide—albeit $400 a month and only when funding was available. He'd had scant income in the three years since leaving the public defender's office. Lewis wrote about the year leading up to Christic's formation:

> I had no formal job. Activists took me in to sleep on couches. They fed me or gave me some money. In New Mexico, I did a day or two of manual labor. In Tulsa, I took a part-time job with the public defender's office. . . . It was sort of a barter system—legal work for food, a room or couch, or gas money. This is why I hitchhiked and rode Greyhound buses, which really impressed on me the stratification of society and the pain and hurt in life. Ride all night on a Greyhound and sit near the back, and you see some broken lives—alcohol addiction, broken relationships, and lots of the things found in country songs.

Christic's founding team included Sara Nelson as executive director, Sheehan as general counsel and public policy director, Hager as legal director, and Lewis as a staff attorney. Father Bill Davis, a Jesuit priest, was also heavily involved. Their goals were to: "represent victims of injustice before courts and create a factual basis for political education"; "help citizens understand that single cases of injustice are often symptomatic of deeper threats to the freedom of every U.S. citizen"; and "help grassroots activists and religious communities organize for effective political change."

After the meeting in Washington, DC, Lewis returned to the antinuclear movement in Oklahoma, where he'd represent himself and other protesters in the aforementioned trial for the June 2, 1979, occupation of the Black Fox plant. Then, at the end of September 1979, he traveled a thousand miles to join protesters for a second demonstration at the nuclear plant in Barnwell, South Carolina.

Southeastern Natural Guard Movement in South Carolina

Southwestern South Carolina was a hotbed of corporate and government nuclear activity. In the 1950s, the federal government spent $260 million to construct the Savannah River Site (SRS) nuclear reservation on 310 square miles spanning Aiken, Allendale, and Barnwell Counties. First, however, towns and communities standing in the way were destroyed using eminent domain—the power of the government to take private property and convert it into public use. For the SRS land, the public purpose was refining materials for nuclear weapons. Gil Scott-Heron sang about the potential dangers of the SRS in his song "South Carolina (Barnwell)."

In 1971, Chem-Nuclear Systems began operating a radioactive waste disposal facility in Barnwell County. Also in 1971, Allied-General Nuclear Services began constructing, in Barnwell County, a plant designed to recycle uranium and plutonium from the fuel rods used to power nuclear reactors. Lewis and his former law partner, Bob Warren, were part of a protest against the plant in April 1978.

The Southeastern Natural Guard, a coalition of twenty environmental justice groups, planned three days of antinuclear activities to begin in Barnwell County on September 29, 1979, and culminate in civil disobedience. Approximately fifteen hundred people gathered in Barnwell for seminars, a performance by Graham Nash, and a march alongside the facility's fences while chanting slogans like "Hell no! We won't glow!"

On October 1, 1979, approximately 161 demonstrators, including Lewis, were arrested for trespassing during simultaneous protests at the SRS and Allied-General plant. Shortly thereafter, most of the protesters were released on fifteen-dollar bond. They later pleaded nolo contendere, meaning they accepted convictions as though guilty pleas had been entered but didn't admit guilt. Lewis, however, chose jail over the bond. He explained in his journal, "I needed a rest break; so, I did the ten days in jail as respite."

Lewis and Warren represented thirty protesters arrested at the SRS. Their five-day jury trial began on January 29, 1980. Lewis and Warren presented a necessity defense. Lewis told jurors, "There are two very basic things involved. First is the fundamental right to free speech, which is far older than the trespassing law. Second, there is the defense of necessity." About a dozen of the protesters testified in their own defense. During closing arguments, South Carolina Assistant AG Buford Mabry warned jurors that a not guilty verdict would be a slippery slope: "If they come on the yard this week, they'll be on the porch the next, and then the house the following week."

The jury found the defendants guilty. Six demonstrators who were considered the ring leaders were given the maximum sentence—thirty days in jail, suspended upon payment of a one-hundred-dollar fine. The remaining defendants were sentenced to twenty days in jail, suspended upon payment of a thirty-five-dollar fine. Warren remarked at the time, "The Savannah River Plant is the most dangerous plant in the world. What has come out in this trial has terrified me."

Around the same time, Lewis and Warren also represented Susan Lott, a former accountant at the Chem-Nuclear facility. She was fired in October 1978, after filing a sex discrimination complaint with the EEOC. A year later, she reported to the South Carolina AG that Chem-Nuclear was illegally receiving liquid radioactive waste from other utility companies and had buried at least three tanker trucks that were too contaminated to save. The South Carolina AG's Office opened an investigation, which the NRC and DOJ later joined. Lott then alleged, under oath, that Chem-Nuclear buried highly radioactive spent nuclear fuel rods in violation of state and federal law.

Lott told reporters that after the state investigation began, she and her family received threatening phone calls and suffered attempted break-ins at their home. Lewis and Warren asked state authorities to seek immunity from prosecution for Lott in return for her testimony about under-the-table payments between various other utility companies and Chem-Nuclear officials. However, in April 1980, the government issued a report concluding that no evidence was found to substantiate Lott's allegations.

Protest at the Pentagon

The Coalition for a Non-nuclear World organized four days of activities to take place in Washington, DC, in late April 1980. The events included a prayer vigil in front of the White House, a rally at the Washington Monument, lobbying at the Capitol, and civil disobedience at the Pentagon and Department of Energy. The coalition sought an end to uranium mining on Native American lands, construction of nuclear reactors, and production of nuclear weapons. The coalition's organizing materials read, "If we—who are so concerned about the escalating nuclear threat—are not willing to make sacrifices, such as risking jail, then how can we expect to convince the general public to take more moderate steps. . . . Put your body and convictions on the line."

On April 28, 1980, approximately twelve hundred demonstrators heeded the coalition's call. They used their bodies and objects to block Metro stations, traffic, and entrances around the Pentagon to symbolize "shutting down" the US Department of Defense. Protesters also let the air out of Pentagon employees' car tires, displayed banners, threw red paint representing blood against buildings, dressed as black-robed "death figures," and wore white nuclear technician suits and surgical masks while carrying coffins. Hundreds of Federal Protective Service officers arrested more than three hundred demonstrators, shoving and dragging some of them. Among those arrested were Lewis; Benjamin Spock, a famous pediatrician; David Dellinger, a member of the "Chicago Seven"; and Daniel Ellsberg, who leaked the "Pentagon Papers." Some of Lewis's friends and former clients from Oklahoma, Texas, and South Carolina were also in Washington, DC, for the events. The arrestees were bussed to local jails for the night.

The following day, Lewis appeared before a federal magistrate in Alexandria, Virginia. He pleaded nolo contendere—that is, he accepted a conviction without admitting guilt—in exchange for six months of unsupervised probation.

Changing His Role in the Antinuclear Movement

During his first six years as an attorney, Lewis had used the law to achieve positive outcomes for criminal defendants, low-income plaintiffs, antinuclear activists, and others. Nevertheless, he continued struggling with his intensifying contempt for lawyers and the legal system and his growing skepticism of the law as an effective tool for social change. He wrote in his journal in October 1979, "I'm absolutely convinced that within the legal system efforts are not for me. I hate lawyers and wasting time in that charade."

In February 1980, Lewis visited Common Ground, an antinuclear activist commune in or near Snow, Oklahoma. There, he took peyote; vowed to quit lawyering and become a full-time, antinuclear, grassroots organizer; and dumped the contents of his briefcase into a bonfire to symbolically disconnect himself from what he regarded as an oppressive legal system.

While Lewis was deciding to quit practicing law, he also wrestled with difficult questions related to his role in the antinuclear movement and the efficacy of various advocacy tactics. On one hand, he abhorred violence, knew nonviolence attracted more moderate advocates, and witnessed the positive outcomes of peaceful, pre-orchestrated civil disobedience in Oklahoma,

Texas, and South Carolina. On the other hand, Lewis felt that nonviolent civil disobedience wasn't effectuating change quickly enough. His impatience intensified following the meltdown at Three Mile Island (TMI) in March 1979, and spill in Church Rock, New Mexico, in July 1979. His restlessness was also fueled by reading the works of Che Guevara, Fidel Castro, and Regis Debray. "The prime role of a leader is to offer an example of courage and sacrifice," Debray wrote. Lewis was inspired by Debray's foco theory of revolution, which, in short, was that vanguardism by cadres of small, fast-moving paramilitary groups can provide a focus for popular discontent against a sitting regime and thereby lead a general insurrection. Lewis's journal entries at the time reflected his disquiet and desperation. For instance, he wrote:

> I'm still tormented to think of me using violence! But the capitalist system does violence every day—directly and indirectly. Nuclear war seems looming ahead. Maybe internal U.S. strife can redirect everything. . . . My recent readings about guerilla warriors have shown me their unbelievable courage and my frail indecisiveness. Thousands in the past have given their all for the struggle—shouldn't I? . . . What form of revolution is still my burning question. . . . I've . . . wrestled with the question of violence; wrestled with it for over a year, in fact. . . . Somebody has got to "heighten the contradictions" and polarize the issue in order to force Americans out of their apathy. Since nobody else is taking the action, I should. . . .

Lewis acknowledges, in retrospect, that his reflections included "sectarian left regurgitation" and suggest he might have had a messiah complex. However, Lewis also believes that his words reflected justifiable outrage about human suffering and avidity about ending it. He reflected, "It just hurt. All this pain hurts and angers me. Redress needs to comport with the extent of harm. You don't take an aspirin if you're gonna have your leg sawed off. . . . We celebrate the first responders when they run into a building to save a kitten or child. We don't question if they have a messiah complex. We see it as selfless and heroic. But if you start to do it for larger societal goals, or anti-capitalism, then it starts to become pejorative."

Ultimately, early in 1980, Lewis concluded that property destruction would be his proportional response to the dangers of nuclear energy and weapons, and that he'd play a vanguard role in the antinuclear movement.

He can't remember who he consulted about his decision but assumes he told Katie Greene and had the blessing of other Christic Institute staff. He began planning to move to Pennsylvania, near TMI, to organize, commit civil disobedience, and carry out violent direct action, without physically harming people.

Three Mile Island

Three Mile Island is a nuclear power plant built in 1974 atop a sandbar on the Susquehanna River, about ten miles from the Pennsylvania State Capitol in Harrisburg. On March 28, 1979, a reactor at TMI—operated by Metropolitan Edison Company—partially melted down, releasing radioactive material. Confusion, stress, fear, and class action litigation ensued, as well as cleanup that took more than a decade and cost nearly a billion dollars. The meltdown is the most serious accident in US commercial nuclear power plant operating history.

A year later, Lewis and a man, "John," who he'd met along his antinuclear movement lawyering travels were sleeping on the floor of the new Christic Institute office located about a mile and a half north of the US Capitol Building. Two siblings—a priest and a nun—had inherited an old, two-story cobbler shop and donated the building to Christic. John recalled that, while in Washington, DC, he and Lewis mostly survived on grits, Cream of Wheat, and "hobo coffee" and typically traveled by walking, jumping Metro turnstiles, and hitchhiking. They both remember occasionally scrounging up enough money to eat themselves sick at a Hare Krishna buffet restaurant.

They were assisting with preparations for the aforementioned antinuclear events that'd take place at the end of April 1980. One of their assignments was to walk around the Pentagon, determine the best areas for protesters to block entrances and exits, and then draw a map for the demonstration—a "scoping-it-out mission," Lewis called it. They were also planning a trial "escalated hit," in Lewis's words, at TMI.

On April 20, 1980, Lewis and John drove to Pennsylvania. Around 2:30 A.M. the next morning, they snuck onto Metropolitan Edison Company property that was across the river from TMI. They crept to an unoccupied, 805-square-foot trailer that served as a communications center and was twenty feet from the TMI Observation Center. Then, they broke the trailer's windows and poured gasoline and threw lit flares inside. Flames burst through a window, brushing Lewis's face and singeing off parts of his beard and eyebrows. They sprinted to their car and drove straight back to Washington, DC. Meanwhile, firefighters responded to the blaze. They put out the remaining fire and hosed down the nearby Observation Center as a precaution. No one was harmed but the trailer and everything inside were destroyed.

A state police fire marshal investigated and determined the fire was "deliberately set by an arsonist or arsonists." In the meantime, back in DC, Lewis and John scoured national news but found nothing about a fire near TMI. Lewis laid low for a while to avoid anyone seeing his singed face.

John and Lewis went their separate ways. More than forty years later, John still remembered Lewis very fondly, commenting, "I'd do anything for Lewis. I really would. . . . God knows I'm proud of him. I've followed him from afar. Damn proud of him."

Lewis and John had no idea what happened to the trailer until 2022. Lewis wondered whether the fire went out as soon as they ran away, and if so, whether their failure was the result of incompetence or divine intervention. Lewis also questioned whether the power structure had actively concealed their courageous act so others wouldn't be encouraged or inspired to undertake similar actions. Upon learning he'd succeeded in destroying the trailer, Lewis very briefly wondered if his involvement becoming public would put him in jeopardy. However, in his words, he quickly "decided that candor was more important." "Being open is how I've lived my life. I'm kinda proud of the fire and being willing to do something that serious. I don't want to start hiding or ducking now."

Amsterdam

By spring 1980, Jim Garrison, Lewis's friend from antinuclear activism in Oklahoma, had returned to Cambridge University, started two antinuclear organizations, and published his first book. He had also received grant funding to organize an "International Conference on Nuclear Trade." A convening to plan the conference was scheduled for June 1980 in Amsterdam. Garrison recruited Lewis to assist with the events.

Lewis embarked on his first trip abroad on May 29, 1980, several weeks before the convening. He spent a few days with Garrison in England before continuing to the Netherlands.

Antinuclear delegates from various countries attended the convening, which, according to Lewis, quickly became divisive. Participants grew suspicious of each other and argued about whether to focus on nuclear weapons or commercial nuclear power. Moreover, some attendees suspected the Americans of being spies and resented them because of Hiroshima, Nagasaki, and US-made reactors being shipped abroad. Ultimately, the conference never happened.

While their primary focus was organizing the convening, Lewis and Garrison had another reason for being abroad—to procure explosives for antinuclear property destruction. They both recall paying an American woman, who called herself "Mary," to meet them in Amsterdam. Mary claimed to have access to explosives and to be the daughter of Robert Williams, a civil rights leader, founder of Radio Free Dixie, and author of *Negroes with Guns*. Mary was supposed to be accompanied by Ron Karenga, a Black Nationalism activist and professor of Africana studies, best known as the creator of Kwanza; however, she claimed that he was detained at the airport. Lewis can't recall why they met Mary in Amsterdam rather than in the United States. Regardless, according to Lewis and Garrison, Mary strung them along, manipulating their "white guilt" for a free trip to Amsterdam, and they never obtained the explosives.

While in Amsterdam, Lewis wrote a letter to Fidel Castro asking to be trained as a freedom fighter. Unsurprisingly, Lewis didn't receive a response. He realizes, in retrospect, that the letter was naïve and "borderline stupid because surely the FBI and CIA seized the letter."

After the disappointing convening, conference cancellation, and ordeal with Mary, Lewis and Garrison traveled in France and Germany using a borrowed car. Garrison reminisced, "We had a great series of adventures. Just being on the road. . . . Beatles, sex, drugs, and rock and roll. It was the greatest generation. I'm tellin' ya."

Moving On

Regarding his two years traversing the country, broke and fighting nuclear proliferation, Lewis shared, "Talk about livin' free. I'd have a few beers and a joint, look up at the night sky, and think, 'Where am I right now—Texas, Oklahoma, South Carolina?' I had to think for a second or two before remembering where I was." By summer 1980, he had resigned himself to a likely future of prison or death in the name of fighting nuclear proliferation and, more broadly, the energy companies and defense contractors that represented the greed and capitalism he hated.

However, Lewis's fate changed with a knock on the Christic office door. Two lawyers, Earle Tockman and Tom Ono, showed up to meet with Danny Sheehan, Christic's general counsel. However, Sheehan wasn't at the office; so, Lewis met with Tockman and Ono. They discussed recent events in Greensboro, North Carolina—specifically, the killing of communist activists by Klansmen and Nazis, with the complicity of law enforcement. The victims' comrades needed legal assistance. Lewis accepted their invitation to visit Greensboro.

CHAPTER 5

Labor and Racial Justice Movement in Greensboro, NC

Greensboro, North Carolina, has a long, complicated history of racial and class-based tensions. During the first half of the nineteenth century, the city was a hub for Quaker antislavery activity. In the late nineteenth and early twentieth centuries, textile mills brought increased racial and economic diversity to the area. Additionally, the city's historically black colleges and universities—North Carolina A&T State University and Bennett College, both founded in the second half of the nineteenth century—contributed to the development of a local Black middle class.

Nevertheless, white industrialists continued to dominate Greensboro and were determined to resist labor organizing and maintain a Black underclass. In the 1960s, Greensboro was a hotbed of the civil rights movement, including sit-ins at Woolworth's and the uprising at Dudley High School. Additionally, during the 1960s and 1970s, the labor movement gained a foothold in Greensboro as the textile industry boomed across the state.

In 1979, New Left communist groups in Greensboro and Durham, North Carolina, became part of the national Workers Viewpoint Organization (WVO), a Maoist, anti-Soviet organization. Members worked and organized in factories, including textile mills in and around Greensboro. They were also involved in anti-racism causes, such as freeing the "Wilmington Ten"—a group of nine Black men and one white woman wrongfully convicted of firebombing a white-owned business in Wilmington, North Carolina. Additionally, WVO members protested the KKK and other white supremacist groups that racially divided workers, thereby interfering with interracial labor organizing.

The Klan was virulently anti-communist, like much of the country after the Vietnam War and as the Cold War lingered. During the 1960s, there were approximately twelve thousand Klansmen in North Carolina. They thrived among white mill workers and other blue-collar laborers by playing on fears of immigrants and racial minorities "taking jobs" from white people. Although Klan membership declined during the 1970s, the group remained considerable and joined forces with neo-Nazi groups.

In July 1979, the WVO squared off with the KKK and Nazi Party in China Grove, an hour southwest of Greensboro. The Klan was screening "Birth of a Nation" at the local community center. About sixty WVO members and other anti-racism activists staged a counter-protest.

WVO members—some waving bats, sticks, or pipes—chanted "Death to the Klan!" and "Kill the Klan!" while standing face-to-face with Klansmen and Nazis who were aiming weapons back at them. Gorrell Pierce, a KKK leader, said communists and Klansmen were so close they "could feel each other's breath." Law enforcement officers and journalists gathered around the porch while Joe Grady, grand dragon of the Federated Knights of the KKK, preached to the crowd and cameras.

Before the situation turned violent, law enforcement ordered the Klansmen and Nazis to leave. The WVO celebrated by burning the Confederate flag. "There will be revenge for this," Grady promised. Years later, Signe Waller, a WVO member, wrote, "The [WVO] displayed an arrogant triumphalism at and after China Grove. The Klan felt humiliated and grew angrier and more vengeful after China Grove."

In September 1979, Klan and Nazi Party members formed a coalition—the United Racist Front. Meanwhile, to build on momentum from China Grove, WVO members planned a rally, march, and conference to be held in Greensboro. The gathering, called "Death to the Klan," was scheduled for November 3, 1979.

Greensboro-based civil rights activist and WVO member Nelson Johnson applied for a parade permit. The application included the planned march route, listed Morningside Homes as the pre-march assembly point, and stipulated, pursuant to a directive from the Greensboro Police Department (GPD), WVO members would limit the size of their picket sticks and wouldn't carry firearms. Morningside Homes was a public housing community for Black people where WVO members had been working with residents for years. Leading up to November 3, the WVO distributed leaflets about "Death to the Klan" in the community and met with Morningside's Neighborhood Residents Council.

The WVO continued antagonizing the Klan in the weeks leading up to "Death to the Klan." WVO members publicly called Klansmen "too cowardly" to show up at the event and face the "wrath of the people." On an event flyer, the WVO claimed to have "chased . . . scum Klansmen off the lawn" at China Grove. "[The Klan] should be physically beaten and chased out of town," another flyer read. An "open letter" from the WVO to "Joe Grady, Gorrell Pierce, and all KKK members and sympathizers" challenged the Klan to attend, asserting that the rally was meant "to organize to physically smash the racist KKK wherever it rears its ugly head." Nelson Johnson penned his own open letter, which read, "Klanspeople, and your Nazi friends—you are a temporary pest and an obstruction in our fight to end all exploitation and oppression. . . . We will show you no mercy. DEATH TO THE KLAN!!!" During a press conference, WVO member Paul Bermanzohn said, "[The Klan] can and will be crushed. They are cowards, night riders who try to terrorize innocent people. They must be physically beaten back, eradicated, exterminated, wiped off the face of the earth. We invite you and your two-bit punks to come out and face the wrath of the people." Notably, two days before the event, Johnson publicly declared, "We say to Mayor Jim Melvin and the police, stay out of our way. We will defend ourselves."

Meanwhile, the FBI was investigating the WVO, KKK, and Nazi Party. Law enforcement had moles within the Klan and Nazi Party. The FBI had recruited Eddie Dawson, while he was serving prison time for Klan-related activities, to become an informant. He then became a paid GPD informant, with Detective Jerry Cooper as his handler. In July 1979, the Bureau of Alcohol, Tobacco, and Firearms (BATF) assigned Undercover Agent Bernard Butkovich to infiltrate the Nazi Party. Posing as an associate of the party's Forsyth County Chapter, Butkovich offered to sell automatic weapons to the Nazis.

Dawson and Butkovich were involved in the Klan's and Nazi Party's preparations to confront the WVO on November 3. In Black neighborhoods, Dawson posted fliers featuring a lynched body and warning, "Even now, the crosshairs are on the back of YOUR necks. It's time for old-fashioned American Justice." Additionally, Dawson obtained a copy of the parade permit and shared it with the Klan and Nazi Party. He also drove the march route with Klansmen the night before the event. Butkovich encouraged Nazis to bring weapons to the rally. Dawson notified his former FBI control agent and GPD officials that the Klan was planning an armed confrontation on November 3.

The BATF, FBI, and GPD chose not to warn the WVO about white supremacists' plans. Worse still, Deputy GPD Chief Walter Burch decided law enforcement would take a "low profile" at the march, keeping officers out of sight, purportedly to avoid provoking a confrontation with marchers.

In October 1979 the WVO changed its name to the Communist Workers Party (CWP).

The Greensboro Massacre

On the morning of November 3, 1979, approximately thirty-five Klansmen and Nazis gathered at a Klansman's home on the outskirts of Greensboro. The white supremacists discussed plans to confront marchers, studied the march route, and stockpiled weapons, including shotguns, rifles, handguns, nunchucks, knives, brass knuckles, clubs, chains, tear gas, and mace. Detective Cooper, who was surveilling the house, reported his observations to GPD headquarters.

Meanwhile, marchers arrived at Morningside Homes, where they sang, chanted, circulated newsletters, made signs, and hid weapons. One person had an effigy of a Klansman with a noose around his neck and a sign that read, "KKK Scum." The media began arriving. Law enforcement was noticeably absent, despite the history and violent rhetoric among the communists and white supremacist groups, Dawson's and Butkovich's involvement in planning a confrontation and their warnings, and Cooper's observations that morning. Two patrol officers responding to a domestic disturbance just a few doors down from the march staging area—the intersection of Everitt and Carver Streets—were suspiciously ordered to leave the area. Additionally, members of a GPD tactical squad assigned to monitor the rally were taking an early lunch break elsewhere.

At approximately 11:00 A.M., Dawson hurried Klansmen and Nazis into vehicles and then boarded the lead car with Virgil Griffin, the grand dragon of the North Carolina Knights of the KKK. They led a caravan of nine vehicles toward Morningside Homes. Cooper, accompanied by a police photographer, followed the caravan and radioed in its movement toward the rally; however, he reportedly couldn't reach his superiors on duty because they weren't using their radios.

Twenty minutes later, the caravan approached Morningside Homes, where forty to fifty demonstrators, children, and residents were gathered. Someone noticed a Confederate flag on one of the cars and cried, "Here comes the Klan!" Dawson shouted at Paul Bermanzohn, "You wanted the Klan, you communist son-of-a-bitch? Well, you got the Klan!" A Nazi gestured toward the demonstrators and yelled, "Remember China Grove?" The groups heckled each other. White supremacists screamed, "niggers," "kikes," and "commie bastards." Marchers chanted "Death to the Klan!" and "Ku Klux Klan, scum of the land!" Cooper again radioed from his unmarked car: "Okay we got nine or ten cars . . . now at the parade formation point. . . . They are driving through and heckling. . . . They're scattering."

A marcher hit the lead car carrying Dawson and Griffin with a picket stick. The vehicle swerved toward a second marcher who dodged and kicked the car. Demonstrators began banging caravan vehicles with their hands, feet, and sticks.

Klansmen and Nazis stopped, exited their vehicles, and, armed with various weapons, moved toward the intersection. A brawl ensued. Cooper announced the fight over the police radio and advised, "You better get some units in here." GPD officers finally headed to the scene but failed to arrive before the confrontation turned deadly.

At 11:23 A.M., two Klansmen fired weapons into the air. One of them yelled, "Shoot the niggers!" Other white supremacists retrieved firearms from their vehicles and opened fire at demonstrators. Some of the communists fired back. In eighty-eight seconds, according to shifting and unreliable accounts from the FBI, thirty-nine shots were fired—twenty-one from locations occupied by Klansmen and Nazis, including the first shots, and eighteen from locations occupied by CWP members. Cooper didn't attempt to intervene; instead, he watched from his car while the police photographer snapped photographs of the violence.

Uniformed officers finally arrived at 11:25 A.M. They stopped a van carrying twelve Klansmen and Nazis, arresting all of them and confiscating the weapons and ammunition inside. GPD officers allowed the other caravan vehicles to speed away. Stunned demonstrators and bystanders emerged from hiding places and wandered around the intersection. Some of them screamed and cried; others voiced outrage about law enforcement's tardiness.

Five CWP members died—four at the intersection and one two days later. Cesar Cauce—a Cuban immigrant, Duke University graduate, and union organizer—was hit on the head with a stick and shot in the chest. Sandra Neely Smith—a Black woman, Bennett College graduate, nurse, civil rights activist, and union organizer—was shot above her eye while she was looking for children to protect. James Waller, "Jim,"—president of a local textile workers union, a medical doctor, and cofounder of the Carolina Brown Lung Association—was shot in the back, lungs, and heart. Michael Nathan—chief of pediatrics at a community health center—was shot in the face as he ran to help Waller. Nathan died two days later, after being sworn in to the CWP on his deathbed. William Sampson, "Bill,"—a Harvard Divinity School and University of Virginia Medical School graduate and union steward—was shot in the heart while returning fire at Klansmen.

Other CWP members and allies were badly injured. Paul Bermanzohn, a Duke-educated medical doctor and cofounder of the Carolina Brown Lung Association, was shot in the head and arm. He survived following brain surgery but sustained permanent paralysis on his left side. Jim Wrenn was shot nine times—including twice in the head and once in the chest—after attempting to pull Michael Nathan to safety. He survived after undergoing brain surgery and being on life support for a time. Nelson Johnson was cut on the hand and stabbed through the arm. Don Pelles, Tom Clark, Rand Manzella, and Frankie Powell were wounded by shotgun pellets.

Four CWP members were arrested. After police officers wrestled him to the ground and put a boot on his neck, Johnson was arrested for "inciting a riot." While trying to aid Johnson, Willena Cannon was arrested for "interfering with an officer." Police also arrested Manzella for gun possession and James Carthen for disorderly conduct.

No Klansmen or Nazis died; one suffered an injury; and only the van occupants were arrested on November 3. The next day, two additional Klansmen were arrested on murder and conspiracy charges.

The ordeal on November 3 came to be known as the "Greensboro Massacre."

Legal Team

In spring 1980, families and friends of the deceased formed a nonprofit—the Greensboro Justice Fund (GJF)—and began fundraising for a civil lawsuit. The fund was primarily staffed by widows Marty Nathan and Dale Sampson. Its advisory board included doctors, religious leaders, professors, and activists. The GJF's legal team initially consisted of Stewart Kwoh and Tom Ono, who practiced together in Los Angeles, as well as Gayle Korotkin and Earle Tockman, who the CWP sent to Greensboro just days after the massacre.

Korotkin was small in stature and exceptionally introverted—"quiet as a church mouse," said Lewis. After serving as an AmeriCorps Volunteers in Service to America member in Chicago and an employment counselor in the Bronx, she earned a law degree from New York University. She then spent nearly four years as a tenant organizer and legal services attorney in New York

City. Signe Waller, wrote in her book, *Love and Revolution,* "Gayle Korotkin, a lawyer friend of CWP head Jerry Tung from New York and an unassuming, self-effacing person, volunteered to stay in Greensboro indefinitely to do whatever necessary for justice in our case. Over the next six years, she lived, slept, ate, spoke, wrote, and dreamed Greensboro."

In many ways, Tockman was the opposite of Korotkin. According to Lewis and others, Tockman was loud and hotheaded. He joined the WVO in Chicago and in 1976 was among the ranks that the organization's leadership sent to work and organize in factories. Prior to the massacre, Tockman provided legal services for Sandra Smith and met other CWP members in North Carolina.

LEWIS JOINS

Earle Tockman and Tom Ono turned to the Christic Institute for legal help. Lewis accepted their invitation to visit Greensboro. First, however, in July 1980, Lewis and Katie Greene attended the ten-day Black Hills International Survival Gathering. The antinuclear event drew approximately twelve thousand participants from around the world to a ranch east of Rapid City, South Dakota. Lewis and Greene drove from Oklahoma to South Dakota in Greene's old Subaru. Along the way, they slept in a cornfield because they couldn't afford a motel. At the ranch, they stayed in a tent, despite scorching temperatures. The gathering included workshops about genocide of Native Americans, destruction of family farms, and alternatives to nuclear energy. There were also concerts and speeches by John Trudell and Sandinistas. Lewis wrote about their trip, "We were reading Che and Fidel; trying to figure out how best to make a difference, end the madness, and be young and in love. . . . We had a blast."

Then, Lewis and Greene traveled to Columbia, South Carolina, for an antinuclear movement meeting. Afterward, they visited Lewis's parents in Bethune and Greene's parents in New York, hitchhiking for part of the trip after Greene's car broke down. Finally, the couple went to Greensboro to meet with massacre survivors and CWP lawyers.

Initially, CWP members in Greensboro were taken aback by Lewis and Greene. Marty Nathan was quoted in Sally Bermanzohn's book, *Through Survivors' Eyes*: "And these hippies . . . came to town. Lewis had a thick southern drawl, long hair, and he never wore shoes. . . ." Tockman recalled, "They were like a counter-cultural couple. . . . They weren't wearing underwear kinda thing. . . . We were like, 'What the fuck?' . . . When they came down, they were like in a different world. They were like from Mars; like from fuckin' outer space." Signe Waller said Lewis and Greene looked like they "had just been wandering all over," "living in tents or cars," and "in the rough for a while." Nelson Johnson wrote that he, as "a rural, Black 'son of the South,'" was "cautious" of Lewis's "distinct, white southern accent."

CWP members quickly warmed to the couple. Johnson recalled, "It did not take me long to discern in Lewis a deep sense of integrity, a profound understanding of structural social injustices, and a fierce determination to struggle for a more just society and a more peaceful nation." Lewis "immediately understood the issues and dynamics of the [massacre], the place and the time," Marty Nathan wrote. Tockman said of Lewis and Greene, "They were terrific. Everybody loved them. Everybody trusted them."

CWP members played a videotape of the massacre for Lewis and Greene, who described the footage as "horrifying and heartbreaking." Widows and victims also shared their painful stories. "We were moved by the depth of their personal loss and by their commitment to work tirelessly to attain justice on behalf of loved ones who had been slain or injured," Greene wrote.

Nelson Johnson, his wife, Joyce Johnson, and the existing legal team members convinced Lewis that he'd be foolish and self-centered to give up practicing law because radical groups needed lawyers to assist in defending and building movements. They helped him understand that "the issue was not whether to be a movement lawyer but how to be a movement lawyer," according to Lewis. Tockman recollected about Lewis, "He's on his way to blow something up. And we're like, 'Woah, slow down, man. . . . Let's talk about this. . . . That's some anarchist shit and it won't get you anywhere.' Who knows what would've happened to him if he hadn't met us." "No shit the legal system is oppressive and corrupt, but you can use it for the movement," is how Lewis summarized their message. Elizabeth Wheaton wrote in her book, *Codename Greenkil: The 1979 Greensboro Killings*:

> The years of battling the combined forces of the government's Nuclear Regulatory Commission and the nuclear corporations had left him embittered toward the legal system and the capitalist state. . . . Pitts considered himself a self-made revolutionary who had forsaken the practice of law. . . .
>
> Pitts' return to legal work was inspired, he explained, by Gayle Korotkin and the other lawyers who were representing the

Communists. "They told me, 'Look man, cool out. Revolution takes utilizing all forms of struggle, which includes legal, particularly when the legal system is used to convey the illusion of democracy and fairness.'"

Lewis and Greene were sold. He was moved by the tragedy, eager to be back in the South, and excited to work with the young CWP revolutionaries. Moreover, life on the road was lonely; he longed to establish roots in a community and have a full-time relationship with Greene. Regularly being in one place would allow him to more fully be a movement lawyer. Likewise, Greene looked forward to helping with massacre-related public education and organizing and to being with Lewis more. She shared:

> My decision to move to Greensboro with Lewis to work on the case meant that I would be putting the completion of my undergraduate degree on hold, . . . moving to an area of the country . . . I never thought I would live, . . . and, most significantly, . . . making a commitment to my relationship with Lewis.
>
> Lewis and I were . . . an unlikely pair. Lewis was 33, the oldest of four children raised in a small Southern rural community, divorced, and well along his chosen career path. . . . I was 23, a middle child of six children raised in a suburb of New York City, working on my undergraduate degree, trying to figure out "which way forward." Rather than focusing on these differences, in fact giving little thought to them, I was attracted to Lewis' passion for and commitment to public interest work, to his easy manner with people, to his kindness and compassion. Ultimately, I fell in love with Lewis because he recognized and celebrated my strengths, as well. He valued in me what I valued most in myself.
>
> Being with Lewis was the easy part. The challenge: believing that I was not jumping on the back of his white horse, that I would remain true to my own journey, that my work in Greensboro would be of value and valued. Taking a leap of faith—in myself, in our relationship—I said "yes" to Lewis, to Greensboro, to uncertainty, to a new beginning.

Christic Institute's board agreed to take the GJF on as a client and deploy Lewis to Greensboro. Years later, he told the Associated Press, "It was kind of unsettling, being our first year as a public interest law firm, funded primarily by religious groups, and dealing with a case that involved communists and Klansmen, guns, shooting deaths and all of that."

Lewis abandoned his plans to move near TMI and focus on antinuclear activism, agreed to be chief legal counsel for the GJF, put a copy of the Constitution back in his briefcase, and moved to Greensboro with Greene in August 1980. Signe Waller wrote, "An outstanding people's lawyer, Pitts . . . was exactly the kind of lawyer we needed to lead the legal fight for justice in our civil rights suit. A skilled legal strategist, Lewis understood the relationship between political activism and the courts. He was deeply committed to democratic processes and to people at the grassroots." In 2018, during a gathering with massacre survivors, Lewis recalled, "I came here trying to be a studied terrorist. . . . But these people talked to me. . . . So, I take the earring off, get a haircut, put on some underwear, buy a tie, and start with the process."

OTHERS JOIN

The GJF still needed more lawyers on its legal team—called the "Legal Alliance for Greensboro Justice." Stewart Kwoh, Tom Ono, and Earl Tockman were called away for other work. Danny Sheehan was on the team but had other time-consuming Christic Institute responsibilities. What's more, neither Lewis nor Korotkin was licensed to practice in North Carolina.

Therefore, Lewis recruited Carolyn McAllaster to join the team. McAllaster had a practice in Durham, where she'd represented several CWP members and supporters, including in trespassing and vandalism cases in the aftermath of the massacre. Lewis's passion and fearlessness in speaking truth to power appealed to her. Furthermore, McAllaster, who became a clinical professor of law at Duke University, explained to *Duke Law News* that she joined the legal team because "it seemed . . . really clear that there was a wrong done," "the actions of the police . . . were really disturbing," and "there needed to be strong representation for folks who were victims."

Lewis, Korotkin, Sheehan, and McAllaster were joined by Flint Taylor, a founding partner of the People's Law Office in Chicago. Lewis didn't know Taylor personally but had followed his work representing the families of Fred Hampton and Mark Clark, Black Panther Party leaders murdered by police officers. Through his work with Black Panthers, Taylor had developed connections with the Black Nationalism faction of the CWP and with Tockman.

Finally, dozens of volunteer paralegals, law students, and other lawyers from across the country contributed to the Legal Alliance for Greensboro Justice.

State Prosecution

By the end of 1979, the Guilford County DA had charged fourteen Klansmen and Nazis with first-degree murder, felony riot, and conspiracy. Then, in May 1980, a grand jury indicted four CWP members for felony riot and other charges. A GJF newsletter read, "By prosecuting both the Klan/Nazis and the CWP at the same time, the state wants to make it look like a shootout between 'two fringe groups.'"

Four Klansmen and two Nazis were prosecuted for murder. The trial, which began on August 4, 1980, was a debacle. Jury selection ended with all ninety-four prospective Black jurors eliminated and an all-white seated jury. Prosecutors later admitted that five jurors were pro-Klan or anti-communism, including the foreman, who was an anti-Castro Cuban immigrant and called the KKK a "patriotic organization." Additionally, CWP members refused to testify for the prosecution in order to avoid possible self-incrimination and legitimizing what they viewed as a sham trial. Some massacre survivors were arrested for attempting to force their way into the courtroom; others were held in contempt for shouting critiques during the proceedings; and one emptied a vial of skunk oil in the courtroom. Moreover, the prosecution didn't call Eddie Dawson or Bernard Butkovich to testify. Finally, according to Flint Taylor, "The lawyers for the Nazi and Klan defendants used every emotional weapon at their disposal—anti-communism, racism, and patriotism, wrapped around a self-defense claim."

On November 17, 1980—after hearing from about 130 witnesses, receiving approximately six hundred pieces of evidence, and deliberating for more than thirty-five hours—the jury returned not guilty verdicts on all counts. According to one news report, "Twenty-five policemen lined the walls of the courtroom as the verdict was read and police riflemen perched on surrounding rooftops." *Washington Post* coverage began, "At a distance, the not-guilty verdict from Greensboro conjured up the Old South at its worst: A white jury acquits Ku Klux Klansmen of killing five people." The acquittals emboldened white supremacists. Nazi Party leader Harold Covington announced plans to create a "Carolina Free State"—a home for racists, free of non-white people.

"This state has a history of racism, this state has a history of resistance to authority, . . . and it is well-suited to this," he claimed.

After the not guilty verdicts, the DA dropped all the charges against the remaining Klansmen and Nazis, as well as the charges against CWP members.

Civil Lawsuit Filed

On the one-year anniversary of the massacre, Lewis and the rest of the legal team filed a $48 million civil lawsuit—$18.3 million in actual damages, plus $29.7 million in punitive damages—in the US District Court for the Middle District of North Carolina. The plaintiffs included eleven individuals who were wounded or arrested on November 3, as well as survivors of the five dead. They named over eighty defendants, including Klansmen, Nazis, Dawson, Butkovich, BATF and FBI agents, GPD officers, and city officials.

The plaintiffs brought the lawsuit under four federal statutes that originated with the Civil Rights Act of 1871, also known as the "Ku Klux Klan Act." One of the statutes, the Anti-Klan Act, gave victims of racially motivated conspiracies the right to sue conspirators for money damages. The essence of the claims was that federal, state, and local officials conspired with Klansmen and Nazis to violate the rights to freedom of speech and assembly and to equal protection of the laws of persons killed, injured, or arrested at the rally. The complaint defined the group of persons targeted as "communists and/or labor organizers and/or civil rights activists who were organizing black and white workers equally into unions." The lawsuit also alleged four violations of state law: wrongful death, assault and battery, malicious prosecution, and abuse of process.

Key facts relied on by the plaintiffs included: Federal agent Bernard Butkovich encouraged Nazis to bring weapons to the rally; police informant Eddie Dawson shared the march plans with Klansmen; Dawson told authorities, and Detective Cooper radioed in, that a caravan of armed white supremacists was headed toward the rally, but law enforcement didn't intervene; the GPD captain responsible for intelligence failed to maintain contact with Cooper and other officers; and law enforcement never warned demonstrators, purposely took a "low profile," and were absent when the encounter began.

Federal Prosecution

For nearly two years, the GJF and its allies campaigned for the "decidedly unsympathetic Reagan Department of Justice," in Flint Taylor's words, to prosecute Klansmen and Nazis under federal civil rights laws. They circulated petitions, wrote letters, lobbied in DC, picketed at the FBI's regional headquarters in Charlotte, and persuaded the Greensboro City Council to pass a resolution calling for DOJ involvement.

Finally, in March 1982, the Justice Department convened a grand jury to investigate the actions of Klansmen and Nazis on November 3. The GJF wanted the grand jury to also indict federal officials, especially Butkovich, for their role in the massacre. So, on April 20, 1983, Lewis and Nelson Johnson, accompanied by a television cameraman, walked into the federal courthouse in Winston-Salem holding ten packets of information about the federal government's involvement for the grand jury. The jurors, however, were at lunch. When Lewis and Johnson attempted to leave the packets for jurors, Thomas Brereton, an FBI agent and the grand jury's lead investigator, threatened them with jury tampering charges and seized the packets as "evidence."

The GJF pressed for Brereton to be replaced as the FBI's lead agent assigned to the case. Lewis and Korotkin wrote to the prosecuting US attorney, Kenneth McAllister, explaining that Brereton had a conflict of interest due to his relationship, prior to the massacre, with the GPD and Eddie Dawson. Brereton had even employed Dawson to perform carpentry work in his home. Lewis and Korotkin also accused Brereton of being hostile toward the CWP, erasing twenty to thirty minutes of a Klansman's taped confession, withholding and manipulating other evidence, and obstructing justice. Finally, they called Brereton's accusations of jury tampering by Lewis and Johnson "baseless and irresponsible." Brereton, however, wasn't removed from the case and his findings were included in the FBI's report on the massacre. He said, "Both groups had the mentality of juvenile gangs. . . . What happened in Greensboro was that these rival gangs met face-to-face and just blew up."

On April 22, 1983, after hearing from approximately 150 witnesses and recessing for months at a time, the grand jury finally indicted six Klansmen and three Nazis on fourteen counts of civil rights violations. Neither Butkovich nor any other federal agent or official was indicted.

SPECIAL PROSECUTOR

The GJF urged the Justice Department to appoint an independent special prosecutor for the federal criminal trial. Lewis and other legal team members argued—in letters to the Justice Department, a motion and appeal in federal court, and a lawsuit against the US AG—that the Ethics in Government Act required a special prosecutor. They alleged the DOJ and FBI were part of the underlying conspiracy against the CWP, and thus, Justice Department lawyers had a conflict of interest. GJF representatives also hand-delivered to the AG's office a petition with more than 1,100 signatures of Greensboro residents demanding appointment of a special prosecutor and released a list of approximately two hundred individuals—including attorneys, professors, clergy members, celebrities, elected officials, and civil rights leaders—who likewise called for a special prosecutor.

Nevertheless, the Office of the AG, US District Court for DC, and US Circuit Court of Appeals for DC found insufficient evidence of a conspiracy by high-ranking government officials to require appointment of a special prosecutor.

TRIAL

Judge Thomas Flannery, a Nixon appointee, presided over the trial. Four days before the trial began, Flannery prohibited witnesses from discussing their upcoming testimony with the media. The US Court of Appeals for the Fourth Circuit denied the GJF's petition for a writ of mandamus overturning the gag order.

On January 9, 1984, the trial began with jury selection, which was closed to the public. Four newspapers unsuccessfully contested, in court, the closure of the proceedings. The process ended with another all-white jury. In the *Washington Post*, Lewis assailed jury selection in the two criminal cases as "reflecting the systematic exclusion of black people from the political process."

The trial lasted more than three months and involved 120 witnesses and hundreds of exhibits. This time, Butkovich and CWP members testified, and Dawson was a defendant. FBI experts presented evidence showing where shots originated on November 3 and matching bullet fragments in victims to guns of Klansmen and Nazis. Scientific evidence confirmed that Klansman David Matthews killed four people with buckshot pellets. Video evidence showed Klansman Jerry Paul Smith firing at a helpless fallen body. The defendants argued that the FBI's evidence was misleading and inaccurate and that they merely acted in self-defense after being fired upon first by a communist mob.

On April 15, 1984, the jury acquitted all nine Klansmen and Nazis, including Dawson. White supremacists celebrated and CWP members wept in the courtroom. Widow Dale Sampson told the *New York Times*, "This is a real go-ahead for the Klan and Nazis to kill people." Likewise, widow Signe Waller shared with the *Washington Post*, "It begins a process of legitimately killing people for their political views."

Lewis explained to reporters that the civil rights charges against the Klansmen and Nazis were unnecessarily brought under a narrow provision in federal law. Specifically, for thirteen of the fourteen counts the prosecution chose to bring, the government bore the burden proving the defendants were motivated by racial animus, thereby allowing the defendants to claim they were, instead, motivated by anti-communism and patriotism. Similarly, Sheehan told the media, "The government avoided charging the Klan and Nazis with what they actually did . . . , which was to kill people because they were communists and labor organizers who were bringing whites and blacks together. The government didn't do that, because it was involved in instigating the Klan and Nazis to do just that, to disrupt communist efforts." Flint Taylor wrote that a different federal statute "would have permitted a showing of either racial or political (i.e., anti-communist) animus."

Three weeks later, about 250 people, including Lewis, marched through downtown Greensboro to protest the acquittals. He told the *Washington Post*, "The mayor and the Chamber of Commerce keep saying, 'Let's put this behind us. Good grief, let's not air this whole thing.' . . . But right now it's going to remain a black eye for Greensboro because this is the place where people were killed on TV in broad daylight and no one was punished for it."

Civil Trial Preparation Challenges

Marty Nathan wrote, "The third trial was our last chance for justice. . . . The civil trial was the first time we could have *our* lawyers try the case." However, according to Signe Waller, "The civil rights suit was a steep uphill fight, with obstacles littering the path all the way." The obstacles included a lack of resources, the volume of pretrial preparation in a relatively short amount of time, obstruction by the defendants and their attorneys, the need for the plaintiffs to acknowledge their own mistakes, and the legal team's internal tensions.

LACK OF RESOURCES

Pervasive anti-communist sentiment and the GJF's association with communism made fundraising for a controversial lawsuit even more difficult. Therefore, the GJF made strategic decisions to change its name to the Greensboro Civil Rights Fund (GCRF), remake its board of directors with outside allies, and collaborate with more mainstream national coalitions. To combat red-baiting, the GCRF produced literature that situated the massacre among celebrated historical struggles for civil and human rights. Additionally, the GCRF secured endorsements from dozens of famous individuals, including Michael Douglas, Joan Baez, Harry Belafonte, and Pete Seeger; and numerous organizations, such as the ACLU, Congressional Black Caucus, National Council of Churches, and National Lawyers Guild (NLG).

The GCRF raised funds from grants, individual donors, newsletter subscriptions, and speaking engagements. Lewis traversed the country, primarily with Marty Nathan, speaking at fundraising events. They lugged around a Betamax machine, which "weighed a million pounds," to show "gruesome video footage" of Michael Nathan's "face being blown off," Lewis said. Finally, the GCRF utilized a nationwide network of volunteers to minimize expenses.

VOLUME OF PREPARATION

The federal judge who presided over the civil case, Robert Merhige Jr., stayed discovery until the end of the federal criminal trial and then ordered the parties to complete all discovery within only four months. In that time, Lewis and the other attorneys had to take depositions and represent the plaintiffs during their depositions; interview witnesses; review tens of thousands of pages of subpoenaed documents, criminal trial transcripts, and materials from grand jury proceedings; draft, respond to, and litigate pretrial motions; prepare for jury selection; discuss trial strategy with the plaintiffs and organizers; and perform a variety of other tasks.

The plaintiffs' lawyers took nearly two hundred depositions. For Lewis, "obtaining good depositions from bad guys" was a highlight of the case. For example, Lewis recalled, FBI Agent Richard Goldberg became so agitated under intense questioning that he leapt out of his seat with a leg cramp.

Lewis also attempted to elicit information from Roland Wayne Wood, the local Nazi Party chapter leader at the time of the massacre. They met at a truck stop located a half-hour from Greensboro. Lewis wrote, "I found a cheap Dictaphone-type gadget small enough to drop into my boot. I ran a wire from my boot into a mic clipped into my shirt. He knew I was one of those 'commie lawyers,' but we also figured he was pissed at the BATF for getting them in all this mess. So, I met him to talk, with Gayle sitting alone at another table, not too far away. She was carrying a .38 pistol to 'cover me.' . . . In the end, Wood didn't spill any beans and no incident occurred."

OBSTRUCTION BY THE DEFENDANTS

According to Korotkin, the government defendants' attorneys "fought discovery tooth and nail." She explained that they "limited the kinds of questions their agents could answer," found "an excuse" to end depositions when they "were going badly for their clients," and withheld documents until it was too late to digest the information and follow up.

Additionally, the Klansmen and Nazi defendants filed counterclaims and a demand for $40 million in damages. They alleged that the plaintiffs, on November 3, attacked them and deprived them of their constitutional rights because they were white, Christian Americans who opposed communism. During the trial, Judge Merhige ruled that the counterclaims had to be tried before a separate jury, thereby defeating the purpose of pursuing counterclaims, which was "mucking up the civil trial," according to Lewis. The defendants didn't pursue their claims further.

OWNING MISTAKES

Trial preparation was also emotionally difficult for CWP members. Marty Nathan explained the "painful" process: "We had spent years defending ourselves from the media's propaganda barrage against us. For the first time, we began to talk about our own shortcomings, because we had to be able to explain our errors to ourselves before we could explain them to a jury. We knew that if we didn't talk in court about our mistakes, the defense would present them in the worst way."

One such mistake, according to Sally Bermanzohn and Nelson Johnson, was calling the rally "Death to the Klan." Bermanzohn and others also believed changing their name from Workers Viewpoint Organization to Communist

Workers Party was a misstep. Johnson said he also regretted the "letter that called the Klan members cowards and challenged them to come from under their rocks and face the wrath of the people."

INTERNAL TENSIONS

The biggest internal tension for the plaintiffs' lawyers was the theory of the case—that is, how to characterize the defendants' motives for the jury. Flint Taylor and the plaintiffs wanted to portray the massacre as a high-level, anti-communist, US government-backed assassination of CWP members because they were the vanguard of the working class. Danny Sheehan, on the other hand, believed the theory ought to be that government officials refrained from stopping the attack because of "class-based, invidious, discriminatory animus" they harbored against the demonstrators based on their political beliefs and efforts to support Black workers. Sheehan said the CWP's "theory was vastly beyond the reality of the jury," which would "see the strident political purposes" and would not "want to be part of an ideological statement." Lewis appreciated the pros and cons of both approaches.

The competing theories and how they were handled exemplified differences between Lewis's and Sheehan's approaches to lawyering and litigation. Sheehan said he didn't think using the civil trial to further a political message or organizational line was appropriate, and he was more narrowly focused on legal issues. In contrast, Lewis believed in breaking down barriers between lawyer and client, adopting clients' goals, and participating in the broader movement. He chose a legal tactic not based on the likelihood of "winning" in the traditional sense, but rather in consultation with the community and based on the tactic's potential for empowering activists and advancing grass-roots movements.

In Greensboro, Sheehan was supportive of the CWP's goals, but largely anti-communist. Unlike Lewis, Nelson Johnson said, Sheehan didn't fully appreciate the CWP members as individuals or their collective goals, and thus, they didn't trust Sheehan. Sheehan described CWP meetings as "terribly didactic," "strident," and "freshman politics." He viewed the CWP as "rigid," "unpleasant," "unattractive," and "self-conscious," and himself as "comparatively sophisticated." Sheehan shared that he didn't have any loyalty to the CWP as an institution or political party, and had only "an arm's length, dialectical relationship" with others involved. He did, however, praise Lewis for building local relationships that were broader, deeper, and richer than his own.

Sheehan said that, compared to himself, Lewis and Taylor had a higher level of "simpatico" with the ideological line of the CWP. Joyce Johnson recalled that Lewis, unlike Sheehan, was "part of the local fabric."

According to Lewis, Sheehan's connections with religious institutions and fundraising responsibilities for Christic Institute may have contributed to him keeping the plaintiffs at arm's length. "Danny was seen as an opportunist who, at times, would play the anti-communist angle to ingratiate himself with the D.C. liberal, ACLU, and churchy types," Lewis wrote. Indeed, Sheehan wrote in his autobiography that the WVO changing its name to CWP "resulted in a public relations nightmare for Sara—who was trying to raise money from . . . former Silkwood supporters and church people to defray the expenses of the trial."

Lewis had to mediate tensions between Sheehan and CWP members and Taylor, while also navigating his own frictions with Sheehan. Sheehan said trial preparations "strained" his relationship with Lewis and resulted in "growing estrangement" between the two of them. He and Lewis both felt personally hurt by the tensions. Lewis wrote, "The situation was complicated because Danny had some kernel of truth in his position about how best to win over the largest number of supporters and funders. But, of course, compromise must have limits to ensure adherence to principled beliefs about the root causes of injustice, oppression, and racism. I felt Danny's beliefs tended to be in the minority on the legal team, abstracted, and too easily anti-communist. Yet, I love Danny and appreciate the sacrifices he has made to be a lawyer for People's justice."

Once Sheehan realized "winning," as he defined it, wasn't the primary goal for the plaintiffs or the rest of the legal team, he played only a minor role in the case. He wrote in his autobiography, "Since I was unable to persuade the WVO plaintiffs to permit me to present my proposed theory of the case to the jury, I felt like I was trapped in a bad dream."

Civil Trial

The plaintiffs' in-court trial team primarily consisted of Lewis, Flint Taylor, and Carolyn McAllaster. Korotkin and others continued diligently working behind the scenes.

On March 11, 1985, jury selection began in the Winston-Salem federal courthouse where the trial would take place over the next three months. Lewis asked that a prospective juror be excused after he said, "Blacks should stay with Blacks," and another be dismissed because he said communists "should go back to Russia." However, Judge Merhige allowed both men to remain in the venire. Defendant Roland Wayne Wood—wearing a shirt that read, "Eat Lead You Lousy Red," and representing himself—asked Merhige to question potential jurors about their ties to the United Way, which he alleged contributed to "race-mixing." Merhige denied the request. The seated jury ultimately consisted of five white people and one Black person. The lone minority served as jury foreman. He'd participated in civil rights demonstrations and said, during voir dire (i.e., the process through which potential jurors from the venire are questioned by either the judge or a lawyer to determine their suitability for jury service), he can't respect any man who hides his face under a white hood to express his beliefs.

Two weeks later, opening arguments began in a courtroom packed with reporters, sketch artists, CWP members and supporters, and white supremacists. Lewis told jurors, "In the two previous trials, prosecuting officials had the interest of concealing or at least not emphasizing the role of agents provocateurs." He talked about how the exercise of constitutional rights without fear of violence, irrespective of political beliefs, "makes the system work." He asked jurors to consider what would've happened if the Lions Club planned an event in Greensboro and police knew communists were headed to attack them. "Our forefathers and foremothers would be as mad as a hornet in a jar that these plaintiffs were killed, not because they were communists but because . . . it erodes all our rights," Lewis said. He described how Klansmen and Nazis went to the march "with full military capability to provoke something, to retire to their arsenal, and then to complete the task of killing." Taylor informed jurors that Dawson encouraged Nazis and Klansmen to approach the march while police officers were ordered to posts away from the scene. McAllaster explained that CWP members carried weapons to the rally for self-protection but weren't prepared to use them. An attorney representing the GPD and city officials declared, "The conspiracy lies with the plaintiffs. The plaintiffs were out to seek people who wanted to redress grievances with the government, infiltrate them, and stir up trouble with the authorities and the police." He warned jurors that the plaintiffs would portray the case as a struggle between Blacks and whites; instead, he claimed, "This is a case of the Communist Party against the City of Greensboro."

Lewis, Taylor, and McAllaster presented the plaintiffs' case over eight weeks. McAllaster primarily handled direct examination of the plaintiffs, while Lewis and Taylor focused on questioning Klansmen, Nazis, and law enforcement witnesses. All told, they called seventy-five witnesses, including two cameramen who filmed the massacre; an FBI expert who testified about the order and origination points of the gunshots; sixteen of the plaintiffs or family members of the victims; and thirty of the defendants. In addition to describing the events of November 3, the plaintiffs shared with jurors their anti-Klan and pro-communism beliefs, their decision to become labor organizers, and the admirable qualities of their dead compatriots.

When Roland Wayne Wood, then head of Aryan Crusaders for Christ, was sworn in on the stand, he performed a Hitler salute. Taylor questioned Wood about his prior anti-communist and anti-Semitic behavior and the five white skulls pinned to his lapel. Wood claimed that the skulls stood for "the five attacks . . . committed against" him "by communists" when he "tried to express" his "freedom of speech." Taylor asked, "You are proud that you're a racist, aren't you?" Wood responded, "Yes sir. . . . I believe that my country is occupied. And I will fight as my forefathers fought to give me a free Christian republic." Later, while still on the stand, Wood sang to the tune of "Jingle Bells":

> Riding through the town
> In a Mercedes Benz
> Having lots of fun
> Shooting the Jews down
> Rat a tat tat tat
> Rat a tat tat tat
> Shot the kikes down
> Oh what fun it is
> To have the Nazis back in town

Wood was also involved in the most awkward moment of the trial for Lewis. In a courthouse bathroom, Wood began using the urinal next to Lewis. Wood was six inches taller and 150 pounds heavier than Lewis, who silently pleaded with himself, "Please, please, please don't accidentally piss on his leg. He'll kill you!"

Lewis elicited testimony from KKK leader Virgil Griffin that, at his rallies, he advocated for violence and "having a hundred dead niggers in the street." Griffin also said all communists "should be charged for treason against the U.S., put in front of a firing squad, and shot."

To establish law enforcement liability, Taylor questioned GPD informant Dawson and Lewis questioned BATF Agent Butkovich. Dawson testified that he twice telephoned a GPD detective on the morning of November 3 to report the caravan of vehicles carrying armed white supremacists and that he was surprised by the absence of police when the caravan arrived at Morningside Homes. Butkovich admitted that his undercover role involved giving Nazis the "opportunity to violate the law." Additionally, the plaintiffs' attorneys called current and former GPD personnel. Officer April Wise testified that a police dispatcher ordered her and another officer to leave the staging area shortly before the shooting began. William Swing, GPD chief at the time of the massacre, conceded he believed Klansmen would show up at the rally and do anything to get even with the CWP; and while in the command center on November 3, he knew Klansmen were headed to the rally but didn't order officers to the scene. Finally, Lewis called Robert di Grazia, a former Boston police chief and consultant for police departments across the country, as an expert witness. On the stand, di Grazia accused GPD officers of not following accepted police practices with respect to informants and properly training, supervising, and disciplining officers. Di Grazia also testified that the GPD produced incomplete reports designed to justify its failings and contributions to the massacre.

The plaintiffs rested on May 17, 1985. Shortly thereafter, Judge Merhige ordered fifteen of the sixty defendants—the former city manager and fourteen GPD officers—to be dropped from the suit. "I'm glad I wasn't driving through Greensboro on November 3, 1979, because I guess I'd have been sued too," Merhige quipped. Earlier, during a conference in chambers, Merhige scolded the plaintiffs' attorneys: "You people have done a disservice to your own clients. You sued everybody. . . . You didn't have a snowball's chance in hell, and I'm satisfied you had no evidence when you brought your lawsuit. . . . Stop wasting time and costing the government thousands and thousands and thousands of dollars, and everybody else here, needlessly, foolishly. For what? Publicity?"

The legal team acknowledged, in retrospect, that the lawsuit named too many defendants. Notes from the team's post-trial debrief read, "Why we didn't cut down defendants: We were always one step behind because of pressure to go to trial before the evidence was ready or we had time to digest it. . . . Couldn't let loose of bad guys politically or emotionally, didn't have detached view. Also, we dug in vs. judge's efforts to tell us how he thought it should be done. Politically we had to condemn all the bad guys, but then maybe should have dropped some. By time we thought about it, didn't want to because of possible legal consequences."

Lewis believes that Merhige, through his rulings and comments, played defense against the plaintiffs and shaped the trial to fit his predetermined opinion about the case. Moreover, Lewis described Merhige as "a tyrant in the courtroom," who'd "belittle" and "intimidate" people. He also said Merhige taped to the attorneys' podium a copy of the rule allowing judges to fine lawyers deemed to have wasted the court's time. Despite their ongoing tensions, Merhige wrote, four years after the trial, "I found Mr. Pitts to be a well-mannered, competent and dedicated attorney."

The remaining defendants took only four days to present their case. They attempted to show that the CWP members provoked the confrontation, Klansmen and Nazis acted in self-defense, and police acted reasonably and responsibly. The GPD defendants called their own police consultant, who testified that no probable cause or reasonable suspicion existed to stop the caravan. The defense rested on May 24, 1985.

The plaintiffs' attorneys divided up their closing argument. Taylor addressed the roles of Klansmen and Nazis. He asked jurors to "stand up for" the victims and justice, and to "bring back a verdict . . . to say to Klansmen and Nazis and police and general officials that they can't do this, not in America, not in . . . 1979." Lewis handled the role of law enforcement. He began by admitting that he was "as nervous as that long-tailed cat." He reminded jurors that communists were entitled to "equal protection of the laws." Lewis made clear that the plaintiffs weren't besmirching all law enforcement; however, he also stressed, "None of us want nor should we tolerate irresponsible law enforcement." "How many times one officer could have done one thing to stop the violence?" he asked jurors. He pleaded with jurors to reject the notion that Black people, civil rights advocates, and communists are "so undeserving of constitutional rights that it's okay to kill them." Finally, McAllaster told jurors the plaintiffs had a "history of commitment to social justice issues" and were working for "a better world" and "the good of mankind." She asked, "What were the sinister motives behind their beliefs, their belief that people with brown lung deserved treatment, that Black people should have civil rights, that poor people should have food and clothing? What's sinister about that?"

In their closing, attorneys for the defendants argued that, on November 3, event organizers sought confrontation, media attention, and martyrdom. To advance these goals, the attorneys claimed, CWP members misled law enforcement, which was otherwise ready to protect and serve. The city attorney called the CWP "a fringe, radical, political cult" that "infiltrated" textile mills.

On June 5, 1985, closing arguments ended. All told, the trial involved 101 witnesses and more than 100,000 pages of documents filed with the clerk's office. McAllaster said the trial was one of the most all-consuming things she has ever done. Lewis similarly said the trial was nonstop—day after day of just enough time for showers, meals, and six or seven hours of sleep. Judge Merhige even dragged the lawyers into court on Saturdays to hear motions without the jury present.

After eleven and a half hours of deliberation over two days, jurors reached a verdict on June 7, 1985. For the wrongful death of Michael Nathan, the jury found eight defendants jointly liable: GPD Lieutenant Paul Spoon and Detective Jerry Cooper; Eddie Dawson; Roland Wayne Wood and two other Nazi Party members, Jack Fowler and Mark Sherer; and two Klansmen, David Matthews and Jerry Smith. The jury awarded $351,500 to widow Marty Nathan. Additionally, the jury found Wood, Fowler, Matthews, and Smith liable for assaults on Michael Nathan, Tom Clark, and Paul Bermanzohn. The jury awarded $1,500 to Clark; $38,359.55 to Paul—his exact out-of-pocket medical expenses; and an additional $3,600 to Marty Nathan.

The jury cleared the remaining thirty-seven defendants, including all the city officials and federal agents, of any wrongdoing. Moreover, the jury didn't find any defendants liable for conspiring to violate the plaintiffs' civil rights, failing to protect marchers, inadequately training and supervising officers and informants, or falsely arresting two demonstrators. Finally, none of the other injured plaintiffs were compensated and nothing was awarded to the estates of the other four CWP members killed.

REACTIONS

Privately, the plaintiffs and their attorneys were largely disappointed and outraged. However, Lewis kept their spirits high, and publicly, they put a positive spin on the verdict. Nelson Johnson said Lewis helped the plaintiffs appreciate the significance of the outcome and persuaded them to focus on the positives. Sally Bermanzohn's book included the following recollection from Marty Nathan: "It was horrible. . . . It was a terrible blow. . . . We left the courtroom stunned but quickly regrouped. Lewis Pitts argued that it was a victory—a southern jury finding the cops complicit with the Klan is a huge victory—only the second time ever that the cops had been found jointly liable with the Klan, despite their long history of complicity. So, Nelson, Signe, Dale, and I went out to talk to the press, holding each other's arms high for victory."

Lewis told the Associated Press, "We're very pleased a jury of North Carolinians has found not only that Klansmen and Nazis shot and killed Michael Nathan, but that they also found police informants and police liable in his death." During a press conference, with Lewis sitting between Nathan and Waller, the plaintiffs described the verdict as a "beacon of hope for victims of governmental abuse of power, police brutality, and corruption across the nation" and "a contribution in the struggle for local official accountability and for the rights of all to speak, assemble, advocate change, and organize for power in order to bring about positive change." Flint Taylor wrote, "Plaintiffs' initial disappointment at what appeared to be a compromise verdict soon gave way to the realization that a substantial victory—but not complete justice—had been obtained. After nearly six years and three trials, a southern jury had finally convicted a good number of the main actors in the November 3rd massacre." A *New York Times* editorial read, "The findings show that North Carolinians understand the need to resist forcible interference with free speech and assembly. Rights are rights, even for radical dissenters. The jury also made clear that police may not yield the streets in the name of neutrality. The verdict set the proper limit: tough talk is permissible; terrorism is not."

While CWP members and their lawyers had mixed emotions about the verdict, they seemingly had unanimous praise and appreciation for Lewis's work and leadership. In 2017, Nathan, Waller, and Taylor shared their reflections about Lewis's work. Nathan wrote:

> I don't know anybody who didn't immediately fall in love with Lewis. He was incredibly energetic, smart, radical, funny, brave and handsome to boot. . . . In retrospect, our task . . . was impossible. Yet Lewis never expressed a moment of doubt; just highly analytical fury couched in Southern dialect at the horror of the crime inflicted on us.
>
> Lewis was so smart as a lawyer, so sensible—he could translate law into human rights—so loving of the oppressed, knowledgeable in the deepest ways of the racist complexities of Southern society and so absolutely fearless, that even now, nearly 40 years later, my heart begins to ache at the gift that he gave to us who

were pretty much ground into the dust by our grief, horror and fear. He became one of the best friends I have ever had, helped me and my friends more than anyone could have ever expected, paid pinto-bean salary, sleeping on the floor, and all because of a flaming sense of justice that I think is only ever encountered among history's heroes.

He cut through the arguments with good sense and great research. . . . He was almost always right and was humble and funny in his approach. He won the hearts of his plaintiffs, the judge, ultimately the jury, even as he went nose-to-nose with some of the nastiest men—official, legal and criminal—I have ever seen.

Waller called Lewis "compassionate, fair and honest"; "an extraordinary human being"; and "an American hero." She continued,

One of the most admirable traits of Lewis as a lawyer was that he was not trapped by the legal B.S. as so many lawyers are. Because his primary allegiance is to Democracy, he knows that many of the most vital social justice issues have to be resolved in the streets, not in a court of law. He always has a very holistic legal strategy that includes people's participation in taking a stand for what is just.

Lewis helped give us the closest thing to a victory that we could expect in the civil rights suit. . . . He is truly a people's lawyer and a radical revolutionary, in the best sense of these terms. I admire Lewis more than I can describe and . . . feel so privileged to be his friend.

Taylor wrote, "Lewis was and is a terrific lawyer, and an even better friend and human being. Fearless, yet compassionate, a real leader, a southern gentleman, with a great sense of wry humor, a practical intellectual with a keen sense of radical politics, racism, and fascism."

The Greensboro Massacre work was the most complex, time-consuming, and high-profile of Lewis's career. The civil trial verdict, which Lewis considers his greatest professional accomplishment, gives him immense joy, even if the plaintiffs didn't obtain the full justice they deserved. Lewis's experiences in Greensboro validated his decision to recommit to being an attorney and strengthened his resolve to continue being a lawyer who defends and advances grassroots movements for social justice.

What's more, moving to Greensboro led to new and lasting relationships. For decades, Lewis remained close friends, and collaborated on future social justice work, with Nelson and Joyce Johnson, Marty Nathan, Signe Waller, Flint Taylor, and Gayle Korotkin. Also, in August 1982, amid the Greensboro Massacre campaign, Lewis and Katie Greene married at the courthouse in Greensboro. The next day, surrounded by family and friends in the Johnson's backyard, they exchanged vows under a large shade tree and celebrated. Finally, on June 13, 1985, less than a week after the Greensboro Massacre civil trial verdict, Katie Greene gave birth to Stephen Daley Pitts. Lewis caught Stephen, cut his umbilical cord, and bathed him. He shared, "It was all amazing and miraculous!" Greene wrote, "Lewis and I fell in love at a time when we were . . . fully engaged in social justice work. . . . We shared . . . a vision for a future in which the well-being of all, including our planet, would prevail. We felt a passion for each other and for our common purpose. . . . Stephen was born of that shared love and commitment."

CHAPTER 6

Defending Black Movement Leaders and Activists (Part 1)

During the first half of the 1980s, the Greensboro Massacre campaign consumed most of Lewis's time as a Christic Institute staff attorney. However, he also worked on two campaigns that involved defending Black, grassroots, social justice movement leaders: Eddie Carthan in Mississippi and Fred Carter in West Virginia. These experiences—together with his desire to lead an organization focused exclusively on racial justice movements in the South—led Lewis to start Christic Institute South (CIS).

Eddie Carthan

When the Voting Rights Act of 1965 was codified, only about seven percent of eligible Black people in Mississippi were registered to vote and the state's only Black local elected officials were the mayor and city councilmembers of an all-Black town. Just five years later, the percentage of eligible Black registered voters in Mississippi ballooned to sixty-seven percent. By 1982, Black elected officials controlled the political machinery in half of the Mississippi "Black Belt" counties, including Holmes County in the heart of the Mississippi Delta.

In western Holmes County lies Tchula, a farming town of about one and a half square miles and sixteen hundred residents, the vast majority of whom are Black. Tchula's extreme poverty is well documented. The *Washington Post* described the town as "haunted by stray dogs and boarded-up buildings." A *Guardian* article titled, "Poorest Town in Poorest State," read, "Economic decline has brought with it a creeping malaise smothering the optimism that gripped the town when segregation ended."

Tchula may be best known for its former mayor—Eddie Carthan. Born in 1949, Carthan was raised in a shack on land his family purchased as part of a New Deal project that involved dividing former plantations into parcels to distribute to Black tenants. He spent his childhood attending a segregated school and picking cotton in Tchula. He was a Freedom School student and accompanied his grandfather to civil rights events. (Freedom Schools were first developed by the Student Nonviolent Coordinating Committee during the 1964 Freedom Summer in Mississippi to "provide an alternative education for African American students that would facilitate student activism and participatory democracy," wrote educational historian Jon N. Hale.) After graduating from college, Carthan returned to Holmes County to be a teacher and small-business owner.

In 1972, Carthan was elected to the Holmes County School Board. Then, at age twenty-eight, he defeated white opponents in Tchula's mayoral race, becoming the first Black mayor of a Mississippi plantation town since Reconstruction and the first Black man ever elected mayor of a biracial town in the Mississippi Delta. Black candidates also won four of the five seats on Tchula's governing board. Carthan adopted "a loose ideological conception of black power for black people," "was idealistic," and "held fast to principles such as egalitarianism, participatory democracy, and human freedom," according to Professor Minion K. C. Morrison. Carthan's victory was celebrated by Black people and civil rights activists across the South.

After the election, John Edgar Hayes Sr., the one remaining white alderman and a wealthy plantation owner and cotton farmer, launched a divide-and-conquer campaign among local Black leaders. He recruited Roosevelt Granderson and Jason Gibson—two Black aldermen who feared losing their jobs at white-owned businesses—to form a dissident majority. Together, they reduced Mayor Carthan's monthly salary from $600 to $60; refused to attend meetings, thereby preventing quorums required to conduct municipal business; refused to pay the city's telephone and light bills; raised property taxes on Carthan's supporters; and changed the locks at city hall to keep Carthan out of his office. Worse yet, Carthan and his family received threatening letters and phone calls.

The small town's racial tensions received national attention. The *Washington Post* reported about how "Tchula's white power structure lashed back." A *Newsday* article read, "Jolted by the election of a black, Carthan says, the white establishment of Tchula made it impossible for him to administer the city. . . . Soon meetings of the city council were marked by bitter arguments and emotional outbursts. Some townspeople carried guns to the monthly sessions; Carthan kept his pistol in an open briefcase. From Carthan's point of view, his woes are easily explained. 'As soon as you speak out against the system, they classify you as a smart nigger,' he says. 'Then they go after you.'" The *New York Times* also covered Tchula: "The soil of Tchula's and Mr. Carthan's troubles is a rich mixture of political enmity, ignorance, struggles for economic control of a town with 30 percent unemployment. . . . All are steeped in decades of racial mistrust that is magnified by blacks' efforts here and elsewhere to share, if not seize, political control."

Despite extraordinarily difficult circumstances, Mayor Carthan experienced early success. He secured more than a million dollars in federal funding for Tchula, in addition to private investment; created eighty new jobs; initiated a nutrition program to provide meals to senior citizens; built public housing, a daycare center, and a health clinic; and paved streets where segregated Black residents lived.

Still, racial tensions boiled over in April 1980, when Tchula's police chief stepped down for health reasons. Carthan selected John Dale, a Black police officer, as acting chief. Meanwhile, Hayes, Gibson, and Granderson arranged to have Jim Andrews, a white businessman who'd lost the mayoral race to Carthan, appointed as the permanent police chief on April 30, 1980. That night, and into the early morning, Carthan, Dale, and five other armed men confronted Andrews at the police station and demanded his resignation. Andrews refused, a scuffle ensued, gunshots were fired, and a bullet grazed Andrews.

Andrews pressed charges against Carthan, Dale, and the other five men—collectively known as the "Tchula Seven." Then, Andrews's sister-in-law, County Probate Judge Deane Taylor, referred the case to a grand jury, which indicted the Tchula Seven for aggravated assault against a police officer. Taylor said of Carthan's claims of racism, "That's behind us. It's nonsense and ridiculous."

A jury convicted the Tchula Seven in April 1981. Circuit Court Judge Webb Franklin, a white Republican, sentenced each defendant to three years in prison but suspended the sentences (i.e., decided they wouldn't have to serve the sentences if they met certain conditions) for all of them, except Carthan. A federal judge later reduced Carthan's sentence to nine months.

While out on bond before beginning his prison sentence, Carthan was required to leave office because of his felony conviction. The board of aldermen installed Roosevelt Granderson as mayor pro tempore. Granderson was a teacher, basketball coach, and employee at the Jitney Jr. convenience store.

Granderson retained his mayorship after winning election in June 1981. Days later, he was shot and killed execution-style at the Jitney Jr. The killer or killers also stole $5,000.

Police arrested two Black men, Vincent Bolden and David Hester, for Granderson's murder. Bolden and Hester had extensive criminal records and were visiting Tchula from Illinois at the time of the murder. Hester was the first cousin of Joseph Carthan's brother-in-law. Joseph was Eddie's brother.

Bolden and Hester spent months in jail before cutting a deal with the white prosecutor in exchange for testifying that the Carthans hired them to kill Granderson and stage a robbery. In April 1982, a grand jury indicted Eddie and Joseph for capital murder and armed robbery. Their alleged motive was revenge for Granderson taking over the mayorship.

In five years, Carthan went from mayor and successful business owner to facing three years in prison for aggravated assault and the death penalty for murder. NBC News reported, "Eddie Carthan's dream has turned to dust. This is still a Mississippi town he knew as a child, where the power looks white and the poverty looks Black, and the plantation is still a way of life." Carthan told *The Guardian*, "The whites couldn't accept a black mayor. Not just in Tchula—across the delta. If I was successful here, that would have encouraged other towns and cities to elect black officials, black mayors."

Many individuals and organizations believed Carthan was framed and stepped up to support him, including the National Conference of Black Lawyers and the Mississippi Conference of Black Mayors. Amnesty International sent an observer to Tchula. Black farmers raised funds for Carthan's bail. While awaiting trial, he traversed the country raising awareness about his case and funds to mount a defense.

Holmes County United League Director Arnett Lewis asked Christic Institute to help with Carthan's case. Lewis and Danny Sheehan, Christic's general counsel, agreed to assist amid their ongoing Greensboro Massacre work. Mary Ellen Fitzmaurice, another Christic attorney, also worked on the case.

They helped the "National Campaign to Free Mayor Eddie Carthan" with fundraising, community organizing and education, investigation, and legal work. While in Holmes County, Christic Institute staff traveled in an old blue car they dubbed "The Justice Machine." In his autobiography, Sheehan described their accommodations in Tchula and the dangers of civil rights work in the Mississippi Delta: "We all moved into an old farmhouse. . . . One night . . . we heard a commotion outside. Twenty carloads of Klansmen had shown up, driving around the house, flashing their headlights, and shouting racial epithets at us."

The campaign held strategy meetings at the home of three Catholic nuns who were engaged in local racial justice advocacy: Beverly Weidner, Loretta Beyer, and Louise McKigney. Weidner recalled that they too experienced intimidation, including nails in their driveway to cause flat tires and Beyer's bedroom window being shot out.

Lewis also worked closely and developed a friendship with Carthan's local defense attorney, Johnnie Walls Jr., a Black Mississippi-native and former legal services attorney who'd gone into private practice. Lewis remembered Walls teaching him about Mississippi's racist history and helping him "see the false charges, overt defiance of Eddie's mayoral authority, and law enforcement's attack on African American leadership."

Lewis, Walls, and Sheehan decided to file a motion to dismiss the charges, arguing the prosecution ought to be barred from proceeding due to "outrageous government misconduct." In *United States v. Russell*, Supreme Court Justice William Rehnquist formally introduced the defense into law. He wrote that there may be cases "in which the conduct of law enforcement agents is so outrageous that due process principles would absolutely bar the government from invoking judicial processes to obtain a conviction."

Lewis contacted Arthur Kinoy—Center for Constitutional Rights cofounder, Rutgers Law School professor, NLG leader, and one of Lewis's role models and mentors—for his thoughts about the motion. Lewis also turned to Gayle Korotkin—then CWP lawyer and one of his cocounsels in the Greensboro Massacre campaign—for her help with research and writing. Lastly, Lewis requested expert assistance from Manning Marable. At the time, Marable was a history and economics professor and part of the Race Relations Institute at Fisk University. He later founded the Institute for Research in African American Studies at Columbia University and won a Pulitzer Prize for his biography of Malcolm X. According to Lewis, Marable jumped at the opportunity. Marable later wrote, "Carthan's election was an intolerable threat to the racist power structure of Holmes County, and indirectly, of the entire state. . . . Change in a repressive society does not come about without opposition."

The motion described the means white people used after Reconstruction, the civil rights movement, and passage of the Voting Rights Act "to keep Blacks from having meaningful representation in the political process." The motion alleged that the "new wave of attacks" included efforts "to discredit and destroy Black elected officials," such as the concocted charges against Carthan. Finally, the motion characterized the charges as an attempt by the local white power structure to frame and "legally lynch" a Black leader.

To Lewis's surprise and delight, Circuit Court Judge Arthur Clark granted the defense's request for a pretrial hearing on the motion. The defense team attributed Clark's decision to the pressures of local organizing and national scrutiny. "Mississippi had to at least make an effort to appear fair about their legal lynching," Lewis believes.

Lewis, Walls, and others educated the community about the motion and organized around the hearing date. Decades later, Lewis wrote about the hearing:

> As we expected, the judge denied the motion. But the reframing had occurred! The word-of-mouth buzz galloped around the county. The historical and current racism was being named in the white man's courthouse. The truth of the testimony resonated like a "Negro spiritual" and similarly moved people toward the confidence that "We Shall Overcome." . . . What matters is the courtroom was packed with African American folks, seemingly straight out of the fields. I remember bandanas aplenty in the audience and loud, church-like "Amens!" throughout Manning's testimony. The audience listened as Manning, an educated African American, articulated the suffering and injustices that they and their ancestors had experienced. They watched as Manning stood toe-to-toe with the establishment; and as Manning countered and effectively responded to the judge's efforts to derail or halt the history lesson being delivered in that courtroom. It brings chill bumps to my body this many years later just to think about it—a good example of People's lawyering linked with community organizing to educate and empower the civil rights movement.

Before the trial began, the judge granted the defense's motion to sever the trials of Carthan and his brother. Eddie would be tried first.

On October 19, 1982, jury selection began. Walls asked prospective white jurors if they belonged to a white supremist organization, such as the KKK, and if they'd ever used the word "nigger." One potential juror replied, "I don't think you'll find many white people who haven't." Ultimately, an all-Black jury was selected—a victory Carthan attributed to the diligence and skill of Lewis, Walls, and Sheehan. "Carthan's team of defense attorneys . . . demolished the prosecution's efforts to pack the jury with white racists," Marable wrote.

Organizing efforts continued during the trial. Supporters rallied outside the courthouse, holding signs that read, "Free the Tchula 7." On October 23, an estimated 2,500 people marched seven miles across Jackson, to the state capitol building. Charles Evers, former mayor of Fayette, Mississippi, warned the crowd, "If they get away with this here, they will try it in other places around the country." Mickey McGuire, with the National Black United Front, proclaimed, "America is watching you, Mississippi. . . . We are not going to stand by and watch you slaughter and throw Black people in the creek like you did Emmett Till."

Meanwhile, inside the courthouse, the prosecution maintained that greed, jealousy, and bitterness drove Carthan to arrange the robbery and murder. Bolden and Hester testified that Carthan promised them $20,000 to kill Granderson and stage a robbery.

Lewis, Walls, and Sheehan argued that Carthan was framed by the "white power structure" and the murder was related to drug dealing between Hester and Granderson. Carthan's wife, Shirley, testified that she and Eddie were hosting guests at their home on the same evening he supposedly met with Bolden and Hester. Willie Brown, who had shared a jail cell with Bolden for five months, testified that he overheard Bolden admit to not knowing or recognizing Carthan. During closing arguments, Carthan said, "I'm here to be made an example. When you fail to become a little boy with the power structure, this is what will happen to you."

On November 4, 1982, after deliberating for only forty-five minutes, the jury acquitted Carthan. His supporters cheered and danced in the crowded courtroom. Outside, they faced off with hooded Klansmen who were calling for "removal of all Black murderers from office." On the courthouse steps, Carthan declared, "This is a victory for all people who want to achieve equal treatment under the law. The bell has struck for liberty and justice and peace."

Lewis credits his experiences in Tchula with expanding his understanding of the lasting impacts of slavery and white supremacy, the lengths the power structure will go to disrupt and discredit the Black liberation struggle, and the importance of framing a cause in legal pleadings for public consumption. Additionally, Lewis said the campaign deepened his appreciation for the "beauty and dedication of known and unknown African Americans who struggle for equal justice."

In 2018, Carthan reflected on Lewis's and Sheehan's work: "I knew that they were extremely serious, extremely dedicated because they were risking their lives to do what they did. And it was a danger for Lewis Pitts while he was here. . . . Had it not been for them, I would not be alive today. I thank them. I thank God Almighty for them." Shirley Carthan said Lewis "was a drum major for justice and had a heart for God's people."

Fred Carter

After contracting pneumoconiosis, Fred Carter, a Black coal miner in West Virginia, was forced to quit working in 1959. Pneumoconiosis, more commonly known as "black lung," is an incurable disease caused by prolonged inhalation of coal dust.

Subsequently, Carter became active in Miners for Democracy and vice president of the Black Lung Association. He also applied for medical benefits on behalf of himself and other former miners under the Federal Coal Mine Health and Safety Act of 1969, known as the "Black Lung Act." The act established a benefits program for coal miners who were totally disabled due to pneumoconiosis and for surviving dependents of miners whose deaths were caused by black lung. Carter secured compensation for approximately 1,800 former miners and survivors. According to Carter, he wasn't paid for his services; instead, he was merely reimbursed for related expenses.

By 1975, Carter and approximately 225,000 other sick miners and dependents still hadn't received compensation and benefits from the grossly underfunded federal program. Carter lobbied Congress for additional funding and lobbied against legislation that'd make obtaining benefits even more difficult.

In June 1982, Carter announced his candidacy for president of the United Mine Workers of America (UMWA) union. The National Knights of the KKK campaigned against Carter and for his white opponents. Worse still, in August 1982, days after the nominating period for the UMWA elections ended, a grand jury indicted Carter in the US District Court for the Southern District of West Virginia.

US Department of Labor officials and law enforcement officers claimed Carter had engaged in illegal activities from September 1977 to July 1981. He was charged with fourteen misdemeanors related to allegedly accepting $21,000 in fees for handling miners' cases without the Labor Department's pre-approval. He was also charged with two felonies: lying to a federal official when asked if he was charging fees for black lung cases and impersonating a federal officer. At age sixty-one, Carter faced up to twenty-two years in prison.

After his court-appointed attorney advised him to plead guilty, Carter sought private counsel. He retained John Taylor, the white son and grandson of coal miners who had contracted black lung; a native West Virginian, union activist, and solo practitioner who represented people in cases involving claims for black lung benefits, Social Security Disability Insurance, and workers' compensation; and former general counsel for the UMWA District 17.

In January 1983, Taylor contacted Lewis through NLG connections. Lewis agreed to cocounsel Carter's case. They got to know each other while traveling to mining towns in hollers. Lewis wrote, "It was great being with those people. Based on their mining labor, they already had a class analysis and fighting spirit. They had no trouble seeing our evidence as showing the criminal case against Carter was politically motivated. . . . They felt solidarity with Fred as a miner and advocate for miners, even though he was African American. Plus, the trips with John gave us time to exchange life stories and for me to learn more from him about mining labor struggles and the history of the area." Lewis also spent time getting to know Carter at his home in Kimberly, West Virginia.

Christic Institute formed the "National Campaign Committee to Defend Fred Carter," which included UMWA members, religious leaders, and representatives of organizations working on mining health and safety issues. They publicly reframed the prosecution of Carter as an attack on lay advocate programs, the black lung movement, and Carter's UMWA presidential campaign. The UMWA's newspaper read, "The Reagan government hopes that by prosecuting Carter they will be able to intimidate all lay-advocates from taking cases." A campaign committee packet read, "Fred Carter is an outspoken black man who refused to stay 'in his place.'"

The campaign committee also pressured US Attorney David Faber to drop the charges. Its petition to Faber read, "We, the undersigned, believe the charges against FRED CARTER . . . are trumped up. We believe the charges are an attack aimed at weakening Lay-Advocate Programs, thus preventing disabled workers from receiving just compensation for industrial diseases." Lewis and Taylor recruited the NLG to join the lobbying efforts. NLG President Michael Ratner demanded the dismissal of all charges against Fred Carter. A few days later, Johnny Colon, NLG's vice president, wrote to Faber, "The timing and nature of the charges resemble very closely the frame-up charges against Mayor Eddie Carthan of Tchula, Mississippi, another black leader. The Carter case reeks also of political prosecution."

Lewis and Taylor filed three motions for dismissal of the charges against Carter. Their "Motion to Dismiss Based on Invidious Discrimination and Selective Prosecution" alleged that, due to Carter's race and First Amendment activities, federal officials initiated the indictment "to chill the Defendant's activities, discredit him and destroy his effectiveness and means of livelihood." Their "Motion to Quash Based on Outrageous Government Conduct" claimed the prosecution abused the grand jury system by withholding exculpatory information and leading witnesses. Rulings on these motions were delayed until after the trial. A federal magistrate dismissed their third motion, which argued the applicable statute about accepting fees was unconstitutionally vague—that is, the law didn't adequately specify the legally required or punishable conduct.

Federal District Court Judge Charles Haden presided over the trial, which began with jury selection on May 23, 1983. Approximately seventy Carter supporters filled the courtroom. The seated jury included eleven white jurors and only one Black juror. At the start of the trial, the prosecution dropped two of the misdemeanor charges.

The prosecution called fifteen miners or miners' relatives who testified they'd paid Carter fees—ranging from $500 to $3,200—for representing them in black lung cases. Additionally, a Labor Department official testified he couldn't locate any fee petitions from Carter, which he was required to submit in order to legally collect the alleged payments.

Two days into the trial, Lewis obtained evidence that the US Attorney's Office had withheld discovery, made false statements to the judge, and coached witnesses. That night, Lewis called Judge Haden's home to relay the information. Haden, in turn, took the unusual step of giving the defense access to the grand jury files. Lewis found a memo from US Attorney Faber to Assistant US Attorney Larry Ellis, the lead prosecutor in Carter's case. According to the memo, eight days after Carter's indictment, an administrative law judge (ALJ) said he hoped the prosecution was successful because Carter had long been a thorn in the side of judges. Lewis's case notes read, "The Grand Jury Proceedings were nothing short of a total and complete effort to smear the character of Fred Carter. Carter Elliott, the Department of Labor special agent, trashed Fred's ability and competency as a lay representative." Additionally, according to Lewis's notes, Elliott described "Fred as a big man with a rough voice that appeared and looked like Sonny Liston, creating the impression that Fred went around and physically beat-up old widows in order to take money from them."

After the prosecution rested, Judge Haden granted Lewis and Taylor's motion to dismiss the felony charges for impersonating a federal official and making false statements to federal officials. The following day, Haden also dismissed a misdemeanor charge because the clerk had misplaced critical evidence.

During the defense's presentation, Carter testified that he accepted money only as reimbursement for expenses, such as acquiring medical records, arranging medical exams for clients, and paying for travel, lodging, and food. Lewis and Taylor also attempted to show that the federal government framed and prosecuted Carter to end his bid for UMWA president and undermine the black lung movement. However, Judge Haden precluded the defense from calling the special agent who seized Carter's files and who, according to Lewis, was a CIA agent.

On May 28, 1983, the jury convicted Carter of the eleven remaining misdemeanors. He faced a maximum sentence of eleven years in prison and a $11,000 fine. Haden delayed sentencing to allow time to rule on the defense's post-trial motions. After the verdict, Lewis said he'd appeal because jurors were prevented from hearing evidence of a conspiracy among federal officials to discredit Carter.

Things went from bad to worse for Carter. Ten days after the verdict, he lost a motion for a new trial. Four days after that, he suffered a heart attack. Next, he failed to receive the requisite votes to have his name on the ballot for UMWA president. Finally, in January 1984, West Virginia Governor John Rockefeller denied Lewis's petition to grant clemency to Carter.

However, Carter's conviction was eventually overturned by the US Court of Appeals for the Fourth Circuit, by which time Carter had a different attorney. The court reasoned that the statute under which Carter was convicted didn't apply to him under the circumstances and was unconstitutionally vague. In effect, the Fourth Circuit agreed with the argument in Lewis and Taylor's pretrial motion.

Lewis, of course, wanted Carter acquitted on all charges. However, dismissals of the felonies and some of the misdemeanors were major victories. Additional silver linings for Lewis included learning more about union organizing from Carter and lawyering from Taylor, feeling "solidarity with mining families," "raising hell about the feds," and fighting for a worthy cause. Taylor wrote that Lewis's "experience and expertise in criminal trials" enabled them to expose the US government's "deliberate concealment of exculpatory material" and "resulted in a very well-prepared defense for Mr. Carter."

Christic Institute South Begins

Midway through his Greensboro Massacre work, and shortly after the Carthan and Carter campaigns, Lewis was eager to start his own organization. First, he wanted to control his own schedule and limit his work to the South in order to have more time with Katie and Stephen.

Second, Lewis said "handling" Danny Sheehan was "tiring." Lewis had managed tensions and acted as a buffer between Sheehan and Johnnie Walls in Tchula and between Sheehan and Flint Taylor and CWP members in Greensboro. The sources of friction, Lewis explained, were Sheehan's ego, wild theories, and relatively moderate politics. Moreover, they had differing theories of change and approaches to lawyering.

Third, Lewis recognized a need for an organization specializing in defending elected officials and activists of color who were facing politically motivated criminal charges and other attacks designed to discredit and neutralize racial justice movements in the South. He wrote, at the time:

> There is a shortage of legal resources in the South to deal with these political and legal attacks. Few local lawyers are prepared for an all-out fight against the "good old boy" power structure because they know that being too bold or outspoken on a political case could result in economic sanctions or endanger any political aspirations they have. Existing legal organizations . . . do not begin to meet the needs in less publicized cases, which just as surely threaten basic constitutional rights and grassroots empowerment. As a result of this vacuum, people become demoralized and isolated, and some go to jail for lack of assistance.

His desire to meet this need was shaped by his work on the Greensboro Massacre, Carthan, and Carter campaigns, as well as his ongoing conversations with Gayle Korotkin, Flint Taylor, CWP members, and others.

During the Greensboro Massacre work, Lewis and Korotkin formed a special bond. In 1983, Lewis approached her about starting an organization with him. According to Lewis, Korotkin was extremely hardworking, deeply empathetic, brilliant, widely read, a gifted researcher and writer, and unwaveringly committed to social justice. He accepted her oddness. Korotkin drove a small, old, beat-up car filled with newspapers and boxes of her belongings. She often spent nights sleeping under a desk and occasionally brought stray cats into the office. She was also exceptionally introverted and private. Asking Korotkin to speak publicly was like "pouring salt on a slug," Lewis recalled. He said she never shared anything about her past and "was masterful at immediately flipping the conversation to you telling your own story." Ultimately, her personality and skillset nicely complemented Lewis's sociability and forwardness.

Korotkin agreed to join Lewis, and they began planning to open CIS. Although CIS would be a regional office of Christic Institute and use its 501(c)(3) nonprofit status and fiscal sponsorship, Lewis and Korotkin would have their own board of directors and work plan. The arrangement combined the help with fundraising and public relations they needed from Christic Institute with the independence and "room to romp" they wanted, Lewis said. Christic Institute's other leaders were excited about having a racial justice project based in the South under the organization's umbrella.

Lewis and Korotkin formed a CIS board consisting of Shirley Carthan; Manning Marable; Lewis Brandon, a civil rights activist in Greensboro; John Erwin, a retired textile worker and vice president of the Greensboro NAACP chapter; Naomi Green, a community organizer in eastern North Carolina; and Larry Morse, an economics professor at North Carolina A&T State University and activist with Greensboro's Citizens for Justice and Unity. Apart from Morse, they were all Black.

President Reagan's first term and reelection in 1984 added to their sense of urgency about starting CIS. Lewis and Korotkin wrote:

> In the 1980's we are seeing a period of "turning back the clock" and intensified efforts to undo the gains of people of color and progressive people in the South. These tactics have ranged from Klan terrorism to ideological appeals to "reverse discrimination" and "white rights." The U.S. Justice Department has joined in this by turning from enforcing civil rights to prosecuting those who are working for civil rights.
>
> The purpose of these attacks is clear: to discredit the leaders and their constituency; to disrupt the organizing by draining resources

for legal defenses; and to instill fear and intimidate others so as to deter them from organizing and speaking freely.

Lewis and Korotkin believed community-based, movement lawyering was the most effective approach for them to tackle these Reagan-era challenges and generate lasting change. Their focuses would be like those more recently summarized by the national Law for Black Lives network—"building community power and democratizing the law." Two decades before "movement lawyering" became a somewhat popular term, Lewis and Korotkin wrote:

> It is difficult to defeat politically motivated charges with purely a legalistic defense alone, particularly in southern courts. The legal brief has to be backed up by the "street brief" (e.g., community meetings, petitions, press conferences, marches, other forms of community and wider involvement and pressure). Furthermore, although legal victories help in and of themselves, it is possible to win the legal battle and yet lose the political war of attrition unless public education, organizing, and coalition-building are done to undo the intimidation and reinforce the underlying community efforts for empowerment.
>
> We view litigation as one important tactic, but one always carried out with its twin tactic of a political offensive, consisting of public education and organizing; both tactics serve the strategic goal of empowerment of The People.

Their goals, in no particular order, were to: instill expertise, confidence, and passion in law students and local attorneys; "empower the community by allowing its own chosen leadership to speak and act free from harassment, intimidation, and the threat of becoming the target of a criminal frame-up"; "promote the leadership of women and people of color"; "leave in place a strong community coalition capable of carrying on their work and able to respond to another attack, if necessary"; "discourage future attacks by exposing the political motivations behind criminal charges"; and prevail in court.

In terms of tactics, Lewis and Korotkin envisioned CIS being a "strike force" capable of rapidly deploying education, organizing, and legal advocacy. Their legal advocacy would be designed to not only successfully defend leaders and activists against charges, but also to "shift from defending to exposing," "take the offense against injustice," "challenge underlying injustice," and "raise issues of public concern and draw citizens into action."

Lewis was director and Korotkin was assistant director. She didn't want the spotlight that came with being director and was better than Lewis at research and writing. Lewis had more connections with Christic Institute staff, name recognition from his Greensboro Massacre work, and comfort interfacing with judges, juries, funders, reporters, and others.

From mid-1983 to mid-1985, according to Lewis in a letter to Manning Marable, CIS was in a "conceptualized holding pattern" due to Greensboro Massacre work. Marable wrote to prospective funders, "The challenge of the law is to empower poor people, to free Blacks and rural Southern whites from the fear of selecting their own leaders, or acting within the democratic process on their own behalf without intimidation. . . . Christic Institute-South can play a major role in the ongoing campaign for civil rights in the South. Lewis Pitts, the director, has the training, enthusiasm, and experience which is essential in providing constructive leadership."

CHAPTER 7

Defending Black Movement Leaders and Activists (Part 2)

As soon as the Greensboro Massacre civil trial ended, Lewis and Gayle Korotkin hit the ground running with their new organization. During their first year operating CIS, they played key roles in racial justice movements in Louisiana, Alabama, and North Carolina. Throughout the South, Lewis and Korotkin defended Black advocates who were targets of politically motivated criminal charges and who needed lawyers willing to go on the offensive against vindictive white power structures determined to roll back civil rights.

Pat Bryant and Public Housing Tenants in Louisiana

In 1982, Pat Bryant became the first director of the Southeast Project on Human Needs and Peace—a joint initiative of the Institute for Southern Studies and the Southern Organizing Committee for Economic and Social Justice. Bryant then became director of the Gulf Coast Tenant Leadership Development Project. In that role, he helped one of the project's member organizations in Louisiana—the St. Charles Parish Tenants Organization—build a campaign around three local public housing projects: Boutte, Hahnville, and Des Allemands.

Located approximately twenty-five miles west of New Orleans, the projects had a total of 128 apartments that housed approximately five hundred people. The tenants' campaign focused on rent overcharging, poor maintenance, and uninhabitable conditions. Residents lived with snakes, roaches, rats, holes in walls and ceilings, broken heaters, leaky pipes, faucets without valves, and raw sewage.

In April 1985, Bryant and between sixty and 150 protesters (accounts vary dramatically) began a march at the Hahnville community. Upon arriving at Louisiana Highway 18, they were met by sheriff's deputies who demanded they move from the road to the sidewalk. However, according to Bryant, event organizers had notified the local sheriff's department ahead of time and had been granted permission to march on the road. Additionally, the marchers, including some who were elderly or pushing strollers, refused to comply because the road and sidewalk were separated by a wide, steep ditch filled with mud and water. One marcher told deputies, "We will not be savages any longer."

Deputies arrested thirty-five people, including children, on charges of obstructing a passageway and disturbing the peace by unlawful assembly. Mothers were also charged with contributing to the delinquency of a juvenile. The local jail was too small to hold the twenty-five arrestees who couldn't afford the bond, which had been set at $140; so, they were locked up in the Orleans Parish Prison for the night.

The following morning, the arrestees pleaded guilty to obstructing public passage and promised to pay, in the coming months, a $100 fine and $47.50 in court costs; the other charges were dropped. However, according to Bryant, the pleas were coerced. Specifically, marchers were told they had two options: contest the charges, be charged with a felony, and remain in jail because they were unable to pay bail; or plead guilty to a misdemeanor, go home, and pay a fine later. Additionally, Bryant said, one of the mothers was told she could "either take her three children to jail or give them to someone else." The pressure was applied by the local DA, Harry Morel Jr., who'd later go to prison for demanding sexual favors from women in exchange for his help with their cases; and by State District Court Judge Ruche Marino, who was reportedly a former member of the White Citizens' Council of Louisiana.

On June 1, 1985, about a hundred people gathered for a second march. Bryant told *Southern Exposure*, "We had to press forward because we had some folks down there who were intimidated by the arrests. We had to organize this march quick and make it bigger and more historic to show them that we have right on our side and the cops, who they have feared all their lives, don't have the power to stop a legal freedom of expression." In ninety-degree heat, they marched from Hahnville, over the Mississippi River, to the Destrehan Plantation. Marchers chanted, "Ronald Reagan says cut back, we say fight back," and "We're fired up, can't take it no more!" The march ended without arrests.

Bryant and protesters from the April 14 march needed an attorney to challenge the fines, fees, and coerced guilty pleas. Bryant contacted Anne Braden, cochair of the Southern Organizing Committee, who, in turn, reached out to Arthur Kinoy at the Center for Constitutional Rights. Braden wrote:

Tenant activity in St. Charles Parish is a part of a much wider movement in the Deep South. In the past two years, there has been a mass upsurge of a new tenant movement along the Gulf Coast of Louisiana, Mississippi, and Alabama. The Southeast Project on Human Needs & Peace has served as the catalyst for this movement—training at least 200 new grass-roots leaders who have actually become the organizers of the movement.

Tenants in this area . . . are literally fighting for survival today. Funds for housing have been cut more than anything else under Reagan's budget cuts; the Reagan administration came into office with a specific plan to abolish public housing altogether.

However, the center's lawyers were already stretched too thin. During Braden's conversation with Kinoy, Lewis's name came up. Braden wrote that Lewis could help "relieve the situation in Louisiana" and meet "the crying need for a trouble-shooting sort of lawyer to help grassroots movements, when creative legal action can keep a movement from being killed aborning." She continued, "We talked to Lewis. He was willing—in fact eager—to come and work on the fine situation. But it was a fact he had no money for expenses."

Lewis's first step with all CIS cases was listening to local advocates' experiences, concerns, and goals. He made multiple trips to the St. Charles Parish area, during which he stayed with Bryant and his wife, Clare Jupiter.

On August 27, 1985, Lewis attended a tenant meeting in Boutte and a protest of the local housing authority. His clearest memory of the event was being "hot as hell and sticky" after their bus broke down. Bryant reminisced, "As was often the case, the old school bus would break down. And I would get out, put on a jumpsuit, and make the repairs."

After the meeting and protest, Lewis remained in the area to work with Bryant and local counsel for the protesters, Thomas Divens, on taking affidavits from tenants and appealing the guilty pleas. Bryant shared that he immediately recognized Lewis was a "feisty, young, white lawyer who knows southern traditions and culture." "Those are remarkable assets," Bryant added.

On August 29, two business days before the protesters' deadline for paying the fines and court costs, Lewis and Divens filed two motions in the 29th Judicial District Court. One motion was to vacate the guilty pleas because they were the product of coercion and ineffective assistance of counsel from Bryant's wife. The accompanying memo read, "Ms. Jupiter stepped forward as counsel. . . . She rarely practices in the area of criminal law or constitutional law. The defendants were not fully advised by her of their constitutional rights or any of their several constitutional defenses." The other motion was to disqualify Judge Marino because he allegedly involved himself in the plea-bargaining process, contributed to the coercion, and failed to properly advise the defendants of rights they'd waive by pleading guilty.

Lewis and local advocates also publicly insisted that race played a role in the April 14 standoff between marchers and law enforcement. Bryant told reporters, "This is all part of a larger issue of the way blacks are treated in this parish. They never would have arrested whites for marching on the street." The arrests were "reminiscent of South Africa, where they round up blacks and cart them away," Lewis told the *Louisiana Weekly*.

Marino hadn't ruled on the motions by September 2—the deadline for the defendants to pay. Therefore, Lewis contacted DA Morel, who granted Lewis's request to delay the start of the marchers' sentences pending a ruling on their motions.

On September 6, Marino ordered the guilty pleas vacated based solely on ineffective assistance of counsel. His order read, "ALL other matters denied!" Thus, Marino effectively rendered moot the allegation of coercion by him and the motion for his recusal. Lewis and the protesters were, therefore, unsatisfied.

Lewis wrote to another 29th Judicial District Court judge, Joel Chaisson, asserting that Marino "lost any authority to act" in the case upon the filing of the recusal motion on August 29, and consequently, Marino's order was invalid. Lewis insisted "upon a valid order vacating the pleas." Chaisson didn't respond.

At the direction of local advocates, Lewis filed a motion requesting that Marino's order be vacated based on his lack of jurisdiction and a dismissal "be reissued by a judge with proper jurisdiction." However, before the scheduled hearing on the motion, Lewis unexpectedly received a copy of his own letter to Judge Chaisson. On the letter was a handwritten notation from the court clerk indicating that the pleas were vacated, the charges were dismissed, and the fines and fees would be refunded.

CIS materials read, "The arrests, time in jail, and fines had a chilling effect on further organizing activities by the tenant group. . . . The successful intervention by CIS helped give the tenants a sense of victory and strength in proceeding with their work." Similarly, Bryant wrote, "Lewis was a tremendous advocate who was able to get the state off the back of the movement. . . .

Lewis really knows how to get the job done." Bryant further reflected on working with Lewis: "Lewis is a brother whom I would choose to be in a fox hole with. . . . He should be brought in to teach young lawyers . . . his style of being on tap rather than being on top. . . . We often struggled with lawyers who wanted to dictate organizing tactics and strategies. Lewis was not about that. . . . I often compared Lewis to Mort Stavis, Bill Kunstler, and Arthur Kinoy because of his way to get down to the heart of matters—racism. He was tenacious."

"Greene County Five" and Voting Rights Advocates in Alabama

Federal civil rights laws were antithetical to President Reagan's philosophies on "states' rights" and deregulation. During his presidency, Reagan's antipathy toward civil rights permeated the DOJ. "The DOJ was the nerve center of the Reagan revolution," wrote journalist, author, and voting rights expert Ari Berman. The department dramatically scaled back enforcement of the Voting Rights Act, which Reagan called "humiliating to the South" and attempted to weaken with the help of future US Supreme Court Chief Justice John Roberts. Heather Cox Richardson, a history professor and author, wrote in the *Boston Globe* that "the modern myth of voter fraud" began during Reagan's presidency, "when Republicans recognized that their policies could not attract a majority of voters." Republicans' voter suppression efforts, under the guise of election integrity, included popularizing myths about widespread voter fraud to justify "security" measures—such as voter identification laws and purging voter rolls—and "enforcement" measures to deter prospective voters—such as threats of severe civil and criminal penalties for voter fraud.

During summer 1984, Reagan's Justice Department announced that all ninety-three US attorneys across the country were joining "a comprehensive program to combat voter fraud." The department targeted the predominantly Black counties of Lowndes, Greene, Wilcox, Sumter, and Perry—all part of Alabama's "Black Belt."

The department's motive was clear. In the ten southwestern Alabama Black Belt counties prior to passage of the Voting Rights Act in 1965, few Black people were registered to vote, and whites controlled the political machines. But by 1984, Black registered voters in the counties outnumbered white registered voters, and Black elected officials in those counties accounted for forty-four percent of all such officials in Alabama. Additionally, Black people held a majority of seats on the county commissions and school boards in five of the counties. The region also had several Black mayors and sheriffs. Anne Braden wrote, "All of this frightened the white power structures—the more so because the new black office-holders came to power as part of an organized movement."

The Reagan administration claimed that its voter fraud program was prompted by complaints from Black residents in the area about absentee voting fraud during primaries and elections in 1984. Yet, the FBI began its eight-month investigation in the Black Belt before the 1984 elections.

The Reagan administration targeted absentee voting for two strategic reasons. First, a relatively large number of Black voters were illiterate, elderly, or otherwise unable to understand absentee voting requirements without assistance. Second, many Black residents relied on absentee ballots because they had to find employment outside of their counties, and long work hours and commutes prevented them from voting while polling locations were open.

The FBI reportedly harassed Black voters leading up to the 1984 presidential elections, including appearing at residences and nursing homes demanding to know how individuals had voted. Federal officials transported elderly Black voters in buses, under armed guard, to testify before a grand jury. According to the *Los Angeles Times*, "Hundreds of ballots were confiscated, reams of office files were seized and more than 1,000 black absentee voters were questioned."

The Justice Department charged eight Black voting rights advocates— three in Perry County and five in Greene County—with crimes related to alleged voter fraud. State Senator Hank Sanders of Alabama called the department's actions "a sophisticated re-enactment of post-Reconstruction activities." Georgia State Senator Julian Bond—who'd become chairman of the NAACP and the first president of the Southern Poverty Law Center—called the prosecutions "a vicious conspiracy directed from the White House . . . whose goal is the suppression and destruction of a budding political movement in the Black Belt." Civil rights advocates responded by forming the Alabama Black Belt Defense Committee.

Jefferson Beauregard Sessions III, then US attorney for the Southern District of Alabama, unsuccessfully prosecuted the Perry County advocates. According to the *Washington Post*, the failed prosecution of the three civil rights advocates "sank Jeff Sessions's bid for a judgeship" after Reagan nominated him to the bench in 1986. In 2017, amid Sessions's confirmation hearings to become Donald Trump's AG, Emily Bazelon—a journalist, author, and Yale

Law School professor—wrote in the *New York Times Magazine*, "The Perry County case is a precursor to current Republican claims that voter fraud at the polls is a widespread problem, which Sessions has promoted, even though there is little evidence to support it."

Greene County was the Justice Department's second bite at the apple. The county is the smallest and among the poorest in Alabama; nevertheless, white people viewed the county's politically active Black people as threatening. The *New York Times* reported that the county "nurtured a small and influential group of educated middle-class blacks" who "organized a series of boycotts and demonstrations in . . . the mid-1960's, attracting national attention." Martin Luther King Jr. made multiple visits to Eutaw, the Greene County seat, from 1965 to 1968, by which time all the county's elected officials were Black.

In June 1985, James Colvin, Bobbie Nell Simpson, Bessie Underwood, Spiver Gordon, and Frederick Douglas Daniels—the "Greene County Five"—were indicted on a combined 138 counts related to alleged voter fraud involving absentee ballots. They were accused of voting more than once, furnishing false information to an election official, ballot tampering, mail fraud, and conspiracy. Colvin was mayor of Union, a town in Greene County. Simpson, the only white defendant, was the deputy county registrar and active in registering Black voters. Underwood worked for the school district. Gordon was a nursing home director, city councilman in Eutaw, leader of the local Civic League, national board member of the Southern Christian Leadership Conference (SCLC), member of the County Hospital Board, and deputy voter registrar in Greene County. Daniels was Gordon's assistant at the nursing home.

Sessions prosecuted Colvin first. In September 1985, a federal judge declared a mistrial after the jury failed to reach a verdict. Nine days later, Simpson's trial also ended with a hung jury and mistrial, except for one count for which Simpson was found not guilty. In exchange for prosecutors dropping twenty-four felony charges against her, Underwood pleaded guilty to a misdemeanor charge of improperly handling absentee ballots and was put on probation.

Gordon and Daniels were tried together—Gordon on twenty-three counts, after fourteen charges were dropped just days before jury selection began; and Daniels on nine counts, all of which overlapped with Gordon's. Conviction on each charge carried a maximum penalty of five years in prison and a $10,000 fine. Lewis said federal officials unsuccessfully pressured Daniels to fabricate incriminating evidence against Gordon, who was the "bigger fish" for voter suppression purposes.

Gordon was represented by J. L. Chestnut Jr., who was the first Black lawyer with a practice in Selma, Alabama, marched on the Edmund Pettus Bridge on Bloody Sunday, and represented various civil rights activists, including Martin Luther King Jr., James Foreman, Dick Gregory, John Lewis, Ralph Abernathy, and Joseph Lowery. Leonard Weinglass, dubbed by the *New York Times* as "perhaps the nation's preeminent progressive defense lawyer," joined Chestnut to defend Gordon.

Daniels's defense team initially consisted of two Black attorneys: Carlos Williams, one of Chestnut's law partners, and John England, an attorney from Tuscaloosa. Kim West, a white, local attorney joined the team. Then, about five days before the trial began on September 23, 1985, Lewis was asked to join Daniels's team. Lewis had met Chestnut, England, and other Alabama civil rights attorneys while attending Southern Organizing Committee meetings in Birmingham organized by Anne Braden. Lewis recalled, "I was added . . . since we expected a majority white jury. My southern accent and whiteness were deemed assets."

Gordon's and Daniels's attorneys collaborated and worked out of Chestnut's offices. Williams reflected, "I was awestruck by the caliber of lawyers who answered the call to come down to the Alabama Black Belt to defend the clients. . . . I recall that Lewis had a calm, but confident, demeanor about him. He was zealous and unflinching in his defense of our clients."

During jury selection in a Tuscaloosa courthouse, the prosecution used all six of its peremptory strikes on the prospective Black jurors, leaving Gordon and Daniels with an all-white jury. Lewis accused the government of discriminating against Black people and told the Associated Press, "Our position is not that those white jurors will be unfair, but the Constitution guarantees a cross-section of the community (on juries) and therefore Black representation." US District Court Judge Elbert Bertram Haltom Jr. denied the defense's motion for a mistrial. The Eleventh Circuit agreed to review an emergency request to stop the trial based on the jury composition but allowed the proceedings to continue in the meantime.

During opening arguments, Chestnut said, "We are dealing with elderly, rural, and for the most part, uneducated black folks. We are going to show the effect on them of a white, three-piece-suited FBI man wearing a badge and coming around asking questions." Lewis told jurors, "There has been no voter scam, no ballot stuffing, no voter fraud." He continued, "I am a white Southerner, too, and I know that white Southerners are not all racists. We ask for fairness for all, regardless of color. Don't let anyone appeal to racism."

England later praised Lewis's ability to read and connect with jurors, as well as his willingness to use his white privilege and "southernness" for good.

After the government rested its case, Lewis shared with the Associated Press, "We think that the government witnesses have helped us more than they have helped the government." The defense teams moved for directed verdicts of acquittal based on insufficient evidence and biased jury selection. "There is not an iota of evidence of conspiracy," Lewis told Judge Haltom. Haltom denied the motions without comment. John Nettles, Alabama leader of the SCLC, called Haltom "a disgrace to the judicial system of America."

During closing arguments, Assistant US Attorney Bill Barnett told jurors, "The people in Greene County do not like for some voting merchant to come along and cast their votes." Holding up an absentee ballot box, he said voting is a sacred right that "closely parallels the Ark of the Covenant." During the defense's turn, Chestnut asked jurors to consider why there'd be "a criminal prosecution over eleven absentee votes out of 1,500; eleven votes which changed no race, caused no one to win or lose." Gordon was "a convenient target for those who do not follow his political philosophy," Chestnut said. Lewis told jurors the government brought "puny allegations" against Daniels without "a scintilla of evidence" about criminal intent.

The trial lasted three weeks and involved forty-nine witnesses and more than thirty exhibits. Civil rights organizations held press conferences during lunch recesses. Kim West recalled, "Ladies from the SCLC who had been in the courtroom throughout, would stand in front of the courthouse, hold hands, . . . and pray for the judge and jury."

On October 12, 1985, after eleven hours of deliberation over two days, jurors acquitted Gordon and Daniels of all nine of their overlapping charges. Judge Haltom ordered the jury to continue deliberating for Gordon's remaining fourteen counts. While deliberation continued, the defendants' supporters stood outside the courthouse, arms locked, singing "We Shall Overcome." Lewis told the media gathered outside that the Reagan administration was "trying to repress voting rights in the South at the same time the world [was] outraged about the same sort of repression going on in South Africa." Daniels declared, "I feel great. . . . The Lord is with us, and he hasn't brought us this far to abandon us now."

One of the high points of the case for Lewis was getting to work and share a motel room with one of his role models, Leonard Weinglass. By that time, Weinglass, a Yale-educated criminal defense lawyer, had represented a long list of high-profile, controversial clients, including Jane Fonda, Angela

Davis, Kathy Boudin, John Sinclair, Daniel Ellsberg, and Anthony Russo. Lewis shared, "It was thrilling to be present in Alabama with so many of the civil rights lawyers and activists who had earned such tremendous respect for their long-time work. Working with and rooming with Lenny was such an honor. I watched and observed his every move and tactic."

Alabama State Senator Hank Sanders wrote to Lewis in 1990, "A legal strike force to support community movement, as represented by CIS, is critical. Too many traditional legal organizations have grown conservative in the kind, extent, and time frame of support provided. . . . I cannot forget that you provided immediate, aggressive and effective legal assistance in 1985 when there was another serious attack on key Alabama Black Belt leadership in voter prosecution cases (so-called voter fraud cases). You helped in the overwhelming victory."

Larry Little

Larry Little helped start and lead the first Black Panther Party chapter in a southern city. The Winston-Salem, North Carolina, chapter registered voters and offered free breakfast for school children, sickle cell anemia testing, and ambulance services. Little later became a Winston-Salem alderman.

In 1984, Little played a significant role in forming the Darryl Hunt Defense Fund. Hunt, a nineteen-year-old, Black man from Winston-Salem, was wrongfully convicted of raping and murdering a white woman and sentenced to life in prison. Little helped uncover evidence favorable to Hunt. Shortly thereafter, Little was falsely accused of misspending monies from the defense fund and threatened with indictment. Additionally, Donald Tisdale, the local DA who prosecuted Hunt, demanded the defense fund's financial records and threatened to seize its assets. According to CIS materials, Tisdale's baseless allegations and threats were retaliation against Little and calculated to disrupt and chill the defense fund's efforts.

Lewis, Korotkin, Douglas Harris, a state ACLU attorney, and Jeffrey Bryson, a local Black attorney, came to Little's defense. They filed motions in Forsyth County Superior Court, including one arguing that making the defense fund's financial records public would violate contributors' First Amendment rights to freedom of speech and association.

In August 1984, Judge Preston Cornelius heard arguments on the motions. Tisdale accused Little of "trying to hide something" by not releasing financial records. Lewis responded, "We are trying to protect the First Amendment."

Later, Lewis said, "If [Tisdale] wants to bring a charge, that's fine and we can defend against it. He shouldn't be allowed to hang a cloud over a good-faith effort by a group of citizens." Cornelius ruled in Hunt's favor, finding the state had no right to an accounting from the defense fund. Thereafter, attacks on the defense fund and threats against Little by the DA's office stopped.

Lewis reflected, "I went to raise a fuss about First Amendment rights and the government trying to create fear and chill a movement. I tried to be a bulldog and model being bold, assertive, and vigorous. Most white lawyers are three-day old Coke with no fizz. I tried to hoot and holler." CIS materials read, "Defense Fund supporters demonstrated a renewed energy and feeling of their strength from their ability to defeat the legal tactics designed to hinder efforts."

Cozelle Wilson

In 1984, two-term Democratic governor James Hunt Jr. and two-term incumbent Republican Jesse Helms battled to represent North Carolina in the US Senate. According to the *New York Times*, "The campaign was the most expensive Senate race in United States history" at that time and "one of the most mean-spirited in the nation" that year. The *Washington Post* read, "The Helms-Hunt battle invites superlatives and has been described here as Armageddon, a holy war, a crusade, a fight between good and evil and a battle between the Old South and the New South."

Thomas Farr, who former president Trump twice unsuccessfully nominated for a federal judgeship, served as legal counsel to Helms's US Senate campaign. Thomas Ellis, a partner at Farr's law firm, was called "the backroom architect of Helms' rise to political power" by the *Washington Post*. The Southern Poverty Law Center reported, "In 1984, Helms, Ellis and Farr used their vast political network to suppress African American votes and scare up white resentment in Helms' campaigns for senate. . . . The campaign circulated photos of . . . Hunt with African American leaders . . . and cited Hunt's support of voter registration, the Martin Luther King, Jr. holiday—the vote for which Helms infamously filibustered in the Senate—and the reauthorization of the Voting Rights Act."

To gain an advantage in the race, the Grand Old Party (GOP) launched a "Ballot Security Program," despite little to no legitimate evidence of voter fraud. The program's primary purpose was to suppress voting in Democratic areas of the state with large percentages of racial minorities.

As senator, Helms arranged for his former aide, Sam Currin, to become the US attorney for the Eastern District of North Carolina. During Helms's reelection campaign, Currin wrote to officials in forty-four eastern North Carolina counties threatening vigorous enforcement of election fraud laws and announcing that FBI agents would be stationed throughout the region before and during the election. Moreover, US attorneys and FBI agents in North Carolina held a joint press conference to threaten prosecution for voter fraud. Finally, Republicans placed threatening Ballot Security Program posters and "ballot security squads" in predominantly Black communities.

The Ballot Security Program also targeted specific Black leaders, such as Cozelle Wilson. Wilson lived her entire life in Lenoir County, North Carolina—mostly in Kinston, the county seat. She was an ordained minister, active in her church, and a leader in the Eastside Neighborhood Improvement Association and local NAACP chapter. She also became a volunteer "special registration commissioner"—a person authorized to accept voter registrations from qualified individuals.

During the first week of October 1984, Wilson and student volunteers from Elizabeth City State University, a historically Black university in northeast North Carolina, registered 205 Black housing-project residents to vote. According to Wilson, "They were mostly older people, who have never had their names put on the book because they were denied the right to register in the past."

A week later, at the Lenoir County Board of Elections meeting, the white county supervisor of elections alleged that registration forms from Wilson had inconsistent handwritings, and thus, should be subjected to closer scrutiny. The board declined to take action. Additionally, the state board of elections denied the North Carolina Republican Party's request to purge voter rolls of individuals who'd been registered by Wilson.

However, after gaining a majority of seats on the county board of elections in July 1985, Republicans pushed for criminal charges against Wilson. In September 1985, the local DA, Donald Jacobs, had a grand jury indict Wilson on felony charges of registering voters contrary to law. At age sixty, Wilson faced up to ten years in prison for allegedly allowing college students to assist too much with registrations and failing to require identification from every registrant.

Wilson retained Paul Jones, who'd opened a private practice in Kinston after serving as the managing attorney of Eastern North Carolina Legal Services. He was also president of the local NAACP chapter. Then, according to Jones, after rumors of federal charges against Wilson began swirling, the state NAACP contacted Lewis because of his reputation and experience with federal litigation. However, a CIS memo presents a different story:

> We first became aware of Rev. Wilson's case through the director of legal services for eastern North Carolina, who was concerned that nothing was being done around the case and asked if we could help.
>
> When CIS became involved, in December 1985, . . . the case wasn't perceived as an important political case locally, no organizing was being done around it, and Rev. Wilson's attorney was essentially waiting to see what the prosecutor would do.
>
> We undertook a legal and political offensive to bring the real issue out into the open, to make voter intimidation a public issue, and to unite people around Rev. Wilson and in defense of Black voting rights. A strong offense would be the best defense of Rev. Wilson.

During the first few months of 1986, Lewis and Korotkin filed three pretrial motions. The first was to quash the indictment for "outrageous government misconduct." CIS used the motion to frame the prosecution as a "politically and racially motivated" attempt "to intimidate and chill Black citizens from voting." The motion read, "Rev. Wilson has been made a pawn and an innocent victim of the partisan maneuvering and trickery behind the most heated and expensive Senatorial race in U.S. history." Likewise, Lewis told the media that Wilson was being "used as a political ping-pong in the Helms-Hunt race." Lewis and Korotkin also filed a motion to quash the indictment for lack of particularity because it didn't identify who Wilson supposedly registered improperly. Finally, they filed a motion for production of FBI records related to the investigation of Wilson.

Consistent with CIS's community-based lawyering approach, Lewis and Korotkin combined their legal work with education and organizing. They collaborated with the NAACP, Black Workers for Justice, and other organizations to hold community meetings, meet with clergy, and present at churches. The events were pep rallies for Wilson's defense and Black voter turnout. Lewis and Korotkin also recruited NLG members, ACLU staff, and law students to respond to additional reports of voter suppression. Additionally, Lewis and Korotkin teamed with the Rainbow Coalition to send a mass mailing asking supporters to write to DA Jacobs and demand the dismissal of

charges against Wilson. CIS materials highlighted how the case had "implications far beyond the effect on" Wilson, how "a strong counterattack [was]
crucial to prevent [her] case from being the first of a series," and how the case
presented an opportunity to build "community strength to deter further such
attacks," including "an interracial grassroots church coalition . . . to link and
support all the local struggles."

Lewis and Jones met with Jacobs and members of the Lenoir County
Board of Elections. According to Jones, after Jacobs refused to dismiss the
charges against Wilson, Lewis declared, "You do what you have to do, and
we'll just have a trial." Lewis and Jones reminded Jacobs that a partisan prosecution of a well-respected Black community leader, in a county that was
nearly forty percent Black, wouldn't bode well for his reelection prospects. Afterward, Lewis wrote to Jacobs, accusing him of "intimidat[ing] and chill[ing]
Black voters"; failing to "grasp the seriousness of the issue" and "deep history
of racism" in eastern North Carolina; and having "a total lack of sensitivity" to
the Black community.

On May 7, 1986, the eve of the first pretrial hearing, Jacobs dropped the
charges against Wilson. CIS materials read, "The prosecutor was forced to
dismiss the charges . . . after CIS exposed the racist political maneuvering
behind the indictment and united diverse groups against the prosecution."
Wilson told reporters, "I will continue to work hard for my people. This case
has given me an even greater desire to do more." The NAACP's state field director told the *Carolina Peacemaker*, "A victory like this helps to strengthen the
minority community. Had we lost, people would have been more hesitant in
registering voters or even voting. It could have set the community back years."
Manning Marable called Wilson "a symbol of courage and hope in an era of
Reaganism and renewed racism."

Two weeks after the charges were dropped, Lewis wrote to Robert Brad-
shaw, state chair of the Republican Party, and US Attorney Currin to notify them that CIS had fully investigated the Ballot Security Program, would
be monitoring the election, and was "prepared and eager" to expose them if
charges were refiled. The letter accused them of "shameful indifference to
Black people's struggle for the fundamental right to vote" and "perpetuat[ing]
the tragic effects of the poll tax, literacy test and Ku Klux Klan in disenfran-
chising Black people." CIS also issued a press release about the letter.

Jones said Lewis "thought you had to fight fire with fire," "was very, very
aggressive," and "was an advocate who believed in taking no prisoners and

winning." Jones added, "If you push Lewis, he's gonna push you twice as much as you pushed him. No one could ever accuse Lewis of not representing someone zealously." Jones, who became a state court judge, recalled that Lewis's style was effective in Wilson's case because locals had never witnessed anyone push back so fiercely against attacks on Black people. In fact, Jones said Wilson wasn't indicted on federal charges because, at least in part, "Lewis was going to be a barrier."

Bobby Ward

Bobby Ward was a Black manager at one of the largest post offices in Chattanooga, Tennessee, and president of the local NAACP chapter. He advocated against employment discrimination within the US Postal Service and local fire and police departments.

An audit of Ward's post office supposedly revealed falsified vending machine revenue reports and an unreported excess stock of stamps. Consequently, he was removed from his position. He lost appeals to the US Merit Systems Protection Board and then to an ALJ.

CIS represented Ward in his appeal to the US Court of Appeals for the DC Circuit. Lewis and Korotkin argued that Ward actually had revenue overages and was a good employee. Moreover, they alleged he was targeted as retaliation for his advocacy against discrimination and for affirmative action. Lewis recalled, "Gayle, as usual, wrote a totally shit-kicking brief." The brief's conclusion read, "The agency should not be permitted to bootstrap a scintilla of suspicion with a scintilla of speculation, apply 'heads-I-win-tails-you-lose' logic and come out with 'substantial evidence' to justify the firing of a man who has spent his life serving the Federal Government."

Lewis argued the case before a three-judge panel in October 1987. The DC Circuit found there was insufficient evidence of Ward falsifying financial records and that his failure to report excess stock was "more than mistake" but "less than fraud." The opinion read, "In light of Ward's 34 years of heretofore unblemished service to the federal government, we remand to the Board for a mitigation of the penalty."

In March 1988, an ALJ reduced Ward's punishment from termination to a demotion. The judge also ordered the Postal Service to award back pay and benefits to Ward and $10,000 to CIS for attorney's fees.

Operation Mushroom Cloud

In the late 1970s, the FBI and DOJ launched an initiative that involved targeting Black elected officials for prosecution, often for alleged corruption. The program—called "Operation Frühmenschen," which is German for "primitive man"—was premised on the belief that Black people were intellectually and socially incapable of managing governmental institutions. As part of the program, the FBI and Internal Revenue Service (IRS) initiated "Operation Mushroom Cloud" in 1987. The operation was prompted by a white businessman who reported that Black elected officials in Greensboro and Winston-Salem were accepting bribes and using their positions for profit. The businessman had a reputation for racially discriminatory employment practices and was disgruntled about not receiving city contracts.

The operation, which became public in August 1989, involved wiretaps, undercover agents, and subpoenaed bank and organizational records. The media dubbed the alleged criminal activity a "vote buying scheme." The operation targeted only local Black leaders, including: Earl Jones, a Greensboro city councilmember; Rodney Sumler, a political consultant, newspaper publisher, and vice president of the local NAACP; Larry Womble, a Winston-Salem alderman and founder of North Carolina Black Elected Municipal Officials; Vivian Burke, a Winston-Salem alderwoman; and Patrick Hairston, president of the local NAACP and a former Winston-Salem alderman.

In addition to serving on the Greensboro City Council, Earl Jones was an attorney, chair of the local NAACP's Legal Redress Committee, and director of the Guilford Community Action Program, a nonprofit that assisted people with housing and employment. In August 1989, officials publicly announced Jones was a target of Operation Mushroom Cloud and the subject of a grand jury investigation. However, after two years of investigation, there wasn't any incriminating evidence against him. In fact, Jones had repeatedly rejected bribes offered by undercover agents posing as business owners who needed zoning changes before relocating their factories to the area.

Jones's legal team consisted of Lewis and Korotkin; Romallus Murphy, a Black attorney for the North Carolina NAACP; and Douglas Harris, a local white attorney. Jones and his attorneys went on the offensive. In September 1989, they filed a motion in the US District Court for the Middle District of North Carolina asking for a judge to oversee any remaining investigation of Jones. The petition also requested an order directing the US attorney to present exculpatory evidence to the grand jury, inform grand jurors about the

FBI's history of misconduct and racial discrimination, and prevent further leaks of information. The "Statement of Facts" in support of the petition described "the legacy of slavery," "barriers to Black political empowerment," the FBI's "history of violating civil rights," "racism within the FBI," and IRS "tax collectors as political police." At a press conference to announce the petition, Lewis accused federal authorities of intentionally leaking information to ruin the reputations and careers of Jones and other officials, "solely because they're Black." Jones told reporters, "This is what is being used against us now instead of ropes, bullets, and firebombs." In October 1989, Lewis, Murphy, and Harris filed a second petition in which they requested all pleadings related to the investigation of Jones be unsealed.

US Magistrate Russell Eliason, a former US attorney, recommended that a federal judge deny the petitions. Eliason claimed the petitioner's allegations of racial bias were "simply superfluous." Lewis reacted, "Such an attitude by certain federal judicial officials has played a major role in the persistence of racism and racial discrimination in our society. It is imperative that the district court overrule the magistrate." Lewis and Jones's other attorneys filed a response in January 1990. They wrote, "To pretend that race is not a factor in defining the merits of the issues in this case . . . suggests not a misguided attempt at 'color-blindness' but rather a fundamental hostility to the types of issues raised by petitioner."

The following month, a federal judge adopted Eliason's recommendation and denied the requests. However, in July 1991, shortly after other local Black leaders were indicted, Jones learned he was no longer under investigation. Jones said of Lewis, "He was always a person committed to justice. He pursued equal justice for all. He actually lived that mantra in his life's work." Jones described Lewis as an "extremely competent" and "excellent lawyer," who was "bold," "aggressive," and a "bulldog."

Around the time the cloud hanging over Jones was lifted, Lee Faye Mack, another Black advocate ensnared in the Operation Mushroom Cloud net, would need Lewis's skill and bulldog mentality. Mack was born into a sharecropping family. Known as "Mother Mack" by the local Black Panther Party, she was a reverend, activist, organizer, friend of Larry Little, and Winston-Salem resident. After working at the local Urban League, she became vice president of People Are Treated Human (PATH), a local charity working to reduce crime and drug abuse. Mack also directed I've Known Trouble, which became the Back to Life Center. The center offered drug and alcohol rehabilitation, support groups, food distribution, and a variety of other programs.

In June 1991, Operation Mushroom Cloud produced federal indictments of Mack, Larry Womble, Patrick Hairston, and Rodney Sumler. The charges included extortion, mail fraud, money laundering, obstructing justice, racketeering, and conspiracy. Mack, at age sixty, faced up to fifty years in prison and a million dollars in fines. The indictment alleged she falsified charity records to funnel bribes for her three codefendants and committed perjury before a grand jury in fall 1989. Mack had told grand jurors that Sumler, who chaired PATH, had nothing to do with preparing a list of contributions to the organization, but prosecutors claimed Sumler had created a phony list and asked her to lie. The "Winston-Salem Four," as they came to be known, all pleaded not guilty.

Lewis and Korotkin joined Gregory Davis, a local Black attorney, in representing Mack. CIS got involved because, according to Korotkin, the charges against Mack were "another unjustified and dangerous attack on black leadership." Korotkin wrote, "Such investigations and prosecutions have become an occupational hazard for black leaders and officials. They uncover little actual wrongdoing but grab headlines and taint reputations." Lewis told the *Winston-Salem Chronicle*, "The government's case is a series of disgruntled white businessmen who resented black elected officials who responded to the needs of their constituents for a return of economic benefits into their community. . . . If it were white aldermen, white charities, white lobbyists, none of this would be nearly as questionable."

According to Lewis, he and Korotkin sought to "flip the script"—from Mack being portrayed as a criminal to Mack being understood as a victim of government corruption and racism. They'd taken the same approach in representing Eddie Carthan, Fred Carter, Pat Bryant, Frederick Douglas Daniels, Larry Little, Cozelle Wilson, Bobby Ward, Earl Jones, and others.

In October 1991, Lewis and Davis asked Federal District Court Judge Richard Erwin to order prosecutors to turn over data on all federal investigations of public officials for the previous five years. The defense team hoped to use the information to prove a pattern of selective prosecution. However, after Lewis said he thought the prosecution was racially motivated, Erwin sniped, "What you 'think' is for a college debate."

The prosecution filed a motion for an order "precluding mention at trial of alleged selective racial prosecution." Mack's defense team opposed the motion "as premature, overbroad, dangerously vague and non-specific, and an unconstitutional restriction of her right to cross-examine witnesses and present a defense." On March 23, 1992, when Mack's trial began in the US District

Court for the Middle District of North Carolina, Judge William Osteen Sr. granted the prosecution's motion. Osteen was a former Nixon-appointed US attorney and was nominated to the bench by George H. W. Bush.

The seated jury consisted of six Black jurors, five white jurors, and one Hispanic juror. During opening arguments, Davis told them, "The evidence will show that Lee Faye Mack is guilty . . . of trying to feed the hungry, clothe the naked, and give direction to those who are less fortunate." He preemptively conceded that Mack's bookkeeping was sloppy, but added, "That's not the crime she's charged with."

Two weeks after the trial began, the prosecutor dropped the conspiracy and racketeering charges against Mack. A *Winston-Salem Chronicle* article described her reaction: "Mack could not hide her emotion. . . . She closed her eyes and held her chin high as a line of tears silently traced its way down her round cheeks." Since these charges were the only two shared among the Winston-Salem Four, Judge Olsteen bifurcated their trial. Mack and Sumler would be tried separately from Womble and Hairston.

During a recess on April 7, Mack reiterated the defense's theory of the case to press: "I see this as an attack on . . . the Black community as a whole. They are . . . pitting the Black community against each other, weakening the strength of the leadership and causing the leadership to spend money for legal defense." On the witness stand, Mack acknowledged she'd mistakenly told the grand jury that neither she nor Sumler prepared the donations list. However, she also explained that, at the time, she'd misunderstood the assistant US attorney's question. Additionally, she testified that the list accurately represented contributions to her organization, with the possible exception of a $1,500 contribution. Finally, Mack said she didn't record the contribution, didn't know who did, and hadn't seen the check or cash; and instead, Sumler told her that he'd received the donation and used the funds for renovations to the Back to Life Center.

Jurors began deliberations on May 21. At a press conference in front of the courthouse, Mack's daughter said, "The American judicial system, from the FBI and police on the street to the judge in the courtroom, is racist and irrefutably biased against Black people." Lewis again told reporters the investigation was racially motivated and criticized Judge Osteen for not allowing a selective prosecution argument. Jurors reached a verdict after eighteen and a half hours of deliberation. They acquitted Mack of obstruction of justice (falsifying records) but convicted her of perjury (lying to the grand jury).

In August 1992, Osteen sentenced Mack to five months in federal prison and an additional five months of house arrest. Afterward, Mack addressed observers in the courtroom, many of whom were crying: "The only thing I did was serve. At no time did I do anything I know was wrong." As she left the courthouse, Mack shouted, "Glory! This is a rejoicing time!"

Nearly two and a half years later, the US Court of Appeals for the Fourth Circuit reversed Mack's conviction. The court reasoned that, during the grand jury proceeding in which she supposedly committed perjury, "the prosecutor did not use the requisite specificity in questioning, despite Mack's apparent confusion or evasion."

Lewis would later work with Mack's daughter, Hazel, at LANC. In 2023, Hazel wrote,

> Lewis understood how the arms of the legal system can be used politically. He understood the landscape immediately and came in as co-counsel on mom's case. What I and others soon learned was that Lewis was not bluster. He had a command of the legal issues. He brought research skills and resources. He and his small team of committed legal warriors became essential in the effort to mount a legal defense for mom. He worked tirelessly. But what he also brought was his understanding of the political nature of the case. He had waged these types of battles before.
>
> What I want to say to Lewis is this—your life's work mattered and still matters. . . . First, it matters because, notwithstanding being viciously attacked by the most powerful within the bar, judges and prosecutors in the legal system, you helped many along the way. My mother's case was just one prime example. Second, your protest advocacy worked to shine light on the unjustness within the legal system. Whether you won or lost in the moment, is not the ultimate measure. Your willingness to weigh in against the odds allowed a voice for the voiceless. Third, you affirmed the voices of those outside of the legal system who were unwilling to be quiet. You held a mirror up to the unjustness of the legal system and those upholding that unjustness.

CHAPTER 8

Movement to Restart Local Government in Keysville, GA

Lewis and Gayle Korotkin continued building CIS on the heels of successful campaigns in Louisiana, Alabama, and North Carolina during the organization's first year. They opened an office in Carrboro, North Carolina, a town just west of Chapel Hill. The office was in the Plowshare Center, an office building and hub of movement organization activities and resources. Lewis and Korotkin raised enough money to pay themselves modest salaries and employ a part-time office administrator. They also hired a Black full-time community organizer/fundraiser, Ashaki Binta.

Growing up in Gary, Indiana, Binta was politically active and learned about challenges facing working-class people from her mother, a nurse's aide, and father, a mental hospital orderly and a juvenile probation officer. After earning a journalism degree from Valparaiso University, Binta moved to Chicago, where she worked for the local Service Employees International Union and food justice cooperatives. She then moved to North Carolina to work with Black Workers for Justice and *Southern Exposure*, the Institute for Southern Studies' journal of politics and culture.

Binta applied to CIS because she needed a steady income, wanted to develop fundraising skills, was drawn to the concept of movement lawyering, and shared Lewis and Korotkin's revolutionary politics. Their first campaign together was in Keysville, Georgia.

Keysville

The town of Keysville is just over one square mile in eastern Georgia—mostly in Burke County. During the last century, the town's population has fluctuated between about 180 and 380.

In 1933, Keysville's white residents shut down the local government, thereby eliminating all public offices, municipal services, and tax collection. Publicly, they claimed the city's tax base was too small to support municipal services. Privately, they feared a takeover of local government by Black residents who were about eighty percent of the town's population.

With no city government, conditions for Keysville's residents went from bad to worse. There was no water or sewer system, no police or fire department, and few lit or paved roads. Rain caused sewage, which had been emptied into the creek, to wash onto people's yards and seep into well water. Some elderly residents couldn't carry buckets of clean water to their homes, if they could even find a working spicket. Moreover, after *Brown v. Board of Education* in 1954, white residents closed rather than integrate Keysville's only public school; subsequently, the nearest public school was eighteen miles away. The only jobs were at the white-owned Keysville Convalescent and Nursing Center, which employed about fifty-six people.

The plight of Keysville's Black residents is well documented. For example, a March 1987 *Los Angeles Times* article described Keysville: "Along some streets in black neighborhoods here, as many as four to five families are forced to share water from a single well. Old-fashioned outhouses are still in use. . . . Garbage bursts from overstuffed public dumpsters . . . , littering yards and roads. . . . Civil rights activists contend that . . . the problems here are typical of those in hundreds of other rural communities below the Mason-Dixon line where blacks form a majority of the population but remain politically disenfranchised and economically disadvantaged." A *Newsweek* profile, in September 1987, called Keysville "a town that time forgot" and "like something from a time capsule buried in the Old South." "Blacks, who are the ones with the outhouses, live in ramshackled houses in a poor neighborhood known as 'the Quarters,' while whites live in relatively nice . . . homes in another part of town," the profile continued.

In the mid-1980s, Emma Gresham and others began fighting to end Keysville's apartheid-like conditions and bring hope to its Black residents. Gresham's father was an African Methodist Episcopal pastor and teacher; her mother was a church missionary and Sunday school teacher. Gresham attended Boggs Academy in Keysville, which was founded and operated by the Presbyterian Board of Missions for Freedman and was Georgia's first accredited secondary boarding school. After graduating from Paine College in Augusta, she spent the next three decades as an elementary school educator, primarily working with children who had disabilities.

Gresham and her husband, Quinten Gresham Sr., a fellow Boggs Academy alumnus, lived in Augusta, Georgia. He was a decorated World War II veteran and retired civil service upholsterer. In 1980, after their children were grown, the Greshams put a mobile home on family property in Keysville. On weekends, they stayed in the trailer and attended Keysville's Mount Tabor AME Church.

Fire Sparks a Movement

In 1985, tensions in Keysville reached a tipping point when fire departments in three surrounding counties refused to respond to a mobile home fire in the town's Black community. The incident prompted a group of Black residents, including Emma Gresham, to air their grievances during a meeting with Herman Lodge, a civil rights advocate and Burke County commissioner. They learned from Lodge, who had recently found a copy of Keysville's forgotten charter inside the Burke County courthouse, that the town hadn't relinquished its incorporated status in 1933 after all. The 1890 charter called for annual local elections on January 6. Although Keysville had functionally ceased to exist, its charter was never officially invalidated.

Soon thereafter, Keysville's Black residents began a movement to reestablish a city government. They started by forming Keysville Concerned Citizens (KCC), an advocacy organization with about twenty-two initial members. Turetha Neely, a spokeswoman for the group, said, "We're tired of having to live like this. We've got kids coming up, and we want a better life for them." Gresham commented, "We're a town with no hope, no jobs for young people—and if a house catches on fire, it just burns. We have apartheid 25 miles from Augusta." The former director of the ACLU's Voting Rights Project, Laughlin McDonald, who'd join the struggle in Keysville, wrote, "Black political participation was always about dignity and respect, and about repudiating the myths of Reconstruction that blacks were incapable of voting and holding elected office. But it was also about such intensely practical matters as bringing running water, paved streets, and fire protection to the long-neglected black community. Nowhere was that more evident than in . . . Keysville, . . . which became a modern-day crucible for the opposing forces in the struggle for equal voting rights."

Gresham told the *Augusta Chronicle* about her first KCC meeting, "I said, 'I better not say nothing, because if I talk my husband accuses me of going to meetings and when I leave there, I'm an officer of something because I talk too much.'" She proved him right, quickly becoming the group's president.

Obstacles to Democracy

KCC's primary goal was to hold local elections as soon as possible—specifically January 6, 1986. However, the group faced a variety of obstacles.

State law required officials appointed by the local governing body to conduct municipal elections. However, with no governing body in Keysville to make appointments, there weren't local election officials. So, at the request of KCC, the Burke County attorney requested guidance from State AG Michael Bowers about how to reactivate the municipal government. Bowers detailed four options: Ask the governor to appoint local election officials; file for a judicial order directing the governor to appoint a local governing body; conduct a town meeting to elect temporary officials; or request the Georgia General Assembly pass an act providing temporary officers and a method of election.

KCC and Burke County officials chose to hold a town meeting. Turetha Neely and Joseph Upton Cochran, the white owner of the town's general store, were elected cosuperintendents of elections. In accordance with the 1890 town charter, there ought to have been elections on January 6; however, Cochran refused to sign off. Neely distributed copies of an election announcement anyway.

The other major obstacle was Keysville's white residents. The town's population was approximately eighty percent Black, which virtually assured a majority or all-Black local government. Desperate white people lashed out.

First, they argued that establishing a government and basic services, such as a water system, would lead to unacceptably high taxes. One white resident declared, "I have a well. Seems if they want something bad enough, they can get it. If they want water and sewage, let them pay for it." Cochran said Black residents not having wells was "a matter of priorities," and "those who need better wells could build them."

Second, white residents claimed Black residents were incapable of governing. Geneva Marshall, who owned Keysville's nursing home with her husband, said local Black people "can't even keep bread in their homes, much less keep up any obligations to the city."

Third, white residents accused Black residents of seeking revenge and engaging in "reverse discrimination." "They're trying to do to us what they say we did to them back in the 1960s," James Poole said.

Lastly, white residents asserted that the pace of change was too fast. Cochran told *Newsday*, "In my opinion, they're just doing too much too fast and if they don't watch out, it's going to get us into a whole lot of trouble. I'm very upset about this." Another white resident told a reporter, "I'd rather see things go along like they're going now. We're doing alright."

David Treadwell, who covered Keysville for the *Los Angeles Times*, called white residents' conduct "a still-classic pattern in the rural South." American University Professor Binny Miller characterized the situation in Keysville as "a compelling tale of racial strife."

1986 Elections

Gresham filed to run for mayor and five other Black residents filed to run for the new city council positions. Becoming mayor would mean ending her teaching career and living full-time in her Keysville mobile home. Gresham told the *Washington Post*, "I could see that the children were not going to school like they should, . . . we had too many dropouts and . . . Keysville was never getting anything." As for the white townspeople, she said, "I decided to love the hell out of them."

White residents, on the other hand, refused to run because they claimed the elections were illegal. "I just wish it could really quiet down," one said.

Under Georgia law, municipalities weren't required to hold an election if a candidate was unopposed after the filing deadline. Consequently, on December 30, 1985, at 10:30 A.M., the Black candidates who had filed were sworn into office by a Burke County judge. Emma Gresham, as mayor, and five Black council members would form Keysville's government, or so they thought.

Five hours after the swearing in, six white Keysville residents obtained a restraining order from State Superior Court Judge Albert Pickett preventing Gresham and the councilmembers from taking office and halting elections in Keysville. The purported basis for the order was that the town's obscure boundaries made identifying eligible voters and candidates impossible.

Keysville's boundaries were fixed by the state legislature when the town was incorporated in 1890. State law extended the borders "one-half mile in every direction from the schoolhouse." However, the whites-only schoolhouse had been demolished, without a marker to pinpoint its previous location. Black residents had a map of Keysville showing borders that'd make them the town's majority; white residents had their own map, which would give them a majority.

On January 17, Judge Pickett issued a preliminary injunction, continuing his prohibition on conducting municipal elections in Keysville. The swearing in was nullified and there'd be no election in 1986.

CIS Joins the Movement

KCC needed support fighting the town's wealthier and more politically connected white minority. Gresham's daughter, a reporter, knew someone who'd worked with CIS and suggested that her mother reach out to the organization for help. Gresham recalled part of her first call with Lewis:

> GRESHAM: Aren't you white?
> LEWIS: Yes.
> GRESHAM: You don't want to bother with this.
> LEWIS: You're fighting for justice aren't ya?
> GRESHAM: Yes, we are.
> LEWIS: Well, I believe in justice.
> GRESHAM: Well, if you believe in justice and you wanna fool with people who don't have any money, maybe you should come.

Days later, Lewis and Korotkin were staying in the Greshams' home. Mrs. Gresham recalled, "He found his way down here. . . . He brought another lawyer, female, who doesn't eat meat. And I was cookin' biscuits and sausage and bacon that mornin' . . . a big southern spread. She sat there and ate coffee and a biscuit. Pitts ate all that he could eat." During their initial visit, Lewis and Korotkin were given a tour of Keysville and attended a community meeting to hear from Black residents.

After discussing the visit, Lewis, Korotkin, and Ashaki Binta decided to join the movement in Keysville. Regarding why they chose to get involved— for no money, on the side that'd been losing, in a tiny town three hundred miles away—Lewis wrote, "Easy—the injustice was obvious; the racism was obvious; and this was a classic example of a Black Belt-type community being thwarted from the basic right to govern themselves and self-determination. Plus, the soul, spirit, and determination of the Greshams, Neelys, and others was so hospitable to our mission that it was a hand-in-glove fit." Similarly, Korotkin told the *Los Angeles Times*, "It's like the civil rights movement never happened in these places. The 'Whites Only' signs are gone, yet institutional barriers to real political, economic and social power on the part of blacks are still there." Lewis explained in a "Memo to Special Friends" that Keysville could "be a showpiece for the substance of what the Civil Rights Movement is seeking—empowerment and self-determination."

For more than two years, Binta made monthly trips to Keysville, often for weeks at a time. Lewis and Korotkin made the ten-hour round-trip drive from North Carolina more intermittently, but still nearly every month, staying for about a week each time. The *Winston-Salem Journal* read, "In many ways, Keysville is an example of how Christic South works. Rather than taking its battle only into the courtroom, Christic South organizes entire communities."

During Lewis's visits to Keysville, he stayed with the Greshams. In his book, *Fire in the Heart: How White Activists Embrace Racial Justice*, Professor Mark Warren shared Lewis's reflections on staying with the Greshams:

> It's 7:30 in the morning. She's making breakfast, and we're getting ready to go to some meeting about struggling to get the movement going. She's on the telephone, talking to maybe a state representative or a newspaper reporter, and stirring the grits, and leaning over and pulling biscuits out; she put sugar in the biscuits to make them good. You can't put a price tag on that. Getting to know her and be part of that, and having her hug me, and me hug her, and replicate that with all these characters that are out there. That's what I've gotten out of this, man. So, when I use that word "solidarity" with people, it really means something.

Gresham shared that Lewis "knew how to talk to everyone" and was "a very intelligent, caring, and loving person." She recalled "something so different about" CIS: "Really and truly, the first time they came, the church was about full because they wanted to see . . . these white people who are going to come and defy these other white people here and be brave enough to come and do this sort of thing. And then, when they started visiting the homes of the [white people] and talking to them . . . we said, 'They are crazy.' But they did! . . . And then, they came back again! And again! And again! We started saying, 'These are *our* attorneys. These people are working with *us*.'"

CIS's organizing efforts included coalition building. For instance, CIS arranged for the National Council of Churches' Racial Justice Working Group to send a delegation to Keysville to "investigate the continuing struggle of Black Keysville residents to exercise their basic democratic right to reactivate town government."

Additionally, Lewis recruited Laughlin McDonald—a fellow South Carolina native and director of the ACLU's Voting Rights Project—to handle most of the movement's traditional legal work, such as pleadings, briefs, and hearings. They'd known each other since Lewis practiced in South Carolina. Lewis described McDonald as "an absolutely wonderful person and lawyer" who "understood the importance of organizing, and thus, gave CIS plenty of room and support to do so while he so ably handled" the legal work. McDonald wrote, "Keysville and Burke County have such a long and extensive history of racial discrimination in voting and all areas of life that working with someone as sane and sensible as Lewis made the litigation far less traumatic."

One of CIS's primary objectives was working with the Greshams and Neelys to strengthen KCC and help its members understand their rights, the long history of the struggle for voting rights in the Deep South, and that "they were the movers of history, not the supreme court or lawyers," Lewis shared. Emma Gresham wrote, "We did not have any expertise in how to do any of this. We didn't understand the dynamics of power. Pitts did. He would sit on the floor of a little shack the men had built for our Concerned Citizens office. . . . We were so happy to hear, to listen; and we celebrated every time we had a small victory. Pitts encouraged us." "We've been extremely careful about not coming in and organizing everything ourselves or making the decisions for them," Binta said at the time.

Together, CIS staff and KCC members canvassed door-to-door, distributed leaflets, held monthly meetings and rallies, trained residents on how to vote, and generated press coverage. Additionally, CIS recruited Sally Alvarez to create a twenty-minute video about the struggle in Keysville. Alvarez was a union organizer and communications specialist, and married to Joe Alvarez, a CWP member who organized around the Greensboro Massacre.

Additionally, CIS and KCC teamed with Henry Key to investigate the town's boundaries. Key was Keysville's oldest resident at age ninety-three. He was the son of an enslaved woman and her legal owner, Joshua Key Sr., a reverend for whom the town is named. Henry Key took a group of visitors and local residents to where the schoolhouse at the center of Keysville's boundaries had been located. Lewis recalled that Key "was a card" who "used old-timey phrases, like 'green as a grasshopper'" and "was smiling all the time."

Lewis reflected on how CIS staff were viewed by Keysville's Black residents:

Gayle and Ashaki were naturals at fitting in. Ashaki, being African American, connected innately because of her passionate support for building leadership in the Black Belt South and her deep political experience. Gayle, being white, connected nevertheless because of her obvious empathy, yet not paternalistic ways. Gayle was as humble as anybody you've ever met, but if need be, she could dazzle with her knowledge of history and civil rights legal precedents—all in a non-elitist, folksy way. You just knew both of them were there for good purposes and had the courage to face down the racist power structure in whatever form it appeared.

Mrs. Gresham, in effect, sponsored and vouched for us anywhere and everywhere. The Keysville folks were trusting and, with Mrs. Gresham's blessing and our non-traditional approach, we were all fully accepted. We were a non-traditional law firm in that we came to them, walked the streets, visited homes, went to church, and weren't afraid or ashamed to be passionate about the injustice they faced and to show our emotional solidarity. We did not have an "office" down there; our office was their community meetings, church, and front porches.

The African American folks made us feel right at home. They showered us with love. They opened their homes to us. Folks were so salt-of-the-earth; oozing with decency and honesty; with a fighting spirit, but not with any hatred or desire for retribution.

Keysville's white residents, on the other hand, resented CIS staff. Upton Cochran claimed, "We've never had any racism here. We all grew up together." He blamed "outside agitators" for the racial tensions. Binta said she received threats from "KKK types," and in response to county law enforcement and Klansmen intimidating potential Black voters, she, Mr. Gresham, and other Black residents organized an armed self-defense committee to patrol the Black community.

Moreover, CIS staff reported that white residents repeatedly disrupted the town meetings, threatened cross burnings, and alarmed older Black residents with claims they'd lose their homes because of tax increases. Additionally, CIS shared with supporters, "White residents used their control of the town's only place of employment (a nursing home) to carry out economic reprisals against residents involved in the reactivation efforts," and "a 'city limits' sign was found with a heart drawn on it, and a bullet hole shot through the heart."

Lobbying

With help from CIS and the ACLU, Keysville's Black residents lobbied elected officials to facilitate local elections. They asked the Burke County Board of Elections to call for a special election; a week later, the board denied the request. Additionally, they unsuccessfully pleaded with Burke County's representatives in the General Assembly to introduce legislation to reactivate Keysville's government.

The primary target of their lobbying was Governor Joe Frank Harris because the Georgia Constitution stipulated, "When any public office shall become vacant by death, resignation, or otherwise, the Governor shall promptly fill such vacancy unless otherwise provided by this Constitution or by law." Yet, Harris refused to act, claiming the town's boundaries were too indeterminate for him to make appointments. He also rejected Gresham's invitation to visit Keysville. Finally, Harris snubbed a petition, signed by about a third of Keysville's residents, urging him "to follow the law and fill the vacancies."

In January 1987, Lewis and McDonald asked Harris to appoint election officials. In response, Harris's attorney claimed the governor didn't have "authority to fill the vacancies in the city government." Lewis and McDonald replied to Harris, "Your failure to act . . . and your reliance on an unsupported interpretation of the Constitution . . . manifest insensitivity and indifference at best. The message to Black citizens of Georgia and to the world, is likely to be that . . . the rights of Black citizens are not respected in Georgia." Similarly, Lewis told a crowd gathered at Keysville's Mount Tabor AME Church that Harris was behaving like a "racist" and "political pickpocket," which Lewis defined as "a public official who looks you in the eyes and spits platitudes about racial equality, all the while keeping the poor and oppressed at bay with his fast-moving hands below eye-level."

In March 1987, Lewis, Korotkin, Binta, about thirty-five Black Keysville residents, and others staged a protest on the steps of the capitol building in Atlanta. They carried signs displaying slogans such as, "Keysville, Ga.: City Without Hope," and chanted, "Keysville, Georgia, another South Africa."

CIS and KCC recruited others to lobby Harris. For example, they had Donald Leiter, executive director of the Georgia Christian Council, and

Joseph Lowery, president of the SCLC, visit Keysville and write to Harris. "Civil rights leaders view the dispute as an important test in the fight to win political and economic power for blacks in the rural South," the *Chicago Tribune* reported.

In April 1987, Lewis and McDonald sent Assistant State AG Jeff Lanier a "final attempt to urge the Governor to act" in which they accused Harris of unconstitutionally refusing to fill the vacancies because doing so "might offend the white minority."

Lawsuit

On April 29, 1987, after approximately six months of unsuccessful lobbying efforts, KCC, CIS, and the ACLU sued Governor Harris and other state officials in federal district court. The complaint alleged violations of the Voting Rights Act of 1965 and requested Harris be enjoined from failing to recognize Keysville as an incorporated town. "The purpose and result of the refusal of the Defendants to fill the existing vacancies in the mayor and council and superintendent of elections of Keysville is to deny or abridge the right of blacks to vote on account of race or color," the complaint read.

During a press conference at the SCLC headquarters in Atlanta to announce the lawsuit, Lewis told reporters, "The issue really is water and sewage and democracy." He accused "some whites in the community" of wanting "to sabotage any efforts at incorporation." He said Harris and other state officials "totally abdicated" their "duty to ensure democracy, elections, equal protection and due process to the black residents of Keysville," and their "inaction and feeble excuses [were] classic examples of institutional racism." "It was emboldening for the people to go file a lawsuit in federal court, flanked by Reverend Joseph Lowery of the SCLC," Lewis recalled.

Breakthrough

The litigation was short lived. Less than two months after the lawsuit was filed, at the urging of the Georgia Legislative Black Caucus, the Georgia General Assembly enacted legislation allowing for reactivation of Keysville's government. The law, which took effect in July 1987, provided that "in the event that all seats on the governing authority of a municipality are vacant, the elections superintendent of the county in which the municipality is located shall have the authority to call for a special election to fill the vacant offices and to conduct, or to appoint a superintendent of elections for the municipality for the purpose of conducting, the special election."

Elections in Keysville were scheduled for January 4, 1988. However, pursuant to the Voting Rights Act of 1965, Burke County first needed preclearance from the US AG. County officials prepared a call for the election, as well as a map of Keysville designating areas from which residents would be allowed to vote. CIS and KCC made mailing the preclearance package—an otherwise simple legal step—an event to fuel the movement. They organized a march to the post office, inviting all Keysville residents, as well as the SCLC and NAACP. Lewis recollected, "We explained what that moment meant and how such laws came into being—a history lesson connecting them to the rich legacy of voting rights struggles. The mailing of a letter was like a baby step in the empowerment to next walk, then run." The Justice Department granted preclearance, in addition to Lewis and Korotkin's request to send federal observers to monitor the elections.

A slate of six Black candidates—Gresham for mayor and five others for city council—formed the Keysville for Justice Committee, adopted the Keysville Progressive Slate Platform, and pledged "to give every citizen, regardless of race, sex, or creed, the opportunity to participate in a democratic government."

Meanwhile, white residents again turned to Judge Pickett. On New Year's Eve in 1987, he granted their request for an order preventing elections "until such time as the municipal boundaries for the town of Keysville have been properly determined." Later that day, Black residents, represented by CIS and the ACLU, filed a motion in federal district court. A judge held a hearing, reversed Pickett's injunction, and enjoined the white defendants from failing to conduct the precleared elections on January 4. A federal three-judge panel later held that a state court can't reschedule or halt a precleared election without prior approval from the Justice Department.

1988 Elections

On the evening of January 3, 1988, Joseph Lowery delivered an impassioned sermon in a packed Keysville church. The next day—election day—Binta and local advocates provided voters with carpools, babysitters, and hot food.

About ninety percent of eligible Black residents and eighty percent of eligible white residents voted in Keysville's first election in fifty-five years.

In total, 140 ballots were cast. At age sixty-four, Gresham was elected mayor by a margin of ten votes over Upton Cochran, the white store owner who previously attempted to prevent elections. Additionally, Black candidates won four of the five city council seats. James Poole Jr., the lone white candidate elected, defeated his Black opponent by two votes. According to McDonald, KCC had endorsed James Poole Jr. in order to promote a multiracial new government.

On the day of the election, several white residents filed a complaint with the County Board of Registrars challenging the eligibility of forty-one voters. The board dismissed the complaint. The white residents also lost challenges in state and federal court.

Civil rights leader Benjamin Chavis Jr. reported about the "historic election with national implications" and gave credit to CIS for "work[ing] in and with the community day after day, to plan strategy and to organize the voter mobilization and registration campaign." The *New York Times* acknowledged CIS's role in the successful movement and reported, "The political battle here has been closely watched as a model effort by blacks in the rural south to seize electoral power and improve their living conditions."

On January 15, Keysville's newly elected leaders were sworn into office. Keysville's Black residents celebrated with hymns, prayers, speeches, and a jubilant fish fry. Gresham became the second Black female mayor in Georgia. The *Chicago Tribune* reported, "The civil rights movement came late to Keysville. Until recently, racism went unnoticed and unnamed, as unremarkable in the routine of things as outhouses, hush puppies and chewing tobacco. Life between blacks and whites was so peaceable that Emma Gresham used to tell other blacks proudly that Keysville wasn't one of those towns that needed to be marched in or marched on. . . . Now she wonders if racial peace once prevailed primarily because blacks had no power."

Governing

James Poole, the only white member of city council, stopped going to council meetings. He said, "If they wanna gov-un, let 'em move tuh somewhere where they got one. Let us alone out her. We wuddint causin' nobody no trouble. . . . I don't believe Keysville will ever get off the ground. . . . I don't buh-lieve the type of people who live here care enough about our town or government to keep it goin'."

Mayor Gresham and the other councilmembers, all without salaries, went about governing. A church-owned, double-wide trailer atop cinder blocks served as both city hall and the community center. Wires, bent nails, and naked lightbulbs hung from the saggy, leaky ceiling. They paid for utilities, telephones, and supplies using a portion of KCC's membership dues and proceeds from chicken dinner fundraisers.

Despite inadequate facilities and funding, Gresham and councilmembers improved conditions in Keysville. They paid Mr. Gresham twenty-five dollars a week to pick up townspeople's trash and deliver it to the dump. Additionally, they arranged for a Burke County sheriff's deputy to drive through town and check in at city hall at least once daily. Mrs. Gresham and her friends started a literacy program for residents and Junior Concerned Citizens, a leadership development and community service group for local teenagers.

Under Gresham's leadership, Keysville would eventually have a library, post office, health center, water and sewer system, fire station, and municipal building that housed the town hall, police station, and water treatment department. The city also installed streetlights, built a playground, and started an after-school program. One commentator described Gresham's approach to politics as "a blend of tireless persistence and faith." "The changes that came to Keysville were nothing short of remarkable and owed much to the spirit of local residents who persevered against the odds and refused to succumb to the racial fears and distrust that had for so long gripped the white community," McDonald reflected. A *New York Times* reporter wrote that Keysville had come "to symbolize for some the determination of rural blacks to win such basic services as water, sewers and garbage collection in the face of opposition from white voters who fear higher taxes, as well as a surge of black political power."

After seventeen years as mayor, the "Queen of Keysville" retired in 2005. She received numerous honors and awards for her leadership and service.

Mutual Adoration

"Keysville was never the same after Lewis Pitts came," Gresham told a radio documentarian in 1989. She continued working with CIS. In December 1991, she wrote to the organization's supporters and prospective funders:

> [CIS] not only helped us legally win our case, but they also taught
> us how to organize our community and helped motivate us to

struggle toward our goals. They helped us do what we thought could never be done.

. . . We are forever grateful to [CIS] for helping us.

I have agreed to serve on the Board of Directors of [CIS] because I know first-hand of their commitment to the thousands of African Americans in the Southeast living in conditions similar to—and worse than—those in Keysville. I want to make sure that Keysville survives, but I also want to ensure that when the next group of concerned citizens—and our numbers are indeed many—challenges their oppression, [CIS] will be . . . able to fight with and for them.

On January 20, 1992, Gresham was the keynote speaker at the annual Martin Luther King Jr. commemoration at Hilton Head High School. She credited CIS with helping KCC and called on her "son," Lewis, who was sitting with Mr. Gresham, to stand and be recognized.

About a year before her death in March 2018, Gresham reminisced, "Pitts really taught us courage, faith and belief in ourselves. . . . [He] put his life on the line for a few poor, undereducated, black people who had been robbed of . . . our dignity. . . . I called him my son. . . . I'd trust him with my life. I love Lewis Pitts. I still pray for him." Lewis told the *Augusta Chronicle* that Gresham "was a great public servant and public official" who "operated from the heart and . . . that goodness center of trying to help people and make the ideals that we like to talk and sing about in our nation, make them a reality." He wrote, "Mayor Gresham was a person with a golden heart; always sweet as honey. While she had a folksy, country way and manner, she was also very bright and sharp. You could not help but falling in love with her."

Lewis Pitts, his younger brother, Paul, and their parents, Lewis Sr. and Martha, in their home in Clinton, SC (Oct. 1950).

Lewis Pitts (left) and his siblings, Paul, Margaret (back), and Helen (front).

Lewis Pitts as a student at Wofford College.

Lewis Pitts addressing jurors during the trial of Comanche Peak Life Force protestors in Somervell County, TX. Courtesy of the *Texas Observer* (Dec. 14, 1979). Photo by Frederick C. Baldwin.

Greensboro Civil Rights Fund members (1985). From left: Lewis Pitts, Gayle Korotkin, Marty Nathan, and Nelson Johnson. Courtesy of the University of North Carolina at Chapel Hill, Louis Round Wilson Library Special Collections, Southern Historical Collection.

Greensboro Civil Rights Fund members on the steps of the federal courthouse in Winston-Salem, NC (1985). From left (excluding children): Nelson Johnson, Victoria Osk, Andrea Bernstein, Marty Nathan, Pamela DiStefano, Gayle Korotkin, Flint Taylor, Linda Delaney, Jill Cahill, Signe Waller, Carolyn McAllaster, Shelley Wong, Curtis Pierce, Lewis Pitts, Dale Sampson, and Daniel Sheehan.

Christic Institute South staff. From left: Ashaki Binta, Marcia Still, Alan Gregory, Gayle Korotkin, and Lewis Pitts. Courtesy of the University of North Carolina at Chapel Hill, Louis Round Wilson Library Special Collections, Southern Historical Collection.

Christic Institute South staff. From left: Susanne O'Sullivan Stearns (not staff), Czerny Brasuell, Lewis Pitts, Alan Gregory, and Gayle Korotkin. Courtesy of the University of North Carolina at Chapel Hill, Louis Round Wilson Library Special Collections, Southern Historical Collection. Photo by Jerry Markatos.

"Come Home to Keysville Day" in Keysville, GA (Summer 1988). From left: Katie Greene, Lewis Pitts, Stephen Pitts, Quinten Gresham Sr., and Emma Gresham. Courtesy of the University of North Carolina at Chapel Hill, Louis Round Wilson Library Special Collections, Southern Historical Collection.

Bob Warren and Lewis Pitts speaking to reporters outside the federal courthouse in Raleigh, NC, during the trial of Timothy Jacobs and Eddie Hatcher (1988). Courtesy of Julie Dews.

Timothy Jacobs's extradition hearing in the Madison County courthouse in Wampsville, NY (Feb. 1989). From left: Alan Rosenthal, Lewis Pitts, and Timothy Jacobs. AP Photo/Commentucci.

Lewis Pitts interviewing his client Louise Wilson at the Cooper River Cemetery on Daufuskie Island, SC. Courtesy of the University of North Carolina at Chapel Hill, Louis Round Wilson Library Special Collections, Southern Historical Collection.

Selma Movement against Racial Tracking (SMART) and the Best Educational Support Team (BEST) advocates and their lawyers outside the city jail in Selma, AL (Aug. 18, 1990). From left: Connie Tucker, Carolyn Gaines-Varner, Faya Ora Rose Touré, and Lewis Pitts. Courtesy of the University of North Carolina at Chapel Hill, Louis Round Wilson Library Special Collections, Southern Historical Collection.

SMART and BEST advocates and their lawyers outside the city jail in Selma, AL (Aug. 18, 1990). From left: Richard Walker, Gayle Korotkin, Lewis Pitts, Bruce Boynton, Kenyatta Gaines, Maurice Watson, Carlos Williams, and Kindaka Sanders. Courtesy of the University of North Carolina at Chapel Hill, Louis Round Wilson Library Special Collections, Southern Historical Collection.

Antinuclear protest at the Carolina Power & Light Company (CP&L) headquarters in Raleigh, NC (Oct. 17, 2000). From left (seated): Jim Warren, Carrie Bolton, and Lewis Pitts. Courtesy of the North Carolina Waste Awareness and Reduction Network.

Advocates for Children's Services staff and interns before a rally and march in Raleigh, NC, organized by the North Carolina State Conference of the NAACP and local African Methodist Episcopal Zion Churches, to protest the Wake County Board of Education's decision to end the district's socioeconomic diversity plan (July 21, 2010). Back (from left): Keith Howard, Lewis Pitts, Laura Schwartz, Destyni Williams, and Jason Langberg. Front (from left): Erwin Byrd, Cary Brege, Mary Irvine, and Kristin Weissinger. Courtesy of Cary Brege.

Lewis Pitts and his wife, Spoma Jovanovic, attending a rally against North Carolina's transphobic House Bill 2 "bathroom bill" at College Park Baptist Church in Greensboro, NC (Apr. 3, 2016). Courtesy of Lena Mattson.

Lewis Pitts speaking at a press conference in defense of Zared Jones's attorney, Graham Holt, at the International Civil Rights Center and Museum in Greensboro, NC (Sept. 5, 2019). Standing (from left): Joseph Alston, Nelson Johnson, Hurley Derrickson, Lewis Pitts, T. Anthony Spearman, Bob Foxworth, Daran Mitchell, and Wesley Morris. Seated (from left): Hester Petty, Marilyn Clayton, and Signe Waller. Courtesy of *Triad City Beat*. Photo by Sayaka Matsuoka.

CHAPTER 9

Detour to Expose
the Iran-Contra Affair
and Those behind
a Bombing in Nicaragua

During CIS's work in Keysville, Danny Sheehan, Christic Institute's general counsel, asked Lewis to help with a case involving drug and weapons trafficking, money laundering, assassination attempts, militias and mercenaries, and the CIA, Pentagon, and White House. For Lewis, working on the case would mean significant time away from CIS and racial justice movement lawyering, as well as his family. An Associated Press article read, "Keeping the commitment to his work, Pitts said, has been more difficult since his son was born three years ago. 'It's a challenge in the demands put on my time,' he said. 'I don't want to be a halfway father and a halfway social justice advocate. The problem is in finding good role models. I know some people who are great at lawyering in the movement, but have absolutely screwed up their family lives,' he said. 'And there are guys who do Little League and all that, but have essentially given up their social justice advocacy.'"

Despite his concerns, Lewis jumped at the opportunity to work on a high-profile, complex case with national and international implications. "The adrenalin was pumping like a fire hydrant," he recalled.

Contragate

In 1979, the Sandinista National Liberation Front and other socialist and communist groups overthrew the government of Nicaragua's president Anastasio Somoza Debayle, ending forty-six years of dictatorship by the Somoza family. With support from Cuba and the Soviet Union, Sandinistas governed Nicaragua from 1979 to 1990.

The Sandinista regime was opposed by right-wing, counterrevolutionary rebels, known as "contras." Many contras were former members of the Nicaraguan National Guard and other groups that fought for Somoza. Much of their funding came from the cocaine trade; they also received money, weapons, and operational and military support from the US government. During their war against the Nicaraguan government in the 1980s, contras committed terrorist attacks and widespread human rights violations.

In 1980, with the United States in the fourth decade of the Cold War, presidential candidate Ronald Reagan promised to assist anti-communist insurgencies around the globe. He described the contras as "the moral equivalent of the Founding Fathers," and claimed that a left-wing regime in Nicaragua would spark revolution throughout the region and threaten US security. As president, in November 1981, Reagan secretly signed "National Security Decision Directive 17," giving the CIA authority and $19 million to recruit and support a five-hundred-man force of Nicaraguan rebels to conduct covert actions against the Sandinista government.

Once Reagan's support for the contras became public, Congress passed the Boland Amendment in December 1983. The amendment prohibited the CIA, Defense Department, and other government entities involved in intelligence from using funds "for the purpose of overthrowing the government of Nicaragua."

Nevertheless, the Reagan administration continued covertly supporting the contras through two loopholes. First, the wording of the Boland Amendment implicitly gave the CIA permission to offer aid to the contras, so long as the stated purpose wasn't overthrowing the Sandinista government. Second, the Reagan administration used the National Security Council (NSC), rather than the CIA or Defense Department, to conduct covert activities in Nicaragua. Reagan instructed Robert McFarlane, his national security advisor and head of the NSC, to assist the contras through the loopholes.

In 1984, Congress passed a strengthened second Boland Amendment that made support to the contras almost impossible; yet, over the next two years, Reagan and his associates still managed to funnel approximately $88 million in support to the contras.

During his State of the Union address in February 1985, Reagan outlined key concepts of his foreign policy, which came to be known as the "Reagan Doctrine." He claimed that supporting "freedom fighters" who opposed the "Sandinista dictatorship of Nicaragua" was "self-defense."

The following March, Reagan delivered a nationally televised speech to generate support for his $100 million aid package for the contras. He told the American people that the Nicaraguan government was a national security threat and had "launched a campaign to subvert and topple its democratic neighbors" and a "takeover of Central America."

Funding for support to the contras came, in part, from the Reagan administration's secret and illegal arms sales to Iran. The CIA and Lieutenant Colonel Oliver North, an NSC staff member, facilitated the transfer of funds, with approval from Rear Admiral John Poindexter, Robert McFarlane's successor as head of the NSC. North assumed Poindexter had Reagan's blessing. The scandal became known as the "Iran-Contra Affair" or "Contragate."

La Penca Bombing

Edén Pastora, leader of the Southern Front of the Sandinista National Liberation Front, began serving as Nicaragua's deputy interior minister in 1979. However, he became frustrated with Sandinista leaders, resigned his ministerial post, and voluntarily exiled himself from Nicaragua in July 1981.

In 1982, Pastora formed his own group, the Democratic Revolutionary Alliance, which opposed "pseudo-Sandinistas" for their repressiveness, inadequate assistance to campesinos and aboriginal peoples, and failure to live up to Socialist and Marxist ideals. He joined forces with contras, despite their political differences, thereby accessing US resources.

On May 1, 1984, the CIA gave Pastora an ultimatum: join forces with the US-backed contra group, the Nicaraguan Democratic Force, and agree to follow CIA dictates within thirty days, or lose US funding and support. Pastora called a press conference to denounce US pressure and announce his refusal to join.

The press conference took place on May 30 at a Democratic Revolutionary Alliance camp in La Penca, a remote area of the jungle in Nicaragua. During the event, a bomb exploded, killing eight people, including three journalists, and injuring at least twenty-one others. The bomb was meant to kill Pastora. He survived, albeit with serious wounds. Among the injured was Tony Avirgan, an American freelance television cameraman and radio reporter covering the press conference for ABC. After doctors operated on him in Costa Rica, Avirgan was flown to a Philadelphia hospital.

The US government quickly blamed Sandinistas for the bombing. On behalf of the Committee to Protect Journalists and the Newspaper Guild, Avirgan and his wife, Martha Honey, a journalist herself, initiated an investigation of the bombing. During the investigation, one of their witnesses was killed, and they were followed by unmarked cars, threatened, framed for drug trafficking, and accused of being spies for a CIA-funded, right-wing organization.

In October 1985, Avirgan and Honey presented their findings at a press conference in Costa Rica. They concluded that contras hired an assassin to kill Pastora; John Hull and a group of Cubans in Miami were working with the CIA and Oliver North's Contragate network to run contra operations in Costa Rica; and Hull and others in the network played a role in the bombing.

Hull, an American farmer in Costa Rica, was virulently anti-communist and an extreme foe of Nicaragua's Sandinista regime. His land served as a clandestine base for contras, who used the farm's airstrip to transport wounded combatants, American-supplied weapons, and cocaine. He reportedly had five CIA-funded bodyguards and a network of local informants.

Within days of Avirgan and Honey's press conference, Hull sued them in Costa Rica, alleging libel and defamation and demanding a half-million dollars in damages and court costs.

Lawsuit Filed

According to Danny Sheehan's autobiography, a reporter asked him to assist with defending Avirgan and Honey against Hull's lawsuit. Sheehan wrote that, in fall 1985, he flew to Costa Rica to meet with the couple.

After they prevailed against Hull, Sheehan persuaded Avirgan and Honey to join Christic Institute in a Contragate lawsuit. Honey wrote in the *Tico-Times*, "Tony and I, out of a combination of fear and a desire to have more help with our investigation, agreed to become plaintiffs in a lawsuit brought by . . . the Christic Institute. The institute's lead lawyer, Daniel Sheehan, claimed to have a great deal of information that dovetailed with what we had found in Costa Rica."

In May 1986—six months before Contragate became mainstream news—Christic filed a $24 million lawsuit in the US District Court for the Southern District of Florida. The legal team primarily consisted of Sheehan, Lewis, and fellow Christic lawyers Rob Hager and Lanny Sinkin, as well as numerous pro bono attorneys. They positioned themselves as "private attorneys general" filling "a prosecutorial gap."

The lawsuit was filed under the federal RICO Act. Best known as a government tool to prosecute organized crime, the act also provides for private civil actions and remedies. For their RICO claim to succeed, the plaintiffs had to prove three elements. First, they had to demonstrate that an enterprise of individuals or entities engaged in racketeering activities—that is, certain felonious acts. The plaintiffs alleged a "secret team" of current and former US government officials, contras, mercenaries, drug smugglers, and other anti-communist extremists committed murder, drugs and weapons smuggling, and other racketeering activities for more than twenty-five years in Nicaragua, Cuba, Vietnam, and Iran. To prevail, the plaintiffs wouldn't be required to prove that all individual members of the enterprise were directly connected to the bombing.

Second, the plaintiffs had to prove injury to business or property. They asserted that Avirgan suffered injury to his person (burns and cuts), property (recording equipment), and business (he couldn't work without his equipment).

Finally, the plaintiffs had to show that the enterprise's racketeering activities caused the injuries. The plaintiffs alleged the bombing was carried out by a Libyan assassin, Amac Galil, who posed as a reporter covering the press conference. Moreover, they alleged Galil was paid $50,000 by the enterprise, which wanted Pastora dead because he refused to merge his Democratic Revolutionary Alliance with the US-backed Nicaraguan Democratic Force.

Among the twenty-nine named defendants were former high-ranking government officials, including: John Singlaub, a retired Army general and CIA leader, head of various anti-communist organizations, and a fundraiser for the contras; Richard Secord, a retired Air Force general and the point man in creating a network to supply weapons and drugs to the contras; Robert Owen, a former national security advisor and secret emissary to the contras for North and others; Theodore Shackley, a former CIA leader alleged to have supplied weapons to former Nicaraguan dictator Somoza, among others; and Thomas Clines, a former CIA official who supplied arms to the contras.

The plaintiffs also named John Hull; Albert Hakim, an Iranian businessman and arms dealer; Jorge Luis Ochoa Vazquez and Pablo Escobar, Medellín cartel leaders alleged to have supplied cocaine for the enterprise; Sam Hall, an American former mercenary imprisoned in Costa Rica for spying on the Sandinista government; Thomas Posey, head of an ultra-right-wing group that recruited mercenaries and sent resources to the contras; Rafael Quintero, a CIA operative and professional assassin who helped coordinate supply flights to Nicaragua; Adolfo Calero, leader of the Nicaraguan Democratic Force alleged to have aided in the press conference bombing and creating an arms pipeline through Hull's ranch; and Francisco "Paco" Chanes, a Miami-based drug smuggler alleged to have imported cocaine from Hull's ranch, purchased weapons for the contras, and financially sponsored the bombing.

Christic didn't name any US government officials—despite the alleged involvement of President Reagan, Vice President Bush, and others—because doing so would've resulted in skilled Justice Department attorneys joining the defense team. Moreover, Christic sought to avoid possible dismissal of the case under the political question doctrine, which allows courts to refrain from adjudicating inherently political questions considered to be more properly resolved by the legislative or executive branch.

Broader Campaign

The lawsuit was part of Christic's broader Contragate Project, the goals of which included justice for the La Penca bombing victims and public accountability for those responsible, the end of the secret team and violence by the contras, and "restoration of [the] Constitution by creation of an enlightened United States foreign policy based on law and morality." Avirgan told the *Sun Sentinel* that they aimed to start a "grassroots movement" to "revamp the national security apparatus of the United States."

Christic formed a "Contragate Project Advisory Board" that included religious leaders; Joseph Lowery, president of the SCLC; Eleanor Smeal, former president of the NOW; and Robert Drinan, a former congressman and Georgetown Law professor. Additionally, Christic developed a "Communications Alliance" of more than fifty organizations committed to disseminating information about the Contragate Project.

Christic staff participated in events across the country. For instance, Lewis spoke at a "Peace Lunch Forum" at North Carolina State University, where he told attendees that the defendants "represent the epitome of organized crime" and "seek to take over whole nations." Lewis, Sheehan, and others also traveled to Hawaii to generate support and donations at the Association of Trial Lawyers of America conference. They stayed at Kris Kristofferson's house in Maui for about a week. Lewis summarized the trip: "It was pretty groovy."

Evidence Emerges

Publicly emerging details about Contragate buttressed the institute's claims of covert racketeering activities by the enterprise. In December 1985, the Associated Press published a story about Reagan approving Oliver North's proposal to create a private aid network to fund Nicaraguan rebels. In early 1986, US Senator John Kerry convinced the Foreign Relations Committee to investigate the Reagan administration for illegally providing aid to the contras in Nicaragua. Next, in October 1986, Sandinista soldiers shot down a cargo plane flying over Nicaragua. Eugene Hasenfus, the sole survivor, was an ex-Marine with links to the CIA. The Nicaraguan Defense Ministry said the plane was carrying weapons, ammunition, and other military supplies. Evidence strongly suggests Hasenfus helped fly the supplies to contra mercenaries in Nicaragua for North's network. He was a "kicker"—the crew member assigned to push cargo out the plane's open rear door into the forests below.

In November 1986, *Ash Shiraa*, a Lebanese magazine, broke the Iran-Contra story, confirming the US government had been secretly selling arms to Iran in an effort to secure the release of seven American hostages held in Lebanon. A few weeks after that, US AG Edwin Meese announced that arms sales proceeds were diverted to fund the contras' war against Nicaragua's Sandinista government. Oliver North admitted he'd diverted arms sales funds to the contras in Nicaragua, with John Poindexter's knowledge, and assumed President Reagan and Vice President Bush knew about his efforts. Finally, in December 1986, Reagan commissioned the Tower Commission and AG Meese called for independent counsel to investigate the Iran-Contra scandal.

The *Washington Post* reported that Christic's claims "gained credibility when the details of the Iran-Contra affair began to surface later in the year," and the institute "was the first to reveal the existence of a private contra supply network linked to the White House." "Enough of the case's allegations have been admitted or verified to win the . . . policy center greater credibility," the *Boston Globe* read.

The emerging details bolstered Christic's fundraising. Its spring 1988 newsletter boasted, "New offices have opened in Los Angeles and San Francisco to support the lawsuit. Fifty thousand people now receive the Institute's reports on Contragate." Donations were "pouring in" to Christic, the *New York Times* reported. The *Christian Science Monitor* read:

The scene inside the cramped, shabby rowhouses of the Christic
Institute hardly conjures up images of "L.A. Law." Amid a sea of
clutter, young earnest types wearing anything but three-piece suits
move purposefully about their business. Posters of Karen Silkwood and other causes line the walls, not oak paneling. But then,
this isn't your average high-priced law firm. With the salaries set at
$15,000 a year, nobody's getting rich, but the Christic Institute may
just be getting famous—or notorious, depending on your point
of view. . . . Fundraising has boomed, from $800,000 in 1986 to a
projected $2.3 million for this year. . . . The institute staff is now
at 60 people, up from 13 at the end of 1986. Twenty staff members
recently moved to Miami for the trial.

Trial Preparations

Chief US District Judge James King, a military veteran and Nixon appointee, presided over Christic's Contragate case. The defendants asked King to
dismiss the lawsuit. In response, Sheehan took the unusual step of filing his
own affidavit, which provided "a detailed, specific narrative of the defendants'
criminal activities and the Christic Institute's investigation of them." In January 1987, King denied the defendants' motion to dismiss—a major victory for
Christic. However, King also limited the scope and time for discovery.

Discovery was, nevertheless, a massive undertaking. Fortunately, more
than forty lawyers volunteered to assist with the case. Lewis viewed the large
number of well-respected, pro bono attorneys from across the country as evidence of the lawsuit's merit. For example, Anthony Cunningham—founder
of Trial Lawyers for Public Justice and onetime president of the Academy of
Florida Trial Lawyers—assisted. Lewis built an especially close relationship
with Leonard Schroeter, who was active in the NAACP Legal Defense Fund,
ACLU of Washington, and other progressive organizations. Lewis's primary
role in the case was coordinating and collaborating with the pro bono lawyers.
His friendliness, southern charm, and trial experience made him well suited
for the role.

Starting in May 1987, Christic's staff and volunteers took approximately
seventy-five depositions. During this time, Lewis made frequent three-to-
four-day trips to DC, where he stayed in an old Catholic convent with other
institute staff.

Lewis spent about two weeks in Costa Rica interviewing and deposing witnesses, including Edén Pastora. Back in the US, Lewis attempted to interview Jack Terrell, a leader of an American paramilitary group, Civilian-Military Assistance, and Jesus Garcia, a Cuban military veteran, Dade County correctional officer, and alleged liaison between anti-Castro organizations and North's network. However, according to Christic records, Terrell and Garcia refused to go on the record after prosecutors threatened them with indictment.

Operation Bushwack

Lewis also led a Christic initiative—called "Operation Bushwhack"—within the broader Contragate Project. In 1988, George H. W. Bush was leading Michael Dukakis in the race for president. Bush claimed ignorance of Oliver North's activities; however, the institute had evidence of Bush's involvement in Contragate and other nefarious activities during his time heading the CIA and as vice president. Operation Bushwack involved using discovery in the Contragate lawsuit to publicly expose Bush's unscrupulous activities during his campaign for president.

Sheehan publicly claimed that, in 1976, Bush, then CIA director, permitted creation of a secret team to hide "private racketeering enterprises" from the Carter administration. In response, Bush told the *New York Times*, "If any of these little left-wing outfits like the Christic Institute have something [on me], let's see what it is. Let the American people have it examined and have a fair resolution made." Abundant evidence has since emerged showing Bush, as reported by the *Washington Post*, "participated in elaborate efforts to induce third countries to give military support to the Nicaraguan contras in return for favors and aid from the United States at a time when Congress had banned direct American military aid to the rebels," and then attempted to cover up his involvement.

As part of Operation Bushwack, Lewis accompanied Michael Withey, a Seattle-based public interest lawyer, to depose Donald Gregg, a former CIA official who became Bush's national security advisor in 1982. About six months after the deposition, *Rolling Stone* published an investigative report that read:

> The denials of Bush and Gregg are part of a continuing cover-up
> intended to hide their true role in the Reagan administration's

secret war against the Sandinista government of Nicaragua. Bush and Gregg were, in fact, deeply involved in a previously undisclosed weapons-smuggling operation to arm the contras that began in 1982, two years before the much-publicized Iran-contra operation run by . . . Oliver North and financed by the sale of missiles to Iran. This earlier operation, known as Black Eagle, went on for three years, overlapping North's operation. The idea of both operations was to circumvent congressional restrictions on the CIA and the Pentagon. . . . They were the instruments of a secret U.S. foreign policy carried out by men who constituted a kind of shadow government.

On May 19, 1988, Lewis deposed Sam Watson, Gregg's former deputy and Bush's advisor on Latin America. The *Baltimore Sun* reported:

Watson spent the afternoon . . . testifying under oath about Panama and the Nicaraguan rebels and having his credibility challenged by a slight young lawyer with a modified "punk" haircut.

It was indignity enough for the gentlemanly, soft-spoken adviser, Col. Sam Watson, to hear the attorney, Lewis Pitts, deliver a veiled threat of subjecting his taped testimony to sophisticated lie-detection techniques.

When questions zeroed in on what he and the vice president had known in the past about General Noriega's drug trafficking, Colonel Watson acted on instructions from his Justice Department lawyer and invoked executive privilege.

The source of this discomfort for the Bush camp is an 8-year-old group of left-liberal legal activists . . . operating from a cluttered storefront building . . . in one of the most depressed sections of inner-city Washington.

Their well-publicized efforts, including inviting reporters to pre-trial depositions conducted in borrowed rooms, are greeted by the government and the Bush campaign with anger and contempt.

Whatever the ultimate outcome of the case, the Christic probe has helped to shed new light on Mr. Bush's . . . staff's awareness of covert U.S. support for the contras during a period when U.S. military aid was banned by Congress.

Lewis wrote, "It was a heady experience being in the midst of such a national scandal as it unfolded. Every news cycle brought the potential for another exposure and bit of the scandal."

Defendants Mobilize

Meanwhile, the defendants and their allies launched a counteroffensive, denying accusations and attacking Christic. Richard Secord told a congressional committee the lawsuit was "the most outrageous fairy tale anyone has ever read." Adolfo Calero alleged the institute had close ties to the Nicaraguan embassy in DC. Theodore Shackley called Christic staff "practitioners of character assassination through legal terrorism" and their claims "rubbish."

According to Secord, he spent more than $100,000 from a Swiss Iran-Contra bank account on private detective work and legal fees. He hired a former CIA agent and member of the secret team to dig up dirt on the plaintiffs and Christic staff. Secord claimed the funds were used for legitimate business expenses because the lawsuit could've exposed the enterprise's aid to the contras.

The defendants also fundraised to pay their high-priced attorneys. Singlaub wrote in *Soldier of Fortune*, "If I were back in Vietnam in a firefight, then I'd ask for an airstrike to blow the bastards away. But to win this fight we need money. To fight the damned Christic Institute lawsuit takes money."

Given the nature of the case and the defendants' pasts and rhetoric, Christic took out extra insurance on Sheehan, Lewis, and other staff. "I began to wear a cross necklace as my silent way of seeking protection—even though I wasn't a true believer," Lewis shared.

Summary Judgment

Christic hired tractor trailer drivers to transport documents, equipment, and other trappings needed for trial to Miami. Staff established temporary offices at Florida International University.

However, on June 23, 1988, just five days before the trial was to begin, Judge King granted summary judgment for all twenty-nine defendants. King found much of Christic's proposed evidence to be inadmissible and the admissible evidence to be insufficient to prove the defendants' actions were the proximate cause of Avirgan's injuries. In his decision, King noted that Sheehan "delayed orderly discovery for many months" while refusing to reveal the identities of seventy-nine witnesses he alleged to have knowledge of the defendants' complicity. King found that all the witnesses were "totally unknown to Mr. Sheehan," didn't know him, had never spoken to him, denied the statements he attributed to them, or "did not furnish any statements that would be admissible." Christic staff and the plaintiffs "must have known prior to suing that they had no competent evidence to substantiate the theories alleged in their complaint," King wrote.

Sheehan told reporters, "The judge made this decision in order to stop this case from going to trial before the upcoming election. . . . I think it is a judicial disgrace. . . . We are embarrassed for the court." Years later, Lewis shared similar sentiments, "The facts, particularly those exposing Daddy Bush just as the election was rolling around, were too explosive to be allowed, and thus, King dumped the case. . . . The case was dismissed for political reasons, not because we didn't have enough proof and facts to justify going to trial."

The defendants reacted arrogantly and spitefully. Thomas Spencer, one of Singlaub's attorneys, threatened "to file some actions for malicious prosecution and defamation." Singlaub wanted Sheehan disbarred and told the *Christian Science Monitor*, "I feel sorry for all the innocent people who have been conned into contributing to this hoax."

In August 1988, the Council for Inter-American Security held a celebration and fundraiser for the defendants, who the Council dubbed "victims of the Christic Institute." Attendees included Pat Buchanan, Strom Thurmond, and Orrin Hatch. The Council's president told the *Washington Post* that Christic was "selling" a "conspiracy story" in order to "get donations." US Senator Gordon Humphrey called Christic staff "sleazebags" who were conducting "legal guerrilla warfare at the cost of hundreds of thousands of dollars." "I want to put my foot on the head of the Christic serpent and see it crushed," Congressman Bob Dornan said. He also told attendees that the institute spread "poisonous lies" and engaged in "a horrible, lying frenzy, attacking one American organization after another."

Sanctions

Worse still, in February 1989, Judge King ordered the plaintiffs to pay eight defendants a total of more than a million dollars for attorney's fees and court costs. Avirgan, Honey, Sheehan, and Christic were jointly and severally liable for the sanctions, which were awarded pursuant to Rule 11 of the Federal Rules of Civil Procedure.

Rule 11 allows for "appropriate sanctions" against a party to federal litigation if, after the party has notice and a reasonable opportunity to respond, a judge determines the party violated Rule 11(b). Rule 11(b) requires written representations to a court not be presented for any improper purpose, such as to harass, cause unnecessary delay, or needlessly increase the cost of litigation; claims, defenses, and other legal arguments be warranted by existing law or by a nonfrivolous argument for extending, modifying, or reversing existing law or for establishing new law; factual contentions have evidentiary support or will likely have evidentiary support after a reasonable opportunity for further investigation or discovery; and denials of factual contentions be warranted on the evidence or reasonably based on belief or a lack of information.

The sanctions against Christic coincided with a nationwide increase in the use of Rule 11 by Republican-appointed federal judges who sought to chill civil rights plaintiffs and attorneys. For example, Rule 11 sanctions were levied against ACLU attorneys who were representing people with AIDS in southern Texas; former US AG Ramsey Clark, who was representing civilian victims of the US bombing in Libya; and NAACP Legal Defense Fund Director Julius Chambers, who was representing plaintiffs in an employment discrimination case against the US Army. Then Fordham Law Professor Georgene Vairo conducted a study of Rule 11 and concluded it was "being abused by particular judges and lawyers" and "chilling meritorious litigation and effective advocacy." Holly Burkhalter, then associate director of Human Rights Watch, told the *New York Times* the sanctions against Christic were "certainly going to have a chilling effect on any other public interest group that attempts to dig beneath the surface."

Christic appealed the summary judgment and sanctions to the US Court of Appeals for the Eleventh Circuit. Trial Lawyers for Public Justice, the Alliance for Justice, Public Citizen Litigation Group, legal scholars, and religious organizations filed amicus curiae (friend of the court) briefs supporting the institute. In June 1991, the Eleventh Circuit affirmed the summary judgment, reasoning that the plaintiffs' evidence was "scant, almost nonexistent, on the important issue of causation." The court also upheld the sanctions, writing, "Sheehan could not have reasonably believed at the time of the filing of the complaint and the signing of the affidavit that the complaint was well-grounded in fact. Particularly is this true of the affidavit with its unknown, nonexistent, deceased sources, its fabricated testimony, and the deceptive style used to mask its shortcomings. It is obvious that if the appellants knew (must have known) prior to filing this lawsuit that they had no competent evidence, then, this complaint was not well-grounded." A year later, the US Supreme Court declined to hear the case.

Retaliation

The defendants, their attorneys, and conservative commentators continued disparaging Christic staff, referring to them as "courthouse terrorists," "vigilantes, riding the range of defamation," and "left-wing legal hoodlums who specialize in separating gullible Christians from their money." Charley Reese, a nationally syndicated columnist, called on the IRS to "take a hard look at" the institute's tax-exempt status and for congressional investigations into Christic's "foreign ties." A *Wall Street Journal* editorial suggested Congress repeal the RICO Act "before it holds other innocent defendants hostage to the likes of the frivolous Christic suit."

The media piled on Sheehan. For instance, the *New York Times* read, "The vast majority of the 79 witnesses Mr. Sheehan cites as authorities were either dead, unwilling to testify, fountains of contradictory information or at best one person removed from the facts they were describing." *Mother Jones* reported, "Ask these journalists, experts, Capitol Hill investigators, and former CIA agents, many of whom are sympathetic to Danny Sheehan's general critique of covert operations, and they will tell you that his gorgeous tapestry is woven of rumor and half-truth and wish-fulfillment. In Danny Sheehan, they see a man in whom passion has overcome reason." Lewis wrote about the coverage, "With the history of the judicial system being so often wrong (*Dred Scott*; *Plessy*; etc.), it is disappointing how easily some folks couldn't resist joining in the 'discredit and shoot the messenger' tactics."

Moreover, details of a rift between Sheehan and the plaintiffs emerged. Even before Judge King granted summary judgment, Avirgan told the *Christian Science Monitor* that he and Honey had "sometimes been uneasy" with Sheehan's deductive leaps in the case. After the Rule 11 order, Avirgan released a statement that read, "As plaintiffs in the suit, Martha Honey and I struggled for years to try to bring the case down to earth, to bring it away from Sheehan's wild allegations. Honey wrote in the *Tico-Times*, "Over time we and a handful of lawyers, journalists and private investigators . . . became disillusioned with Sheehan's wide-ranging conspiracy theories and often sloppy attention to detail." She also told a reporter that she and Avirgan "had a very serious falling out" with Sheehan.

Moving On

Despite the time away from his family and CIS, summary judgements, and sanctions, Lewis is proud to have worked on the Contragate campaign and doesn't regret the detour. He reflected:

> I never once argued, in court or out of court, any fact or legal position I did not believe was accurate. Yet, I knew—we all knew—that proving the elements of the case would be very difficult given the high political stakes and establishment opposition coming from not only Judge King but also highbrow media . . . and "liberal" think-tanks. . . .
>
> We must've had over 100 non-Christic Institute lawyers, including all the renown folks from Trial Lawyers for Public Justice, legal scholars, civil rights groups, etc., who studied the pleadings and evidence and decided to help us do discovery and submit amicus briefs supporting us and condemning the sanctions. . . .
>
> The Contragate case underscores how important it is to expose and teach . . . that the predominant role of the legal system has been to protect the elite few and discredit those of us who sincerely attempt to use law as a tool for social change and to actually establish justice.

While Lewis kept up with Christic's appeals, his involvement in the Contragate case largely ended after King granted summary judgment. Lewis explained, "Being away from home and Katie and Stephen was agony." He also needed to turn his time and attention to Robeson County, North Carolina, where CIS joined a movement against racism and corruption in the justice system.

CHAPTER 10

Movement against Corruption in Robeson County, NC (Part 1)

Christic Institute South emerged from its infancy and entered a strengthened fundraising position after successes in Louisiana, Alabama, North Carolina, Georgia, and elsewhere. Lewis, Gayle Korotkin, and Ashaki Binta had sufficient resources to hire a third attorney.

Alan Gregory graduated from the University of Maryland, where he was president of the Black Student Union and involved in the anti-apartheid movement. He attended Antioch School of Law and then worked briefly for Congressman John Conyers. After learning of CIS's anti-racism, movement-building approach to lawyering, Gregory sent his resume to Lewis and Korotkin. They were eager to hire a young, promising Black attorney.

After working on the tail end of CIS's campaign in Keysville, Gregory and his new coworkers joined a movement against corruption and oppression in Robeson County, North Carolina.

Robeson County

In the 1980s, Robeson County was consumed by drugs and violence; its crime rates were among the highest in the state. The *Los Angeles Times* reported, in 1988, "Robeson County, . . . on the Interstate 95 'cocaine alley' leading from Florida, has become a major drug trafficking center where the murder rate is double the state average." According to *Southern Changes*, the county had eighteen unsolved murders from 1975 to 1988, "including execution-style killings said to be drug related." Among the unsolved murders was that of Joyce Sinclair, a Black woman killed soon after being promoted to a supervisory position at a textile mill. On Halloween night, in 1985, white men kidnapped, raped, and murdered Sinclair, and then dumped her body on land where the KKK held a rally the previous year.

Widespread poverty and economic inequality also plagued the county. Robeson is one of the poorest large counties in the US. Its population of about one hundred thousand—which is approximately forty percent Native American (mostly Lumbee), one-third white, and one-quarter Black—is racially segregated. In 1988, the *Charlotte Observer* described the county as "not a place where heroes—or hope—flourish" and as "haunted by" poverty, oppression, racial division, drug trafficking, violent crime, tension, anger, and distrust.

Allegations against the Robeson County Sheriff's Department included using excessive force, accepting bribes, refusing to pursue leads about drug trafficking, tipping off drug dealers before raids, and racial profiling. Sheriff Hubert Stone publicly supported drug dealers. For example, in 1985, he testified to the "good character" of a man indicted for possessing more than four hundred grams of cocaine. In another case, he wrote to a prosecutor and judge expressing support for a man arrested for attempting to purchase five hundred pounds of drugs from undercover agents. Stone was also openly racist. He told *GQ*, "Cocaine, we still have a problem with, especially among the Indians. . . . Most of the drug dealers that are arrested are one race—Indian. The blacks are on crack. Most of the Indians stay on coke. . . . Anytime you look down the street and you see a black and an Indian guy, you've got crime. . . . If they're running together, something's up. We always know when we spot a car and see 'em—an Indian and a black—there's gonna be some crime. We have to keep a firm hand on 'em."

Sheriff Stone's son, Deputy Kevin Stone, also had suspected connections to drug dealers. In 1986, $50,000 worth of drugs and other evidence went missing from an evidence locker. Kevin was one of only two deputies with a key to the locker. During the trial of the men indicted for stealing the evidence, a State Bureau of Investigation (SBI) agent testified that he suspected Kevin of aiding the defendants.

That same year, Deputy Stone killed Jimmy Lee Cummings, a local Native American. Shortly before his death, Cummings said he feared for his life because he bought cocaine that was stolen from the sheriff department's evidence locker and was being watched by Kevin. Kevin claimed he acted in self-defense, even though Cummings was unarmed and merely swinging a plastic bucket. Less than two weeks after the killing, and following only twelve minutes of deliberation, a coroner's jury issued a highly unusual verdict that Cumming's death was "either an accident or self-defense." Moreover, the jury didn't call Kevin to testify, other law enforcement officials presented conflicting accounts of the killing, and Cummings's family wasn't provided adequate notice of the inquest.

Another problem in Robeson County was Joe Freeman Britt, the local DA from 1974 to 1988. Guinness World Records dubbed him America's "deadliest prosecutor" because he racked up forty-seven death sentences. Britt also reportedly prosecuted racial minority defendants at higher rates; sought unreasonably high bails; discouraged plea-bargaining; manipulated court calendars to cause defendants to have to appear every day for weeks until their case was finally called; told indigent defendants they'd have to repay the state if they requested a court-appointed lawyer; and otherwise pressured defendants to waive their right to counsel. Britt's distant cousin, who later became DA in Robeson County, told the *New York Times* about Britt, "He is a bully, and that's the way he ran this office. People were afraid of him. . . . They were intimidated by his tactics."

In 1983, Maurice Geiger, a former Justice Department attorney and then director of the Rural Justice Center, released a multiyear study of Robeson County's justice system. "In all my experience in criminal justice I have never seen a jurisdiction in the United States with such a consistent disregard for fundamental due process, a prosecutor's office so pervasive in its abusive practices, or a judicial attitude that so condones those practices," he declared.

In 1987, the North Carolina Commission on Indian Affairs released a report finding that, in Robeson, bonds were excessive, indigent representation was poor, and Native Americans served more time than white people who had the same sentences. Britt countered, "You've got to remember one thing about these reports. They are consumer-oriented—and who's the consumer? . . . These activist groups have received big bucks. . . . Their reports have to reflect a problem or the funding will dry up." He also said of criminal justice reform organizations and advocates, "It's going to be a cold day in hell before they run the district attorney's office."

Brief Positive Momentum before More Heartbreak

Less than a month after Cummings's death, a multiracial coalition formed Concerned Citizens for Better Government in Robeson County. Led by John Godwin, a Lumbee civil rights activist, the group registered voters and advocated for merging the county's five segregated school systems and creating a public defender office to replace the hodgepodge of court-appointed private attorneys. The coalition's meetings drew hundreds of community members, including Timothy Jacobs and Eddie Hatcher.

Born in July 1968, Timothy Jacobs spent most of his life living in Robeson County. Jacobs, who's part of the Tuscarora people, was known on the national Native American powwow circuit for his good looks and dancing skills as a child. As a teen, he spent time at the Red School House, an Indian-controlled community survival school in St. Paul, Minnesota, where he met Native American leaders who had been involved in the American Indian Movement. After graduating from high school, he continued living with his mother, Eleanor, a school cafeteria worker, and his father, Mancil, a painter at Pembroke State University (i.e., now University of North Carolina at Pembroke). Jacobs worked intermittently as an artist and construction worker.

Thirty miles northeast of Robeson County, Eddie Hatcher was born John Edward Clark in September 1957. His mother was a traveling nurse and Tuscaroran. He dropped out of school and obtained a GED. Hatcher then moved to Robeson County before bouncing among homes, colleges, and jobs across the state. He became an alcoholic and had a criminal record for misdemeanors.

In 1987, Hatcher, Jacobs, and other Concerned Citizens members generated momentum for change in Robeson County. For example, in April, their march and rally drew approximately one thousand residents into the streets. Then, a Lumbee civil rights leader and active Concerned Citizens member, Julian Pierce, announced his candidacy for a new superior court judgeship in Robeson County. He was the first director of Lumbee River Legal Services, involved in the movement for federal recognition of the Lumbee tribe, and sought to become North Carolina's first Native American judge. He stepped up to run against Joe Britt, who'd already announced his candidacy. Pierce campaigned against drug trafficking, racism in the justice system, and corruption in the county.

However, tragedy struck again on January 12, 1988, when a young Black man, Billy McKellar, died of bronchial asthma in the Robeson County jail. He'd been ill for three days while sheriff's deputies withheld his asthma medication and medical attention. A deputy finally put McKellar in chains to take him to the hospital; however, after McKellar defecated on himself, the deputy refused to transport him. By the time an ambulance arrived at the jail, McKellar was dead. He spent the last two months of his life in a cage, awaiting a first court date for alleged car theft. Sheriff Stone callously declared, "He's not the first person to die in that jail, and he won't be the last."

Hatcher's Maps

John Hunt was confined to the Robeson County jail for nine months while awaiting trial on armed robbery and assault charges. According to Hatcher, when he visited Hunt at the jail on January 23, 1988, Hunt shared information about corruption and drug trafficking in the county, including the location of maps showing drug dealers and their connections to law enforcement and public officials. In a letter to Sheriff Stone, Hatcher threatened to release evidence of illegal activity by the sheriff's department, including by Deputy Stone, unless the sheriff released Hunt.

The next day, Mac Legerton, founder of the Center for Community Action, called Mab Segrest. Segrest cofounded North Carolinians Against Racist and Religious Violence and was working in Robeson County. Legerton told Segrest that he was sending her someone who needed help.

On the morning of January 25, Hatcher and Segrest met in his hotel room. He showed her the maps and told her that he feared for his safety because Sheriff Stone knew he possessed them.

Each of the next three days, Segrest and Hatcher attended meetings at the CIS office. Segrest wrote in her book, *Memoir of a Race Traitor*:

> I called [CIS] and asked for help. Bless their hearts and busy schedules, they said I could come over immediately to their office. . . . I picked up Eddie . . . and we drove over. . . .
>
> When we got to the Carrboro office, I introduced him to Gayle Korotkin and Alan Gregory, [CIS] lawyers. After hearing his story, Gayle asked us to come back the next day when Lewis Pitts, [CIS]'s director, would be in the office.
>
> Lewis . . . is more impatient with the failure of the law than any lawyer I have ever met, and it doesn't take judges long to detect his attitude. . . .
>
> Lewis wanted to help, but he had to see the evidence first before we could do anything.
>
> That night, Eddie headed back down to Robeson County. . . . Eddie called me to pick him up at the Raleigh bus station the next morning. I drove him over to [CIS]. . . .
>
> Lewis looked at the maps and shook his head. They were rough, hand-drawn. Anyone could have done them.

"These are just not self-substantiating enough, Eddie," he said. "We can't go public with this." . . . Eddie was disappointed, to say the least. Lewis worked out a plan to help get the source of the maps out of jail to see if he could substantiate the story. On Thursday, Eddie headed back to Robeson. We were supposed to hear from him.

Lewis was preoccupied with the Contragate campaign; so, he recommended his friend and former law partner, Bob Warren, to be Hatcher's attorney. Warren dropped everything and, on January 29, he and Gregory drove to Robeson County to meet with Hatcher.

Hostage Crisis

In an oral history interview, Timothy Jacobs told the University of North Carolina's Center for the Study of the American South that, on January 30, Hatcher showed him the maps and told him about threats from Hubert and Kevin Stone. Jacobs said, "And so, it really scared me, it frightened me. . . . Eddie had really stumbled on something that was a very big deal." Throughout the weekend, according to Jacobs, law enforcement officers were parked outside Hatcher's apartment and Hatcher received threatening phone calls. Jacobs explained in the interview that they decided to forcibly occupy the offices of the *Robesonian*, a daily newspaper in Lumberton, because they thought "it would bring the attention of the world." He shared, "I come from a long line of Tuscarora people, who have fought in Robeson County, in one form or another, for many generations. . . . If it's in your blood, if it's in your DNA, then that's what you do. You do what your ancestors did. You fight for justice, you fight for survival and you fight for the right to exist."

Mab Segrest wrote in her memoir, "I got to the office early on a Monday morning, with no word from Eddie. The phone rang, and it was Gayle. 'Have you heard from Eddie? We just got a call from him. He claims he's taken hostages at the Robeson County newspaper office.' Oh shit."

Shortly before 10:00 A.M. on February 1, 1988—armed with a pistol, two sawed-off shotguns, and a knife—Hatcher and Jacobs entered the *Robesonian* office building. Jacobs chained the front door shut while Hatcher walked toward the rear of the building, yelling at everyone to move to the front lobby. Most employees thought they were being robbed. About a dozen people fled through the back door. A reporter hid under a desk. Hatcher and Jacobs herded the seventeen or so remaining hostages into an interior room.

Approximately one hundred heavily armed sheriff's deputies and SBI and FBI agents surrounded the building. Negotiators huddled in a nearby van. Some onlookers expressed sympathy for Hatcher and Jacobs, and even heckled law enforcement officers.

Inside, Hatcher and Jacobs spoke, via phone, with various media outlets. They told reporters, "The great fire of oppression is out of control and no longer are we able to put out their fire with humility and reverently requesting. No longer can we assume our rights will be acknowledged or that the great white government will enforce those rights. Should we fail to act now, we shall fail a people."

Hatcher yelled at the newspaper's editor, Bob Horne, "Get the governor on the phone!" Hatcher and Jacobs presented Republican Governor James Martin with their demands, which were: they be allowed to surrender to the FBI, not local authorities; John Hunt be released from the Robeson County jail or at least transferred to a jail in another county; and the governor appoint a special prosecutor and task force to investigate the charges against Hunt, corruption in the sheriff's department and DA's office, and Billy McKellar's death.

Throughout the ordeal, Hatcher was significantly more volatile and aggressive than Jacobs. Hatcher falsely claimed the doors were rigged with explosives; announced, "I'm ready to die here today"; threatened to kill hostages if law enforcement entered the building or the governor didn't return his call; and paced back and forth, repeating, "I'm getting a headache, and when I get a headache, I get foolish." Jacobs, in contrast, according to Horne, "spoke softly and easily" and said "'Yes sir' and 'No sir.'"

Hatcher and Jacobs released about half of the hostages during the first few hours of the standoff—one because she had heart problems, three who weren't *Robesonian* employees, two in exchange for lunch, and one swapped for cigarettes. Hostages were allowed to smoke, eat, talk, and walk around. They reported, afterward, that Hatcher and Jacobs were mostly polite and courteous. Some hostages helped answer phones and negotiate a resolution. Understandably, most of them were also quite scared; however, many later said that, as the day wore on, they felt less threatened.

Late in the day, Governor Martin, through his chief of staff, Phillip Kirk, agreed to Hatcher and Jacobs's demands. None of the demands were "of an unreasonable quality," Martin told the Associated Press.

Finally, at about 8:00 P.M., having achieved their objectives for the day, Hatcher and Jacobs ended the ordeal. Hatcher gave Horne the maps and told him to give them to the FBI. Then, after releasing the remaining seven hostages, Hatcher and Jacobs threw their weapons outside, peacefully surrendered, and were arrested. They were driven two hours to the Orange County jail. No one was injured during the ten-hour ordeal.

The next day, Horne wrote in the *Robesonian*, "I don't believe these two men held any hostilities toward *The Robesonian* or that they had any intentions of hurting anyone. I do believe they sought to call attention to perceived problems in Robeson County that they believe scream for serious investigation. And I believe they succeeded in obtaining that attention." He told reporters, "I don't think you can necessarily condone what they did. I don't think you can say it's right, but I don't know of anything else they could have done that would have achieved the attention they succeeded in attracting." "I believe they accomplished more in ten hours than has probably been accomplished in a hundred years," Horne later told a grand jury.

Defense Attorneys

The day after the hostage crisis, Hatcher and Jacobs appeared in federal court where they were formally charged with using firearms to take hostages, making and possessing illegal firearms, and other crimes. A week later, a federal grand jury indicted the men.

On February 17, 1988, Hatcher and Jacobs had their first detention hearing. About a hundred supporters, some wearing beadwork and rawhide, traveled in a motorcade from Robeson County to the federal courthouse in Fayetteville. After a four-hour hearing, US Magistrate Wallace Dixon ordered Hatcher and Jacobs to await trial in the federal prison in Butner, North Carolina. In his order, Dixon slammed the defendants, describing their "degrading criminal acts" as "no different than those of the Palestine Liberation Organization (PLO) or other international terrorist groups" and "deserving of substantial punishment and national condemnation." Hatcher and Jacobs needed a team of experienced, skilled, gutsy attorneys.

Hatcher retained William Kunstler, who was known for representing high-profile defendants, including American Indian Movement leaders Dennis Banks and Russell Means. However, Kunstler was preoccupied with another case and Hatcher refused to be represented by another lawyer; so,

Kunstler advised him by phone. Kunstler's colleagues at the Center for Constitutional Rights, Ronald Kuby and Stephanie Moore, also aided in Hatcher's defense. Barry Nakell—a University of North Carolina law professor who'd worked with Lumbee and Tuscarora communities, advocated for various social justice issues in Robeson County, and become friends with Hatcher—also joined Hatcher's team. Finally, three local attorneys contributed to Hatcher's defense: Horace Locklear, Kenneth Random, and Bruce Cunningham Jr.

Jacobs retained CIS attorneys Lewis, Korotkin, and Gregory, as well as Bob Warren. Jacobs's team and Hatcher's team agreed to collaborate. CIS materials read, "We must uphold the right of oppressed people to protest and to act against injustice, poverty, and wrongdoing which take away their internationally recognized human rights." "The plantation owners—Stone and Britt—can no longer rule their little fiefdom like they have . . . ," Lewis announced to reporters. Lewis later explained, "The Institute, although it did not condone the tactics used by the two men, believed they were entitled to a vigorous defense that informed both the jury and the public about the conditions that forced them to act in desperation."

Organizing amidst Heartbreak and Terror

In the two months immediately following the takeover, momentum toward positive change picked up again. In February 1988, Governor Martin appointed a task force to receive information regarding corruption in Robeson County; John Hunt was released on bond; and presidential candidate Jesse Jackson visited the county, drawing national attention to local issues. The following month, the North Carolina Human Relations Commission began creating a Robeson County Human Relations Commission. Also, a measure to merge the county's five segregated school systems passed with record voter turnout among Black and Lumbee residents. Then, Governor Martin floated the idea of immunity for anyone who came forward about drug dealing in Robeson County. However, by the end of the month, positive momentum again screeched to a halt when tragedy struck twice in just four days.

On March 22, 1988, John Godwin, the leader of Concerned Citizens for Better Government in Robeson County, died in a car accident. On the day of Godwin's funeral, just weeks before the judgeship election, Julian Pierce, a

Lumbee activist and candidate running against prosecutor Joe Britt, was murdered. Pierce's body was discovered face down, with three shotgun blast holes, in his kitchen. According to Mab Segrest, "There was a resonance between the two deaths, a one-two punch, which made each more devastating." The front page of the *News and Observer* declared, "Murder of Activist Dims Hope in Robeson."

Sheriff Stone initially said, "It just looks like he was actually assassinated. . . . I never thought anything like this would ever happen—to kill somebody over an election." But then, just three days after Pierce's death, Stone announced the case was solved and the main suspect, John Goins, a twenty-four-year-old Lumbee man, was dead from an apparent suicide. Goins was the boyfriend of Pierce's fiancée's daughter. According to Stone, Goins killed Pierce in a domestic dispute because Pierce and his fiancée barred Goins from seeing her daughter. Deputy Stone coldly declared, "It's Indian killing an Indian. That's all it is, thank God."

Shortly thereafter, SBI Director Robert Morgan announced that he was satisfied with the sheriff's department's findings. Morgan blamed "all the trouble in Robeson County" on a "small minority within a minority" and a "few troublemakers," and said a racially diverse community is "naturally going to have some difficulty."

Activists, on the other hand, believed Pierce's death was an assassination. Reportedly, Pierce had been threatened and feared for his life and carried a briefcase filled with documents that'd expose drug-related corruption within the sheriff's department; however, the briefcase was never found. Anne Crain, project director at the Rural Assistance Fund in Lumberton, told the *Christian Science Monitor*, "I haven't heard anybody who believes [Pierce died from a domestic dispute]. On the surface of it, it is so convenient for the justice system."

In the face of tragedy, local Black and Native American advocates pressed forward. They organized the Robeson Justice Committee "to bring support in for Hatcher and Jacobs and to help rid Robeson County of the corrupt establishment . . . waging a war on the Indians, blacks and poor whites." To fundraise, they sold T-shirts, hats, bumper stickers, food, and raffle tickets for homemade items. The *Philadelphia Inquirer* described the committee's office as "a tiny, ramshackle room in Pembroke, equipped with a sagging sofa, naked light bulbs and a copying machine."

CIS's Work

For more than fifteen months, CIS staff worked side by side with local advocates. A *News and Observer* article titled, "Robeson Case Fits Lawyers' Cause," read, "Lawyers at the Christic Institute South don't wear ties or socks, and they don't talk about billable hours. They talk about 'empowerment of the people.' Lately they've been talking about empowerment of the people in Robeson County." A profile of CIS in the *Robeson County Leader* read, "Words like 'empowerment,' 'grassroots movements,' and 'power structure' come easily to Pitts, as naturally to him as his ACLU-vintage attire: cowboy boots and jeans matched beneath buttoned-down shirt, tie, and corduroy jacket. But in his voice these buzzwords of boulevard leftists lack the amateur's glib self-righteousness and glassy-eyed fanaticism. Both he and his coworkers at the CIS headquarters in Carrboro pronounce their terms carefully, measuring them against the gravity of the case. And they are convinced that if ever a case were made for those terms, it is the Hatcher-Jacobs trial." Lewis explained to the media that the work in Robeson County was "very, very important" because it was about "a fundamental issue of empowerment" in areas where racial minorities were "the majority in terms of an electorate, but . . . cut away from power."

Lewis wrote, "As was our standard operating procedure, we needed to be among the People to understand their issues, gain their trust, and build hope." He built an especially close relationship with Jacobs's mother. In 2017, Lewis reflected on being with Eleanor while Timothy was jailed awaiting trial:

> She so missed her son. Ms. Jacobs showed me his room. She went to his closet, showed me some of his clothes, and smelled them, saying how much she missed him. Such a basic, primal love of mother for child—I cried on the inside. It felt like a cosmic moment of insight that this was a just cause and fight, and it had to be waged with all-out energy, vigor, and creativity. I had other similar moments . . . that conveyed we were carrying out the rich legacy of fighting for justice and against hundreds of years of oppression against Native People—and government misuse of law and order and the so-called "rule of law."
>
> I remember, during this time, listening to an album by Delaney and Bonnie, and their song "Rock of Ages." It's a classic country

hymn, salt-of-the-earth in flavor, close enough to my country roots to tap into my own memories of church, revival, etc.

I was steeped into feeling the pain of Robeson County dirt poor folks and our fight for right. I was alone and listening. I broke into sobs of emotions and empathy; felt compassion and moral outrage cascade all over me; and thought of my welcomed duty to fight with and for these people. Even today, it brought back chill bumps.

Eleanor recalled that Lewis was "like family," made her feel like they'd known each other for years, and put her more at ease. Timothy said Lewis was willing to fight back against the government and went out of his way to get to know Jacobs and the Tuscarora community; and therefore, Timothy trusted Lewis.

During long days in Robeson County, CIS's community organizer Ashaki Binta worked with local advocates to build a multiracial coalition, organize community meetings, conduct voter registration teach-ins, and collect more than twenty thousand signatures on a petition demanding Hatcher and Jacobs be released from jail pending trial. She spent nights in the homes of local Native American families. Binta also organized events in Raleigh, Durham, and Chapel Hill to drum up broader support.

Meanwhile, Bob Warren investigated the drug trade and corruption in the county. He and a professional investigator, who'd spent fifteen years as a homicide detective, interviewed more than a hundred locals and compiled a report of more than a thousand pages. Warren also established a "lawyer bank" of experienced criminal defense and civil rights attorneys to advise or represent witnesses who feared retaliation. Jacobs praised Warren for going above and beyond typical defense attorneys, including bringing toiletries and food to the jail. Jacobs also spoke highly of Gayle Korotkin, recalling she "was like the brainchild" and "always optimistic."

Alan Gregory also traveled to Robeson County nearly every week. He tracked down evidence, registered voters, took affidavits about the sheriff's department's violence and corruption, and collected signatures on a petition to impeach Sheriff Stone. Additionally, Gregory teamed with Al McSurely, a North Carolina-based civil rights lawyer, to lobby state Black elected officials for legislation that'd create a special committee to investigate conditions in Robeson County. CIS staff also supported calls for a US congressional investigation and a special prosecutor.

Decades later, Lewis wrote about movement lawyering in Robeson County, "The deep and wonderful feelings from working with those people remain central in my heart and core—the feeling of being part of their struggle, the historical legacy of the 'leveling spirit' and thirsting for justice, and the solidarity around equal justice for all."

CIS staff and Warren persisted in the face of ongoing intimidation and harassment in Robeson County. Lewis compared the local power structure's methods to COINTELPRO—the FBI's series of covert, often illegal projects during the 1950s to 1970s that involved surveilling, infiltrating, discrediting, disrupting, and neutralizing progressive political organizations and civil rights movements. "The fear factor was incredible and for good reason—death and law enforcement violence were rampant," Lewis wrote.

Gregory said, "When we would drive down there, we'd be scared as heck, especially coming down those country roads late at night." He remembered learning to handle a gun and target practice with CIS staff. Binta recalled someone attempting to plant drugs under a trailer where she was staying with a local advocate, as well as mysterious individuals appearing at their community meetings and spreading rumors, sowing confusion, and creating division. Warren reported that, while driving through Lumberton, a bullet shattered his windshield; and an anonymous caller later claimed it was a warning shot. He told the Associated Press, "But we are not going to be intimidated. We are not going to stop the investigation." Warren began wearing a bulletproof vest, hanging a flak jacket on his driver's side door, carrying a shotgun, and using rental cars. CIS staff installed an alarm system at their office and began traveling in pairs.

The harassment continued during the federal trial in Raleigh. During the trial, Warren spent most nights at Lewis and Katie Greene's home in Chapel Hill, including while Lewis was away working on the Contragate case. Lewis wrote, "Katie was upset that I had him stay there as the danger he faced might've caused harm for her and Stephen. I think I was too blinded by adrenaline from the cases to grasp her legitimate point. I thought she wasn't being committed enough. I now believe I was wrong." Lewis and Warren also stayed at a hotel in Raleigh for a few nights. They learned that someone had reported to police seeing three men wearing ski masks and loading automatic weapons near the hotel. According to Warren, the license plate of the masked men's vehicle belonged to a recent murder victim in Robeson County.

Hatcher Flees

At a hearing on July 5, 1988, having already served 155 days behind bars, Hatcher and Jacobs were released on $100,000 bonds. Jacobs's supporters carried him atop their shoulders out of the federal courthouse in New Bern, North Carolina.

However, prosecutors successfully appealed. Hatcher and Jacobs were ordered to turn themselves in to authorities. Jacobs immediately surrendered. Hatcher, on the other hand, ran, and a warrant was issued for his arrest.

Hatcher ended up in New York City, but one of his attorneys, Ronald Kuby, convinced him to return to North Carolina. Federal authorities arrested Hatcher when he arrived at Raleigh-Durham International Airport.

Judge Boyle

Judge Terrence William Boyle presided over Hatcher and Jacobs's federal criminal trial. Boyle, a former legislative assistant to Senator Jesse Helms, was first appointed to the bench by Ronald Reagan.

Years after the trial, George W. Bush nominated Boyle to the Fourth Circuit. In response, The Leadership Conference on Civil and Human Rights wrote to senators, "Judge Boyle's record reflects a deep and abiding hostility to civil rights cases based on race, gender, disability, and age." Lambda Legal warned that Boyle's "record showed a clear hostility towards civil rights claims and blatant disregard for the law." An analysis by People for the American Way found that "Boyle's record reveals a troubling history of espousing a damaging neo-federalist philosophy from the bench that is particularly harmful to civil rights." Senator Edward Kennedy released a statement about Boyle's nomination:

> Judge Boyle is an example of a nominee chosen for his radical views, not his qualifications. . . . His decisions have been reversed or criticized on appeal more than 150 times, far more than any other district judge nominated to a circuit court by President Bush. Too often, these reversals took place because he made the same mistake more than once. . . .
>
> Time and again, the conservative Fourth Circuit has ruled that Judge Boyle improperly dismissed cases seeking protection for

important individual rights, such as the right to free speech, free association, the right to be free from discrimination, and even the right to a fair and lawful sentence in a criminal case.

Mab Segrest wrote that Hatcher and Jacobs's trial was "likely one of the most contentious in recent North Carolina history" and "a running battle between Lewis and Bob" and Boyle.

Federal Criminal Trial

On September 26, 1988, family, friends, and other supporters of Hatcher and Jacobs caravanned to the federal courthouse in Raleigh for the first day of the trial. A Tuscaroran musical group wore headdresses and played drums outside the courthouse. The courtroom was full; crowds overflowed into the lobby. Hatcher and Jacobs wore blue jeans and Native American-style shirts and jewelry. CIS staff and Warren surrounded Jacobs at a table. Warren wore his standard gray suit and red suspenders. He also wore a necktie, but only after Boyle ordered him to wear one. Lewis wore his trusty cowboy boots.

During jury selection the following day, the defense team and prosecutor exchanged accusations of racial discrimination. The prosecutor used six peremptory strikes to eliminate Black and Native American individuals from the jury pool. US Attorney John Stuart Bruce claimed the defense engaged in reverse discrimination by using ten strikes against white prospective jurors. Ultimately, the seated jury consisted of nine Black and three white people.

The defense team planned to argue necessity—that is, Hatcher and Jacobs reasonably believed their actions were necessary to avoid imminent harm and there weren't adequate alternative means of avoiding the harm. Importantly, this defense would give them a legal justification for using the trial to bring further attention to the fear, violence, corruption, and injustice in Robeson County.

During opening statements, Warren told jurors the evidence would show "a long history of intolerable discrimination against Indians, Blacks, and poor whites living in Robeson County"; "how the lives of poor people in Robeson County are controlled by members of the drug underworld . . . under the protection of law enforcement"; and Hatcher and Jacobs "believed that they were going to be killed because of what they had found out about the drug underworld and saw no way out." "The defendants should be found not guilty of all the charges brought against them because the defendants were justified in doing what they did," Warren suggested.

However, later in the day, in response to a motion from the prosecutor, Boyle ruled that the defense couldn't argue necessity. He wrote, "A direct causal connection cannot be established between the taking of innocent hostages on the one hand, and the alleviation of alleged drug-trafficking and official corruption or alleged threats to the defendants' lives on the other. This is not to say that hostage-taking could not be an effective means toward those ends, but that whatever effectiveness it would have could only be indirect." Additionally, Boyle said to Lewis, "The perpetrator of harm must be the object of your action. Necessity is not available to private citizens who take vigilante action."

Lewis told reporters the prosecution's motion showed "how desperate the federal government" was to prevent exposure of the sheriff department's involvement in drug trafficking "because the next logical question is if it's so rampant and visible, why haven't the federal prosecutors done something about it." An article about the day's events read, "Relations between the judge and defense team have grown increasingly testy, and on Wednesday the judge warned defense lawyers that they could be charged with contempt of court."

The testiness continued Thursday during testimony from Raymond Godfrey, a reporter for the *Robesonian*. US Attorney Bruce began asking Godfrey about US Attorney Sam Currin's previous comment that there was "a perception among drug dealers that they can operate at will" in Robeson. Judge Boyle interrupted Bruce and asked him, "Do you want to open up that area?" Lewis objected, accusing Boyle of "helping the government when [Bruce] was about to make a foolish mistake that would have opened up the door on this issue." Boyle overruled the objection. Shortly thereafter, jurors were excused, and then Lewis told Boyle, "My objection is to you participating as part of the prosecutorial team. I am shocked at what just occurred. I wonder if you would like to pull up a chair at the government's table." Three decades later, Alan Gregory laughed as he recalled how the courtroom "went wild" when Lewis told Boyle to "pull up a chair." "I already held him in such high regard, but when I saw that, he became like an icon," Gregory said about Lewis.

On the fifth day of the trial, Lewis moved for charges to be dropped based on outrageous government conduct. He said to Boyle, "Mr. Bruce is trying to create the impression that drug trafficking and corruption is not present in Robeson County, which is an outrageous position for any government official to take, especially when the US Attorney's Office has evidence to support forty drug indictments in the county." In turn, Bruce accused Lewis of pandering to the press and other spectators. Lewis asked Boyle to order Bruce to allow the defense to privately review the drug-related indictments. Boyle denied the motion to dismiss and withheld a decision about Lewis viewing files. A profile of CIS in the *News and Observer* read:

> The lawyers, who represent Mr. Jacobs, seem to welcome every notebook and television camera outside the courtroom as a tool to influence what happens inside.
>
> The prosecutors are trying to contain the case to the courtroom and a simple question: "Did the defendants take hostages?" . . .
>
> Nevertheless, the defendants and their lawyers maintain, the question is not so simple. They say the defendants were driven to such a desperate and dangerous act by a county government that is corrupted by drug dealing and oppresses minorities, and a myopic legal system that refuses to see it. . . .
>
> The wrongs they see in Robeson County have become their cause, while acquittal of the defendants is their immediate goal. And though they deny publicity is their sole aim, it is certainly their friend and partner.
>
> "We handle and conduct cases in such a way that raises these social justice issues to public awareness," said P. Lewis Pitts. . . . "We are in this work to right these wrongs. The issues are what attract the attention."

The same day, *Robesonian* editor Bob Horne testified. While being cross-examined by Lewis, Horne said the defendants appeared rational for most of the takeover, the atmosphere was calm after the first few minutes, and their demands were reasonable. At one point, Lewis asked Horne, "Haven't you described Eddie Hatcher and Timothy Jacobs as the conscience of the community?" "Yes," Horne responded. However, the prosecution then called about a dozen other hostages, most of whom testified they had nightmares and felt unsafe at work after the ordeal.

On October 6, 1988, the defense made a written proffer of evidence to support a necessity defense. A proffer is a presentation of evidence at trial for admission or rejection by a judge. Boyle rejected the evidence. Lewis explained, "Boyle's goal . . . was to prevent the public from hearing our evidence about what a corrupt place Robeson County was at the time." So, Lewis and the other attorneys shifted their focus to convincing jurors that Hatcher and Jacobs lacked criminal intent when they took over the *Robesonian*—in other words, they acted to save the lives of Hatcher and others, not with malicious intent to commit crimes.

During the week of October 10, Boyle continued delivering blows to Hatcher and Jacobs. First, Boyle dismissed CIS's subpoenas of Robeson County officials, including Sheriff Stone and Deputy Stone. He called the subpoenas an "unreasonable" and "oppressive" "fishing expedition." Additionally, Boyle rejected the defense's request for self-defense to be included in the jury instructions. Finally, he refused to allow Maurice Geiger to testify about the Rural Justice Center's findings regarding corruption, dysfunction, and mistreatment in the county's justice system.

Boyle did, however, dismiss the hostage-taking charges against Jacobs, reasoning that the prosecution failed to present evidence that Jacobs made a demand on the government himself or aided Hatcher in making a demand. Consequently, Jacobs's charge of committing a violent crime with an illegal firearm was also dismissed.

After a three-week trial, Hatcher delivered his own closing argument, which Kunstler helped him write. Hatcher asked jurors, "When those sworn to uphold the Constitution won't, what do you do"; and "Can you imagine 60,000 frightened, abandoned people crying out?" He continued, "From 150 miles away, they're crying out—some are faint; they're tired; they're wore out. Please don't abandon me and Timmy." Hatcher's voice cracked and his lips quivered. Tears welled in the eyes of Jacobs, his attorneys, and jurors. Supporters sobbed in the courtroom.

Lewis delivered the closing argument for Jacobs. Despite Boyle's previous rulings, Lewis argued that Jacobs acted out of necessity and reminded jurors, "The law recognizes, at some point, drastic action is necessary." He asked the jury to scrutinize key words in the indictment—specifically, "knowingly, willfully, intentionally, *and maliciously*." Lewis explained that when Hatcher and Jacobs seized the newspaper, they acted no more irrationally than similarly persecuted figures in the Bible. "Before God tapped Moses to lead the people out of slavery, Moses had murdered an Egyptian," Lewis said. He told jurors the courtroom was a "temple of justice" and "fairness was a hallmark of the ministry of Jesus." An Associated Press profile of Lewis read, "The religious symbolism, he said later, was more than just a rhetorical flourish from a lawyer's bag of tricks. 'My grandfather was a Methodist minister,' said Pitts. 'But I got totally turned off to institutional religion in college.' 'Eventually I came to understand that God is love, and love is what you do to people who inhabit this earth—not some distant heavenly place,' Pitts said. . . . 'Trying to relieve the suffering of others gives purpose to your life,' said Pitts. . . . 'There's not anything else, is there?'"

In his closing argument, US Attorney Bruce urged jurors to abandon any sympathies for Hatcher and Jacobs, focus on the siege, and ignore claims of drug trafficking and public corruption. "What can start out as a kernel of good intentions can make a person get carried away and do something that's entirely illegal and improper," he told the jury.

After closing arguments ended, the jury spent eighty-five minutes deliberating before being dismissed for the day. They returned on October 15, 1988, and reached a decision after five hours of deliberation. Boyle warned everyone in the courtroom to remain quiet and seated while the verdict was read. The foreperson then announced the verdict for Hatcher and Jacobs: not guilty on all counts.

"Thank you, Jesus," someone shouted as soon as the verdict was announced. Ashaki Binta jumped out of her seat and jubilantly screamed. Jacobs slumped in his chair, held up by CIS staff. With tears in his eyes, Hatcher stood and turned toward the back of the courtroom. Supporters leapt to their feet and rushed to envelop both men. Lewis wept with relief. The verdict was "absolutely euphoric," he recalled.

A white juror hugged Hatcher in the courthouse hallway and said, "God bless you. . . . You're a good boy." Two jurors said they didn't think Hatcher and Jacobs acted with criminal intent. Mab Segrest wrote, "In spite of all the court's hostility, the jury found Hatcher and Jacobs 'not guilty' on all charges, to the amazement of everyone but Lewis, who knew he had the case won as soon as he had the Black-majority jury."

As people filed out of the courthouse, Lewis told reporters, "The jury realized that when people face those conditions, it is inevitable that they will rebel." He called for the US Attorney's Office to bring drug trafficking cases in Robeson County, for Sheriff Stone to be removed, and for Joe Britt to be barred from taking judicial office. Sheriff Stone remarked, "All circuses have come to an end. Now we have to wait and see where the clowns have their next show at the taxpayers' expense."

An editorial in the *Charlotte Observer* read, "Obviously the allegations that Mr. Hatcher and Mr. Jacobs made about conditions in their county were not only credible, but persuasive enough to convince the jury that they acted without criminal intent. . . . If where there's smoke there's fire, it's amazing

Robeson County hasn't been engulfed in flames for years, and the jury's astonishing verdict adds a lot more smoke. There are simply too many rumors and assertions of corruption and injustice there for state and federal officials to ignore."

The Robeson Defense Committee held a celebration and fundraiser at West Robeson High School on October 25, 1988. Hatcher received a standing ovation, played the piano, and announced, "The jury has come back with its verdict. It says, 'Joe Freeman Britt, you're guilty; Hubert Stone, you're guilty; Kevin Stone, you're guilty!'"

However, good news was once again short lived. Less than two months after the federal trial acquittals, Jacobs and Hatcher were indicted on state criminal charges.

CHAPTER 11

Movement against Corruption in Robeson County, NC (Part 2)

Lewis and others worked to build on the momentum from Eddie Hatcher's and Timothy Jacobs's acquittals in federal court. For example, on October 28, 1988, Lewis and Barry Nakell, one of Hatcher's lawyers, met with the Governor's Task Force on Robeson County and gave members more than a hundred pages of documents showing law enforcement complicity in widespread drug trafficking in the county. Lewis told the media afterward, "Even though the trial is over, and they were acquitted of all charges, the problems of corruption and lawlessness still exist in Robeson County. And we were asking them to do whatever they could do to try to bring some solution to those problems."

Then, in November 1988, Lewis and Nakell met with State AG Lacy Thornburg. After Thornburg claimed the county's main problem was division among people, Lewis accused him of victim-blaming. Thornburg kicked Lewis out of his office. Lewis told the *Robeson County Leader*, "Thornburg has said to me, since the October trial, that the problems in Robeson are no different from those of other counties . . . and that everything is relatively under control. That's bullshit, frankly—it's not an objective, honest description of what he knows goes on there. What we have to do in Robeson County, he said, is 'help people learn how to get along.' That's outrageous! Either it's blatant racism and insensitivity because the people who're dying and being oppressed are black and Indian, or the tentacles of the drug cartel have reached into Raleigh." "I see nothing but platitudes and false descriptions of what's happening there," Lewis shared with the *Charlotte Observer*.

Additionally, local advocates and CIS staff started a petition to the Robeson County Superior Court demanding that Sheriff Hubert Stone and his son, Deputy Kevin Stone, be removed, pursuant to state law, for unfitness and willfully engaging in misconduct and corruption. Advocates planned to submit the petition—as well as county residents' complaints collected by CIS attorney Alan Gregory—to the new DA, after the current DA, Joe Britt, became a judge in early 1989.

State Charges

Local organizing continued under a cloud of rumors that Hatcher and Jacobs would be charged under state law. The *New York Times* reported, "A month after two Indians were acquitted of all Federal charges filed in connection with their armed seizure of the local newspaper, the conflicts they stirred up show little sign of abating. A movie deal, the threat of a lawsuit by a former hostage, uncertainty over whether the men will face state charges of kidnapping—all these continue to arouse strong feelings."

DA Britt fueled the rumors, telling the *Fayetteville Times*, "There is an SBI task force operating down here, brought in at my request. . . . In addition to analyzing the Hatcher, Jacobs matter under state law, we are expanding our inquiry to include a possible pre-takeover conspiracy involving other parties." The same day, according to Lewis, a *News and Observer* reporter informed him that CIS attorneys, as well as Bob Warren and Barry Nakell, were targets of the conspiracy investigation.

Lewis and Nakell wrote to Britt requesting a meeting and asserting that the agreement Hatcher and Jacobs reached with the governor's office to end the siege precluded the involvement of Robeson County law enforcement in a state prosecution. They also wrote to James Trotter, the governor's general counsel, detailing why Hatcher and Jacobs shouldn't be prosecuted again—specifically, Lewis and Nakell argued, the state system should respect the federal justice system and federal jury's verdict; state prosecution would effectively, albeit not technically, violate the Fifth Amendment's prohibition on double jeopardy; the local DA's office ought to, instead, focus on true injustices in Robeson County; and another prosecution would stir strong passions and protests in the community. Neither Britt nor Trotter responded.

A month before leaving office to become a judge, Britt called a special grand jury session. On December 6, 1988, a Robeson County grand jury indicted Hatcher and Jacobs on fourteen counts of second-degree kidnapping, which carried a total maximum prison sentence of 420 years.

Lewis believes the state charges were intended to "keep persecuting men who had the courage to speak out" and chill free speech by intimidating those engaging in First Amendment activities, such as petitioning for removal of the Stones. Ronald Kuby and William Kunstler, Center for Constitutional Rights attorneys who'd help represent Hatcher in state court, accused Britt of "prosecutorial misconduct" and being "vindictive." The Robeson Defense Committee called on the community to "demand that the state drop the charges and launch an immediate investigation into the reign of terror, lawlessness, and discrimination in Robeson County." The *Durham Morning Herald* editorial board wrote, "The spirit of the constitutional guarantee against double jeopardy is trashed in the state's vindictive decision to try the two Indians. . . . The much-needed healing of Robeson County will not be served by this uncalled-for prosecution."

Hatcher and Jacobs Run

When the indictment was issued, Jacobs was in New York. He called a Raleigh television station to say he wouldn't be returning to North Carolina. A warrant was issued for his arrest.

Hatcher was arrested and then released, after the National Council of Churches posted his bond. Soon thereafter, he fled. Following a stint on a reservation in New York, he sought sanctuary with Shoshone-Bannock people in Idaho.

Jacobs ended up in the Onondaga Nation territory in New York. *Newsday* read, "The story of how Timothy Jacobs got to New York is the story of how a rural community, already beset with age-old problems of poverty, lack of education, and racial divisiveness, is now struggling with a modern problem: a cocaine epidemic. Add to that charges that local law officials are involved in the drug-trafficking and that the criminal justice system is providing different standards of justice for the rich and the poor, and the atmosphere in Robeson County is one of violence, suspicion and fear."

Jacobs was eventually arrested near Syracuse, after leading law enforcement on a high-speed chase and crashing into an unoccupied school bus. He was arraigned and jailed as a fugitive, pending a decision about extradition to North Carolina.

On December 16, 1988, the National Council of Churches posted Jacobs's $25,000 bond in New York. While awaiting a decision about extradition, he lived on the Onondaga Reservation, where Dennis Banks, a founding member of the American Indian Movement, had taken refuge from the US government in the early 1980s.

Extradition Fight

CIS led a campaign against Jacobs's extradition. Lewis wasn't licensed in New York, and therefore, needed local counsel. He reached out to fellow NLG member, Alan Rosenthal. Rosenthal had started the Syracuse Law Collective, which handled criminal defense and civil rights cases, including police misconduct matters. One of his law partners, Joe Heath, represented the Council of Chiefs for the Onondagas. Rosenthal said of Lewis's invitation to collaborate, "I was an easy mark and readily accepted." He described Lewis as a "kindred spirit fighting for underdog causes." Rosenthal thought Jacobs wasn't a "sophisticated" or "politically developed" advocate, had gotten caught up in "something beyond his capacity," and was largely along for the ride with Hatcher. Nevertheless, Rosenthal also knew, in his words, "There was a right and a wrong side in the case." So, he agreed to cocounsel with Lewis.

During the extradition fight, Lewis made multiple trips to New York, where he stayed at Rosenthal's home. A highlight for Lewis was visiting a longhouse (a type of long, rectangular home built from wood and bark) on the reservation where Jacobs had taken refuge. There, Lewis addressed the community's elders about why they shouldn't permit law enforcement to enter their sovereign land to arrest Jacobs. Another highlight was attending a fundraiser for Jacobs, sponsored by the Rainbow Coalition and Syracuse Black Leadership Congress and featuring Jacobs performing traditional dances in Native American garb.

Lewis lobbied North Carolina Governor James Martin and New York Governor Mario Cuomo. He wrote to Martin:

> The ends of justice require that you not pursue extradition and that the charges be dropped against both defendants because this prosecution is tainted by abuse of power for the vindictive, improper purpose of deterring exercise of First Amendment rights to organize and to end the reign of terror in Robeson County. . . .
>
> Now is a chance for a change in Robeson County. You and the new district attorney will be held accountable for what use you make of the opportunity—whether the laws and powers of the State are used to improve conditions for residents of Robeson County or are used to continue the state of affairs characterized by lawless law enforcement, oppression, and discrimination. . . .

Two days later, Lewis wrote to Cuomo, requesting he direct the New York AG to exercise "discretion not to extradite Mr. Jacobs because his departure from North Carolina was based upon a reasonably grounded fear for his life and therefore was involuntary." In a second correspondence to Cuomo, Lewis noted, "Our concern is only heightened by the fact that when the District Attorney who procured the indictment in bad faith, Joe Freeman Britt, assumes his judgeship, he will be replaced by John Richard Townsend, his acknowledged clone and protege." Townsend had been Britt's assistant DA for eight years.

CIS staff encouraged others to join the lobbying efforts. A group of North Carolina leaders—including elected officials, professors, clergy, and civil rights advocates—wrote to Cuomo, requesting an investigation into the extradition. Additionally, the Onondaga Council of Chiefs in New York issued a letter of support for denying extradition. The National Center on Institutions and Alternatives submitted a report to Cuomo about Jacobs's extradition, which read, "Suspicious deaths, murders and 'suicides' continue. . . . Official intimidation of those who support Eddie Hatcher and Timothy Jacobs continues. It is within this continued climate of fear and injustice in Robeson County that Eddie Hatcher and Timothy Jacobs were indicted."

Nevertheless, Governor Martin wrote to Lewis, "It is my duty under the Constitution and laws of this State to seek the extradition of fugitives from justice who have been charged here in North Carolina." Lewis told the media that Martin was "knowingly colluding with the likes of Joe Freeman Britt and Hubert Stone in continuing the oppression and intimidation of the people of Robeson County."

Then, on January 10, 1989, Governor Cuomo signed a warrant for Jacobs's arrest and an extradition order. Lewis and Rosenthal petitioned for a court order invalidating the extradition warrant and moved for an "Evidentiary Hearing on the Likelihood of Irreparable Miscarriage of Justice if Forcibly Extradited."

Lewis and others traveled from North Carolina to New York for the extradition hearing. Alan Gregory said, "We drove in a damn van all the way from Chapel Hill to New York, man. It was a perilous journey. We had about ten people in the van. It was snowy and treacherous. I thought to myself, 'What am I doing?' It was freeeeezing."

Madison County Judge William O'Brien III presided over the three-day extradition hearing, held the week of February 27, 1989. Throughout the hearing, monks outside the courthouse played drums at a continuous beat in the snow. Rosenthal said "the friction" between Lewis and Judge O'Brien, and between Lewis and the local DA, Neal Rose, "was as ever present as the drumbeat."

During the first day, Lewis and O'Brien battled over the admissibility of evidence about corruption in Robeson County. O'Brien told Lewis such evidence wouldn't be considered because Jacobs's extradition, not his claims of corruption, was the sole matter at hand. Nevertheless, Lewis submitted affidavits, and called a variety of witnesses to testify, about conditions in Robeson County and risks associated with extradition for Jacobs.

Lewis also got under O'Brien's skin by repeatedly moving for a mistrial and for O'Brien to recuse himself. O'Brien sustained, without explanation, several of DA Rose's objections to Lewis's questioning of witnesses. A local reporter wrote, "After sustaining a number of Rose's objections, O'Brien became so flustered at Pitts' inquiries that he refused to answer any of the attorney's questions. 'I think your honor has gotten so angry that you are no longer making fair judgments,' Pitts said. 'This hearing is a waste of time.'"

Rose called only one witness—James Bowman, a North Carolina SBI agent. Bowman acknowledged drug problems and rumors of corruption in Robeson County; however, he also claimed there wasn't concrete evidence to support Jacobs's specific claims.

Lewis spent most of the following morning cross-examining Bowman and continuing to butt heads with Judge O'Brien. Rosenthal said Lewis had a "bulldog notion" of "sinking his teeth into something," even when the odds were against him. The following exchanges occurred in court:

> O'BRIEN: Please keep your feet off the backs of the chairs. This is a courtroom, not a movie theater. Excuse me, Mr. Pitts. I'm trying to maintain decorum. Any problem?
>
> LEWIS: No. I'd just like the same consideration for the life of Timothy Jacobs as we do for the backs of the chairs. . . .
>
> O'BRIEN: Mr. Pitts, I thought we had an agreement or understanding.
>
> LEWIS: Well, I can't sit by here when you can make a ruling like that. . . .
>
> LEWIS: And I think the record will reflect, if it doesn't, the objection was prompted by the Court.
>
> O'BRIEN: That's absolutely, unequivocally and positively untrue.

O'Brien eventually ordered Lewis, Rosenthal, and Rose into chambers, where he excoriated Lewis: "The purpose of the chambers conference is to heretofore, once and for all and lastly and finally, admonish Mr. Pitts . . . to accept the Court's rulings without engaging the Court in a dialogue as to the reasons why the Court has ruled as it has, without engaging the Court in a discourse over whether the Court's being fair." O'Brien called Lewis's conduct "uncalled for" and "contemptuous," and threatened to immediately end the hearing and extradite Jacobs.

The judge then directed his ire at Rosenthal: "I accepted your application that Mr. Pitts be admitted to practice in this state for the purpose of . . . this case, and I'm directing you now as a member of the bar of this state to direct him and to admonish him . . . , or whatever you feel you need to do, to have him comply with the rules of this Court and to respect the Court . . . ."

O'Brien asked if Rose had anything to add for the record. Lewis interrupted, "Can we do this in open court?" O'Brien denied Lewis's request, ordered him not to mention the conference in court or to reporters, and threatened to hold him in contempt and stop the proceedings if he violated the order.

Rose took his opportunity to chastise Lewis. He called Lewis's conduct "totally offensive," "unprofessional," and "contemptuous." Rose continued:

> His conduct went well beyond any claim of vigorous representation of a client. It included colloquy. It included trite remarks to the Court and in open court solely for the purpose of demeaning the Court and . . . of just making a big show and a big splash.
>
> Furthermore, I have newspaper accounts of Mr. Pitts conducting himself in a similar manner in . . . North Carolina during the federal trial connected with this case where . . . he abused the federal judge. There are newspaper accounts and personal accounts of his sanctimonious conduct, his contemptuous conduct; and as he sits there now smugly having been afforded . . . an opportunity to practice in . . . New York, when he obviously wouldn't qualify to do so either by education, training or professional demeanor, I . . . want to make a record so that he doesn't get admitted . . . again in this state.
>
> Furthermore, . . . if there was any member of our local bar or a member of the state bar who conducted himself as he has, I would make a report . . . so that Mr. Pitts's record of performance and

his lack of professionalism can be a record in New York State and elsewhere around the country because I think it's a disgrace.

After Rose finished grumbling, Lewis told O'Brien that the hearing had become "a farce and a mockery" and "an exercise to guard against accusations made about drug trafficking and law enforcement officials." Lewis added, "I think that the Court's just-given comments . . . speaks volumes as to the injustice that is occurring today, and . . . that the Court's issuance of a gag order . . . is indicative of the similar guarding of the law enforcement officials in an effort to prevent, in an open trial, the citizenry and public . . . from knowing the real situation that my client faces if forcefully sent back to Robeson County."

During the third and final day of the hearing, the acrimony subsided. News coverage read, "Pitts apologized to the judge for his behavior at the start of today's testimony. That came after Jacobs complained on Wednesday that the constant bickering between the judge and the attorney had taken on a personal edge and muddled the point of the extradition hearing." Maurice Geiger, Director of the Rural Justice Center, wrote that O'Brien was "constantly combative" with Lewis, "insulting toward witnesses," and "absolutely unable to objectively handle the matter before him."

On March 14, 1989, O'Brien ordered Jacobs to be extradited and revoked his bail. For more than an hour, while some of Jacobs's supporters stood with their backs to O'Brien, the judge explained the bases for his decision, which were that Governor Cuomo didn't have discretion about whether to extradite Jacobs; there was insufficient evidence, other than the *Robesonian* siege, of Jacobs being an outspoken advocate; Jacobs wasn't harmed while previously jailed and out on bond in North Carolina; Jacobs's acquittal in federal court demonstrated he could get a fair trial in North Carolina; reports of corruption and danger in Robeson County were rumor, gossip, and innuendo, which primarily pertained to Hatcher, not Jacobs; positive changes were underway in Robeson County, including a new public defender and DA; and North Carolina had a statute that'd allow Jacobs to petition for the state prosecution to be moved to a court outside Robeson County. Lewis told reporters that O'Brien's ruling was "absolutely contrary to the evidence."

At Lewis's request, a New York Appellate Division judge granted a temporary stay of O'Brien's ruling. However, on March 21, 1989, the full appellate division declined, without comment, to continue the stay or review the extradition decision.

The next day, Lewis publicly announced that Jacobs wouldn't appeal to New York's highest court because Robeson County authorities had assured Jacobs that, upon his return, they'd support reasonable bail, and he wouldn't be jailed in the county. However, Robeson County DA Richard Townsend claimed that no such promises had been made, and, in fact, he'd oppose bail altogether.

Jacobs told reporters that he was really tired of running, felt like a year of his life had been wasted, and regretted helping Hatcher. Additionally, he confirmed an Associated Press report that he'd called *Robesonian* editor Bob Horne to apologize to him and the other hostages. Jacobs wanted them to understand that he and Hatcher "had tried other things for years" and the siege "was the only choice" they had. He told the *Fayetteville Observer*, "Of all the people involved on Feb. 1, I probably feel worst of all. . . . It's been a living hell."

Hatcher and Jacobs Return

On March 23, 1989, Jacobs returned to North Carolina. Lewis arranged for Alexander Charns, a Durham-based criminal defense attorney, to join Jacobs's defense team.

The following day, they appeared in Robeson County Superior Court. However, at the hearing, Judge Anthony Brannon, a former prosecutor, repeatedly advised Jacobs that he was entitled to "conflict-free counsel," implying CIS was more concerned with its own spotlight, and perhaps with Hatcher's interests, than with Jacobs's well-being. Brannon told Jacobs, "I am prepared to appoint you a well-known, successful criminal defense lawyer . . . who never gets his own clients' interests confused or wound up with anyone else's, or with some other cause." The judge then told Charns, "I don't know who's paying you to be here. I don't know what interests or motivation there may be, nor do I intend to inquire." Brannon set bail at $100,000, and appointed James Parish, a private attorney based in nearby Fayetteville, to represent Jacobs.

Meanwhile, Hatcher fled from Idaho, after a Shoshone-Bannock Trial Court judge issued a warrant for his arrest. A month later, he visited the Soviet Union's consulate in San Francisco to request political asylum. Bewildered Soviets contacted American authorities, rebuffed his request, and told him to leave. FBI agents arrested Hatcher as soon as he stepped off consulate property. In May 1989, after a couple of months in a San Francisco jail, Hatcher was extradited to North Carolina, where he was jailed while awaiting the state criminal trial.

Civil Lawsuit

On January 31, 1989—while Hatcher and Jacobs were on the lam, and the day before the one-year anniversary of the hostage crisis—the Robeson Defense Committee filed a lawsuit in the Federal District Court for the Eastern District of North Carolina. Lewis represented Jacobs and his mother. Barry Nakell, William Kunstler, and Ronald Kuby represented the remaining plaintiffs—Hatcher, his mother, and other Native American and Black members of the committee. The nineteen named defendants included Governor Martin, AG Thornburg, former DA Britt, current DA Townsend, and Sheriff Stone. The plaintiffs alleged the defendants violated the First, Fifth, Sixth, and Fourteenth Amendments by participating in a campaign of intimidation and harassment to suppress political dissent. At a press conference, Lewis said, "In this lawsuit, we hope to put Robeson County—not the people but the power structure, which for decades has punished enemies and rewarded friends—on trial."

The plaintiffs sought to deter the state prosecution of Hatcher and Jacobs and enjoin the defendants from interfering with Lewis and Jacobs's relationship. According to Jacobs's mother, Eleanor, SBI Agent James Bowman—the same agent who testified in New York against Jacobs's extradition—showed up at her house in December 1988, whereupon he insisted that CIS was "using Timothy to make a name for themselves" and "Timothy should fire Christic and get local lawyers." A week later, Bowman called Eleanor when Lewis and Gayle Korotkin happened to be at her home. They taped the conversation, during which Bowman pushed Eleanor to urge Timothy to fire Lewis, plead guilty, and testify against Hatcher.

Additionally, the plaintiffs sought to preclude the defendants from further harassing participants in the campaign to remove Sheriff Stone. The alleged harassment included SBI agents questioning campaign supporters and seeking membership rolls for the Tuscarora nation; mysterious cars parked outside the Robeson Defense Committee's office; and the sheriff's department pressuring the local school system to ban the committee's continued use of district facilities for meetings.

At a press conference to announce the lawsuit, Lewis said residents of Robeson County "are a changed people." He explained, "No longer will they sit by and take the reign of terror and the oppression, and this lawsuit reflects their changed attitude. They are calling the emperor naked. That's the positive spirit here one year after the takeover." The lawsuit demanded at least $10,000 in damages from each defendant and a judgment "declaring unconstitutional the campaign of intimidation and harassment," including the state criminal charges.

Judge Malcolm Howard—a former prosecutor, lawyer in the Nixon White House, and Reagan appointee—presided over the civil case. In February 1989, the plaintiffs moved for expedited discovery. In turn, the defendants requested a protective order from discovery, alleging the plaintiffs were improperly seeking information to use in the state criminal case. Howard sided with the defendants and prevented all discovery. Lewis reflected, "Think about that. If discovery was legitimate in the civil case, then what would be wrong with it being used in the criminal case?"

Before the order preventing discovery was lifted, the plaintiffs moved to dismiss their own lawsuit for three reasons. First, through his court-appointed attorney, Jacobs had arranged a plea agreement, thereby rendering moot the plaintiffs' Sixth Amendment claim that some of the defendants were interfering with Lewis's representation of Jacobs. Second, CIS and the Robeson Defense Committee lacked sufficient financial resources to both continue the civil case and aid in Hatcher's defense. Third, harassment by the SBI and sheriff's department subsided after the lawsuit was filed.

On May 2, 1989, a little more than three months after the lawsuit was filed, Howard granted the plaintiffs' motion to dismiss. Notwithstanding, the plaintiffs hoped to raise public awareness about the issues raised in the lawsuit during Hatcher's criminal trial.

Guilty Pleas

Two days after the lawsuit was dismissed, Jacobs, represented by his court-appointed attorney, pleaded guilty to all fourteen counts of second-degree kidnapping and agreed to testify against Hatcher. However, when he returned to court on June 19, 1989, Jacobs said he wouldn't testify against Hatcher after all. Jacobs was sentenced to six years in prison and an additional six years of a suspended sentence with supervised probation. In court, Jacobs apologized to the hostages. Afterward, he told the media, "I fought for my people, so I can go [to prison] with my head held high"; and "I'd like to be remembered as . . . an American Indian activist who tried to do something for his people." Lewis shared his perspective in the Christic Institute's newsletter:

> Under the circumstances, we agreed with Timothy's decision to plead guilty. . . . I certainly understand why Timothy did not want to gamble his liberty on getting a fair trial from the corrupt system.
>
> The hostage taking may have been wrong, but the result was to end once and for all the obscurity of this small, impoverished county ruled by drug pushers and corrupt officials. The citizens of Robeson County now know that they are not alone, that they have allies around the country, and that they have the power to organize for their rights.
>
> There's a long and hard road ahead for the people who live in Robeson County, and a long struggle before the dealers are jailed and corrupt officials removed from office. But the people already have begun to take the first steps.

Eventually, Hatcher also decided to cut his losses and plead guilty to the state criminal charges. On Valentine's Day 1990, he was sentenced to eighteen years in prison.

Jacobs ultimately served only two years of his six-year sentence before being released on parole. Hatcher was paroled after five years.

Sanctions

In June 1989, the state defendants filed a motion seeking Rule 11 sanctions against Lewis, Kunstler, and Nakell. Rule 11 of the Federal Rules of Civil Procedure—the same provision used against Christic Institute in the Contragate case—is supposed to ensure that claims brought in federal court have merit and aren't filed for an improper purpose, such as harassing, delaying, or needlessly increasing litigation costs. The defendants sought attorney's fees and court costs, calling the lawsuit "a propaganda and plea-bargaining tool." In their motion, AG Thornburg wrote, "Such misconduct holds to public ridicule and scorn high state officials . . . when no evidence suggests even one of these officials ever violated his professional responsibility or his public trust." The county defendants filed a similar motion less than a month later.

Lewis told the Associated Press that the AG's office was "shooting the messenger rather than looking at the substance of the message." Specifically, he said, "The state has elected to spend their resources and try and drain our resources on this issue rather than looking at the deplorable conditions of corruption and lawlessness in Robeson County." Lewis also pointed out to the media that the lawsuit "wasn't detrimental to the defendants" because the plaintiffs withdrew their complaint only three months after filing it.

The plaintiffs' attorneys filed motions for an evidentiary hearing on the Rule 11 motions and sanctions against the defendants "for filing their frivolous Rule 11 motion." Lewis, Kunstler, and Nakell retained Morton Stavis, cofounder of the Center for Constitutional Rights, to be their lead attorney.

In September 1989, having ignored the request for an evidentiary hearing, Judge Howard heard two hours of oral arguments regarding whether Lewis, Kunstler, and Nakell violated Rule 11. David Blackwell, an attorney in the state AG's office, told Howard, "The whole basis of their suit was hearsay, surmise, and suspicion. Much of their evidence they manufactured themselves." Stavis told Howard the request for sanctions contained "very mean and nasty personal attacks on counsel," and said, "It is time that the bar realizes that civil rights lawyers are not easy hunting." The *News and Observer* reported, "It was the legal equivalent of a stone-throwing contest. . . . The two sides clearly had considerable disregard for each other."

Three weeks later, Howard ordered Lewis, Kunstler, and Nakell to collectively pay $92,834, the full amount of the defendants' combined expenses, as well as $10,000 each for punitive sanctions. Moreover, the judge barred them from practicing law in the Eastern District of North Carolina until the full amounts were paid. He also denied the plaintiffs' motion for Rule 11 sanctions against the defendants.

Howard reasoned that the plaintiffs' attorneys never intended to litigate the lawsuit, but rather brought the case to generate publicity for their broader campaign, embarrass county and state officials, secure leverage and discovery for the state prosecution of Hatcher and Jacobs, and intimidate prosecutors. "In summary, the court finds that the entire complaint is tainted by improper purpose, and that counsel failed to conduct a reasonable inquiry into the factual and legal allegations they were making," Howard wrote.

Lewis told the *Winston-Salem Journal*, "The message is clear. People dare not challenge the state. People dare not tell the truth about Robeson County." Nakell called the sanctions "judicial McCarthyism." They published a handout, which read:

We believe the sanction was in part retaliation for our successful defense of Eddie Hatcher and Timothy Jacobs of all federal charges. . . .

This order is part of a recent trend to use Rule 11 to gag civil rights lawyers. It seriously affects lawyers, but the ultimate losers are citizens who have been deprived of their rights by public officials and who will now find it more difficult to obtain lawyers willing to challenge these officials. . . .

Our only regret is not having pursued the suit. . . .

What this says about the Federal court system as a forum for vindication of constitutional rights and the Federal judiciary as a "neutral" referee is tragic; what is says about social reform through litigation is sobering.

Lewis, Kunstler, and Nakell appealed to the US Court of Appeals for the Fourth Circuit. All three judges on their panel were Reagan appointees; one was a former prosecutor and assistant to Strom Thurmond. The panel, in September 1990, upheld Howard's finding that attorneys' fees and sanctions were owed but overturned the amount because the appellants were entitled to a hearing on the matter at which they could address their financial ability to pay.

Lewis, Kunstler, and Nakell filed a petition for a rehearing before the entire Fourth Circuit. A dozen religious and civil rights organizations—including the SCLC and Southern Organizing Committee for Economic and Social Justice—jointly filed an amicus brief supporting the petition. The organizations argued the sanctions were part of a pattern of "closing the courthouse doors" to grassroots activists who "have been marginalized because of their race, color, or economic status," and take legal action to secure constitutional rights. The North Carolina ACLU, Academy of Trial Lawyers, Association of Black Lawyers, and NLG Chapter also filed supporting amicus briefs.

Nevertheless, in October 1990, the Fourth Circuit denied their petition for a rehearing. Then, Lewis's petition for a writ of certiorari to the US Supreme Court was denied.

Lewis, Kunstler, and Nakell turned their attention to the district court hearing ordered by the Fourth Circuit. They collected and filed affidavits from twenty individuals who swore to the veracity of facts in the lawsuit. Lewis submitted the taped conversation between SBI Agent Bowman and Jacobs's mother, as well as his own affidavit, which read:

Doing the type of work I have been doing and intend to continue to do has caused me and my family . . . to have to live from
paycheck to paycheck. My wife has been working as a substitute
teacher for a year-and-a-half. . . . We are barely able to make [our]
house payments. . . . Both automobiles frequently need repair and
are not likely to last much longer. . . .

I have no confidence that anything I say now or any evidence I
provide to the court will make any difference, and I frankly think
it is a waste of time to try to respond point by point to each distor-
tion. If the facts, the law or my sworn word made any difference,
the case would not be in this posture. If I did not have a responsibility to my wife and child, to my colleagues and to our present
and future clients to try to minimize the impact of this sanction,
I would be loath to lend an air of legitimacy to such a travesty by
responding at all.

Although the hearing was supposed to be solely about the amount of
fees and fines, Lewis pushed Howard to revisit whether Rule 11 was violated.
During proceedings in August 1991, Lewis told him, "I want to talk now about
the state and county's effort to invent a history of misconduct on my part,
and . . . the Court's embracing that—" Howard interjected:

Things in your brief did trouble me. . . . You said Columbus coming to America began a legacy of conquest, genocide, slavery, and
theft. . . .

So don't start lambasting me. I think you better tell me what the
sanctions should be in your case and why. . . .

My decision was made, the Fourth Circuit confirmed it.
Whether you like it or not, you've got to live with it, and whether
or not I like it, I've got to live with it. I don't enjoy being here
today. I'd just as soon my original opinion had become the law of
this case but it wasn't. So, I'm coming back and want to hear you
tell me what the appropriate sanction should be in the case, not
re-litigate the case. I ain't going to do that.

Lewis continued: "Well, Your Honor, as you can probably tell, I don't give
much of a flip about the money. . . . It's personal anguish. . . . I feel the need
to go down the street and reach out to people and say, let me tell you what

really happened. . . . Attacking and destroying movements for democracy and equality under the guise of the law . . . is legalized repression, which is just a sophisticated way of talking about fascism."

North Carolina-based civil rights attorney, Al McSurely, who attended the hearing, wrote to Lewis, "Your oral argument yesterday was a masterpiece. . . . Honesty is revolutionary these days. . . . If a few breathing holes for the human spirit are not kept open, then all that is left are desperate acts of desperate people. You said that yesterday—but better yet—you demonstrated it boldly, courageously and honestly. I was right proud of you."

In September 1991, Howard reduced the sanctions to $50,000 for Lewis, Kunstler, and Nakell, jointly. Undeterred, Lewis again appealed to the Fourth Circuit, arguing that Howard disregarded the court's directive to consider Lewis's ability to pay, improperly punished Lewis for his political views and insistence about not having violated Rule 11, and should've recused himself. Lewis asserted in his brief that Howard's "extremely injudicious" actions were "driven less by facts and legal niceties . . . than by the court's unwillingness or inability to be objective about the facts and the law when confronted with an unacceptable message brought by unacceptable messengers." Two months after oral arguments in May 1992, the Fourth Circuit ordered Howard to further reduce the amount of the sanctions.

In July 1993, Howard issued an amended order further reducing the sanctions to $43,325. Lewis and Barry Nakell unsuccessfully petitioned the US Supreme Court for a writ of certiorari. The Committee to Defend Civil Rights Attorneys paid the sanctions for Lewis.

The Rule 11 sanctions in the Contragate and Robeson County cases took a heavy emotional toll on Lewis. He reflected on how his "feelings of personal worth and integrity took a big beating":

> All I had "accumulated" as a public interest lawyer for all those years was a good reputation for honesty, integrity, and adherence to principles, and demanding the same from government. My work has never paid much money; my personal worth or satisfaction came from doing good work and always acting with integrity and honesty; always seeking to achieve the highest moral standards; never exaggerating a claim or allegation. I would always teach students, interns, and staff: there is no need to exaggerate; the truth is bad and unjust enough.

The powers that be had reframed my work as dishonesty. It was
such a powerful and devastating official attack on my professional
reputation and credibility—like a judicial COINTELPRO. It
made me furious and confirmed my views that the legal system
primarily serves to protect the status quo. . . .

I wasn't chilled or guilt-ridden because I knew we never violated any of the prongs of Rule 11. Our purposes in both cases
were to uphold basic law and expose corruption by government
officials. I was mostly morally outraged, yet it was hard not to feel
hopeless. . . .

In fall 1989, while the Rule 11 orders in the Contragate and Robeson
County cases were being appealed, Lewis and his CIS colleagues remained
focused on movement lawyering and their racial justice mission. They were
heavily involved in a movement being led by Black residents of Daufuskie
Island, South Carolina.

CHAPTER 12

Movement to Protect Gullah Culture on Daufuskie Island, SC

The 1990s ushered in significant changes for CIS. Ashaki Binta left CIS to work with Black Workers for Justice in eastern North Carolina and focus full-time on her biggest passion—labor organizing among people of color. Lewis, CIS's assistant director Gayle Korotkin, and CIS's staff attorney Alan Gregory hired Mia Kirsh and Czerny Brasuell to join them.

Kirsh spent a decade in a farmworker movement before meeting her husband, who had learned of Christic and its Contragate case during his involvement in social justice movements in Central America. They moved to Chapel Hill, where they met Lewis and Korotkin. Kirsh started volunteering for CIS. Shortly thereafter, Lewis and Korotkin hired her as a part-time communications director. Kirsh wrote, "I thought Lewis was passionate, charismatic and amazingly southern, with his South Carolina drawl. Being a Northerner, I had not met many or any Southern civil rights folks. What struck me was how brave he, and others, were—living here 'in the belly of the beast' and trying to stand up against racism and the corruption of the good 'ol boy system. . . . I felt really honored to be able to work alongside Lewis and the others—who really walked the walk, not just talked the talk."

Kirsh did a bit of everything for CIS, which she described as a "bare bones, seat of the pants, little engine that could." She handled administrative tasks, conducted research, and produced the organization's newsletter.

Brasuell, a Black woman, was hired to replace Binta as CIS's director of development and community organizing. She had earned degrees from New York University and the University of Massachusetts at Amherst, taught courses at the City University of New York (CUNY), and served as director of the Third World Center at Princeton University, where she mentored Michelle Obama. Immediately prior to joining CIS, Brasuell worked at a Durham-based racial justice organization while pursuing her doctorate at the

University of North Carolina at Chapel Hill. She wrote about joining CIS, "The positions I held and the way in which the organization formulated a cohesive plan of action around the cases was a dream job. I was able to work in critical positions, with colleagues and within an organization, that mirrored my politics, my concerns, and my priorities. It was the perfect meld. Lewis was the perfect Director."

Finally, in June 1991, CIS moved to downtown Durham. The organization's newsletter explained: "CIS recently moved from an old house in Carrboro, NC (primarily a liberal white community) to a third floor suite on the 'Black Wall Street' of Durham, NC (thought of as one of this country's major strongholds of African American political and economic power). Although most of [CIS]'s work is spread out in many areas of the South, we are also cognizant that we are now in a diverse African American community and our work may have local impact as well."

These changes occurred while CIS staff were in the midst of a movement on Daufuskie Island.

History of Daufuskie

Daufuskie Island is approximately five miles long by three miles wide, and surrounded by Mungen Creek and the Cooper River, Calibogue Sound, Intracoastal Waterway, and Atlantic Ocean. Located in Beaufort County, Daufuskie is South Carolina's southernmost sea island. The island isn't connected to the mainland by bridge; most Daufuskie residents and visitors travel there by ferry or water taxi from Hilton Head or Bluffton, South Carolina.

During the nineteenth century, enslaved Africans tilled fields of indigo and cotton on Daufuskie. Plantation owners and their families spent much of each year away from the island, allowing enslaved people to retain much of their African culture.

After the Civil War, two of Daufuskie's remaining plantations were divided into parcels that were sold to newly freed Black people. Consequently, the island became home to a large population of formerly enslaved people. They were among the founders of Gullah language and culture.

Around the turn of the century, a new oyster cannery and logging boom drove Daufuskie's population up to about three thousand. However, over the next four decades, a boll weevil invasion, the Great Depression, and pollution from the Savannah River caused businesses to close and people to leave.

Daufuskie's primary industry became tourism after publication of Pat Conroy's *The Water Is Wide* in 1972. He wrote that Daufuskie "is beautiful because man has not yet had time to destroy" it. By 1980, Daufuskie's population had dwindled to about sixty, and the island was left with only a store, two-room schoolhouse, and church.

The island's nomination for the National Register of Historic Places, in 1982, read, "Daufuskie's population of fifty-nine is primarily black. They live on small (two to ten acre) tracts, much of it is 'heirs property,' a complicated legal condition which makes the land extremely vulnerable to loss of ownership." A CIS publication read:

> Daufuskie has been shackled with what some might call benign neglect. . . . The reality is that government and most social agencies on the mainland had no knowledge and even less concern about what was or was not occurring on Daufuskie. Common amenities of life were missing—any system of trash removal/disposal; medical care . . . ; means of procuring food and other commodities; boat service to the mainland or other islands. . . . For African Americans in the U.S., the continued existence of Daufuskie represents a phenomenal testament to the resiliency of a people determined to hold on to and pass on a culture which was considered at best without value, and at worst non-existent.

The Wilsons

Louise Wilson and her daughter, Yvonne, were two of the island's remaining residents. Louise was a fourth generation Daufuskie native and descendant of enslaved parents who once inhabited the island. Yvonne was born in April 1953. Louise worked multiple jobs, including catching and selling crabs, while Yvonne attended an elementary school that'd been built to segregate the island's Black children.

At age thirteen, Yvonne moved to Savannah to complete secondary school. She then completed one year of college in New York, before spending the next decade and a half living in Savannah, Hilton Head, and Bluffton, and working as a cosmetologist and waitress. In her mid-thirties, Yvonne moved back to Daufuskie, where she worked as a teacher's aide and school bus driver. A *Los Angeles Times* reporter wrote, "Yvonne Wilson's trailer is crowded with animals and children. It smells like Ajax. A goat, Jack, is tied up outside. . . . Wilson is a short, vital . . . woman who wears combat boots. . . . She's a Gullah, one of 23 remaining on Daufuskie. . . . Wilson is a modern Gullah, someone who doesn't regularly use the traditional dialect but understands it, someone who works a mainstream job Monday through Friday but might spend a weekend at a Gullah reunion banging on a goatskin drum and singing African songs."

Invasion of Daufuskie

Charles Cauthen, a real estate agent in Hilton Head, learned that a family was selling its property on Daufuskie, which amounted to forty-seven percent of the island. He created a development plan for the land and assembled a group of investors, including the chief executive officer (CEO) of Halliburton. On behalf of the group, the Daufuskie Island Land Trust, Cauthen purchased the land for $4.5 million in 1980.

In 1984, International Paper Realty Corporation purchased more than one thousand acres—the entire northeastern portion of the island—from the trust for $8.5 million; and Melrose Company purchased 720 acres on the eastern and southeastern portions of the island from the trust for $6.5 million. The sales included most of Daufuskie's oceanfront land.

By the mid-1980s, developers began ravaging the island as part of a projected twenty-year, $500 million "transformation." Melrose Company began building Melrose Plantation on the eastern property and Bloody Point Club and Resort on the southeastern land. Both areas would become private golf clubs and residential communities, with membership fees of at least $50,000. In 1986, International Paper founded the Haig Point Club. Membership required purchase of a plot for construction of a home.

By 1991, nearly half of the island's 5,000 acres had been "developed," alarming the Wilsons and other Daufuskie natives. Yvonne told the *Beaufort Gazette*, "For generations, this island has been an open community. You could go anywhere on the island. It didn't matter who you were. People shared. If someone caught fish everyone had fish. That is no longer true. Half this island is now off-limits." She shared with the *Los Angeles Times*, "We used to think we had a lot. But when you see people building big houses and wearing beautiful clothes and having nothing else to do but lie around in the sun, you start to say to yourself, 'Gee, I've been fooling myself all this time.'" "We're becoming an endangered species," she expressed to the *New York Times*. Louise declared to the *Charlotte Observer*, "They want to rule 'Fuskie and they're not gonna do it. I'll die and go to hell first. Yessir, boy, this place sure gone down." Lawrence Jenkins, another Daufuskie native, told the *Washington Post*, "I'll tell you how I feel and I ain't gonna tell you no lie. They done bought Daufuskie from under us, might as well say."

Daufuskie's Black residents couldn't afford the island's skyrocketing property taxes, which allowed banks and county tax collectors to seize their land to sell to developers. A South Carolina Tax Commission investigation concluded that they were unaware of, or misunderstood, tax law. *Newsweek* reported, "Some white landowners with valuable waterfront property are paying less in taxes than blacks with land in the interior. The whites took advantage of a generously applied agricultural exemption in the tax code. . . . Ed Gay, the island's former tax assessor, says the tax breaks were available to everyone, but that the 'whites are more educated than the blacks and they understood what we were talking about.'" Beaufort County Council Chairman Bill Bowen—a white attorney who handled banking, construction, and real estate matters—callously insisted that residents who couldn't afford the taxes should sell their land and leave.

Moreover, developers bulldozed woodlands, rerouted roads through fragile wetlands, eroded beaches, and polluted water and wildlife with pesticides used on golf courses. "We have become a people afraid of what we eat and drink," Yvonne said. The *Washington Post* read, "Hunting deer and rabbit, long-time residents used to roam that land freely. Now, there are fences and 'No Trespassing' signs to keep them off land where vacation cottages, small inns, golf courses, riding paths and beach clubs now stand."

Lewis and others viewed the inequitable burdens of exploding property taxes, land consolidation by white developers and homeowners, and environmental destruction as symptoms of racism. Reverend Joe Agne, a member of the National Council of Churches' Racial Justice Working Group, called the development "cultural genocide" and told the *Chicago Tribune*, "This is one more case where rich people are taking land from poor people. The more land they lose, the closer their culture is to being extinct." Henrietta Canty, a Georgia legislator, called the tax assessment handling "covert racism." Pulitzer Prize winning journalist Jeffrey Gettleman wrote in the *Los Angeles Times*, "Daufuskie was no longer a tranquil refuge for families of former slaves. It was an emerging high-class resort, complete with pastel cottages, rising property values and rich white people swinging in hammocks." Pat Conroy called the invasion "an American tragedy," and said in a speech, "I still read about

Daufuskie Island and much of what I read makes me sick. . . . The great threat to blacks in the Sea Islands is that white people find their land beautiful. Blacks no longer have to fear the Klan. Now they have to fear golf courses and country clubs." Jimmy Buffett sang about the destruction of culture and land on Daufuskie in his song "Prince of Tides."

Cooper River Cemetery

The land being destroyed by developers included the Cooper River Cemetery, a sacred African burial ground. The cemetery lies on the west side of Daufuskie Island, where the Cooper River Plantation was located during the nineteenth century. After the Civil War, the plantation's owner divided his five hundred acres into smaller plots and sold them to formerly enslaved people. These formerly enslaved people and their descendants believed souls of the dead entered the Cooper River's waters from the burial grounds in order to access the Atlantic Ocean, make the voyage home to Africa, and join the spirit world.

By 1971, an estimated forty-five people were buried in the Cooper River Cemetery. Most graves weren't formally marked for various reasons. Some families couldn't afford headstones, headstones had been stolen or destroyed, and African traditions called for placement of "grave goods"—such as plates, spoons, medicine bottles, and other household belongings—atop graves, instead of headstones. Louise Wilson's father, grandmother, grandfather, aunt, great-uncle, and cousins are buried in the cemetery. She wanted to be buried there with her family.

However, in 1979, John Scurry, "Jack," took ownership of the land on which the cemetery is located. In January 1985, he transferred the title, which included a dock, to Cooper River Landing and Properties, Inc. Scurry was president, and his son, William, was secretary, of the company. Scurry hired Joe Harden Builder to construct a welcome center cottage, parking lot, and pathways, which he then leased to Melrose Plantation.

Louise and Yvonne Wilson, and other Black Daufuskie residents, claimed the cottage was built atop part of the Cooper River Cemetery. They cited an 1884 land survey map, which showed at least one acre—identified as "graveyard"—that covered all land at the juncture of the Cooper River and a small creek. They further asserted that, since the survey, the cemetery had grown to include an additional, contiguous acre. Additionally, locals told the *Los*

Angeles Times that they'd witnessed construction workers tossing headstones and bones into the Cooper River during construction of the cottage.

Developers, on the other hand, claimed the cemetery was only a half acre and had eroded into the Cooper River prior to construction; and thus, the welcome center wasn't on the burial grounds. They also alleged that the cemetery had been neglected and abandoned. Bud Bates, a local white real estate agent, told the *Chicago Tribune*, "If you don't care enough about your ancestor to let a tree grow through the grave, then you don't give a damn."

CIS Joins the Nascent Movement

In fall 1989, Henrietta Canty, a Black Georgia legislator who owned land on Daufuskie Island, contacted CIS regarding racial disparities in property taxation. Lewis, Korotkin, and Brasuell visited Daufuskie to investigate. They learned that the problems facing the island's Black residents also included environmental degradation, cemetery desecration, and inadequate public services, such as ferry transportation.

For the next few years, CIS staff, the Wilsons, and other advocates and island residents campaigned against corporate developers and their allies. Lewis wrote, "We used our typical model: combined tactics of litigation, public education, and community organizing to serve the strategic goal of building and protecting the people's movement for justice, self-determination, and self-government."

While working in the area, Lewis stayed with friends of friends and supporters of the campaign, such as Joann Dimond. She was a white Hilton Head resident who raised funds and support for the campaign. Lewis also spent a night in a rustic cabin that the Penn Center—a historic landmark and African American cultural and educational center—built as a retreat space for Martin Luther King Jr. Asked about his most vivid initial impression of Daufuskie, Lewis wrote, "The mosquitoes were so damn big! I brought one back, clasped into a notebook, to show Katie and Stephen."

Community Organizing and Education

CIS staff decided not to pursue legal action over the taxation issue because of their limited resources and the exceedingly low likelihood of success before, in their words, the "Reagan-influenced federal judiciary." Instead, they believed that helping to build a strong grassroots movement ought to be their immediate focus.

Lewis recalled disagreements among local Black residents about the development. Some welcomed new jobs, even low-paying ones, and increasing property values, albeit with higher taxes. This dynamic made organizing more "delicate and complicated," he said. According to Brasuell, CIS staff and local leaders organized community meetings and canvassed door-to-door, figuring out who "was angry or outraged enough to speak out" and "wanted to take control of their own struggle."

Most of the people organizing and being organized were Black women. Lewis recalled, "Czerny was fantastic in her work with Yvonne and other island women to empower and train them in skills needed to be an activist leader, such as making an argument, public speaking, and reading and learning the history of the struggle for racial justice and justice for women. Yvonne soaked this up like a sponge."

A CIS priority was "strengthening the leadership of the Daufuskie Island Community Improvement Club with the goal of making it an effective interracial vehicle for addressing the many common problems confronting the people." The club began as part of the War on Poverty but needed to be reactivated after two and a half decades of dormancy. In September 1989, Yvonne became the club's president. During the first year under her leadership, the club secured the island's first public dumpster and garbage pickup by Beaufort County. The club also helped defeat a measure—proposed by William Scurry—that would've limited the time tour boats could stop at the public dock, thereby reducing opportunities for locals to sell food and goods.

Additionally, CIS staff recruited outside allies to support local efforts. For instance, they formed a Daufuskie Island Project Advisory Board, which included Pat Conroy; Guy and Candie Carawan of the Highlander Center; Tyrone Pitts, director for racial justice for the National Council of Churches' Division of Church and Society; Mike Espy, US congressman from Mississippi; Emory Campbell, executive director of the Penn Center; and others.

CIS staff also connected the club with Mayor Emma Gresham and Greenpeace. At the annual Daufuskie Day Festival, Gresham spoke about her experiences in Keysville. Greenpeace brought attention to environmental degradation on the island.

Moreover, CIS staff arranged for twenty-five members of the National Council of Churches' Racial Justice Working Group to tour Daufuskie. During a press conference afterward, spokesman Reverend Joe Agne announced that the group had observed "oppression by race," "human greed destroying the unique Sea Island culture and environment," and "a genocidal approach to so-called development." He noted that including "plantation" in the name of Melrose's community was the "ultimate insult." The Working Group's subsequent report found "unconscionable racism destroying a viable and proud culture" and "the worship of profits at the expense of people."

The Prophetic Justice Unit of the National Council of Churches collaborated with CIS to sponsor a similar fact-finding mission to Daufuskie. Approximately thirty religious leaders met with executives from Haig Point, visited burial grounds, and were briefed by Lewis and Brasuell. Melrose Plantation executives refused to meet with the delegation. The unit concluded that the island's crisis was deliberate "cultural genocide and racial exploitation and oppression." The council called for congressional hearings about the plight of remaining Daufuskie natives who were "refusing to be driven from their homes and land."

CIS's organizing and education efforts also included media and letter-writing campaigns. CIS staff brought *60 Minutes* to the island and the campaign was covered in umpteen national newspapers. In a letter to Daufuskie property owners, Lewis outlined problems with "attempting to turn Daufuskie into another Hilton Head." CIS staff aided Louise Wilson in writing to island residents:

> I am 72 years old and am a fifth generation Daufuskie native and resident. I was born on Daufuskie in the days of horses and buggies, clean air and water, when beaches and roads were open to everyone, and concern for one another was a heartfelt expression of our common status of God's children. . . .
>
> Our way of life was certainly not luxurious, but there is value in a simple life. We worked hard, raised our own food, sewed our own clothes, raised our children to be self-sufficient, productive and caring members of the community. We were, and are, proud of our unique culture, which we preserved through the horrors of abduction and slavery, and which kept us together as a people for over three hundred years. . . .
>
> Melrose and Haig Point Plantations are building resorts . . . all over the island without regard for my history, my culture and my feelings. . . . I am poor in money, yet rich in heritage, but what will I have to leave my daughter and my grandchildren except a

landscape of golf courses and plantation homes? Doesn't my past
and their future count?

Joann Dimond wrote to "fellow landowners," describing how "the Beaufort
County resort economy is built upon racism" and the development involved
"low paying jobs," "cultural destruction," "segregation," and "paternalistic attitude." "If you are silent, then you become complicit," she concluded.

Ethics Complaints

In addition to organizing and education, CIS and the plaintiffs used ethics
rules to go after developers and raise awareness about collusion. For example,
in January 1990, CIS released a report about how Wes Jones was, at once, a
member of the Coastal Council, which managed permits and was supposed
to protect the natural environment, and a lawyer for Melrose, which requested
permits from the Coastal Council. The report read, "These two different roles
impose conflicting duties and involve conflicting loyalties. . . . You don't ask
the fox to guard the hen house. You don't ask lawyers for developers to regulate developers."

Jones was also appointed by South Carolina Governor Carroll Campbell
as the state's representative on the Coastal States Organization, a national
nonprofit that represents governors on legislative and policy issues related
to sound management of coastal resources. Lewis brought Jones's conflict of
interest to the attention of Campbell, who, according to CIS materials, was
a member of Melrose Plantation and brother-in-law of Jones's law partner.
Lewis urged Campbell to remove Jones, calling the conflict of interest "dis-
graceful and an insult to the fine populace of S.C."

Lewis and Yvonne filed a complaint against Jones with the South Carolina Ethics Commission. They alleged that Jones violated a state ethics law
(Section 450), which read, "No person shall serve as a member of a government regulatory agency that regulates any business with which that person
is associated." Specifically, they accused Jones of identifying himself as legal
counsel for Melrose in materials submitted to the Coastal Council in March
and May of 1989, and "using his position as a public official for his own personal benefit as well as that of his client."

The Ethics Commission found probable cause to support the allegations
and scheduled a hearing for December 1990. However, before the hearing, the

Coastal Council filed a petition in the South Carolina Supreme Court, arguing that councilmembers were exempt from Section 450. Lewis and Korotkin unsuccessfully moved to intervene. They claimed the Ethics Commission and Coastal Council were colluding to avoid the hearing and conceal facts regarding Jones's and other councilmembers' conflicts of interest.

The state supreme court heard oral arguments in June 1991. Despite his failed motion to intervene, Lewis stood and asked the justices for three minutes to address "a material misrepresentation of fact." His request was denied.

In October 1991, the court issued an opinion that Lewis called "doublespeak and gobbledygook." The decision read, "The dispositive question in this case is whether Coastal Council 'regulates any business.' . . . We conclude that Coastal Council regulates the preservation and utilization of coastal resources. . . . Although Coastal Council may incidentally affect various aspects of a business, it does not specifically regulate any particular business."

Undeterred, Lewis petitioned the court for a rehearing. He also encouraged the State Ethics Commission to "seek appropriate amendment(s) to make it clear that Section 450 forbids coastal developers and their agents from sitting on the Coastal Council" and "proceed promptly with Ms. Wilson's complaint." While the complaint was pending, Jones was elected chairman of the Coastal Council.

The commission found that Jones didn't violate Section 450. The commission noted that, while Jones's firm appeared before the council, Jones himself never represented Melrose on a matter before the council or served on any council committee that ruled on a Melrose request. Lewis responded to the commission's director, "I find the Decision and Order dishonest and your continuing silence about these matters to be complicity in the dishonesty. . . . These calculated omissions serve to protect Jones as he . . . hurts the fine people of my home state. Shame, shame, shame. . . . This is nothing more than a systemic scam. Meanwhile you and your staff remain silent as church mice."

Cemetery Lawsuit Complaint

On September 7, 1990, Lewis and Korotkin filed a lawsuit in the Fourteenth Circuit Court of Common Pleas in Beaufort County about desecration of the Cooper River Cemetery. They brought the case on behalf of six Black people who were descendants of individuals buried in the cemetery and wished to be buried there themselves: Louise and Yvonne Wilson; Paul Johnson and his mother, Lillian Spencer; Samuel Jenkins; and Frances Jones. Jenkins had four grandparents, two great-grandparents, and three uncles buried in the cemetery. Jones was born on Daufuskie Island in 1910, a resident and teacher there for more than three decades, and nicknamed the "unofficial mayor of Daufuskie"; and he had a grandmother and three cousins buried in the cemetery.

The defendants included Melrose Company, Cooper River Landing and Properties, Joe Harden Builder, and Jack Scurry. The lawsuit alleged they trespassed on and desecrated the cemetery in violation of state law and the plaintiffs' "rights to preserve, honor, and memorialize their descendants." The complaint further alleged the defendants were negligent in failing to "properly demark the area of the cemetery," "apply for and obtain consent to the removal of those interred," "employ adequately skilled workers," "use reasonable care to avoid unlawful intrusion," and "preserve the sanctity, dignity and integrity of the cemetery."

The plaintiffs' requested relief included precluding the defendants from maintaining and utilizing the cottage and other areas atop the burial grounds; enjoining the defendants from prohibiting visitors to and burials at the cemetery; declaring boundaries for the cemetery; compensatory and punitive damages for the plaintiffs' "great grief, mental anguish and anxiety"; and reimbursement for the costs of the lawsuit.

CIS staff and the plaintiffs hoped the lawsuit would also achieve four additional goals. First, they intended to fuel local grassroots organizing. A CIS fundraising letter explained, "The suit was designed to put a brake on the land theft and, as importantly, instill a sense of 'fight and win' in the island residents and their relatives and supporters."

Second, they intended to send a message to developers. Louise told *Sojourners*, "It may be a losing battle, but you gotta show some people you're not scared. You got to fight back and let them know you was here when they came." The *Washington Post* read, "Wilson said [CIS] has helped her learn how to challenge the changes on the island. The point of the lawsuit, in addition to removal of the cottage, is to let the developers know that people of the island 'ain't just gonna sit back and be run over because of economics,' Yvonne Wilson said."

Third, the lawsuit was meant to connect the invasion of Daufuskie with systemic racism. At a press conference to announce the complaint, Lewis said destruction of the graveyard was symbolic of the "economic racism and cultural genocide which characterize the new plantation economy of the area." *Sojourners* read, "The lawsuit has ramifications well beyond the future of a small Sea Island. It brings together, says Lewis Pitts, . . . several issues that comprise a plague for African-Americans across the nation."

Finally, the lawsuit was designed to defend the existence of native island-ers and their culture. Lewis shared with the *Savannah News-Press* that the plaintiffs felt "like there has been a threat to totally wipe them out to make a playground for the rich." He explained to the *Chicago Tribune*, "We all lose a sense of history in the ripping apart of this African community. The strength and tenacity it's taken for this culture to hang in there, that's a valuable thing to preserve. There's something to learn from a culture that hangs on like that." *Washington Post* coverage of the lawsuit—titled, "A Touch of Africa Makes a Last Stand"—read, "Islanders and newcomers, in various factions, are at odds over much more, such as who has the right to speak for the island; which roads are to be public and whether they should be paved; who can ride the school ferry that takes students across the water to high school; what Daufuskie will be in years to come; and, perhaps most difficult, whether the price of progress will be the loss of a culture. . . . 'I feel like the Native Americans when they talk about their sacred ground,' said Yvonne Wilson." She explained to *So-journers*, "If we don't fight this, our whole way of life will be lost. It's a survival thing now. We have to survive this plague in the midst of paradise."

In response to the lawsuit and negative press, the defendants publicly claimed the plaintiffs were factually wrong—the cemetery's boundaries were limited to a half-acre plot, which hadn't been disturbed by the cottage. Ad-ditionally, the defendants argued that their work benefited local residents by reviving Daufuskie's economy. Stephen Kiser, a Melrose Company partner, said, "Development is here because people want it." He added, "Cultures do pass, you know. I'm delighted to take the challenge." Lastly, the defendants blamed the conflict on "dissenters" out to make headlines, obviously referring to CIS. Kiser said, "I know they're receiving outside training. It's very ominous to me."

Retaliation

Even before the lawsuit was filed, the plaintiffs, especially Yvonne, faced re-taliation for their activism. For example, Doug Hancock, who operated Mel-rose's dockside store, reportedly yelled threats and racial epithets at Yvonne and other Black residents. Lewis intervened, writing to Kiser, "If this conduct does not stop, we will take every step available to us under civil and criminal law to protect Ms. Wilson and other residents."

Less than a month after the lawsuit was filed, the developers and their supporters staged what CIS characterized as a "coup." During a Daufuskie Island Community Improvement Club meeting at Union Baptist Church, Kiser and his posse unexpectedly appeared. After he distributed new bylaws that allowed officers to be removed by majority vote, his faction immediately ousted Yvonne and the group's other Black leaders and elected new officers. Joyce Richards became interim president. Bud Bates, a member of the white mob, claimed, "Eventually the Christic Institute pretty much controlled the agenda of our meetings. . . . We put a stop to this once and for all." Yvonne told *Sojourners*, "They started cursing and hooting and hollering like crazy people—in the church, no less, in God's house. . . . They went to their cars drinking. . . . I'm thinking, this is how Ku Klux Klan rallies get together; people may kill me. It was shocking and frightening."

In November 1990, Ed Richards—a county-funded boat operator, owner of Island Charter Services, and Joyce Richards's husband—prevented Lewis, Korotkin, and Joann Dimond from riding the only publicly available ferry from Hilton Head to Daufuskie for a club meeting. Richards told them that county officials directed him to only transport residents and school children. According to CIS records, Richards also said that, since they were pursuing litigation against Melrose and his boat docked at Melrose Plantation, the company prohibited him from transporting them. Lewis, Korotkin, and Dimond boarded the boat anyway, and then refused to disembark. Richards called the Beaufort County Sheriff's Department. Three other boats arrived to transport schoolchildren, adult residents, and Richards. Lewis, Korotkin, and Dimond were left behind and missed the meeting.

The following day, CIS held a press conference about the ordeal. Lewis accused developers of "using the armed might of the sheriff's department and the threat of deprivation of human services to literally control, as if in South Africa, who gets to go to Daufuskie Island and who gets to leave Daufuskie Island."

Residents, members, and employees of Haig Point and Melrose Plantation had regular access to private boats for travel to and from the island. For Daufuskie's Black residents, Richards's collusion with developers was especially problematic because no other public ferry service was available.

Developers and their allies also publicly maligned CIS and the plaintiffs. In doing so, wealthy white people portrayed a fictionalized history of racial harmony, blamed "radical outside agitators," played on Cold War-era anticommunist sentiments, and paternalistically claimed to be defending and speaking for local Black residents. An op-ed in the *Island Packet* described the ferry incident as "an obviously staged confrontation, perpetrated by a radical Daufuskie Island faction, and aided and abetted by an alien (to Daufuskie) organization, the Christic Institute South." Wick Scurry, whose father had the cottage built on the Cooper River Cemetery, wrote in the *Island Packet*, "Outside people have . . . caused absolute turmoil, pitting one resident against another." He also told a reporter that "a bunch of people left over from the '60s" were "causing trouble," "trying very hard to make it look like anybody who is doing development on the island is against blacks," and "taking advantage of some of the ignorance of the people around here." Wes Jones, Melrose Company's lawyer and the target of Lewis's ethics complaint, accused CIS staff of being "irresponsible agitators," with "links reaching as far as the Communist Party." In *Island Packet* op-eds, Bud Bates, a white real estate agent, called CIS staff "radicals," "sensationalists," and "specialists in turmoil," who "absolutely do not represent the feeling of Daufuskie Islanders, black or white." He wrote, "It is time now to put things back together, blacks and whites working together as we have in years past. I would like to issue a message to these outside groups: 'You are always welcome to visit here, but don't ever try and tell us how to run our business.'" Bates told the *Beaufort Gazette* that CIS "divided . . . blacks and whites who always got along together." A letter to the editor in the *Savannah Morning News* accused CIS staff of associating with organizations that incite "insurrection in Third World countries," never having "met a 'red' they didn't like," and "openly express[ing] their acceptance of homosexual and lesbian behavior."

Jim Warren, Lewis's long-time friend and executive director of the North Carolina Waste Awareness and Reduction Network (NC WARN), recalled an incident that occurred while he was visiting Lewis on the island: "After Lewis gave a talk to the community folks at a cookout, an angry worker for the development corporation, a white male, confronted Lewis in a heated discussion, up close. . . . He was a big, burly guy intent on intimidating Lewis, but my friend stood his ground, listened to the fellow patiently, and then explained his own position in a manner that de-escalated the situation."

Cemetery Lawsuit Pretrial

On October 11, 1990, the defendants filed their answer to the complaint and a motion to dismiss the case. They argued that, in 1979, a legal proceeding to determine ownership of the land established that the cemetery was a half-acre plot, separate from where the cottage was constructed; and the three-year statute of limitations on challenging that finding had passed. Lewis countered that a platting in 1884, and subsequent maps, showed a one-acre cemetery and the public notice required before the 1979 proceeding was inadequate.

Lewis Hammet, an attorney for the defendants, wrote to Lewis:

> Believe it or not, my clients are more concerned about the sensibilities of Daufuskie residents than you are, and are less concerned with the financial implications of the cemetery issues.
>
> We . . . wish that you had talked to us before your lawsuit, press conferences, and fundraising publication. We have no choice other than to contest your allegations, which we believe to be unfounded, but my clients intend to be good citizens of Daufuskie Island long after Daufuskie ceases to serve your purposes. I hope we can proceed to resolve any legitimate issues without further character assassination and pretrial publicity. Given your agenda, I may be naive in this request.

Lewis fired back, "You seem to hold 'public interest' lawyering in contempt, as do most Establishment lawyers. . . . As for your insinuation that we are using Daufuskie for selfish purposes, I make $25,000 a year representing poor and oppressed people. Who do you represent and how much do you make? . . . If you seriously want to talk about resolving this matter equitably, then call or write with some concrete proposal. Otherwise, see you in court and in the public arena."

In January 1991, Beaufort County Judge Thomas Kemmerlin held a hearing on the defendants' motion to dismiss. Lewis and Kemmerlin had known each other for years. Like Lewis, Kemmerlin graduated from Wofford College and the USC Law School; and they had a mutual friend in Jon Thames, Lewis's favorite law professor. Nevertheless, Lewis was concerned Kemmerlin might be biased against him and his clients because of recent negative press about Christic Institute and CIS. Lewis was also frustrated, sensitive, and insecure because of the Contragate and Robeson County Rule 11 findings. Consequently, during the first hearing, Lewis attempted to explain the sanctions and probe Kemmerlin's possible biases. Kemmerlin acknowledged that Lewis had "represent[ed] awfully unpopular causes" and they "very seldom agreed . . . on any social issue." However, Kemmerlin also said he'd never questioned Lewis's integrity, had "no prejudice whatsoever" against Lewis, and would decide the case based on the facts and law.

Their discussion in open court then shifted to race:

LEWIS: This case is . . . focused around, inevitably, racial issues.

KEMMERLIN: The law of cemeteries is a question of real estate law, and it wouldn't make a bit of difference under the law whether white people or Black people were in this cemetery. It just happens that they're Black. . . . Now, you may raise a bunch of other social issues. . . . None of that concerns me. All I'm concerned about is, under the law, whether the cemetery was taken and desecrated. If it was, you're entitled to damages. If it wasn't, you ain't. . . .

KEMMERLIN: I do not regard it as a racial issue. Even if it was a racial issue, . . . I have no bias or prejudice that would prevent me from giving a fair trial. I frequently say . . . I was born a white man. I have had to pray for years not to have racial prejudice and gradually I think I've overcome it. I did not take communion for thirteen years because I had so much racial prejudice. . . . Four years ago, I took communion again.

After his back-and-forth with Lewis, Kemmerlin denied the defendants' motion to dismiss.

The next pretrial hearing, in April 1991, focused on whether the lawsuit could include the waterway in front of the cemetery. On behalf of the plaintiffs, Lewis explained how a commercial dock constructed adjacent to the cemetery interfered with movement of the dead to the water that provided access to the spiritual world. Kemmerlin characterized Lewis's argument and the plaintiffs' beliefs as a "bunch of junk," and said, "If the spirit can go to Africa by the water, this bridge ain't going to stop it. . . . They're entitled to their beliefs, but they're entitled to their beliefs in the face of all the law in the Western World."

The next day, CIS filed a motion to disqualify Kemmerlin and a supporting memo describing his comments as "undignified," "injudicious," and indicative of "a bias against the religion and culture of the plaintiffs." Before addressing the motion, Kemmerlin ruled the case wouldn't include the dock issue.

Nearly five months later, Judge Kemmerlin held a hearing on CIS's recusal motion. He told Lewis, "Whether the people are Black, red or green has nothing to do with whether they crossed a line. That's the lawsuit." Lewis reminded Kemmerlin of his previous comment about taking communion.

Kemmerlin responded, "I've told you, I grew up in rural South Carolina. I certainly had a prejudice against Black people. I was raised that way." "Why else would you refer to their religious beliefs as a bunch of junk," Lewis asked.

Their heated back-and-forth continued. Lewis accused Kemmerlin of trying "to take out the public interest aspects" of the case, including concerns over racism, environmental issues, and "collusion between public officials and big developers." Kemmerlin responded, "Yeah, but all those things got nothing to do with this lawsuit at this stage." "Well, they absolutely do," Lewis retorted. Kemmerlin directed Lewis to "bring that suit somewhere else." Lewis told Kemmerlin:

> This is ticking you off . . . and you're trying to reshape the case to be a little tiny personal redress between a few people and an innocent boundary line. . . . Judge, do the right thing here for your sake, for the sake of my and your home state.
>
> At least . . . try to allow people to have a sense of faith and integrity of the system of redress because look at what that means if they don't. They get disengaged in the democracy and worse, they engage in self-help.
>
> You're a judge. You've got the power to tell me that this lawsuit can't raise that dock. . . . I want to raise it because it's a public concern. . . . I'm the kind of lawyer that does that, and there is an effort to make these kinds of lawyers extinct.
>
> Somehow, there's something wrong and devious about raising these public broader issues. We're talking about the Constitution; I believe in it. Let me read this quote from the Fourth Circuit; . . . "Civil actions may also involve questions of public concern. . . . The lawyer involved in such cases can often enlighten public debate." Well, this is not the first time that I've had opposing lawyers wave in front of a judge a newspaper article, as if I've committed a sin because I'm telling on his client to the press. That's what we do under the First Amendment, Your Honor.

Lewis referenced another case in which former US Supreme Court Justice William Brennan wrote, "We consider this case against the background of a profound national commitment to the principle that debate on public issues should be uninhibited, robust, and wide-open, and that it may well include vehement, caustic, and sometimes unpleasantly sharp attacks on government and public officials."

Kemmerlin denied CIS's recusal motion. Lewis told the *Beaufort Gazette*, "He goes out of his way to avoid discussing or even looking at the main controversy, which is collusion between developers and public officials." Kemmerlin quipped, "He fights in the press. I don't." *Sojourners* read, "Most court cases, says Pitts, are what he calls 'Piggly vs. Wiggly suing over widgets.' But he says, 'If you bring in gross inequities aimed at systemic change, the judiciary spreads its wings to protect the system. . . . It completely dismantles our constitutional democracy.'"

CIS staff and the plaintiffs pressed forward with trial preparations. They arranged for two experts, Michael Trinkley and Elaine Nichols, to testify about the history and significance of the cemetery. Trinkley is an archeologist and director of the Chicora Foundation, a heritage preservation organization. At the time, Nichols worked at the South Carolina State Museum. She later became the supervisory curator of culture at the Smithsonian National Museum of African American History and Culture. In 2018, she wrote,

> When I first met Lewis, I was immediately impressed and deeply moved by his dedication to his work. He struck me as someone who had given his all to making the world a better and a fairer place for as many people as possible. . . . I recall that he was brilliant and seemed to pay very close attention to the details, which, in my mind made him a formidable adversary, as his opponents probably underestimated his abilities. He was genuinely kind and an altogether lovely person.
>
> I remember him as a model of courage and it moves me to tears. . . . I can only say that he is an American hero and a person of great integrity.

CIS staff also prepared the plaintiffs to be deposed by the defendants' attorneys. Fortunately, according to Lewis, his clients were strong, resilient, and capable. During a deposition held at the cemetery, plaintiff Paul Johnson said to the defendants' lawyers, "I'm hostile toward you people because you're the problem. . . . I know what money and power can do. . . . That's my understanding of what happened here, and it's wrong—and it's about time it was stopped, and I'll do whatever I can to stop you." Lewis recalled the deposition of Louise Wilson, which also took place at the burial grounds:

> As we all walked around this sacred, primitive, and beautiful bit of the island, with water nearby and moss hanging from the trees, the defendants' attorneys were trying to trick Ms. Wilson into an error or contradiction about what she knew about her relatives buried in the cemetery—exactly where were they buried, how did she know, etc. She tried to explain, in her thick Gullah accent, how the customs were not like European cemeteries, with clear cut individual burial sites. The corporate lawyers kept hammering away, sometimes in harsh, challenging ways and sometimes in paternalistic, plantation owner, honey dripping style. They clearly hoped to make a fool out of this elderly and proud woman.
>
> After she had all she could stand of that legal gamesmanship, Ms. Wilson looked up from the ground—so sacred to her, with all its implications of slavery, the theft of the land, and dying culture—stared right at the defense attorney, and, in a voice that echoed around the trees and moss, shouted, "DAMN YOU!" I felt the power of centuries of history, resistance and fightback being encapsulated in those seconds of resistance. It made me even more compelled to continue the fight and gave me some optimism that we would win at least some aspect of the battle. While I can't be certain, it seems her roar of justice penetrated the defendants' attorneys; they ended the deposition right then and there.

In October 1992, less than three weeks before the trial was scheduled to begin, a judge granted the defendants' motion to add another party—the man who'd surveyed the land where the cemetery was located. The defendants argued they were innocent victims of the surveyor's errors. Procedural rules dictated a postponement of the trial for at least another 120 days so the surveyor could prepare his case. Lewis believes the existing defendants were scapegoating the surveyor and leveraging their greater resources to delay the case from being heard by a jury.

Cemetery Lawsuit: Settlement

In August 1992, Joe Harden Builder settled with the plaintiffs for $1,500. The remaining defendants finally settled in May 1993—two years, eight months after CIS filed the lawsuit. Pursuant to the agreement, the cemetery's bound-aries would be drawn to include one full acre, with borders adjacent to the creek and Cooper River, thereby giving the dead direct access to the water. The agreement also included protection of an additional three-fifths of an acre along the creek in order to allow for public access to the river; access rights for the plaintiffs and others wishing to visit loved ones buried in the cemetery; a prohibition on restricting future burials within the one acre; removal of the cottage by the end of 1993; and payment of $12,500 from Melrose Company to the plaintiffs.

Lewis wrote to his organization's board, "While not perfect, we are satis-fied with this result, especially in light of the uncertain outcome of a trial in the Good Old Boys' court system. We get no attorney's fees, but this was in the best interest of the clients and a People's victory over multi-million-dollar developers and their destruction of African American culture and theft of Black-owned land." "Out of the struggle to reclaim the past has come the hope for the future," Korotkin wrote.

Lewis and Yvonne Wilson reconnected in 2017. She said to him:

> You did so much for us; not just the cemetery suit. That was great. . . . God knows we needed to do that. [You built] our confi-dence in times when we felt like we had nobody else. You were like a saint. You came in and made us feel like we were more than we ever felt that we were. . . . I tell ya, without y'all coming to our aid at that time, it would've been lost. . . . When y'all came, it proved to us our worth and it really made us feel worthwhile. . . . It was like, in this time of need, God . . . sent you. . . . I'm not tryin' to put you up on no pedestal or nothin' cause I know you human, but to me, you felt like a light in a tunnel of darkness. . . . You brought me into your family. . . . You made me feel like I was worth something.

CHAPTER 13

Movement to Protect
Abused and Neglected Children

During Lewis's time directing CIS, he became deeply interested in adolescent development and children's rights. His engagement with the issues was spawned by the birth of his son in 1985, meeting Jeanne Lenzer in 1986, and the United Nations (UN) General Assembly adopting the Convention on the Rights of the Child in 1989. While Lewis remained engaged in racial justice movements, the movement for equal protection and due process for abused and neglected children became a second area of focus for him and his organization.

The dissimilarities between the movements were stark. For example, the former primarily involved partnering with people of color from low-wealth communities, whereas the latter involved collaborating with mostly middle- and upper-class white women. However, Lewis focused on a unifying principle: fighting with and for marginalized groups to be empowered, heard, and treated fairly. *The Guilfordian* read, "Explaining the connections between the different kinds of cases he has worked on, Pitts said, 'Blacks, women, and children were told they didn't need rights and that others would take care of them. Clearly that hasn't been the case.' . . . Pitts identifies an overarching theme connecting a lot of his work as 'self-governing democracy.' . . . 'Everybody is valuable. Policies must be fair to everyone.'" Lewis expanded on the common threads in his law review article, "Fighting for Children's Rights: Lessons from the Civil Rights Movement": "A direct connection can be drawn between the inhumane way our system treats children and our historical treatment of African-Americans and women. The parallel is unmistakable when considered in a legal context: Each group has the grim distinction of being seen as less than fully human and thus not as rights-bearing persons in the eyes of the law."

People Allied for Child Advocacy

In March 1986, while living in Durham and attending Duke University, Jeanne Lenzer and five other survivors of child abuse and neglect cofounded People Allied for Child Advocacy (PACA). PACA grew to about one hundred members spanning thirteen states. Members included ministers, lawyers, physicians, and parents, many of whom had experienced abuse as children. They united over a belief that child welfare systems were failing to adequately protect children, especially when those systems prioritized preserving biological families despite extreme physical abuse. Lenzer told reporters that PACA was founded to "expose the lie that abused kids want to stay with their abusers." "We knew the federal and state mandates that force family reunification had betrayed us as badly as the abuse itself," she added.

PACA coordinated "sanctuaries" for children of abusive or neglectful parents. Members used "underground" networks across the country to move children from place to place. After a respite, some of the children chose to return home; others preferred the new, permanent homes that members helped find for them. Lenzer likened the sanctuaries to domestic violence shelters and sheltering refugees of political violence. Lewis told the *Boston Globe* that PACA members were "very riled up" and willing to coordinate the sanctuaries "because there was no one to do it for them when they were children." The Associated Press dubbed the networks a "20th century underground railway."

Lewis was moved by Lenzer's personal story and her organization's work. He and CIS's Assistant Director, Gayle Korotkin, became general counsel for PACA. They provided network organizers, who risked serious criminal charges, with what Lewis called "civil disobedience advising."

Additionally, as general counsel, Lewis and Korotkin advocated for abused and neglected children who were languishing in the child welfare system to have a recognized legal right to petition courts—in their own name and without an adult guardian—to "divorce" their biological parents. Their first case for PACA involved Karen Cooper and her five children. Karen suffered from mental illness. She abused and neglected her children and voluntarily put them into foster care in March 1985. Subsequently, the Iowa Department of Human Services (DHS) placed the children in the care of Larry and Paula Mick.

For the next twenty-two months, the children lived and developed a strong bond with the Micks. Larry and Paula hoped to adopt the kids, who'd begun calling them "dad" and "mom." However, the DHS moved the children into separate foster homes and planned to reunify them with Karen. According to the DHS, the Micks had "overstepped their role" by viewing the kids as their own and loving them too much.

Jane Harlan, the children's appointed guardian ad litem (GAL), initiated legal proceedings to terminate Karen's parental rights. GALs investigate, report on, and advocate for the best interests of child clients in abuse and neglect proceedings. The judge denied Harlan's termination petition and found that Karen could resume her parental role. He reasoned that Karen, with the help of medication and counseling, could manage her mental illness and care for her children.

The day after learning they'd be reunited with Karen, the two oldest Cooper kids attempted to buy sleeping pills to use to commit suicide. Later, the children wept and clung to the Micks as they were forced to say goodbye.

As PACA's attorneys, Lewis and Korotkin collaborated with Harlan on appealing the judge's decision, on behalf of the kids, to the Iowa Supreme Court. Lewis and Korotkin also filed an amicus curiae brief arguing that the children had a constitutionally protected liberty interest in a permanent living situation, and thus, were entitled to due process before being removed from the Micks's home.

In December 1987, the Iowa Supreme Court ruled that Karen's parental rights should've been terminated; however, the court also held that removal of the kids from the Micks's home was in the children's best interests because the Micks inappropriately sought to build a permanent bond with them. The court rejected Lewis and Korotkin's due process argument.

National Child Rights Alliance and Gregory Kingsley

After three or four years, PACA grew to nearly three hundred members, with branches in six states. It was renamed the National Child Rights Alliance (NCRA), which Jeanne Lenzer cochaired with other child abuse survivors. Volunteers continued the sanctuaries, published a newspaper, and spread their message at public events. Lenzer told the Associated Press that the NCRA sought "recognized divorce and support rights for kids." She continued, "Basically, we're just like other civil rights groups. We're about power relationships, but for kids."

Lewis and Korotkin continued collaborating with Lenzer and the NCRA. Their most time-intensive and high-profile case with the NCRA involved Gregory Kingsley.

Gregory's parents were alcoholics and periodically abandoned him, and his father was abusive. At age eight, Gregory had spent nearly all of the first eight years of his life in state custody, including at least three placements in foster care.

During a stint in a boys' shelter in Florida, Gregory befriended George Russ. Russ first visited the shelter as a member of a government commission studying the needs of children. Having had an unhappy childhood himself, he empathized with Gregory. The state child welfare system eventually placed Gregory with Russ, his wife, and their eight biological children in Fruitland Park, Florida.

After spending time as Gregory's foster parents, Mr. and Mrs. Russ wanted to adopt him. Gregory's biological father surrendered his parental rights; however, Gregory's biological mother, Rachel, fought to regain custody of him. Despite extensive evidence to the contrary, Rachel claimed she'd never mistreated Gregory; instead, she argued, her family was struggling to survive poverty. She also claimed her life was on the right track because she was living near supportive family and engaged to be married.

Russ recruited Jerri Blair, his friend and a children's rights attorney, to represent Gregory. Blair was comfortable handling high-profile cases, having prevailed in Florida's highest court on behalf of a fifteen-year-old who was seeking an abortion without parental consent because she feared abusive punishment from her parents. Lewis and Korotkin, as attorneys for the NCRA, assisted Blair and Russ, an attorney himself, behind the scenes.

In April 1992, Blair filed, on behalf of Gregory, age eleven, a petition in Lake County Circuit Court seeking "termination of the parent/child relationship." In other words, Gregory sought a divorce from his mother. Blair argued that the state agency with custodial control of Gregory was inadequately representing his interests and allowing him to languish in foster care. Florida law limited the time a child could spend in foster care to eighteen months; yet, Gregory had been in foster care for over thirty months. Moreover, his GAL hadn't spoken with him during the two and a half years he'd been in state custody.

Judge Richard Singletary presided over the initial hearing in June 1992. The *Orlando Sentinel* read,

Thursday afternoon, the Lake County Courthouse looked a bit like the scene of a presidential press conference. Reporters filled the normally sleepy gallery and spilled onto the sidewalk. . . . Small groups of attorneys and representatives of civil rights and juvenile justice organizations huddled throughout the courtroom, comparing notes and discussing strategies. It was tough to tell that the case attracting such attention wasn't a heinous crime or a long-awaited presidential announcement, but the fate of an 11-year-old boy.

Indeed, the event has had the unmistakable look and feel of a major—even a historic—event. Participants were mobbed by the media as they entered and left the courtroom, instantly drowning in a sea of rolling cameras, bright lights and simultaneous questions. Reporters, photographers and producers were everywhere, some of them thriving on the frenzy. . . . Courtroom Television Network filmed the proceedings. [CNN] sent a four-person crew. . . . There were reporters from *The New York Times*, *The Atlanta Constitution*, Reuters News Service and newspapers, television stations and radio services from across Florida.

After a ninety-minute hearing, Singletary dismissed the case. He reasoned that the Lake County Circuit Court didn't have jurisdiction because the Orange County Circuit Court was already handling the underlying abuse and neglect case opened when Rachel resided in Orange County. Lewis and Lenzer held a press conference where they accused Singletary of dodging the issue and denying Gregory his constitutional rights. Lewis also discussed the case on CNN's "Larry King Live."

A week later, Gregory's legal team filed a petition for termination of parental rights in Orange County. The following day, Lewis and Korotkin filed, on behalf of the NCRA, an amicus curiae brief in support of Gregory and his "divorce" petition. Lenzer told the *Orlando Sentinel*, "This is the most important case that has come along for the legal rights of the thousands and thousands of abused children across the nation who need help."

In July 1992, Orange County Juvenile Court Judge Thomas Kirk held a hearing on the petition. Gregory testified that he didn't want any contact with Rachel. Although highly unusual at the trial level, Lewis was allowed to make an oral argument on behalf of the fifteen children's rights organizations that signed on to the NCRA's brief. He argued Gregory had a constitutional right to file for "divorce" and his petition ought to be granted. Rachel's side claimed Gregory was too young to know what he wanted and was swayed by the material things the Russes could provide. Rachel also contended, as did the Florida Department of Health and Rehabilitative Services, that Gregory, as a minor, had no legal standing to bring such a petition.

Kirk held that Gregory had standing to initiate a termination of parental rights action. The judge reasoned that the Florida Constitution entitles "all natural persons," including children, to access courts and exercise attendant rights, including the right to legal representation. Moreover, Kirk found that Rachel had neglected and abandoned Gregory. Consequently, Kirk granted the divorce so the Russes could adopt Gregory.

The case continued receiving national attention. For instance, Hillary Clinton expressed support for Gregory's cause. At the 1992 Republican National Convention, then presidential candidate Pat Buchanan responded, "Hillary believes that 12-year-olds should have a right to sue their parents. . . . Friends, this is radical feminism."

After the Russes filed to adopt Gregory, Judge Kirk held a trial on their petition in September 1992. *New York Times* coverage read, "The unusual interest in the trial . . . has opened up the normally secretive world of child custody proceedings to the full view of the national press and cable television, which carried the trial live." Gregory, a sixth-grade student who'd spent only seven months living with his mother during the previous eight years, told Kirk, "I just thought [Rachel] forgot about me" and "didn't care anymore."

Kirk found that adoption by the Russes was in Gregory's best interest. According to the *New York Times*, "As soon as the judge ruled, Gregory turned back and smiled at Mrs. Russ. A moment later they hugged. Afterward, his family gave him a baseball cap and shirt embroidered with the number 9 to indicate that he is their ninth child."

Rachel appealed to Florida's Fifth District Court of Appeals. Lewis and Korotkin again appeared in the case on behalf of the NCRA. The *Orlando Sentinel* read, "The 5th District is the first appeal court in the country to rule on the issue, legal experts will be watching the opinion closely. 'The eyes of the nation are still on Florida,' Pitts said." Meanwhile, according to the *Orlando Sentinel*, "Kingsley's biological parents followed the tabloid route, appearing on shows like 'Sally Jessy Raphael' and 'Donahue,' in exchange for staying in swanky hotels overlooking Central Park and riding in limousines."

The Fifth District ruled, in August 1993, that minors don't possess the requisite legal capacity to bring termination of parental rights proceedings in their own right. The court reasoned that, because children like Gregory have a GAL or other adult "next friend" to bring legal actions on their behalf, their lack of capacity due to nonage "does not unduly burden" their "fundamental liberty interest to be 'free of physical and emotional violence at the hands of [their] . . . most trusted caretaker.'" Nevertheless, the Court upheld the termination of parental rights because Mr. and Mrs. Russ, as adults, had filed a separate petition on Gregory's behalf, and evidence of abandonment by Rachel supported termination. Thus, Gregory, while not recognized as a person entitled to be heard in his own right, effectively won, through the Russ's petition, a divorce from his biological parents.

Headlines in the *Washington Post*, *New York Times*, and *Los Angeles Times* read, respectively, "Boy, 11, Can Seek 'Divorce' from Parents, Judge Rules," "Boy Wins Right to Sue Parents for Separation," and "Boy Is Granted 'Divorce' From Natural Parents." The Fifth District chief judge wrote a separate opinion, which began, "This rather ordinary termination of parental rights case was transformed into a cause célèbre by artful representation and the glare of klieg lights."

Reaction to the decision was impassioned and polarized. A lawyer for the Florida Department of Health and Rehabilitative Services warned the case would have "evil and frightening" ramifications. "If a child has a right to choose his family, we're all in trouble," the lawyer declared. Rachel's attorney repeatedly sounded similar alarms, claiming the "dangerous" ruling "opened a Pandora's box" and would "change the whole system," give children "the ability to sue over anything," and "destroy the family even more." The Family Research Council likewise warned of a slippery slope, with one representative telling reporters, "It is inappropriate to unleash a force of lawyers who become examiners of a family to decide whether they think one is unfit and another proper." Another council spokesperson decried, "I can see the day, about ten years from now, when some kid will want separation from his parents just because he wants out, not because of any showing of abuse or neglect." None of their predictions proved true.

George Russ said the ruling was "the right thing legally and morally" and "a great step forward for all children." Lenzer called Gregory "the Rosa Parks of the youth rights movement." Lewis told the media, "Hopefully this will be the first step of sweeping into the ashcan of history the old paternalistic legal mumbo-jumbo that says children have no rights."

A *New York Times* editorial praised Judge Kirk's decision and countered conservative fearmongering:

The decision need not and almost assuredly will not lead to a flood tide of suits by children seeking to "divorce" their parents. Not every child who has been neglected or abused has the maturity to act in his own behalf, even with the help of foster parents like the Russes.

In most cases social service agencies are designated and best suited to determine what setting would be in a child's best interest. But such agencies, understaffed and overworked, are not infallible. It is useful, as a last resort, to have another avenue of legal redress for children in trouble.

Gregory presented just the kind of extreme circumstances in which the divergent interests of a child and parent ought to be recognized by the law.

Likewise, Lewis wrote in an op-ed published in the *Boston Globe*, *The Nation*, and elsewhere:

Gregory and his supporters, believing in the value of a loving, nurturing home for every child, went to court to fight the government bureaucracy. The victory won ensures the right of the child to advocate remaining with his or her parents when the state unfairly seeks to terminate parental rights, as well as to argue for termination of those rights when the state ignores parental abandonment or abuse.

Gregory put a crack in the ancient legal doctrine that children are property and objects of court proceedings, are incompetent and are therefore to be seen and not heard. . . . And what makes me madder than a hornet in a mason jar is that for partisan purposes the Republican strategists are distorting the facts and implications of the Florida ruling. These misrepresentations could inflame emotions and thwart similar judicial recognition of a child's right to be heard. The voices of millions of children who are abandoned, abused or neglected every year in our country are undermined and trivialized by such a campaign ploy.

In 2019, Jerri Blair said of Lewis, "His real purpose in being an attorney was making the law better. . . . He did the stuff that's hard. He had the courage to stand up for things he believed in. . . . I can't tell you how much I admire Lewis."

National Committee for the Rights of the Child

Lewis and Korotkin also became involved in the National Committee for the Rights of the Child (NCRC)—"a coalition of over 40 organizations and child advocacy centers working to improve the quality of life of children in America." Members included the American Bar Association's (ABA's) Center for Children and the Law, American Psychological Association, American School Counselors Association, National Association of School Psychologists, Catholic Charities, Child Welfare League of America, and Save the Children. The NCRC's primary objectives included effectuation of the rights in the UN Convention on the Rights of the Child and adoption of the convention by the United States.

In 1992, Lewis and Korotkin proposed to the NCRC's board creation of the Legal Action Project (LAP)—an initiative to advance, through litigation, the NCRC's mission and the rights of children to access courts and be heard, through their own attorney, in abuse, neglect, abandonment, and custody cases. The initiative would continue and build on work that Lewis and Korotkin had done with PACA and the NCRA. Their concept paper read, "Improving the legal status of children will require two types of changes: (1) ending the denial to children of fundamental constitutional procedural rights enjoyed by adults—basically court access; and (2) establishing children's legal entitlement to having fundamental developmental needs met." Their "longer-range objective" was "to broaden the sphere of enforceable rights for children so that not only are children treated as rights-bearing individuals, but the sphere of their rights includes entitlement to developmentally critical services." The "cornerstone" of their legal arguments, Lewis wrote in a chapter for the book *Children as Equals*, would be "that children are persons, not property, and thereby are entitled to the human dignity of due process of law." Early in 1993, the NCRC's board approved the LAP.

Lewis and Korotkin formed a LAP advisory board, consisting of Connecticut Superior Court Judge Charles Gill; George Russ, Gregory's adoptive father; Cynthia Price Cohen, a child advocate, singer, dancer, and actress; Anne Schneiders, a child advocacy attorney and former nun; Tony Cunningham, a Florida-based attorney with whom Lewis worked on the Contragate campaign; Shari Shink, founder of what would become the Rocky Mountain Children's Law Center; and Nannette Bowler, then director of the Children's Law Center in Grand Rapids, Michigan. Lewis, Korotkin, and LAP board members identified two circumstances under which children's best interests should outweigh parents' right to raise their children: when birth parents abuse, neglect, or abandon their children; and when children have no meaningful relationship with their birth parents, they've been in the custody of others for long periods, and returning to their birth parents would traumatize them.

As directors of the LAP, Lewis and Korotkin traversed the country supporting child advocates. They collaborated with local advocates and filed amicus curiae briefs in courts in Florida, Kansas, New Mexico, New York, South Carolina, and Tennessee. Lewis also argued cases in appellate courts in some of those states. Lewis and Korotkin's most intensive involvement was in campaigns for Jessica (a.k.a. "Baby Girl Clausen") in Iowa and the Grissom children in Missouri.

JESSICA

On February 8, 1991, Cara Clausen gave birth to Jessica in Iowa. Two days later, Cara completed paperwork relinquishing her parental rights. She listed Scott Seefeldt as Jessica's biological father. He relinquished his parental rights on Valentine's Day.

Less than three weeks later, Michigan residents Jan and Roberta DeBoer filed a petition in an Iowa juvenile court to adopt Jessica. At a hearing that same day, they were granted custody of Jessica pending further proceedings. The DeBoers returned to Michigan with her.

However, on March 6, 1991, Cara petitioned an Iowa court to rescind her relinquishment. In an accompanying affidavit, Cara admitted to lying about Jessica's biological father. Daniel Schmidt, Jessica's actual biological father, filed an affidavit asserting paternity and a petition to intervene in the adoption proceedings.

Almost eight months later, an Iowa district court judge held a bench trial regarding paternity, termination of parental rights, and adoption. The judge voided the termination because there was no finding Schmidt had abandoned Jessica. The DeBoers lost appeals to Iowa's court of appeals and supreme court.

Undeterred, the DeBoers appealed to the Michigan Supreme Court. They were represented by Suellyn Scarnecchia, then head of the Child Advocacy Clinic at the University of Michigan Law School.

Lewis, Korotkin, and Nannette Bowler, a LAP board member, filed an amicus brief on behalf of fifteen organizations and fourteen individuals. They asked the court to recognize a constitutional right for Jessica to initiate legal proceedings in which a judge would determine custody based on her best interests. They argued that Jessica had a due process liberty interest in her relationship with the DeBoers and was denied equal protection under the law because she, as a child in the custody of "psychological parents," was granted fewer rights than children in the custody of their biological parents. The brief read, "This case turns on a very broad issue and a narrow issue. The broad issue is whether tradition or the Constitution governs the legal status of the child; i.e., it confronts competing notions of child-as-chattel versus child as rights-bearing person. The narrow issue is whether this 27-month-old child is entitled to a hearing to consider her rights and best interests prior to being forcibly removed from the only home and family she has ever known and being placed with biological parents who are strangers to her."

On June 2, 1993, the eve of the Michigan Supreme Court's hearing, the Justice for Jessi DeBoer Committee and NCRC held a "Together at Twilight" gathering outside the Washtenaw County Courthouse. Lewis was the featured speaker.

The case, viewed as an ideological showdown between parental rights and the best interests of the child, drew national attention. Jessica appeared on the cover of magazines, including *Newsweek* and *Time*, and was the subject of an ABC Sunday night movie, "Whose Child Is This? The War for Baby Jessica." A *Washington Post* reporter dubbed the case "a war of the most savage kind, a war for the body, mind and affections of a little girl." Six members of Congress urged the Michigan Supreme Court to rule in the DeBoers's favor. Elizabeth Bartholet, a Harvard Law professor and family law expert, wrote in the *New York Times*, "The foster care system is crowded with children who live in limbo because we are unwilling to cut their ties to inadequate birth parents and free them for adoption. . . . This same biological bias results in legal barriers to adoption that drives prospective parents away from those children who are free for placement. The DeBoer decision threatens to create yet another barrier, raising the specter that children may be removed months or years after placement simply because a previously unknown father appears on the scene."

In August 1993, the Michigan Supreme Court ruled against the DeBoers. Regarding the LAP's due process argument, the court wrote, "The mutual rights of the parent and child come into conflict only when there is a showing of parental unfitness. . . . The natural parent's right to custody is not to be disturbed absent such a showing, sometimes despite the preferences of the child." The justices also rejected the LAP's equal protection argument because "the relationship between natural parents and their children is fundamentally different than that between a child and nonparent custodians."

After spending the first two and a half years of her life with the DeBoers, Jessica was sent back to Iowa to live with Cara and Schmidt, strangers who renamed her Anna Jacqueline Schmidt. People all over the country watched on television as Suellyn Scarnecchia handed Jessica, who was screaming and crying, to her biological parents and as the DeBoers shook with grief. A *Chicago Tribune* columnist wrote, "Anyone who has ever loved a 2-year-old must cringe at the thought of a little girl's crying inconsolably for the parents who have given her love and security since birth and who will no longer be hers. But then the law cares more about legal technicalities and biological ties than it does about 2-year-olds." *Newsweek* read, "Jessica symbolized every adoptive parent's nightmare. . . . And while congressmen and psychologists argued whose best interests were served by the tug of war, the vast majority of Americans in poll after poll supported the would-be adopters."

Organizing sparked by the case continued. To reflect its new mission of fighting for children like Jessica, the Justice for Jessi DeBoer Committee changed its name to the DeBoer Committee for Children's Rights, and then to Hear My Voice: Protecting Our Nation's Children. It eventually spread to more than fifty chapters in approximately thirty-seven states. Members continued working with Lewis and Korotkin.

The DeBoer Committee's director, Annie Rose, wrote to Lewis in 1994, "Your spirit, your feelings, your perceptions and your insights are the backbone of my relationship with this movement and the organization. I will never be able to thank you enough for everything you have done." In 2019, Rosemary Pomeroy, a volunteer attorney on the campaign for Jessica, shared her memories of Lewis: "I remember distinctly hearing Lewis speak for the first time. I thought, this guy is going to be like Rep. John Lewis—someone who you would follow across the Pettus Bridge in Alabama. . . . If I had been younger and not entrenched with my family when I met him, I may have moved to North Carolina to work [with him]. He was that inspiring. . . . Meeting Lewis and getting to know him served as part of the inspiration for my law practice."

GRISSOM CHILDREN

Candace Losey and Randall Grissom lived in Missouri. After their marriage dissolved in 1990, Candace was awarded custody of their children: Tony, age seventeen; Rachel, age fifteen; and Rebecca, age twelve. Randall had visitation rights.

In August 1991, and again in March 1992, Randall asked the Adair County Circuit Court to hold Candace in contempt for supposedly interfering with his visitation rights. Judge Bruce Normile heard testimony on Randall's second motion. The children testified that their mother didn't prevent them from visiting Randall, and in fact, encouraged them to see him; and they refused to visit because they feared their father and witnessed him drinking excessively, popping pills, and being violent toward and threatening to kill their mother. Moreover, Rachel testified that Randall had molested her and Rebecca. Finally, a psychologist who counseled the children testified that court-mandated visitation would be counterproductive because of their antagonism toward Randall.

Nevertheless, in May 1993, Normile found Candace in contempt, fined her $3,000, and ordered her to pay $3,500 for Randall's attorney's fees. Additionally, the judge placed the children in the legal custody of the Division of Family Services (DFS), with Candace retaining physical custody, so long as she complied with his orders, including bimonthly counseling sessions. Lastly, Normile ordered resumption of Randall's visitation with the children after they completed three joint counseling sessions. Candace filed a notice of appeal.

Candace tracked down Lewis, who she'd heard of while following news about Jessica Clausen. Lewis was the first attorney to express interest in Candace's story. He and Korotkin agreed to represent Candace and her children.

Lewis first met Candace and her children at their home in Macon County, Missouri. Candace recalled Lewis being "so intelligent and so skilled that he quickly could see what violations were happening." She connected Lewis with David Masters, her friend and the local prosecutor. Lewis told the *Kirksville Daily Express*, "We intend . . . to expose this mistreatment, this judicial abuse of children, to the nation." He explained that the LAP got involved because the Grissom children "didn't even have a semblance of due process or protection of their rights" and Candace's contempt proceedings were "an outlandish example of treatment of children as property and not as rights-bearing citizens."

Lewis traveled to Missouri multiple times to visit Candace and her children and work on their case. He spent a lot of time in their home and even accompanied them to an exotic animal auction. Lewis also met them in New York City, where they discussed the case on *The Maury Povich Show* and dined at the Times Square Hard Rock Cafe.

Lewis and Korotkin sought stays of the contempt and custody orders. They also filed a motion to intervene in the proceedings on behalf of the children. Lewis argued the kids should've been heard because the issues before Judge Normile implicated their fundamental rights, including their liberty interests in maintaining "a relationship with a parent free of state interference" and "not being in the custody and control of the State"; right "to due process of law before being deprived of a constitutional or statutory right"; and "statutory right to have decisions concerning visitation and custody be based on . . . [their] best interest." The memo in support of the motion captured the essence of the LAP:

> The custom of excluding children from the proceedings which determine the basic conditions of their lives is inconsistent with fundamental constitutional and moral principles and cannot stand as a bar to the intervention here proposed. It perpetuates the tradition of treating children as property, to be fought over by competing adults, rather than as the independent persons they are.
>
> Recognizing a child's right to bring this action recognizes the human dignity of minors. It is part of a paradigm shift away from children-as-chattel . . . to children as persons, as child-citizens, whose human dignity must be respected.
>
> What African Americans, women and children have in common is the history of being treated essentially as property and as exceptions to the social contract upon which our founding documents declared this nation to be based. In each case, the articulation of the principle that members of each group were constitutional persons came well before society in general and the legal system actually treated them as such.
>
> Recognizing rights of minors which tradition has denied them does not reflect lawlessness but a changing consensus that reflects new humanity toward children, the proper respect for their rights as individuals and greater knowledge of developmental psychology.

Normile denied the stays and motion to intervene. His ruling violated the Grissom children's rights and was "cruel" and "lacking in common sense," Lewis told the *St. Louis Post Dispatch*.

In August 1993, Randall petitioned the circuit court, for the third time, to hold Candace in contempt. He again accused her of interfering with his visitation rights and preventing the children from attending counseling. Normile ordered Candace to appear at a hearing on August 31, 1993.

Four days before the hearing, Lewis and Masters filed, on behalf of the children, another motion to intervene, a request for a continuance because Masters couldn't attend, and a motion to disqualify Normile. Then, mere hours before the hearing, Randall's attorney filed a motion for sanctions against Lewis and Masters. He alleged they violated Rule 55.03—Missouri's version of the federal Rule 11—by filing a motion to intervene they knew would fail because of Normile's previous ruling and appellate courts' dismissals of writs raising the same issue.

At the hearing, Lewis told Normile, "It is an error to proceed without giving the kids the most fundamental elemental due process right of right to counsel." Regarding the recusal motion, Lewis said to the judge, "We have challenged and questioned your neutrality, objectivity, and lack of bias in being able to assess this question of capacity. . . . And I would bet my finest pair of boots back in North Carolina that you will find the way [counsel for Randall] has argued." Normile interjected, "Mr. Pitts, the Missouri Court of Appeals has ruled these issues; the Missouri Supreme Court has ruled these issues in the last month; and I have ruled these issues this morning. There is no further argument that can be had of that matter, and we are now ready to proceed to the Motion for Sanctions." Lewis responded, "We filed legal papers asserting a very solid legal position to represent the interest of these children. . . . Now we are here trying to right that wrong, and we are being blindsided . . . I guess, to intimidate us away from representing our clients, but the intimidation part won't work. I can assure you of that."

Court recessed, at Lewis's request. Normile gave him just fifteen minutes to prepare an argument against sanctions. When the proceedings resumed, Lewis asked Normile to recuse himself for a "manifest display of lack of objectivity." Normile denied the request. The quarreling continued:

LEWIS: It's a farce and a mockery for you to even be entertaining, much less ruling in favor of—as you are bound to do—a sanction against me that is designed to do nothing but to chill and intimidate vigorous advocacy on behalf of these children.

NORMILE: You are to address the motion for sanctions.

LEWIS: I imagine what is happening is that you don't want me to repeat this gruesome record about what has been revealed about this man, Mr. Grissom, by our children with nobody to represent them, and you have not even given the courtesy of following the statutory mandates and granting a guardian ad litem.

One of the concerns that we had in concluding that it was imperative for us . . . to move to intervene . . . was a complete failure on your part to do anything to look out for their interests.

NORMILE: The issue is whether you had any right to intervene or whether it was a frivolous, unnecessary motion, unfair to the parties, harassing them and causing undue delay in the disposition of the issues. . . . Now, address those issues.

LEWIS: You are about to sanction me, and you haven't even looked at this man for his deliberate failure to have drug and alcohol evaluations and screening when he signed a written stipulation that he would.

NORMILE: You are disregarding the directive of the Court. I asked you to confine yourself to argument on the motion for sanctions. . . .

LEWIS: I'm asking this question like a broken record: Who is looking out for the children?

LEWIS: This is institutional immorality, to be . . . turkeying around . . . when the kids can't even be heard.

LEWIS: And you would have whammed those kids without even them having a semblance of elementary due process.

NORMILE: We are here about the motion for sanctions and you are to respond to that.

LEWIS: We proceeded in good faith. . . . The consideration—even the putting on the agenda—that Mr. Masters and I should be sanctioned for seeking to let the voices of the children be heard in a proceeding where they may be removed from their one stabilizing force, that is a kangaroo court, that is a farce and a mockery, and I appeal to you not to play into that.

Normile sanctioned Lewis and Masters and ordered them to pay $200 for Randall's attorney's fees. Normile announced that the LAP's motion to intervene and pleadings were "not well-grounded in fact as to the issue of jurisdiction," "not warranted by existing law," and "unnecessary and frivolous." He added, "I recognize, Mr. Pitts, that an organization of your kind, I am sure, does some considerable good in looking to the interests of children. It is also helped by publicity and notoriety and fundraising resulting from efforts of this kind." Candace said about the sanctions, "More valuable than money of any amount was someone else thinking that our rights were being violated."

Lewis and Masters appealed, arguing that Normile erred by holding the hearing without allowing them adequate time to prepare, proceeding without Masters present, finding they violated Rule 55.03, and presiding over the hearing after demonstrating bias. An amicus brief supporting them was filed by the National Task Force for Children's Constitutional Rights, National Association of Counsel for Children, Center for Constitutional Rights, and Child Advocacy Law Clinic at the University of Michigan. The brief read, in part:

> Even suits and motions destined to lose are sometimes filed reasonably. Bad court decisions must be challenged if they are to be overruled, but the early challenges are certainly hopeless. The first attorney to challenge *Plessy v. Ferguson* was certainly bringing a frivolous action, but his efforts and the efforts of others eventually led to *Brown v. Board of Education*.
>
> The . . . Missouri Rules of Professional Conduct recognizes lawyers' "special responsibility for the quality of justice." The text continues: "It is a lawyer's duty, when necessary, to challenge the rectitude of official action . . ."
>
> Amici respectfully contend that the conduct of these lawyers not only was fully in accord with the letter of the Missouri Rules but, in fact, exemplifies the highest obligations of our professional calling as members of the bar.

The Grissom children filed, through Lewis and Masters, a separate appeal asserting that Judge Normile erred in concluding the children lacked legal capacity to employ an attorney and failing to appoint a GAL for the children.

In December 1993, while the appeals were pending, Rachel sent Lewis a letter and poem titled, "The Cries of a Child." The poem read:

As I walk down the road of life,
I see much hurt, anger and pain.
I hear the cry of a child,
with no food, shelter, nothing to gain. . . .
When it's raining and I am sitting inside, nice and dry,
I hear the cry of a child,
with no roof over its head and its mother,
forever asking why. . . .
Now things have changed.
I can still hear the cry of the child,
but now it is much closer.
I am the one asking why.

Lewis argued the case before the Missouri Court of Appeals in May 1994. The *Kansas City Star* read, "Now, two national children's rights groups are involved in what one group calls 'a modern-day Dred Scott case for children,' comparing the Grissom case to the 1857 Supreme Court ruling that black people were not citizens. . . . 'Today is the day to declare that any child faced with the potential for removal from their loving, bonded family . . . has a right to counsel and access to the court,' Pitts wrote in a 65-page legal argument. 'Any other declaration sends the message that children are less than full people,' wrote Pitts."

The court of appeals concluded that Normile correctly overruled the children's motions to intervene because their interests and Candace's interests "were the same" and she "adequately represented their interests." Regarding the sanctions, the court held that Normile shouldn't have ruled because Randall's attorney failed to provide adequate notice of the motion to Lewis and Masters. Moreover, the court found that, even if there'd been adequate notice, the motion for sanctions should've been denied. The opinion read, "Rule 55.03 was not intended to chill attorneys' creativity. Sanctions should be applied sparingly and with great caution. The pleadings filed by Masters and Pitts were reasonable under the circumstances. . . . The attorneys' attempt to do so was not frivolous, but a good faith attempt to extend Missouri law. We find no evidence of improper motives."

Rachel and Candace remain very fond of Lewis. In 2019, Candace said about Lewis, "You have to think about us as people drowning. Would you ever forget someone who put their hand out and saved you? That's how it felt to us. That's what he did." Rachel wrote, "Lewis changed my life. He stepped in and was such an important role model just when I needed it. He was a stranger who believed me and believed in me when most of those around me didn't. His influence . . . gave me stability and strength as I escaped a horrible childhood. And his passion to give to others served as a map to me as I found my own callings in non-profit work in my own adult life."

The Foundation for the Improvement of Justice gave Lewis its "Child Protection" award in recognition of his efforts on behalf of the Grissom children and many others, efforts for which he didn't charge a single organization or client.

CHAPTER 14

"Majorly Traumatic"
End of an Era

During the early 1990s, Lewis continued playing critical roles in racial justice movements, experienced a meteoric rise as a lawyer on the cutting edge of advancing children's rights, and led an organization that was revered and respected by advocates nationwide. Nevertheless, this period was also the lowest of Lewis's career. Rule 11 sanctions against Lewis for his work in Robeson County and against Christic Institute in the Contragate case were upheld by federal circuit courts in October 1990 and June 1991, respectively; Christic Institute closed and CIS experienced financial collapse; and he had to fight tooth and nail to be admitted to the North Carolina State Bar. He called the years "stressful," "fatiguing," and "majorly traumatic."

Christic Institute Ends

According to Danny Sheehan's autobiography, the IRS, at George H. W. Bush's direction, "went after [Christic Institute] with a vengeance" as retaliation for the Contragate campaign. Sheehan described IRS agents repeatedly appearing at the Christic office to dig through records and other materials. Members of Congress likewise sought to punish and eliminate Christic Institute. For example, then Congressman Robert Dornan wrote about Christic in the *Los Angeles Times*, "It has engaged in blatant political propaganda, attempted to influence legislation, intervened in a political campaign in opposition to a particular candidate, disrupted the judicial system and violated legal canons of ethics. I, along with 19 of my colleagues, have therefore asked the IRS to pull the plug on the Christic Institute's tax-exempt status."

In 1992, the IRS revoked Christic's 501(c)(3) nonprofit status. Consequently, Sheehan and his partner, Sara Nelson, closed Christic and started a new organization, the Romero Institute. In 2017, Sheehan said, "I loved

Lewis," and described him as "the closest thing you'll find to a saint." Nelson wrote:

> Lewis Pitts is one of the best human beings that I have ever met. . . .
>
> His outstanding characteristics were deep and consistent integrity, genuine compassion, clear judgment, and total authenticity. I never heard him say a harsh word to anyone, and he defended the "least of these" with focused passion. He was not afraid to speak truth to power, and he never failed to be outraged and disappointed by the cruelty and injustice of the racism and inequities that abound.
>
> He lived simply and carried only a toothbrush in his back pocket, moving from place to place, working for fairness and justice, trying to make the world a better place. . . . He was deeply offended that the legal profession was bought and sold, and mostly unresponsive to the millions of people who suffer serious inequities and do not have adequate legal representation.

Christic Institute South Ends

Despite CIS's tremendous success, the organization struggled financially. A confluence of factors negatively impacted CIS's fundraising in the early 1990s. First, the Rule 11 findings in the Contragate and Robeson County cases caused reputational damage. Second, Christic Institute was no longer available to assist CIS with fundraising and administrative costs. Third, amidst the recession in 1990 and 1991, many foundations and donors, with diminished assets, scaled back giving. Fourth, the federal judiciary had swung far right ideologically. By 1992, seven of the nine the US Supreme Court justices and two-thirds of federal circuit court judges were appointed by Republicans. Additionally, the Justice Department under Reagan and Bush had largely abandoned civil rights enforcement. Consequently, some funders questioned the efficacy of, and were reluctant to invest in, civil rights legal advocacy.

Meanwhile, Lewis and his CIS colleagues implemented a variety of measures to avoid the same fate at Christic Institute. For example, they formed a new board of directors, with members who were committed to CIS's mission and also had more name recognition and connections to prospective funders.

The new board included three individuals with whom Lewis had collaborated on campaigns: Anne Braden, founder and director of the Southern Organizing Committee for Economic and Social Justice; Emma Greshman, the mayor of Keysville; and Rose Sanders, a civil rights attorney and the first Black, female judge in Alabama. The other three board members were Black professors: Haywood Burns, former general counsel to Martin Luther King Jr.'s Poor People's Campaign, cofounder of the National Conference of Black Lawyers, and then dean of CUNY Law School; John Hope Franklin, then professor of history at Duke University; and Cornel West, then chair of the African American Studies Department at Princeton University.

Lewis pleaded with the new board members to assist with fundraising. In August 1991, he wrote to Burns, "We most definitely need any amount that can be shaken loose at the moment. The enclosed budget is for $275,418 which is still only a new Chevrolet category operation; our present status running at about $12,000 per month . . . is a 150,000-mile used car which barely gets to its destination." The following month, Lewis shared with Franklin:

> [CIS] is financially in a crisis. I am pulling out all the stops and trying or willing to try anything reasonable to secure our funding; otherwise the one resource in the nation which provides experienced and vigorous organizing, public education, and litigation assistance to Southern grassroots African American struggles for economic and racial equality will go belly up and close its doors.

CIS staff also recruited other allies to solicit funding. For instance, Rosa Parks wrote to "friends":

> Lewis Pitts . . . has accepted the torch to continue the fight for freedom and is inviting us to work with him and his colleagues as they fight for justice.
>
> The people they are assisting are in small towns which are overlooked by the national media. They are in quiet courtrooms where success is measured by small achievements and where racism is accepted as normal. They are in places where the words "equal rights" are not used in polite company until a patriotic day is celebrated and sometimes, not then.

Freedom is still not free! It takes money, volunteers, equipment, training and commitment. The team at [CIS] is . . . working with residents of Southern communities to help improve their
future. . . .

We have inherited our historical leaders' and dedicated citizens'
dreams of an America with liberty and justice for all.

Supporting [CIS] will assist in achieving our goal.

Ultimately, not even CIS's track record of success, multifaceted fundraising strategy, and public support from well-known civil rights leaders could
save the organization. CIS staff and board members decided to cease operating as Christic Institute South, as of January 1, 1992. The organization Lewis
poured his heart and soul into ended. The *News and Observer* read:

After . . . years helping the poor and powerless fight unpopular
legal battles, the [CIS] has closed its doors. . . .

[CIS] has been a tireless advocate for the underdog in the legal
battles against powerful corporations and the government.

With the group's reputation for relentless determination, civil
rights advocates say, the demise of [CIS] leaves a void that will be
hard to fill in the struggle to guarantee basic constitutional rights
for the people least able to speak for themselves. . . .

Their presence will be hard to replace, said William Simpson,
legal director of the N.C. Civil Liberties Union.

"When I came across a client who needed more than just legal
help, I sent them to [CIS]," he said. "I don't know where I'll send
them now."

Pitts blames the government and the rule that allows judges to
fine lawyers—a weapon that he and others say is used mainly to
stifle civil rights lawsuits.

"It has severe consequences on lawyers who do the unpopular
cases," said Dan Pollitt, a retired law professor at the University of
North Carolina at Chapel Hill.

But while [CIS's] strong mix of confrontational politics backed
up with litigation helped earn a reputation for helping disempow-
ered clients, it also eventually led to the Institute's downfall.

Southern Justice Institute Begins

Lewis and Korotkin weren't ready to abandon the vision that drove them to create CIS. So, when CIS formally ended on January 1, 1992, they, along with CIS's remaining staff, began operating as Southern Justice Institute (SJI). A couple of months later, after articles of amendment were filed with the North Carolina Secretary of State, CIS legally became SJI.

The new name was designed to eliminate the negative stigma associated with Christic Institute after the Rule 11 sanctions and smear campaigns. Additionally, the name Southern Justice Institute better conveyed the organization's mission.

SJI's staff and board members tried to emerge from the financial crisis. For example, Anne Braden wrote to the Kellogg Foundation:

> Lewis Pitts . . . and others who work with the [SJI] have those very special and unique skills that enable people to empower themselves. . . .
>
> And they are all really selfless, dedicated people. . . . I don't think there is a self-serving bone in the body of any of them. They are . . . totally motivated by a burning passion to help bring real democratic changes in the South and in this country. And they know that if that kind of change is going to happen, it has to come from people who are victims of injustice and oppression. . . .
>
> At the same time they are doing the legal work, they also help people in communities where they go to organize, to tell their story, to build coalitions. They do this because they know that legal battles alone will not win real change. And they do it successfully because they know how to work with people. They don't go into a community trying to impose their will; rather they work as catalysts, helping people find the skills and strength to be their own leaders. . . .
>
> There are many other examples across the South of situations in which the Institute people have made the difference between a movement for justice being crushed—or living to fight another day and, sometimes, bringing change. We who work in various movements across the South have come to count on the fact that when the going is rough somewhere . . . that we can call on Lewis

and Czerny and the others—and if it's humanly possible they will come.

SJI staff also applied for grants from various foundations. In an application to the Congressional Black Caucus Foundation, John Hope Franklin wrote to Congressman John Lewis:

> [SJI] has consistently been in the vanguard of substantive change in the South, and it is facing imminent closure due to lack of funding. . . .
>
> In many cases it has been the only organization to come to the aid of embattled activists, often with only the hope that expenses incurred would be paid with contributions and grants after the work had been accomplished. But those who sweat to execute the tortuous community organizing and litigation, resulting in victory and real empowerment, without accolades or financial sustenance, are ofttimes overlooked after the fact.
>
> Institute staff have no expense accounts, they drive to their clients across the South, they sleep not in hotels but in the homes of their clients, sharing their food, miseries and frustrations; they receive salaries far, far below what their skills and experience would demand in any public or private arena—and they deliver!

Lewis and Korotkin also hoped that adding children's rights to SJI's priorities and starting the LAP of the NCRC would open up new funding streams. They sought financial support from donors and foundations that supported child advocacy.

Meanwhile, Lewis continued working on campaigns already underway when CIS became SJI, including defending Lee Faye Mack in Winston-Salem and working with Black residents of Daufuskie Island. He also took on new racial justice cases. For instance, Lewis and Korotkin represented civil rights icon Gwendolyn Patton in her appeal to the US Court of Appeals for the Eleventh Circuit after she was prevented from running in Alabama as an independent candidate for US Senate. And amid all of this, Lewis also had to battle to be admitted to the North Carolina State Bar.

Bar Admission

By 1993, Lewis had been a lawyer for two decades. He was admitted to practice law in South Carolina, the US District Court for the District of Columbia, three federal circuit courts, and the US Supreme Court. Additionally, he'd appeared pro hac vice in at least eleven states. Pro hac vice is a Latin phrase that translates to "for this occasion." In the US legal system, it means adding an attorney to a specific case in a jurisdiction where the attorney is not licensed to practice in such a way that the attorney does not commit unauthorized practice of law. Collaborating with attorneys who were licensed by the state bar where Lewis was working allowed him to represent antinuclear protesters, racial justice advocates, children, and others. For example, he represented Comanche Peak Life Force activists in Texas through Thomas Mills; Greensboro Massacre plaintiffs in North Carolina through Carolyn McAllaster; Eddie Carthan in Mississippi through Johnnie Walls; Fred Carter in West Virginia through John Taylor; Cozelle Wilson in North Carolina through Paul Jones; Timothy Jacobs in New York through Alan Rosenthal; and Candace Losey and her children in Missouri through David Masters. Lewis still wasn't licensed to practice in North Carolina, where he had lived since 1980, directed an organization since 1985, and appeared in at least four cases. He hadn't previously had the time, patience, or pressing need to become licensed in the state.

However, not being a bar member in North Carolina had caused headaches for Lewis, including, for example, while attempting to represent Jeanne Lenzer. Lenzer, with whom Lewis would later collaborate on child advocacy issues, was a physician's assistant at the state-run Alcohol Rehabilitation Center (ARC) in Butner, North Carolina. In 1985 and 1986, she reported to her supervisor and the SBI that a male attendant at the ARC had sexually exploited male patients. Lenzer also shared with the SBI her concerns regarding the ARC's handling of the attendant's misconduct. Next, she told the director of the state's Division of Mental Health that ARC administrators might have been covering up abuse and she feared reprisal for whistleblowing.

Shortly thereafter, Lenzer's supervisors retaliated against her. They refused to provide her with the medical doctor supervision required for practicing physician assistants; and then, in May 1986, fired her, purportedly for circumventing the chain of command when reporting her concerns. Her internal grievance about the retaliation proved futile.

Lenzer knew CIS handled advocates' controversial and politicized cases; so, she contacted Lewis and Korotkin, who agreed to help her. Lewis explained why CIS accepted a case that deviated from the organization's racial justice and movement lawyering focus: "It was just a damn outrage; and you don't walk away from injustice."

However, neither Lewis nor Korotkin was licensed to practice in North Carolina, nor were they experienced in employment law. So, they recruited Travis Payne to cocounsel with them. Payne and Steve Edelstein, former legal services attorneys, had opened a Raleigh-based public interest law practice focused on employment and civil rights cases.

In spring 1987, Lewis, Korotkin, and Payne filed a lawsuit on Lenzer's behalf in state superior court. The complaint alleged "unlawful separation from employment" and violation of Lenzer's free speech rights. The named defendants included ARC supervisors and state officials. Lewis also filed, in July 1987, a motion to appear pro hac vice through Payne.

During the slow-moving pretrial process, CIS issued a press release accusing John Corne, an attorney in the North Carolina AG's Office, of threatening and intimidating an ARC employee-witness as part of "an established pattern of such harassment and intimidation by the defendants and . . . their lawyers." In May 1989—nearly two years after Lewis filed his pro hac vice motion, but only about three months after CIS's press release—the AG's office announced it would vigorously oppose his motion.

Lewis filed a memorandum in support of his motion, along with affidavits attesting to his legal skills and moral character. The affiants included Sara Nelson, director of the Christic Institute; David Bruck, Lewis's former clerk and colleague at the Richland County Public Defender's Office (who would go on to become a renowned capital defense attorney and professor at Washington and Lee School of Law); Carolyn McAllaster and Flint Taylor, who worked with Lewis on the Greensboro Massacre legal team; John Taylor, Lewis's cocounsel in Fred Carter's case in West Virginia; John England from the "Greene County Five" cases in Alabama; Barry Nakell and Alan Rosenthal, who worked with Lewis on the Robeson County campaign; and Julius Chambers, an acclaimed civil rights attorney.

McAllaster wrote that Lewis was "highly competent," "a zealous advocate," and "of the highest skill and integrity." Taylor described Lewis as "extremely intelligent and forthright, with exceptional legal skills"; "highly principled, unfailingly honest, and uncommonly dedicated to his clients and their case"; and "a lawyer in this highest tradition of the civil rights and pro bono bar, as well as a man of uncommon courage and principle." Bruck wrote, "I have never known a lawyer who brings greater sincerity and commitment to the representation of his clients. I know Lewis to be unfailingly honest and ethical."

CIS released a statement accusing the AG's office of being "motivated by their desire to conceal gross misconduct committed by state officials sued by Ms. Lenzer." The statement continued, "If such distortions and diversionary tactics by the [AG]'s office succeed, the losers will be not just Ms. Lenzer but workers who fear they can be fired for reporting wrongdoing, patients at the mercy of institutions and . . . the public which pays for these institutions but then is denied the right to know what goes on inside them." Additionally, Lewis alleged the AG's office was retaliating for his advocacy in Robeson County and attempting to "prevent exposure of serious injustices" in the county and deny "the people access to public interest lawyers who will represent them with zeal and not be tamed by the 'good old boy' system." Lewis and the Robeson Defense Committee had filed a lawsuit against AG Thornburg only a few months before the AG's office began opposing Lewis's pro hac vice motion.

In July 1989, Superior Court Judge Orlando Hudson held a hearing on Lewis's motion. That day, thirty-seven public interest groups and advocates issued a joint statement in support of Lewis and calling for journalists to investigate opposition to his appearance. They questioned the motivations of the AG's office and accused it of diverting "public resources and public attention from the underlying injustices." "It is of vital importance for all of us involved in issues of social justice to demand that any efforts to 'chill' First Amendment rights to associate, organize, and protest cease immediately," the statement read.

Assistant AG Ann Reid told Judge Hudson that Lenzer had "no right to have this particular lawyer." Reid said of Lewis, "His courtroom demeanor and his demeanor outside the courtroom has not been appropriate . . . He doesn't have any respect for proper courtroom procedure. He's demonstrated that time and again." Hudson told Reid, "I am trying to determine whether you really don't want Mr. Pitts in this case because he is a liberal rabble-rouser who will give you a difficult time."

Famed civil rights lawyer James Ferguson, who represented Lewis at the hearing, told Hudson that Lewis was an "exemplary," "skilled," and "dedicated" advocate who "speaks his mind" and "educates the public." Ferguson accused the AG's office of retaliating against Lewis in response to CIS's press release about witness intimidation.

Hudson granted Lewis's motion because Lewis fulfilled the statutory requirements for a pro hac vice appearance. "He has never been disciplined, and he has never been held in contempt in court," Hudson commented. The *News and Observer* reported that Hudson also "took into consideration the lateness of the state's objection to Mr. Pitts' participation."

Afterward, Lewis wrote to Ferguson, "It was a real honor for me to have you as 'my' lawyer and you can bet your boots I have bragged about it. . . . Plus, as one who likes to consider himself a trial lawyer, it was insightful to see you operate—smooth as owl shit." Many years later, Lewis reflected, "It's amazing what a fight we put up, with all those people having my back. I am mighty grateful to them."

Lenzer's case ultimately settled for $110,000. According to Payne, the case was the first in which a North Carolina state court recognized a claim for civil conspiracy in an employment matter.

However, retaliation against Lewis seemingly continued. In March 1991, House Bill (HB) 309 was introduced in the North Carolina General Assembly. The bill would limit pro hac vice privileges to lawyers domiciled outside of the state. Lewis told the *News and Observer*, "That sounds mighty personal to me. Is the frequency of this issue arising such that it can be anything other than directed at the Christic Institute South?"

Payne recalled telling Lewis during the pro hac vice motion ordeal, "Look, man, we don't need to be fuckin' around . . . and havin' to spend bunches of hours on this shit. Go take the fuckin' bar and get your ass admitted." After HB 309 took effect on October 1, 1991, Lewis couldn't appear in any North Carolina state court case.

So, Lewis finally took Payne's advice and, in October 1992, applied to take the North Carolina Bar Exam. However, his "Character and Fitness Committee Report," a mandatory component of the application, noted five areas of concern.

The first was a complaint, filed by Winston-Salem DA Donald Tisdale with the state bar in late 1985. He alleged Lewis engaged in the unauthorized practice of law while working with Larry Little and the Darryl Hunt Defense Fund. Specifically, Tisdale accused Lewis of holding himself out as an attorney for Sammy Lee Mitchell, who, like Hunt, was wrongly implicated in the killing of Deborah Sykes. Lewis had explained to the bar that he simply misworded his role in a hastily written letter. The bar didn't act on Tisdale's complaint.

The second concern was a grievance against Lewis, filed with the South Carolina Bar by Neal Rose, the Madison County, New York DA in

Timothy Jacobs's extradition hearing. Rose alleged that Lewis "was openly and persistently contemptuous toward the Court"; "constantly argued with the Court"; "repeatedly made snide, very audible . . . remarks toward the Court"; and "made repeated statements to the media in which he called the proceedings a mockery of justice, the Judge close-minded, biased and prejudiced." Rose included partial transcripts from Jacobs's hearing. The South Carolina Bar determined "there was no evidence of unethical conduct" and dismissed Rose's complaint.

The third and fourth areas of concern were the Rule 11 sanctions in the Contragate and Robeson County cases. Finally, the report noted concerns about Lewis's five antinuclear civil disobedience arrests between October 1978 and April 1980.

Lewis took the February 1993 bar exam; however, his results were sealed pending a hearing and decision about his "character and fitness." He recalled being "devastated by even the implication" that he might be "not morally fit."

Harry Harkins generously agreed to represent Lewis, pro bono, in his character and fitness hearing. Harkins previously worked for the North Carolina Board of Law Examiners, effectively serving as its in-house counsel. Then, in private practice, he handled character and fitness hearings for bar applicants.

The board held Lewis's hearing in October 1993. David Blackwell, an assistant state AG and Lewis's adversary in the Robeson County campaign and other cases, testified that Lewis had been unprofessional and violated rules of court. John Maddrey, an attorney for the North Carolina Department of Justice tasked with advising the board, presented a news clip of Lewis implying that the Robeson County civil suit would give him subpoena power to secure otherwise unavailable information about state criminal charges against Timothy Jacobs.

People from across the country expressed support for Lewis. Among the individuals who testified at the hearing were: his wife, Katie Greene; two parents from his son's Cub Scouts group; his friend, attorney Bob Hallman; his law partner, Gayle Korotkin; SJI board members Haywood Burns and John Hope Franklin; his former clients, Emma Gresham and Larry Little; and his former cocounsels, Carolyn McAllaster and Travis Payne. Also, Arthur Kinoy—a well-known civil rights and civil liberties movement lawyer, and Lewis's friend and role model—submitted an affidavit, which read, "In all of my work with Lewis Pitts, I was impressed with his deep commitment to the role of attorneys in conscientiously defending the right to the people of this country to fundamental protections of the Constitution. He always exhibited a profound ability to devote himself intensively to the most important responsibility of lawyers to utilize the judicial processes to protect their clients from harassment and oppression. . . . I regard him as one of the most qualified and dedicated lawyers I have ever worked with."

Others submitted letters to the Board of Law Examiners, including Reverend S. Michael Yasutake, director of the Prisoners of Conscience Project; Douglas Harris, who worked with Lewis to defend Larry Little, the Darryl Hunt Defense Fund, and Earl Jones; and Loretta Williams, a sociologist who served with Lewis on the governing board of the National Council of Churches' Racial Justice Working Group. Marty Nathan, a Greensboro Massacre survivor and civil lawsuit plaintiff, wrote to board members describing Lewis as "a thoroughly honest, courageous, and brilliant human being." His law partner, Gayle Korotkin, wrote that Lewis "exemplifies the highest ideals of the legal profession." Finally, Linda Delaney, who worked with Lewis on the Greensboro Massacre campaign, wrote, "His profound . . . commitment to the poor and disenfranchised combined with his unwavering respect for the law inspired me to launch my own private practice grounded in these same ideals. . . . Mr. Pitts' character and integrity [are] manifested daily in all aspects of his life, not merely within his professional and political endeavors. The serious yet enthusiastic attention he gives his legal cases matches that which he gives the cub scouts, his friendships, his family."

At the hearing, Harkins told board members that Lewis was a contentious and fierce advocate who wasn't always liked, but who was always ethical and honest; and any opposition to Lewis was based on his politics, not his moral character. Additionally, Harkins told them a finding that Rule 11 sanctions are evidence of poor moral character would establish bad precedent—an argument he believes especially resonated with litigators on the board. Years later, Harkins summarized his closing argument: "Whether you like Mr. Pitts, you'd hire him, or you'd elect him president of the local bar isn't the question; the question is whether he has good moral character, and there's not a shred of evidence that he was dishonest or immoral."

In November 1993, the board issued its finding that Lewis possessed the requisite character and fitness to be a state bar member. Twenty-five years later, Harkins reflected, "Lewis chose to use his legal talents for truly the ones who need it the most. . . . He's a person of great principle. . . . Of all the cases I ever handled, this is one of the ones I'm most proud of."

Once his bar exam results were unsealed, Lewis learned that he'd failed—yet another emotional blow during an already disheartening time. Undeterred, he sat for the test a second time, passed, and was sworn-in to the North Carolina State Bar in April 1994.

Southern Justice Institute Ends

While studying for the bar exam, fighting to be admitted to the North Carlina State Bar, and working on various campaigns, Lewis was also toiling to make SJI financially viable. SJI staff had hoped their new name, board, and focus on children's rights would open new funding streams; however, their financial struggles continued.

SJI lacked sufficient revenue to continue employing Alan Gregory as a staff attorney and Mia Kirsh as communications director. Kirsh wrote in 2019, "Lewis was never . . . on an ego trip like so many male leaders at the time. He was passionate about the cause, but also sweet and loved to tell stories . . . ." She called Lewis a "role model," "hero," "brilliant lawyer," and "defender of justice."

Even with reduced expenses, SJI's funding crisis continued. In September 1992, Lewis wrote to SJI Board Member Haywood Burns, "Underneath this trench-fighting, piss-on-the-bad-guys activist lawyer is a frightened little boy—scared my/our work will die unnecessarily and I'll be forced to work for money rather than the 'quest for human completion.'" The following month, Lewis shared with board members, "Now we must think about feeding ourselves and our families. . . . None of us have savings accounts. I picked up unemployment compensation forms yesterday and will file today. Gayle and Czerny are doing the same. We are forced to be applying for jobs." Lewis began receiving unemployment and performing part-time contract work for a local law firm.

SJI plummeted deeper into financial crisis. In June 1993, Lewis and Korotkin reported to SJI's board, "We are fighting like hornets in a mason jar. . . . Financially, planning for survival each week is a sheer act of faith." He conveyed his anguish to Cornel West: "Things have gone from bad to worse. . . . The ship is so low we must jump off else our families starve. We've had no pay since April 1st. My life's blood—this prophetic method of public interest lawyering—is running out of my veins into the ground. . . . All is a mess and my faith is being put to the greatest test yet. This was such a calling for me! Now I don't know how to serve the movement for justice and equality."

After fourteen years spent working side by side—five years on the Greensboro Massacre campaign, six and a half years as CIS, and two and a half years as SJI—Lewis and Korotkin finally called it quits. In June 1994, Lewis wrote to the full board:

> Gayle and I have no other choice but to leave this historic ship as it quickly sinks. We have poured our heart and soul into the struggle for civil rights. . . . We have done it with the goal of empowerment; we have done it in tandem with public education and organizing; we have done it without charging the clients or the movement fees. . . . We are both in grieving and, more accurately, depressed. Please know that we are not simply leaving in search for higher salaries. . . . This is a necessity. Gayle and I have applied for Legal Services type work. Our future is uncertain, but what we can guarantee is that the values and principles of justice and equality that you each so embody will stay with us in whatever endeavors we undertake. . . .

SJI's final newsletter included an open letter from Lewis, which read:

> I am simply flooded with feelings: the powerful legacy we tried to continue from the Greensboro Civil Rights Fund; the strength and dignity of our grassroots clients despite the pain and inequality they experience; the competence, commitment, and strength of four women (Gayle, Czerny, Mia and Ashaki) whom I have had the opportunity to work with . . . ; the . . . loyal supporters who recognize the strategic significance of Southern, grassroots, African-American struggles for equality; the sheer rottenness of the status quo; the lack of judicial neutrality; the fear and intimidation that holds sway over many; the list could go on.
>
> However, looking back I honestly believe our unique approach using organizing, public education, and litigation as "tactics in tandem" to achieve the strategic goal of empowering grassroots folks to fight battles of their choosing was and still is correct. As my mentor Arthur Kinoy has written about his four decades as a "People's Lawyer": "The ultimate test of the appropriateness of a given legal strategy (we would say tactic) could not be solely the likelihood of success within the court structure. . . . The crucial

question was what role it would play at that moment in protecting or advancing the people's struggle." Many people, especially funders, never grasped this concept. . . .

Rest assured that we are diligently attempting to find new, creative ways to utilize the experience gained with SJI to assist the movements for equality, democracy, and human completion.

Korotkin accepted a job at the Land Loss Prevention Project, a nonprofit that provides legal assistance to financially distressed farmers and landowners in North Carolina. Czerny Brasuell began working for a community development corporation. In 2017, Brasuell wrote:

Lewis was a fiery advocate, a passionate lawyer and defender of the rights of those who were essentially without defense and defenders, without resources, and in imminent danger of losing . . . their freedom, their livelihoods, their land and their lives. He had a clear sense of right and wrong, of ethical urgency, of morality in action. . . .

He honestly expressed such admiration and respect for his elders, contemporaries and youth who had struggled so long without respect. . . . He literally sat at their feet and paid homage and it was his example, coupled with the commitment of the staff he put together, that made us welcome and fostered our successes. . . .

One of Lewis' many strengths is that he could inspire people to believe that winning was possible, and not just the big win, but that all the incremental wins (and stumbles) along the way mattered as well. . . .

Lewis was tenacious. . . . He had . . . wild creativity, finding new and different ways to see a problem, leaving the hidebound hoary ways behind. He was willing to be uncomfortable. He didn't condescend. He had a sharp wit and a truly inspired sense of humor, much needed driving on the dark back roads of southern towns in the middle of the night. Lewis was deeply compassionate and deeply outraged by injustice. He did not hesitate to express contempt for those who were complicit in the latter. There was no pretense and no equivocation in his outrage.

As an African American woman with an activist life before meeting and working with Lewis, I could count on the fingers

of one hand—with spares—how many white men I had encountered with an understanding of white supremacy, the antiracist
movement and the importance of people of conscience working
not only in support and understanding of the agendas of people
of color but working in white communities to challenge attitudes,
behaviors and practices. . . . Lewis was prepared to do that. This
self-awareness and the knowledge that activism begins at home
among those espousing the attitudes he professed to abhor and
fight, made Lewis unique. I didn't feel as though I had to hold
back my feelings, my assessments, my criticism, because Lewis was
always self-critical and he didn't fold when situations and discussions became hot. . . . He was consistent, trustworthy, dependable;
intellectually and strategically honest in all the ways those words
matter in crisis. . . .

Lewis wouldn't back down. We didn't refuse a case in spite of
the odds or clear difficulties at the outset. . . . Lewis didn't profit
by his work. He didn't get rich. . . . He chose this work because he
believed in it and lived it.

PART III

Finding Stability while Still Fighting for Justice

(1994–2015)

CHAPTER 15

Civil Legal Aid

By summer 1994, Lewis was disheartened and broke. He was receiving unemployment and performing part-time contract work for a local law firm. To earn extra income, his wife, Katie Greene, delivered newspapers early in the morning before heading to her full-time job as a high school teacher. They had a mortgage, a child, and myriad other expenses. He desperately needed a steady income and a new outlet for his passion.

Lewis had largely come to accept that external forces had ended the full-time movement lawyering portion of his career—at least as the leader of an independent organization. For his own sanity and his family's well-being, Lewis knew he needed to chart a new course. He was still dedicated to being a social justice lawyer. He was also committed to remaining in North Carolina's Triangle region, where he and Greene had established roots since August 1986. They had a home in Durham; their son, Stephen, was starting fourth grade at the neighborhood public school he'd attended since kindergarten; Greene was happy teaching high school in nearby Chapel Hill and volunteering with local advocacy organizations; and Lewis had recently won his fight to become a member of the North Carolina State Bar.

So, Lewis reached out to local friends and acquaintances, including Paul Pooley. At the time, Pooley was an attorney at Carolina Legal Assistance (CLA) in Raleigh. He'd met Lewis while working for the Karen Silkwood Fund and fundraising for Christic Institute. Pooley introduced Lewis to CLA's director, Deborah Greenblatt.

Carolina Legal Assistance

In 1977, the ABA and Wake County Bar Association cofounded CLA to provide civil legal services to patients in North Carolina's state-run psychiatric hospitals. Over time, CLA's work expanded to include impact litigation on behalf of children and adult prisoners with mental disabilities who weren't receiving adequate services. CLA pursued systemic reform through public education, litigation, and public policy advocacy. The organization subsisted on funding from the federal government and attorney's fees.

Lewis became a full-time CLA staff attorney in fall 1994, and the civil legal aid portion of his career began. He knew little about health and disability law and described himself as "quite the peon" in the organization. However, he studied intensely and worked closely with CLA's leaders to learn on the job.

Lewis was immensely relieved to have a full-time job with benefits. Having a stable, adequate income for the first time in two decades was, in his words, "fat city, gravy-type stuff." Nevertheless, Lewis struggled with working in a larger organization—especially one in which he wasn't a leader or embedded in grassroots movements.

Lewis's time with CLA ended after only a couple of years, in part, because funding associated with one of CLA's major class action cases was drying up. To a greater extent, Lewis's departure related to new rules governing federal legal services funding.

Federal Restrictions on Legal Services

In 1964, Congress passed the Economic Opportunity Act as part of President Johnson's War on Poverty. The act established the Office of Economic Opportunity, through which Congress made available, for the first time, federal funding for legal services for poor people.

A decade later, President Nixon signed into law the Legal Services Corporation (LSC) Act. In addition to establishing the LSC nonprofit to administer federal appropriations for legal services, the act imposed restrictions on the types of cases funding recipients could handle, political activities by their staffs, and other activities.

Then, under pressure from the Reagan administration, which wanted to eliminate the LSC, Congress reduced the organization's funding by twenty-five percent, imposed more restrictions on activities by LSC-funded programs, and stacked the LSC's board with members who were antagonistic toward the organization's mission and activities. New board members directed LSC staff to initiate a highly intrusive, exhaustively detailed, resource-draining regulatory compliance monitoring program for LSC's more than three hundred locally administered legal aid programs and specialized support centers.

After Republicans gained control of Congress in the mid-1990s, they cut LSC funding by a third and imposed draconian restrictions on recipient organizations, including prohibitions on specific types of clients (including prisoners, undocumented immigrants, and people facing eviction from public housing for drug convictions); cases (including school desegregation, abortion, voter redistricting, and welfare reform); and activities (including class actions, legislative advocacy, and community organizing).

CLA was part of Legal Services of North Carolina (LSNC), a confederation of legal services organizations, established by the NC Bar association in 1976, through which LSC funding flowed. The restrictions that Congress instituted in 1996 forced CLA to choose one of two paths forward: remain part of LSNC and continue receiving federal funding but forgo critical advocacy strategies and attorney's fees, or leave LSNC and lose federal funding but continue advocating with a full toolbox of strategies and collecting attorney's fees. CLA's leadership chose the latter.

In turn, Lewis had a choice: remain with CLA after its separation from LSNC, or become director of LSNC's new Mental Health Unit (MHU), which would be created using LSC funds CLA would forgo. Eager to lead again and explore new and different types of campaigns, he chose the latter.

Mental Health Unit

In 1996, Lewis started MHU with support from LSNC's executive director, Deborah Weissman. Lewis first met Weissman when they shared a stage as speakers during an event at Syracuse University in the 1980s. Lewis was in the area for Timothy Jacobs's extradition hearing, which he handled with Alan Rosenthal, one of Weissman's law partners at the time. She and Lewis also knew each other through mutual connections in the CWP and NLG. Weissman described Lewis as an "infectiously lovely human being."

They reunited when Weissman began leading LSNC. She was relieved Lewis stayed with LSNC after CLA separated because he always sought to undertake "more and better" advocacy, "was one of the most creative social justice lawyers" she knew, understood they "could still do impact work" with LSC restrictions, and had an "indomitable spirit of resistance."

The MHU inherited from CLA responsibility for coordinating legal services for patients in state psychiatric facilities. At the time, the state operated four psychiatric facilities: Dorothea Dix Hospital in Raleigh, opened as the North Carolina Insane Asylum in 1856; Cherry Hospital in Goldsboro, opened as the Asylum for Colored Insane in 1880; Broughton Hospital in Morganton, opened as the Western North Carolina Insane Asylum in 1883; and Central Regional Hospital in Butner, opened as the John Umstead Hospital in 1947. The MHU would strive to combat persistent problems in the facilities, including inadequate resources, overcrowding, and patient abuse.

The unit was staffed by Lewis; Susan Epstein, a part-time staff attorney; a paralegal; and part-time, contract attorneys who conducted intake at the hospitals. Their office was in downtown Raleigh.

Prior to law school, Epstein was a nurse specializing in mental health. After law school, she practiced in Massachusetts before moving to Durham. She applied to work in the MHU, knowing her nursing background would be an asset.

Epstein first met Lewis at Central Regional Hospital. She accompanied him into the patient unit, where they met a woman who was institutionalized after being accused of child abuse and diagnosed with Munchausen syndrome. Lewis was impressed by Epstein's impromptu primer about the patient's condition and convinced she'd be a great hire.

Lewis, Epstein, and the contract attorneys traveled to the hospitals to offer patients free legal assistance. Lewis mostly covered Dorothea Dix, where he'd pick up a spare key left for him by hospital staff, enter locked wards on his own, and walk around asking, "Anyone want to talk to a lawyer?" Most patients complained to him about delusions, such as fillings in their teeth emitting radio waves, or quality of care issues, like scratchy blankets—neither of which the MHU was designed or equipped to handle. Lewis said, "The issues felt too big to get a handle on. There wasn't enough money for the facilities or evidence of illegality, and we couldn't do class actions." So, he usually attempted to informally resolve legitimate and manageable claims by pleading with hospitals' medical chiefs of staff.

When necessary, Lewis and Epstein filed petitions in North Carolina's Office of Administrative Hearings. However, according to Epstein, even if they prevailed at trial—after months of discovery, depositions, hearings, and expert testimony—the head of the Department of Mental Health could, under state law, disregard orders from ALJs.

Lewis and Epstein also worked on cases involving the Early and Periodic Screening, Diagnostic, and Treatment (EPSDT) benefit, which entitles children enrolled in Medicaid to preventative and comprehensive health care services. The federal EPSDT law requires states to pay for services that are coverable under Medicaid and determined to be medically necessary to treat, correct, or reduce illnesses and conditions.

For example, Lewis and Epstein, with help from Jane Perkins of the National Health Law Program, successfully represented Timothy Jackson. Jackson, a minor, suffered from bipolar and attention deficit disorders, which caused him to exhibit severe aggression and impulsivity. He was prescribed various psychotropic drugs but continued to struggle behaviorally. The entity that managed Medicaid in Jackson's region of the state refused to pay for his admission to the Child Neuropsychiatry Unit at the University of North Carolina Hospital, even though his treating physician determined hospitalization was medically necessary. Lewis, Epstein, and Perkins successfully appealed the denial and obtained more intensive services for Jackson.

A *Charlotte Observer* profile read, "Through constant letter-writing and occasional lawsuits, Pitts has managed to get mentally ill children the help they need in treatment centers. He has sued the state in federal court to force mental health officials to cover the costs of residential treatment for sick children, and travels the state meeting with families who need help. 'I guess I see law as a ministry,' he says." The federal lawsuit referenced in the profile involved an eleven-year-old boy who had been severely abused and needed psychiatric help. He had a history of torturing and killing kittens and smearing feces on walls. However, the North Carolina Division of Medical Assistance approved payment for only about half the cost of the out-of-state, inpatient care recommended by several doctors. So, Lewis and other attorneys sued the state in US District Court. Lewis told the Associated Press, "It's like me saying you're entitled to go out and have a steak supper, here's a quarter. The improper way the rate is set assures that nobody will get this stuff." The state ultimately agreed to pay for the treatment.

During his time leading the MHU, Lewis also helped start Project Health, Education, and Advocacy Link (HEAL). He was inspired to create Project HEAL after visiting TeamChild staff in Seattle, Washington. TeamChild began as a partnership between public defenders and civil legal aid attorneys who were frustrated by children cycling in and out of the juvenile justice system without receiving individualized services and supports to address the underlying causes of delinquency and reduce recidivism. The organization's mission is "to uphold the rights of youth involved, or at risk of involvement, in the juvenile justice system to help them secure the education, healthcare, housing, and other support they need to achieve positive outcomes in their lives." Through Project HEAL, Lewis and his then colleagues, including

Natasha Nazareth and David Amsbary, collaborated with social workers and juvenile court judges, defense attorneys, and probation officers, primarily in Wake and Forsyth Counties. Like TeamChild, Project HEAL provided civil legal services for youths alleged to be delinquent or "undisciplined." For example, Lewis and his staff assisted Project HEAL clients with securing mental health and educational services.

Finally, Lewis served as a member of the Governor's Advisory Council for Persons with Disabilities. He believed the council did little more than meet and rubber stamp, rather than meaningfully address problems. So, Lewis brought clients to council meetings, where together they raised pressing issues and advocated for solutions.

Lewis directed the MHU for about four years. He recalled that his six years of mental health advocacy, including two at CLA, didn't markedly improve his legal skills but did deepen his understanding of "just how miserable the mental health system was in North Carolina." He described the psychiatric hospitals as "pitiful, smelly, and horrible" and "very depressing," and said, "psychiatrists were there mostly for medication management," "technicians used brutal force," and most patients were "drugged out" and "zombied up."

Advocates for Children's Services

In July 2000, Lewis ended the MHU and started Advocates for Children's Services (ACS) within LSNC. He did so primarily because he wanted to focus full-time on children's rights. Lewis broadly defined ACS's mission as ensuring North Carolina's economically disadvantaged children were heard in legal matters impacting them and provided opportunities to grow up healthy, safe, and well educated.

Secondarily, deinstitutionalization in the mental health system reduced the need for the MHU's services. According to one study, between 1980 and 2010, the number of residents in "any psychiatric inpatient or other mental health 24-hour treatment bed" declined by fifty-nine percent in North Carolina.

Lastly, Lewis started ACS because he believed children's issues, relative to his other prior professional focuses, provided a more sympathetic, less partisan vehicle for stimulating dialogue about neoliberalism, austerity, and social, economic, and political change. Child advocacy was the big tent under which Lewis could—with likely and unlikely allies alike—sermonize and organize against capitalism and for participatory democracy. In a collection of essays published by the ABA's Center on Children and the Law, Lewis wrote, "You cannot meaningfully discuss the need for . . . increased appropriation for children without addressing the campaign finance system whereby private wealth from approximately 1% of the population accounts for 90% of all political contributions. That small, elite group of 'players' buys public policy that serves their personal and corporate needs. Then we and the children are inevitably told there isn't enough money to fully fund Head Start; to fully implement the promises of Medicaid services; to pay teachers and have small classrooms."

In 2002, most organizations that comprised the LSNC confederation merged to become one nonprofit—Legal Aid of North Carolina (LANC). Lewis had chosen to house ACS within LSNC and then he decided to continue with ACS as part of LANC because they provided funding and institutional stability and handled most of the administrative and bureaucratic minutia he loathed.

As ACS's managing attorney, Lewis supervised, at any given time, one paralegal, two or three staff attorneys, one or two post-graduate fellows, and one or more interns or volunteers. He also worked on a wide variety of cases, projects, and campaigns. For example, he provided legal advice and representation to children living in poverty—and in some cases, to their parents or guardians—in a variety of matters, such as guardianship and emancipation, juvenile delinquency, and students experiencing homelessness, academic failure, or school suspension or expulsion. Many of his individual cases involved what he termed the three "big federal promises to children": all medically necessary health services for children from low-income families pursuant to the EPSDT component of Medicaid; individualized special education and related services for elementary and secondary public school students with disabilities pursuant to the Individuals with Disabilities Education Act; and timely permanency planning, with health and safety as the primary concerns, for abused and neglected children pursuant to the Adoption and Safe Families Act (ASFA). In addition to his ASFA work, Lewis continued fighting to ensure that abused and neglected children had a voice in legal proceedings impacting their lives.

The cases of Thomas, Kyle, and S. R. are examples of Lewis's work to enforce promises to children under the EPSDT benefit. Chris's case and Crystal's case illustrate Lewis's ongoing advocacy for abused and neglected children.

THOMAS

Thomas was born to a sex worker who used crack. By age three, he had shuffled in and out of foster care and spent time in a psychiatric hospital. He had bipolar disorder, severe attention-deficit/hyperactivity disorder (ADHD), post-traumatic stress disorder (PTSD), reactive attachment disorder, autism, and a low IQ. He would hurt himself and couldn't be left alone.

Thomas was adopted by his foster mother, Kathy, and thus, legally entitled to Medicaid coverage until at least age eighteen. A psychiatrist determined Thomas needed, as a matter of medical necessity, mobile crisis intervention services, home-based services from a team of professionals, and a short-term crisis intervention bed for when he couldn't be stabilized at home. Instead, the local management entity (LME) responsible for pre-approval of services under North Carolina's heavily privatized Medicaid system told Kathy that, if there was a crisis with Thomas after business hours, she ought to call a hotline to get advice; and if that didn't work, she should call the police, which could've led to Thomas being handcuffed, taken to an emergency room, and committed. His psychiatrist told the *Asheville Citizen-Times*, "The criminalization of Thomas or any other patient is an abomination."

Lewis filed a complaint on Thomas's behalf. In April 2005, an ALJ ruled that the services approved for Thomas were inadequate, in violation of Medicaid law, and he was entitled to all the services deemed medically necessary under the EPSDT benefit.

KYLE

Kyle had autism and bipolar disorder; needed therapy to cope with oversensitivity to light, touch, and sounds; wasn't toilet trained; and would kick, hit, and bite when his daily routine was disrupted. Kyle's mother couldn't find appropriate services for him outside of school because they lived in a rural county and the LME wasn't helping.

Lewis brought a lawsuit on behalf of Kyle, who was four years old at the time. In December 2006, an ALJ ruled, "The state may not fail to provide medically necessary service to a Medicaid-eligible child because it is too expensive, not listed in the state plan of services, or difficult to provide." *News and Observer* coverage read, "Statewide changes in mental health care, in which local governments gave up providing direct care in favor of private agencies, are the reason Kyle isn't getting what he needs, his attorney Lewis

Pitts said. 'The so-called mental health reform has been deformed,' Pitts said. 'They're not making the services available for high-needs kids.' . . . Pitts, a legal aid lawyer in Durham, sees a thread running through the cases—the lack of rural mental health care for children. 'We're going to keep taking them one at a time,' he said. 'We're trying to get someone to listen.'"

S. R.

S. R. had significant mental health issues and was in the custody of the DSS. In January 2008, she was put in a juvenile jail because no appropriate community-based treatment was identified for her.

Lewis brought a lawsuit on S. R.'s behalf, alleging the state was violating her Medicaid rights. An ALJ ordered the state to, within one week, create a plan to move S. R. to a psychiatric residential treatment facility (PRTF) where she could receive intensive treatment. The judge signed an order, drafted by Lewis, which read, "As a matter of law, as a matter of fact, and as a matter of human rights and fundamental decency, it is an abysmal failure to us as human beings and as a society . . . for this 14-year-old child to be illegally locked up in a juvenile detention center, and to have been locked up without treatment since January 18, 2008, because the North Carolina mental health system has been unable or unwilling to locate treatment at a PRTF."

News and Observer coverage read, "One of the girl's lawyers, Lewis Pitts, linked the scarcity of intensive treatment to the state's bungled mental health reform, which moved most services into the hands of private companies. 'That's a systematic flaw,' he said."

CHRIS

Chris was neglected and sexually abused by his mother and stepfather. He was also deaf and showing signs of reactive attachment disorder. At age ten, Chris was a ward of the state, but had spent the previous six years living with a loving foster family that had other deaf children and intended to adopt Chris.

Chris's foster mother asked Lewis to represent Chris. Lewis met with Chris using a sign language interpreter and filed a notice of appearance in his ongoing foster care proceedings. Lewis also recruited University of Florida Law Professor Barbara Bennett Woodhouse and her colleague, a child psychiatrist specializing in deaf children, to file an amicus brief with the trial court.

Lewis wrote in an article for the ABA that the LME "refused to even have Chris evaluated, much less provided treatment" in order to minimize costs; and that Chris's GAL met with him only once during his six years in foster care and refused to advocate for his expressed wishes or best interests.

Nevertheless, the judge denied Chris the right to be heard through Lewis. Lewis described in the ABA article what happened next:

> In what appeared to be a retaliatory move against the foster mother for her public advocacy for meaningful representation and treatment for Chris, [social services] decided to remove Chris from the only loving family he had ever known. . . . Extraordinary Writs to appeal the denial of the right to be heard through re-tained pro bono counsel were denied without opinion by both the North Carolina Court of Appeals and North Carolina Supreme Court. . . . Chris was snatched from his family of six years and moved to another town. After several weeks he was moved once again. . . . [Chris] was truly never heard in court.

CRYSTAL

In 1994, Lazalia "Sissy" Urick was seventeen years old, homeless, unemployed, and pregnant with her second child. Sissy gave her first baby to her mother, and her second baby, Crystal, to a friend, Katherine Romero Gaytan, who lived in Hernando County, Florida. Gaytan and Crystal subsequently moved to Wendell, North Carolina, a suburb of Raleigh. According to news reports, court records showed that Sissy gave Gaytan power of attorney for Crystal on July 12, 1994, but then Sissy revoked that power just a week later.

Seven years later, Sissy told law enforcement in Florida that Gaytan had abducted Crystal. Hernando County detectives tracked down Gaytan and Crystal in North Carolina. Gaytan was arrested and charged with abduction during the week of April 16, 2001. The charge was subsequently changed to felonious restraint—that is, allegedly hiding Crystal. Gaytan said she never knew Sissy wanted or was searching for Crystal. Gaytan was released on $25,000 bond. Crystal was put into foster care in North Carolina.

At the time, Sissy was twenty-four years old and none of her children lived with her. Her son, age eight, lived with Sissy's mother; and her other daughter, age five, lived with Sissy's friend. Sissy had another son who drowned in a swimming pool when he was two and a half years old. Earnest Barnett—Crystal's biological father and Sissy's fiancé—had an extensive criminal record and probation violations.

Wake County District Court Judge Anne Salisbury presided over a two-day trial to determine who'd have custody of Crystal. Lewis attempted to represent Crystal in the proceedings, but Salisbury denied Crystal an opportunity to be heard altogether. In April 2001, Salisbury ruled—without having heard Crystal's feelings and perspective—that Sissy and Barnett could take Crystal to Florida. Lewis told the *St. Petersburg Times*, "(Sissy) came up here with her trump card and said, 'I'm the biological mother,' and the court said that's all that's relevant."

The next day, Lewis filed an emergency appeal to the North Carolina Supreme Court, requesting another hearing at which he could represent Crystal. He also requested visitation between Gaytan and Crystal pending the appeal and a stay of Crystal's return to Florida. In the petition, Lewis argued that Barnett never reported his felony convictions to Judge Salisbury and Wake County Human Services failed to thoroughly investigate Crystal's biological parents. "The state has miserably failed in its duty to investigate and present all of the evidence," Lewis told the Associated Press.

Justice Robert Orr granted Lewis's request for an emergency stay and blocked Urick from taking Crystal to Florida. Upon learning of Orr's decision, Gaytan sighed deeply and proclaimed, "Oh, God; oh, that's wonderful." The state supreme court gave the parties a month or so to submit their written arguments. Meanwhile, Crystal remained in foster care.

North Carolina Lawyers Weekly's coverage of ACS's involvement in the case read:

> Workers at a children's advocacy program say the 7-year-old girl caught in the middle of a custody battle between her birth parents and the woman who raised her deserves a voice in court. . . .
>
> "I got involved because this was another example of the legal system treating a child as property, not as a person," said Lewis Pitts, the lawyer who went to court on Crystal's behalf. "Literally, Thursday morning, as I was driving to work, I wept. It was one of those things: 'Somebody's got to do something. If you don't do it, nobody will.'"

Lewis's advocacy on Crystal's behalf was also highlighted in a *News and Observer* profile titled, "Lawyer Seeks Justice for Those Who Can't on Their Own." It read:

> Fifteen years of such conflict on many fronts have grayed Pitts' beard but not the brown hair that falls just below his collar. . . . On the odd day when it's nice outside and he's got the time, he hops on his Honda Shadow motorcycle and hits the road for 50 or 70 miles.
>
> But his work is his life. He turned his legal mind, awakened during Watergate and the Vietnam War, to the anti-nuclear movement, post-segregation racial justice and, more recently, children's rights.
>
> He acknowledges that some people who disagree with him consider him difficult, uncompromising, a headline-seeker. He said he merely demands that the Constitution keep its promise for all children.
>
> Others who toil in the children's-rights vineyard praise Pitts' energy, as well as his willingness to toil the waters for the causes in which he believes.
>
> "There is an important role in the world for gadflies, of which Lewis is one," said Jonathan Sher, president of the . . . N.C. Child Advocacy Institute in Raleigh. "He's good at prodding people's conscience and trying to make sure that as a society, we live up to our own expressed ideals. . . . He is fundamentally about trying to reduce the gap between the rhetoric about children and the reality of how we treat them."

In May 2001, the state supreme court issued its decision. The court denied a new hearing, directed that Crystal be given to Sissy, and ordered the Florida Division of Children and Families to supervise Crystal. The justices reasoned that Crystal had no liberty interest in who'd be her guardian; instead, according to Lewis, the court declared she was property, "to be shipped to the person who happened to possess the original invoice." He wrote to a *St. Petersburg Times* reporter, "What kind of judiciary did we elect that treats little children with such indifference and disrespect?"

The charges against Gaytan were dropped. In the years that followed, Gayton visited Crystal in Florida two or three times a month, regularly talked with her by phone, and sent her clothes for school and gifts. Crystal called Gayton's mother "grandma."

In 2004, Crystal was removed from Sissy's home amid criminal charges of abuse and neglect. Sissy said she wanted Crystal to live with Gaytan. "I'm saddened that what we feared has come true," Lewis told the *St. Petersburg Times*.

INFUSING MOVEMENT LAWYERING
CONCEPTS AND APPROACHES

Lewis infused movement lawyering concepts and approaches into ACS's work—at least as much as possible given LSC restrictions on client eligibility, organizing, and lobbying, as well as pressure to resolve a high volume of cases. He encouraged ACS staff to examine their own privileges and biases, to view the law as a tool and not a solution, see their role as empowering rather than helping, and be unconventional and creative in their advocacy. They viewed clients as primary decision-makers in cases and, more broadly, as partners, activists, and leaders in pursuing systemic reform. Additionally, Lewis and his staff spent significant time in low-wealth communities—including in churches, nonprofits, community centers, and homes—building power by providing "Know Your Rights" trainings, advocacy workshops, and connections to other resources; developing authentic and trusting relationships with clients and advocates; and collaborating with grassroots service-providers, organizers, and other leaders. They provided people of color-led grassroots organizations—including Bringing about Change, in Robeson County, and Parents Supporting Parents, in Guilford County—with data and policy analyses, communication and education tools, and legal services. In 2013, Parents Supporting Parents' leaders, Linda and Leon Mozell and Lissa Harris, wrote, "In all the years that [Lewis] has dedicated to fighting for the rights of children, the fire has not died, nor has it diminished. . . . Thousands of children who have not heard his name have benefited from his work."

ACS's lawyers also used the law to advance systemic reforms. Lewis collaborated with organizations and attorneys working on appellate litigation regarding the state constitutional right to a sound basic education, alternative education for students long-term suspended or expelled from school, and limiting searches of students at school. He also utilized legal strategies to bolster campaigns aimed at resuscitating the State Advisory Council (SAC) on Juvenile Justice, stopping social services agencies from taking foster children's

Social Security benefits, and eliminating indiscriminate shackling of children in delinquency court.

STATE ADVISORY COUNCIL ON JUVENILE JUSTICE

North Carolina's Juvenile Justice Reform Act of 1998 created a nineteen-member SAC to advise the Department of Juvenile Justice and Delinquency Prevention and other state agencies that served youth about systemic reform, budgeting, and other matters. The act required the governor and state supreme court chief justice to cochair and convene the SAC at least four times a year.

However, by May 2003, the SAC hadn't met since 2001. Mike Easley, governor since January 2001, had never appeared at a meeting. According to Lewis, Wake County District Court Judge Russell Sherrill said Easley was "deep-sixing the meetings" and suggested Lewis seek a writ of mandamus directing the governor to properly fulfill his official duties. So, Lewis filed a lawsuit on behalf of six at risk children against Governor Easley and Supreme Court Chief Justice I. Beverly Lake Jr., requesting a writ ordering Easley and Lake to carry out their statutory duties to cochair and convene SAC meetings.

Subsequently, the council began meeting regularly, with Easley and Lake present. In turn, Lewis and his clients withdrew the lawsuit and declared victory in September 2003. Lewis told the *Asheville Citizens-Times*, "It's shocking when you look at how high-ranking officials like the governor and chief justice ignored a legal duty imposed on them. . . . We'll be paying close attention. . . . If the co-chairs fail to provide adequate leadership, we'll definitely [sue] again." Marcia Morey, a district court judge and SAC member at the time and now a state legislator, wrote about Lewis, "He spoke truth to power and I'll always admire him for that."

FOSTER CHILDREN'S BENEFITS

Shortly after John was born in July 1990, a court terminated his biological father's parental rights. About a year later, John's mother, W. G., married T. S. In December 1992, T. S. adopted John. A week after that, W. G. and T. S. bought a house from Habitat for Humanity in Guilford County. W. G., who was addicted to crack, abandoned T. S. and John in April 1993. Four months later, T. S. executed a will in which he devised all his property, including his Habitat house, to a testamentary trust for John, and appointed his girlfriend, C. B., as John's guardian.

In February 1994, T. S. died of cancer, leaving John the house and a Social Security survivor's benefit. C. B. was appointed John's guardian, and, as such, became responsible for his Social Security checks, mortgage payments, and house upkeep. However, in December 1994, Habitat for Humanity notified C. B. and the local court that she was delinquent in making mortgage payments on John's behalf. Worse yet, C. B. had neglected and abused John.

In October 1997, the Guilford County DSS removed John from C. B.'s home and put him in foster care, where he stayed for five months before being placed in the physical custody of his maternal aunt, A. G.

A. G. adopted John in March 2003, thereby ending court supervision of John and becoming the representative payee for John's Social Security benefits of $571 per month. A. G. also received a monthly adoption subsidy of fifty dollars and was responsible for the monthly mortgage payments on the Habitat house.

Fourteen months later, John was placed in a group home after he started acting out. His GAL reported that John didn't want to return to A. G.'s home because she'd mistreated him, he didn't get along with her boyfriend, she only wanted his money, and he was concerned about the condition of his house and losing it to foreclosure.

In July 2004, John was again placed in foster care. A. G. relinquished her parental rights eight months later. The Habitat house was vandalized and fell further into disrepair. The *News and Observer* reported that the house had been boarded up, a condemnation poster was "plastered next to the front door," the fence was "falling apart," and the lawn was "overgrown."

In October 2005, a court ordered that John remain in the legal and physical custody of the DSS. Consequently, the DSS became the representative payee of his Social Security benefits. However, instead of using the money to make payments on his mortgage, the DSS kept the funds to reimburse itself for the cost of John's care—approximately $1,300 per month for room and board at a therapeutic foster home. The Habitat house was valued at approximately $80,000, and Habitat for Humanity held the outstanding mortgage of about $27,000. Because the mortgage wasn't being paid, Habitat initiated foreclosure proceedings.

The Guilford County DSS office wasn't the only child welfare agency taking foster children's benefits to reimburse itself; nationwide, child welfare agencies engaged in similar practices. A *Charlotte Observer* article about John read, "The Congressional Research Service estimates states take about $150 million a year from foster children."

In November 2005, Lewis and the local GAL office sued the Guilford County DSS to force the agency to use John's Social Security benefits to pay the Habitat mortgage. The following month, District Court Judge Susan Bray found the DSS's actions to be unreasonable because John would need the home when he turned eighteen and aged out of foster care. She ordered the DSS to use a portion of John's benefits to pay for the mortgage and repairs to his house.

A *News and Record* reporter described John's life and case as "a story of uncommon cruelty, compounded by layer upon layer of bureaucratic incompetence." The reporter wrote:

> "This is very ugly," said Lewis Pitts, a Legal Aid attorney who represents the child. "All these people were supposed to look out for the welfare of this boy. Instead, they've been pocketing his money. . . ."
>
> But the boy was also left with a stepmother who subjected him to daily abuse for his first seven years. . . . To the doctor at UNC who noted broken bones and cigarette burns on the child, John had confided that the stepmother "would become mean when she smoked the rock."
>
> Enter an aunt, who next adopted John, . . . promising the DSS that she would see to his needs. . . .
>
> What social workers didn't know—for another six years—was that the aunt enlisted the child to sell drugs for her. . . .
>
> With the boy now left in foster care and the custody of the DSS, what at least forced the case into public view was that Habitat was about to foreclose on the vacant house, having received no payments for a year.

The *New York Times* characterized the case as "a legal battle with potential repercussions around the country."

The DSS appealed the decision, arguing Judge Bray exceeded her authority. The North Carolina Justice Center, CLA, the Governor's Advocacy Council for Persons with Disabilities, and other organizations filed amicus briefs in support of John and Lewis. The court of appeals held oral arguments in January 2007.

While awaiting the court's decision, advocates organized a congressional "Briefing on the State Practice of Robbing Disabled and Orphaned Foster

Children of Their Social Security Benefits," to take place in Washington, DC, in July 2007. First Star, a nonprofit organization dedicated to improving the lives of child victims of abuse and neglect, cosponsored the briefing. Lewis served on First Star's board and was scheduled to testify at the briefing with John. However, the DSS, which still had custody of John, didn't allow him to make the trip. Lewis and John's GAL filed a motion for a temporary restraining order and injunction against the DSS preventing John from attending. They argued John's participation was in his best interest and protected speech under the First Amendment. However, uncertainty about his participation caused confusion and stress for John; and so, he ultimately decided not to attend. Lewis still made the trip and testified.

In November 2007, the court of appeals issued a unanimous decision upholding Bray's order, reasoning that her actions were consistent with district courts' duty to supervise the best interests of the child. The opinion noted that, if Habitat foreclosed on the home, John "would receive very little money from the sale and would be homeless when he aged out of foster care."

First Star issued a press release that read, "The issue is the focus of growing legislative and legal battles in the Congress and in the courts. . . . According to the Child Welfare League of America, 25% of foster youth reported experiencing homelessness within four years of exiting foster care. . . . States are aggressively targeting this money, hiring outside companies to help them identify foster children who are, or who should be, receiving Social Security benefits. The consultants track down these eligible children, help them secure Social Security benefits and then help the states divert the benefits—keeping a piece for themselves." Amy Harfeld, First Star's executive director, declared, "This case has national implications and is a major victory for foster children across the country." Lewis told the *News and Record*, "[Counties] are budget-starved. But the answer is not to steal from children. The answer is to come forward and make the public aware that there's a crisis in child welfare spending."

In January 2008, the North Carolina Supreme Court denied a state appeal request. A First Star press release read, "This decision signals the final chapter in a case that began to wind its way through the courts three years ago, bringing national attention to the plight of now 17-year-old John G. . . . This week's court decision reaffirms the lower court's decision in John G.'s favor, and will now set precedent for similar cases involving foster children throughout North Carolina and quite possibly nationwide." "It is our wish that every foster child in America would have such a committed legal team working on his or her behalf," said Harfeld.

SHACKLING OF CHILDREN

Children appearing in Guilford County juvenile delinquency court—regardless of their age, size, offense, or background—were handcuffed and shackled, unless a judge happened to decide restraints were unwarranted. Rebecca was one of the children in chains.

For three years, starting at age eight, Rebecca was sexually abused, including while handcuffed. She had bipolar disorder, PTSD, disruptive behavior disorder, and ADHD. She needed intensive psychiatric care, but no beds were available in mental health facilities.

In August 2006, a delinquency petition was filed against Rebecca because she stole a purse. She spent the next six weeks in juvenile jail and appeared in court four times. During each appearance, Rebecca was handcuffed and shackled, causing her to experience flashbacks to sexual abuse she had endured. Chains connecting her ankles and wrists were attached to a short length of a third chain encircling her waist. Rebecca stood in court, like a slave at auction, unable to wipe her tears.

After Rebecca was arrested, her family retained Ann Marie Dooley, an attorney in LANC's Greensboro office, to advocate for Rebecca's mental health needs. Dooley reached out to ACS staff for their expertise and assistance. Dooley, Lewis, and ACS attorney Keith Howard became Rebecca's legal team. Dooley focused on obtaining appropriate mental health services for Rebecca, then age fourteen; Lewis concentrated on preventing further shackling; and Howard worked on both issues.

They collaborated with Rebecca's delinquency attorney to file, in February 2007, a motion "to prohibit shackling of minor child in court and other public areas absent a judicial finding of need." They argued that indiscriminate shackling of children "violates their rights to due process" by "interfer[ing] with their right to counsel and to participate in the defense of their case," thereby violating the Fifth, Sixth, and Fourteenth Amendments of the US Constitution. They also cited studies about the psychological and emotional harms of shackling for children, especially those with mental health issues or who've been abused, which, in turn, hinder the rehabilitation purportedly provided by the juvenile system. Their motion concluded, "Children, regardless of their status in society, have a right to be protected from being humiliated and psychologically harmed while appearing in judicial courts."

Rebecca's legal team asked Chief District Court Judge Joseph Turner to order that neither Rebecca nor any "detained child appearing in the Guilford County Court be handcuffed or shackled absent a judicial finding that the individual child poses a threat to himself, the safety of others, or a risk of fleeing the Court." Notably, state law prohibited the shackling of adults in court unless a judge determined shackling was necessary for safety or order or to prevent escape. Lewis and his colleagues asked Turner to apply a similar standard to juveniles. The *News and Record* editorial board wrote, "Taking into account all the differences between juveniles and adults . . . it only seems fair that young detainees have some recourse in court, not just a one-size-fits-all standard."

Judge Turner, however, seemed disinclined to rule in favor of the motion. He claimed that "juveniles" needed restraints more than adults because "they are not mature people" and "much more impulsive than adults," and therefore, "don't necessarily exercise good judgment" and are more apt to run or act out in court. He also said, "One of the reasons juveniles are in juvenile court is because they haven't exhibited very good judgment. An adult most times will exhibit better judgment." Regardless, the case ultimately became moot before the motion was heard in court. Tragically, Rebecca later committed suicide.

In March 2007, Turner and six other judges who handled most juvenile cases in Guilford County jointly decided to continue indiscriminately shackling children. "As a broad, across-the-board rule it is better to leave things as they are," Turner said. Lewis told the *News and Record*, "We were extremely disappointed. . . . It's a sad commentary on the lack of sensitivity from the judiciary."

Undeterred, Lewis advocated for a new state law to narrowly limit shackling in juvenile court. By the end of March 2007, HB 1243 was introduced. Lewis led the North Carolina Bar Association's Juvenile Justice and Children's Rights Section in passing a resolution in support of HB 1243 and lobbying the association's board of governors to endorse the bill.

In June 2007, the North Carolina General Assembly unanimously ratified HB 1243 and the governor signed it into law. The revised Juvenile Code prohibits restraint of juveniles unless a judge "finds the restraint to be reasonably necessary to maintain order, prevent the juvenile's escape, or provide for the safety of the courtroom." The new statute also requires, "whenever practical," judges to "provide the juvenile and the juvenile's attorney an opportunity to be heard to contest the use of restraints before the judge orders the use of restraints." Finally, if restraints are ordered, judges must make findings of fact in support of the order. The *News and Record*, which is based in Guilford County, read, "This time it took an act of the legislature to right an injustice that should have been corrected at home."

In 2019, Ann Marie Dooley, now a highly accomplished immigration lawyer, wrote about Lewis, "To date, he is the most inspirational and amazing advocate I have ever worked with!"

CHAPTER 16

"Off the Clock" Activism
and Pro Bono Work

During his time managing the Mental Health Unit and Advocates for Children's Services, Lewis spent leave time and many nights, weekends, and holidays engaging in activism and pro bono work that would've been prohibited by federal regulations if performed during his day job. He explained his rationale for taking on additional commitments: "That's how I am wired. It's what I do. If I'm not throwing myself into helping others struggle for justice, I feel restless, less human, and out of harmony with my value system. A life of study and efforts toward 'good works' is what keeps humans human, and not sucked into the cultural abyss of selfishness, anger, hatred, and materialism." Specifically, while leading the MHU and then ACS, Lewis spent much of his free time lobbying for expansion of healthcare for children in low-income families; continuing to assist movements to protect abused and neglected children; organizing and litigating for campaign finance reform; fighting against transportation of nuclear waste; participating in the Greensboro Massacre truth and reconciliation process; and defending an activist who was prosecuted for protesting the Iraq War.

Children's Health Insurance

In 1997, Congress enacted the State Children's Health Insurance Program (SCHIP), which would provide approximately $40 billion over ten years in federal block grants to assist states in developing or expanding state-level health insurance programs for uninsured children whose family's income was too high to qualify for Medicaid but too low to afford private coverage. SCHIP funding would be critical in expanding and improving mental health services for children in North Carolina.

In spring 1998, North Carolina's Democratic governor and state senate agreed to accept federal funding to implement an SCHIP program. However, the Republican-controlled state house rejected their plan, insisting that tax breaks be included in the legislation and that eyeglasses, hearing aids, and dental services for disadvantaged children be removed.

During legislative proceedings in April 1998, Lewis, Sister Evelyn Mattern from the North Carolina Council of Churches, and Lynn Williams from North Carolina Fair Share unfurled a large banner in the house chamber, hung it from the balcony, and began chanting. The banner read, "Healthcare for kids, not more welfare for the rich." Security removed the banner, pulled Lewis out of the chamber, escorted him to an exit, and pushed him onto the sidewalk.

Shortly before his act of civil disobedience, Lewis released a statement, which read, "Common sense and common morality dictate that the needs of children be above partisan politics and above the 'logic of loot' that now rules our electoral system. Enough is enough. Therefore, I must act according to a higher logic—a logic of love and compassion for all children. . . . I must civilly disobey this institutional immorality."

The *Indy Week* read, "It got Pitts tossed out of the building, though the women were allowed to remain—we're in the South, after all. It also got front-page headlines, with photos, and great coverage on TV, which Williams says turned the tide in favor of the legislation that now guarantees affordable health insurance for every child in our state." Indeed, the general assembly passed, and the governor signed into law, legislation to accept federal funding and implement the SCHIP program, effective October 1, 1998.

Samantha Frazer

At age six, Samantha Frazer was abandoned by her mother, Victoria Frazer, a long-time user of crack and abuser of marijuana and alcohol. Victoria moved to Texas with her boyfriend, leaving Samantha behind in Delaware. For the next four years, Samantha bounced around foster homes.

Meanwhile, Samantha became very close with her therapist, Bonnie Gladu. Samantha spent time with Gladu's family at their home. Eventually, the Gladus decided to adopt Samantha. "I like them all very much and want to be adopted by them and have a real home and a real mom and dad and brothers," Samantha wrote. The DFS in Delaware petitioned the Kent County

Family Court for termination of Victoria's parental rights so the Gladus could adopt Samantha.

Judge William Walls held a hearing on the petition in March 1998. Samantha's GAL urged the court to send Samantha to live with Victoria, who was in drug rehab in South Carolina. Victoria's drug counselor testified that Victoria would be a competent parent. Victoria's court-appointed attorney also argued against termination. According to Lewis, the DFS attorney failed to "vigorously present the case" for termination.

In April 1998, Judge Walls ordered Samantha to live with Victoria in South Carolina. The DFS attorney didn't appeal the decision.

The Delaware chapter of Hear My Voice: Protecting Our Nation's Children began mobilizing in support of Samantha and reached out to Lewis for assistance. Lewis had worked with Hear My Voice on Jessica's case in Michigan. Janice Mink, cochair of the Delaware chapter, had met Lewis at a conference. She wrote, "While listening to him speak, I remember thinking how brilliant, articulate, and compassionate he was, and how he was focused on helping those who were let down by society. I thought, if our leaders had half of the decency that Lewis had, our world would be a great place." Lewis agreed to help. He wrote about Samantha in a compilation of essays titled, *Perspectives on Child Advocacy Law in the Early 21st Century*, "She was treated as an object of the proceeding and not a participant."

Using information from Mink and her chapter cochair, Catherine Hamill, Lewis drafted a four-page complaint for a writ of certiorari (i.e., an order to a lower court to send up a case record for review) to be filed pro se (i.e., on one's own, without legal counsel) by Samantha with the Delaware Supreme Court. The complaint argued that Samantha had a constitutional right to safety and a liberty interest in maintaining her relationship with Gladu, and thus, a fundamental due process right to be heard in court. The complaint read, "My mother never tried to come back and take care of me. She did not even call me regularly, visit me regularly or celebrate holidays like my birthday with me. When she did speak to me, she made promises that she broke. She has not cared for me or loved me. While she has been gone I have lived in different foster homes. I was abused in one foster home and had to be moved to another. My heart has been hurt very badly." The requested relief included recognizing Samantha as a party to a termination of parental rights action, staying Judge Walls's order pending an expedited appeal, and allowing Samantha to maintain her relationship with the Gladus until resolution of the appeal.

Lewis sent the complaint to Mink and Hamill. They helped Samantha, age ten, review and sign it. Then, they filed the complaint with the Delaware Supreme Court on June 2, 1998.

Media outlets nationwide covered Samantha's appeal. ABC's *Good Morning America* featured a live interview with Samantha. CBS's *48 Hours* with Dan Rather aired "Samantha's Choice," which "examine[d] what happens when parental rights clash with a child's desire for a happy home."

On June 19, 1998, the Delaware Supreme Court ruled in Samantha's favor, holding she was an interested party and her "nonage" was "not a bar to the filing of a complaint for certiorari." The court remanded the case to family court to reopen the termination of parental rights proceedings. Associated Press coverage read, "Samantha went to court to divorce her mom. Her legal fight redefined children's rights in Delaware. . . . By giving her legal standing, the Supreme Court essentially guaranteed that children whose parents abandon them can be represented by their own lawyers instead of just the [DFS's] case workers or court-appointed advocates. And spurred by her case, the General Assembly has approved legislation that makes it easier for children to ask for their birth parents' rights to be terminated."

Lewis wrote that "the unique pro se filing by the child accompanied with local and national media" prevented Samantha from being victimized by "institutional immorality" and "a kangaroo court where her voice was never heard." The case motivated him to create and distribute what he called a "barefoot lawyering" packet for nonlawyers who advocated for children like Samantha. The packet included a fill-in-the-blank petition and directions for completing and filing the petition. The instructions read, "First and foremost, just do it! Do not be intimidated by legalisms or treading into the maze of legal obstacles. You now know the core facts and legal/fairness issues better than most lawyers. If the case has already reached the point of needing this Petition, the legal system has manifested its unfairness and business as usual cannot be morally tolerated. You must do it because no one else has." In the packet, Lewis also encouraged advocates to "keep pushing with creativity and media coverage"; get elected officials, community clubs, religious organizations, parent-teacher organizations, and others to support the petition; and file an expedited appeal, if the petition was denied.

Two decades after the campaign for Samantha, Janice Mink wrote, "Lewis inspired me to find and raise my voice, and to challenge the system. . . . He helped me become strong and unafraid to speak my peace in a thoughtful, respectful, intelligent way. I think Lewis is an amazing soul. . . . We need more Lewis Pittses in our world."

Campaign Finance

In the late 1990s, Lewis came across a *Yale Law & Policy Review* article titled, "Equal Protection and the Wealth Primary." The authors, Jamie Raskin and John Bonifaz, argued that "the current campaign finance regime is inconsistent with equal protection" because economic obstacles effectively prevent less affluent candidates from competing for office and, therefore, "denies huge numbers of people meaningful electoral choice and unlawfully degrades their influence on the political process as a whole." Raskin was a law professor at American University; he later became a US congressman. Bonifaz was an attorney at the Center for Responsive Politics before founding the National Voting Rights Institute (NVRI).

Lewis shared the article with James Exum Jr., a former North Carolina Supreme Court chief justice. They discussed bringing the type of campaign finance lawsuit described in the article. Next, Lewis reached out to Bonifaz, who agreed to join him in organizing a coalition to bring a lawsuit in North Carolina. They were joined on the legal team by Exum; other NVRI attorneys, including Gregory Luke; former NC Supreme Court Justice Harry Martin; and Adam Stein, a founding partner of a nationally acclaimed civil rights firm. Seven public interest organizations, including the state NAACP and twelve individuals became the plaintiffs. The individual plaintiffs were a mix of Democrats, Republicans, and independents—all of whom were former, future, and would-be candidates for the state legislature who didn't have access to the requisite funding for viable, competitive campaigns. Democracy North Carolina played a major role in collecting and analyzing data for the case.

In December 1999, the plaintiffs filed in Wake County Superior Court an amended complaint against the state and its board of elections. They alleged that North Carolina "administer[ed] its elections subject to a de facto wealth primary" because candidates without wealth or the ability to raise substantial funds were "systemically excluded" from elections; "persons who have access to wealth pre-select candidates for office through their financial contributions"; and "persons without access to wealth, who cannot contribute financially, are unable to influence the choice of candidates." The plaintiffs brought the case "to secure their constitutional rights to participate in self-government."

They argued that Article I, Section 11 of the North Carolina Constitution required "the state to conduct free and fair elections, in which no economic qualification may affect the right to vote or hold office and in which there is a right to equal participation by all eligible voters." Section 11 reads, "As political rights are not dependent upon or modified by property, no property qualification shall affect the right to vote and hold office." Additionally, the plaintiffs asserted that wealth primaries violated the equal protection clauses of the state constitution because "candidates and voters with neither wealth nor access to it . . . are excluded . . . from equal participation in the political process by which those who set the public policy of North Carolina are selected."

The plaintiffs requested a declaratory judgment that the wealth primary violated the North Carolina Constitution and an injunction ordering the state to provide adequate public financing for elections.

To aid in the lawsuit, the NVRI commissioned a study by an expert political scientist, who confirmed that, in North Carolina, "money is a primary determinant of electoral success, regardless of a candidate's party affiliation, race, gender, district, or previous office held." Lewis wrote in the *Journal of Common Sense*, "Any honest assessment raises crucial issues of corruption and rule by the rich. . . . We have one dollar, one vote rather than one person, one vote. Public policy is bought by the highest bidder."

In February 2000, the defendants filed a motion to dismiss. More than eight months later, Judge Howard Manning Jr.—a Republican, former corporate lawyer—held a hearing on the motion. After another nine months of inaction, he dismissed the case, claiming the plaintiffs failed to state a claim for which relief could be granted.

The plaintiffs appealed. Their brief read, "Without clearly specifying its rationale, the Superior Court's opinion suggests that its dismissal was based on the lack of a right to 'public funding of campaigns' and the lack of 'state action' by Defendants. Plaintiffs, however, do not rely upon some textual constitutional right to public funding. Instead, they allege—and support with substantial empirical data—that North Carolina's electoral system excludes them from meaningful political participation on economic grounds. Therefore, the system violates specific enumerated constitutional rights, for which public funding of campaigns is a possible remedy."

In October 2002, the court of appeals affirmed the dismissal, reasoning that the state constitution doesn't require public campaign financing and "public financing of political campaigns is clearly a legislative issue." Finally, the state supreme court denied the plaintiffs' request for discretionary review.

North Carolina lawmakers did, however, enact the Judicial Campaign Reform Act of 2002, creating a voluntary full public financing program for North Carolina Court of Appeals and Supreme Court elections. The stated purpose of the new fund was "to ensure the fairness of democratic elections in North Carolina and to protect the constitutional rights of voters and candidates from the detrimental effects of increasingly large amounts of money being raised and spent to influence the outcome of elections." The program was the country's first full public financing system for statewide judicial elections.

In May 2019, John Bonifaz, who became president of Free Speech for People, said:

> I think the world of Lewis. I think he's a fabulous advocate. I think that were it not for his energy and enthusiasm about this wealth primary argument, and sharing it with Justice Exum, there would've never been a case in North Carolina. He was the reason why it got sparked. His energy, commitment, and intellect were critical for advancing it. He was not at all afraid to bring a new argument into the court and he was not at all dissuaded when we lost in the first round.
>
> I think we need more lawyers like Lewis Pitts. We need lawyers who are willing to challenge conventional thinking, to challenge others in the legal community, as well as judges, to broaden their understanding of what's required with respect to our constitutional protections, . . . and to be willing to think outside the box, creatively, and innovatively on how we address critical questions of the day that have underlying them serious constitutional rights at stake.

Nuclear Waste

In the late 1990s, Jim Warren inspired Lewis's return to antinuclear activism. Lewis and Warren met in 1987, when Lewis presented about the Christic Institute's Contragate campaign to a Witness for Peace group in Durham. "We were kindred spirits," Lewis wrote. Since then, Warren shared, they've had "a rich and deep friendship." Warren began volunteering for Lewis's organization, CIS, and Lewis joined the board of Warren's organization, NC WARN.

One of NC WARN's campaigns involved the Shearon Harris Nuclear Power Plant in New Hill, North Carolina, about twenty miles southwest of Raleigh. Carolina Power & Light Company (CP&L) proposed, in the late 1990s, to transport nuclear waste from other plants to the Shearon Plant. CP&L ignored NC WARN's calls for public hearings about the proposal.

In October 2000, NC WARN and the Coalition Against Nuclear Imports to the Triangle protested outside CP&L's headquarters in downtown Raleigh. Lewis and other demonstrators held signs and waved flags, while speakers talked about the dangers of nuclear waste. Their declaration, displayed on an easel, entreated CP&L's CEO to sign a formal agreement to hold public hearings. Lewis, Warren, and Carrie Bolton, a Black minister, attempted to enter the building's front entrance to present the declaration but security stopped them. So, they moved to the rear entrance, where they were again intercepted. Having exhausted their options for entry, Lewis, Warren, and Bolton sat down, blocking access to the rear entrance. Minutes later, they were arrested by police for second degree trespass and taken to jail.

Lewis, Warren, and Bolton were released after providing written promises to appear in court. Their pro bono defense attorney, Stewart Fisher, told reporters, "This is a First Amendment issue. CP&L is a public utility and my clients had every right to seek a discussion with its CEO over an issue with such important regional safety ramifications."

A prosecutor dismissed the charges in January 2001. A few days later, NC WARN again demonstrated at CP&L's headquarters. Lewis, Warren, and four others entered the lobby and asked to meet with the CEO about public hearings. They refused orders from security guards and police officers to leave the lobby and were arrested and charged with trespassing.

In March 2001, a state district court judge found Lewis and the other protesters guilty of trespassing. They retained Fisher again and appealed to superior court, where they'd be entitled to a jury trial. George Hausen, then assistant director of LSNC, joined their defense team.

The defendants planned to present a necessity defense—that is, argue they weren't criminally liable because their conduct was necessary to prevent the greater harm of exposure to nuclear waste. However, the superior court judge granted, without first allowing the defendants to make an offer of proof, the prosecutor's motion to prevent them from arguing necessity. The next day, Lewis and his codefendants were convicted of second-degree trespass.

They appealed to the North Carolina Court of Appeals, which affirmed the convictions in December 2002. The decision read, "One with lawful authority may order a person to leave the premises of a privately-owned business held open to the public when that person no longer has a legitimate purpose for being upon the premises."

Lewis and his codefendants appealed to the North Carolina Supreme Court, arguing that members of the public had implicit permission to be in the lobby of the building, where CP&L leased only part of the space and other entities conducted business. Additionally, the defendants contended that the trial court committed reversible error by precluding them from justifying a necessity defense. Lastly, the defendants asserted that the First Amendment prohibited CP&L from regulating its public space in a way that discriminated against individuals based on their beliefs and messages. The court rejected the first two arguments but remanded the First Amendment issue.

The defendants ultimately lost the free speech argument before the court of appeals. Consequently, Lewis received his third criminal conviction.

For more than thirty years, Lewis and Jim Warren have remained close. They spend time together playing guitars, biking, hiking, traveling, attending political events, and, in Warren's words, "finding a way to laugh out loud and unrestrained." "He has helped me so much in political, personal, and spiritual growth and survival," Lewis wrote. Warren shared, "Lewis is the kind of person who, no matter how much time spent together, I always wish there were more." He described Lewis as "amazingly balanced in terms of his place in the world," "always genuinely and actively interested in the people he's around," "always finding ways to validate and enrich friends and strangers," and "an inspiration and mentor." Warren wrote, "Lewis taught me the invaluable lesson that activists usually cannot win big fights just by having the facts on their side; we usually must, at least equally, challenge the way the debate is waged and who gets to decide."

Greensboro Massacre Truth and Reconciliation

Although the Greensboro Massacre trials ended by 1985, related activism and healing has continued for decades. Lewis has been interviewed for numerous books about the massacre and consulted for *Greensboro: A Requiem*, a play that debuted on Princeton University's campus. He has also helped organize and presented at massacre anniversary events. He was part of a campaign that resulted in the Greensboro City Council finally, in 2020, acknowledging the complicity of the GPD and issuing an apology for the massacre.

Additionally, Lewis was involved in Greensboro's truth and reconciliation process, which was conceived during twentieth anniversary observances of the massacre. The Beloved Community Center (BCC) of Greensboro and the GJF initiated the Greensboro Truth and Community Reconciliation Project (GTCRP). Survivors Marty Nathan and Signe Waller explained in the *Poverty and Race Research Action Council Journal* that the GTCRP was "based on the South African model of soliciting public and private 'truth-telling' by victims, witnesses and perpetrators as a way of basing change, and community transformation, on a full and truthful understanding of the violent historical events." The GTCRP spent three years fundraising, hiring staff, establishing democratic processes, and forming a commission.

As a member of the GTCRP's local task force and national advisory committee, Lewis elicited buy-in from Greensboro officials and educated local community members and national partners about the "legal story" of the massacre. He stressed that truth must come before reconciliation, that discussing the relationship between the massacre and First Amendment rights to freedom of speech and assembly must be part of the process, and that a community-based process embodied Article I, Section 2 of the North Carolina Constitution. That section reads, "All political power is vested in and derived from the people; all government of right originates from the people, is founded upon their will only, and is instituted solely for the good of the whole."

In June 2004, a seven-member, independent Greensboro Truth and Reconciliation Commission (GTRC) was empaneled. The commission's mandate read, "The passage of time alone cannot bring closure, nor resolve feelings of guilt and lingering trauma, for those impacted by the events of November 3, 1979. Nor can there be any genuine healing for the city of Greensboro unless the truth surrounding these events is honestly confronted, the suffering fully acknowledged, accountability established, and forgiveness and reconciliation facilitated."

An all-white majority of the Greensboro City Council voted, in April 2005, to oppose the truth and reconciliation process. Nevertheless, over the next year, the GTRC canvassed to solicit information and publicize events, held public hearings and community forums, received oral and written testimony, conducted interviews and research, and developed recommendations.

In August 2005, Lewis testified at one of the hearings. He focused on "concealment" and "deception" by public officials and law enforcement. He declared, "There's been a devastating impact of denying the true facts that are necessary for the citizens to hold accountable their officials. In other words, there has been an undermining of the core, elementary American value of democratic self-government, accountability, and the public's right to know."

The GTRC released its final report in May 2006. The majority of commissioners found that "the single most important element that contributed to the violent outcome of the confrontation was the absence of police"; "it was immoral and unconscionable for the FBI and the Bureau of Alcohol Tobacco and Firearms—which both had their own inside intelligence on the Klan and Nazis about the potential for violence on Nov. 3, 1979—to fail to share that information with local law enforcement"; and "both the GPD and key city managers deliberately misled the public regarding what happened on Nov. 3, 1979, the planning for it and the investigation of it."

Lewis believes that "every bit" of the hundreds of thousands of dollars and thousands of hours spent on the truth and reconciliation process was worthwhile. Above all else, he appreciates that the process was "substantive, bottom-up, democratic self-government in action."

"Free Speech Zones"

Lewis's most time-intensive pro bono endeavor while working for legal aid involved representing his friend, Brett Bursey. Bursey is a long-time social justice organizer, with a lengthy history of protest-related arrests. He calls himself the "oldest living Confederate prisoner of war" because, in 1969, after burning a Confederate flag in front of the USC president's house, he was arrested, jailed, and released on bond, but never prosecuted. He later served eighteen months in South Carolina's infamous Central Correctional Institution for spray painting "Hell No We Won't Go" and pouring red paint—to symbolize blood spilled in Vietnam—inside the Richland County Selective Service Office. The *Charleston City Paper* dubbed Bursey "the state's protest ambassador for decades." *Slate* characterized him as "either the world's greatest protester or a giant, unmitigated pain"; "a thorn in the side of Columbia, S.C. authorities since 1969"; and "a fixture of Lexington County, protesting everything protestable since Nixon and Vietnam."

Lewis and Bursey regularly crossed paths starting in the mid-1970s. In 1975, Bursey cofounded the Grassroots Organizing Workshop (GROW) in Columbia. The organization was primarily funded by its café, which offered beer, food, live music, worker-run co-ops, and meeting space for activists.

Lewis frequented the café and read *POINT*, GROW's monthly newspaper "dedicated to nurturing a statewide progressive movement."

In the late 1970s, Lewis and Bursey joined forces to protest nuclear energy in South Carolina. Bursey was a leader in two antinuclear organizations, the Palmetto Alliance and the Southeastern Natural Guard. Lewis and his law partner at the time, Bob Warren, collaborated with Bursey and his organizations to protest the Allied-General plant in Barnwell, South Carolina in 1978, and the Savannah River Site in 1979. Bursey was among the protesters arrested and represented by Lewis and Warren.

Bursey also had ties to the Greensboro Massacre. He joined the CWP at Lewis's urging. After Klansmen and Nazis were found not guilty in the federal criminal trial, Bursey organized a press conference in front of the Strom Thurmond Federal Building in Columbia to express solidarity with his comrades in Greensboro. Lewis wrote, "I learned much from him and admired his organizing work. I am always amazed at the fine work he does and how he has stayed in the trenches at considerable sacrifice."

In the early 2000s, Bursey was among millions of people worldwide protesting the United States' plan to invade Iraq. Capitalizing on the public's fear in the aftermath of September 11, President George W. Bush, his political advisor, Karl Rove, his AG, John Ashcroft, and other administration officials began establishing "free speech zones"—also known as "protest zones" or "federal protection zones"—to discourage dissent and corral protesters away from the media and Bush's supporters. Secret Service agents worked with state and local law enforcement to create zones, far away from main events, often behind buses, buildings, and other structures. Protesters who refused orders to relocate to the designated areas were arrested. Meanwhile, the president's supporters were allowed near him to create the desired optics.

Lewis explained the "free speech zones" to Molly Ivins and Lou Dubose for their book *Bill of Wrongs: The Executive Branch's Assault on America's Fundamental Rights*:

> Lewis described a "Barney Fife plan" used by the Secret Service and White House Advance Team. "The feds come to town a couple of days ahead of the president's visit and they bring in the local police. Then the Secret Service gets Barney all jacked up about how patriotic this is. 'We got to defend our president,' they say. And they actually tell them, don't let anyone that's protesting be anywhere but in a free-speech zone. 'We're all Americans and

want people to protest and we're giving them their own separate place to do it.'

"If you're not a fan, they . . . sen[d] in Barney Fife and Barney says you're going to be arrested for trespassing or subject to a disorderly conduct order."

Then Barney's left behind in Mayberry, holding a criminal defendant on charges that won't stand up in court. "The Secret Service and the president fly off," Pitts said. "So there's no federal trace of repression. What you've got maybe is a little fight between Barney Fife and the local ACLU. Which looks a lot less totalitarian."

In 2001 and 2002, Bush traversed the country drumming up support for an invasion of Iraq and portraying himself as a champion of freedom. Meanwhile, at each stop—including in Albuquerque, Pittsburgh, Houston, Trenton, Phoenix, and St. Louis—his minions established "free speech zones."

On October 24, 2002, Bush flew into the Columbia Metropolitan Airport for an event sponsored by the Republican Party of South Carolina. The event, held in an airport hangar, was restricted to approximately seven thousand ticket holders. Bursey, then age fifty-two and head of the South Carolina Progressive Network, didn't have a ticket but planned to hold a small protest nearby.

Once Bush landed, authorities cleared people from a "restricted area" near where his motorcade would approach the hanger. Bursey remained in the "restricted area," holding a megaphone and sign that read, "No more war for oil. Don't invade Iraq." Secret Service Agent Holly Abel and State Law Enforcement Officer Tamara Baker approached Bursey and told him to leave the area. According to Bursey, Abel said he had to relocate to the unmarked "free speech zone," but couldn't tell him its location.

Bursey walked away from the hangar to the far corner of the intersection where the president's vehicle would arrive and depart. Bursey said he was standing within feet of Bush supporters. Abel again approached Bursey. She gave him four choices: leave the airport; go to the "free speech zone"; wait in line to get into the hangar, if he had a ticket; or be arrested for trespassing. Bursey said something to the effect of, "I'm in a free speech zone—it's called the United States of America," and made clear he wasn't going to leave. He was arrested, handcuffed, put into a patrol wagon, and driven to jail.

Bursey was charged with trespassing under state law; however, the charge was later dropped. He knew it wouldn't stick because, in 1970, South Carolina's Supreme Court ruled that individuals couldn't be charged with trespassing on public property. In that case, Bursey was one of seven activists arrested for trespassing while protesting President Nixon at the Columbia airport.

However, in March 2003, US Attorney J. Strom Thurmond Jr., under pressure from the Secret Service and Bush administration, filed federal criminal charges against Bursey under an obscure statute. The law, passed on the heels of political assassinations in the 1960s, makes it a crime to willfully and knowingly enter and remain in a restricted area that a president is temporarily visiting. According to multiple reports, Bursey was the first person ever charged under that provision of the statute. Lewis and Bursey suspect the Bush administration viewed South Carolina—with its strong Republican base and conservative judges, and Strom Thurmond's son as US attorney—as fertile ground for establishing legal precedent governing "free speech zones." Bursey surrendered to authorities, pleaded not guilty, and was released with various conditions.

In May 2003, eleven members of Congress, including one Republican and several members of the House Judiciary and Homeland Security Committees, sent a letter to AG John Ashcroft urging him to drop the charges against Bursey. "No plausible argument can be made that Mr. Bursey was threatening the president by holding a sign which the president found politically offensive," they insisted. The letter read, "As we read the First Amendment to the Constitution, the United States is a 'free speech zone.' In the United States, free speech is the rule, not the exception, and citizens' rights to express it do not depend on their doing it in a way that the President finds politically amenable. . . . This prosecution smacks of the use of the Sedition Acts two hundred years ago to protect the President from political discomfort. It was wrong then and it is wrong now."

Bursey was initially represented by two local defense attorneys: Clarence Rauch Wise and Bill Nettles. Wise was four years ahead of Lewis at Wofford College and the University of South Carolina Law School. He'd represented Bursey in his draft board civil disobedience case, and according to Bursey, "blew it pathetically." Like Lewis, Nettles previously worked in the Richland County Public Defender's Office. He also shared office space with Lewis's good friend, Bob Hallman.

After butting heads with Nettles and Wise, Bursey asked Lewis to join his defense team and help politicize the case. Bursey fired Nettles because, according to Lewis, Nettles "revealed his style of inside game and kowtowing to the US attorney and magistrate." Nettles would later serve as the US Attorney in South Carolina.

Lewis took leave from his day job at LANC to codefend Bursey pro bono. *Indy Week* read, "Lewis Pitts' idea of a holiday? It's taking a little time off to go to South Carolina and defend Brett Bursey. . . . How did Pitts, a 56-year-old lawyer with Legal Aid of N.C., come to defend the pony-tailed activist Bursey in a case with national significance? Better to ask, how could he not?" Lewis explained his motivation: "The prosecution was an attack on a grassroots leader and a classic case of needing People's lawyers to help link litigation, media work, and public education and organizing to build and defend the People's movements." In 2017, Lewis said, "[Bursey] courageously refused to walk over to some bullshit 'free speech zone' and be nullified. If more people acted with such courage, we might not be in this neo-liberal, pre-fascist period right now. A hard fight back and unapologetic defense of Brett was needed, and I was lucky to be in a position to lend my head and mouth to presenting the outrage it deserved."

Lewis and Wise requested a jury trial and filed a motion to dismiss based on "outrageous government misconduct." They argued that the totalitarianism-like, content-based suppression of free speech by the Bush administration, Secret Service, and US Attorney's Office was so outrageous that constitutional due process principles barred the government from prosecuting Bursey.

Additionally, the defense filed a "Supplemental Motion for Specific Discovery"—namely, Secret Service records related to "free speech zones." The motion asserted that the additional discovery could show "the federal charges were brought selectively and in bad faith with the intent of preventing and chilling the exercise of constitutionally protected First Amendment rights to free speech, to assemble, and to petition the government for redress of wrongs." The motion included transcripts from another case in which the Kalamazoo, Michigan, police captain revealed that the Secret Service gave specific instructions and orders to suppress free speech during the president's visit there in 2001.

Lastly, Lewis subpoenaed Ashcroft and Rove to question them about how the statute under which Bursey was charged was being used as a political weapon, rather than for its intended purpose—ensuring presidents' safety. Lewis told *Indy Week*, "We wanted the political context of this charge considered. If you can't come out to a political event and just hold a sign, you're unplugging the basic notions of free speech—and that's just so un-American."

Bristow Marchant, the federal magistrate who presided over Bursey's trial, denied all three pretrial motions, as well as motions to enforce the subpoenas for Ashcroft and Rove after they refused service.

Bursey's two-day trial began in Columbia on November 12, 2003. Proceedings were moved to a larger courtroom because of the crowd size.

Lewis and Wise argued that the parameters of the supposed restricted area were so ambiguous that Bursey didn't have adequate notice of, and thus, couldn't comply with, the limitations—in legal terms, they argued the law as applied to Bursey was "void for vagueness." They also argued that the applicable statutory provision was so broad it covered both protected and unprotected speech, and therefore, violated the First Amendment—a principle of judicial review known as the "overbreadth doctrine." Moreover, the defense attempted to establish a pattern of viewpoint discrimination by the Bush administration. Lewis and Wise introduced transcripts from other cases in which protesters were prosecuted for carrying signs critical of the president and called individuals who were with Bursey at the airport to testify about him being singled out.

Secret Service agents testified about the need to create safe passages for the president. Agent Abel described how she'd given Bursey options. Law enforcement officers testified that the areas where Bursey stood were clearly shut down and the content of his sign wasn't an issue. Bursey claimed that the agents and officers lied. According to Lewis, "The bad guys played so fast and loose with the facts and their testimony. . . . We faced a kangaroo court."

In January 2004, Marchant found Bursey guilty of trespassing and fined him $500. Lewis told supporters and reporters that Marchant's decision was "contrary to all of the evidence," "a way to appease the government and the Bush administration," and "sugar-coated with a light sentence to make people think that it was not as outrageous as it was." A *YES! Weekly* reporter wrote, "Marchant decided ultimately that post-Sept. 11 security concerns trump free speech." Indeed, Marchant's decision read, "In this age of suicide bombers, . . . the Secret Service's concern with allowing unscreened persons to stand in such close proximity to a slow-moving vehicle carrying the President is not just understandable, but manifestly reasonable."

Bursey and Lewis believed not fighting the conviction and fine would've been a missed opportunity to try to prevent dangerous legal precedent and raise public awareness about "free speech zones." So, a week after the verdict, he and Bursey appealed Magistrate Marchant's decision for review by a judge in the US District Court for South Carolina. Lewis wrote, "It was the kind of the tenacity I learned from Bob Warren: bite 'em in the ass as a bulldog would, and hold on, even if you're dragged nearly to death."

In September 2004, a judge conducted a hearing and upheld Bursey's conviction and fine. *Slate* read, "Bursey's conviction sharpens the teeth of police threats and gives the discontented one more reason to keep quiet. It's certainly not the end of protest in America. But it's a step in that direction."

Undeterred, Bursey and Lewis appealed to the Fourth Circuit. They were joined by Jeffrey Fogel from the Center for Constitutional Rights. They asserted the trial court erred in finding that Bursey was in a "restricted area" when he was ordered to leave because there weren't physical demarcations of the restricted area and it wasn't yet shut down, as evidenced by people still roaming around near him. Additionally, they argued the prosecution failed to establish intent—that Bursey purposefully engaged in conduct he knew to be unlawful. Their brief contended, more broadly, "The importance of this case goes far beyond the $500 fine imposed and its impact on the defendant. . . . At issue is the rule of law, the obligation of government officials to follow the law and whether an American citizen can be arrested while simply holding a sign critical of the President." People for the American Way, the NLG, and other organizations filed a supporting amicus brief.

Oral arguments took place in Richmond, Virginia, in May 2005. Bursey's friend and supporter, Phil Leventis, a former Air Force brigadier general and then South Carolina state senator, flew Bursey and Lewis on a twin-engine turboprop airplane to Richmond. The presiding judge began the hearing by declaring, "This is an uncommonly silly prosecution." Nevertheless, the Fourth Circuit upheld the conviction and fine, reasoning that the restricted area was sufficiently cordoned off by officers who were positioned around the perimeter; the area was off-limits for everyone—protesters and supporters alike—except authorized personnel; and Bursey intended to enter and remain in the area, which he knew to be restricted.

In December 2005, Lewis and Fogel filed a petition for a writ of certiorari with the US Supreme Court. However, the following month, the court announced it wouldn't hear the case. "This is a disturbing precedent that will limit the First Amendment rights of all Americans," Lewis told the Associated Press. The following month, Lewis and Bursey held a press conference and rally outside the federal courthouse, where they raised more than enough money to pay the fine.

Bursey and Lewis subsequently learned the ACLU had obtained the White House's *Presidential Advance Manual*, dated October 2002, and marked, "Sensitive—Do Not Copy." The Justice Department heavily redacted the manual before turning it over. The remaining text nevertheless demonstrates the Orwellian nature of the "free speech zones":

> There are several ways the advance person can prepare a site to minimize demonstrators. First, . . . work with the Secret Service and have them ask the local police department to designate a protest area where demonstrators can be placed, preferably not in view of the event site or motorcade route. . . .
>
> The formation of "rally squads" is a common way to prepare for demonstrators by countering their message. This tactic involves utilizing small groups of volunteers to spread favorable messages using large hand-held signs, placards, or perhaps a long sheet banner, and placing them in strategic areas around the site.
>
> These squads should be instructed always to look for demonstrators. The rally squad's task is to use their signs and banners as shields between the demonstrators and the main press platform. If the demonstrators are yelling, rally squads can begin and lead supportive chants to drown out the protestors (USA! USA! USA!). As a last resort, security should remove the demonstrators from the event site. The rally squads can include, but are not limited to, college/young republican organizations, local athletic teams, and fraternities/sororities. . . .
>
> Once a group of demonstrators has been identified, the advance person must decide what action to take. If it is determined that the media will not see or hear them and that they pose no potential disruption to the event, they can be ignored. On the other hand, if the group is carrying signs, trying to shout down the President, or has potential to cause some greater disruption to the event, action needs to be taken immediately to minimize the demonstrator's effect.

Lewis wrote, "It was all so damn outrageous. The executive branch rigging protest and discrediting folks sincerely protesting. Yet, like the history of creeping fascism in Europe, it's ignored as merely an increment and not as the blazing warning of things to come."

The manual supported the allegations in Lewis and Bursey's outrageous government conduct motion. Additionally, the manual wasn't provided in discovery before Bursey's trial. However, they'd already exhausted traditional appeals.

Lewis turned to Michael Tigar, a professor and legendary trial lawyer, for help. Tigar's former clients include Terry Nichols, Angela Davis, and Scott McClellan. Lewis and Tigar knew each other from Tigar's time teaching at Duke University. Tigar shared that Lewis "has the courage to do what must be done" and "is a superb mentor for younger lawyers, law students and all those with whom he works." Tigar agreed to join Bursey's legal team, along with Joyce Cheeks, then interim executive director of the South Carolina ACLU.

In December 2007, they filed a writ of coram nobis in federal district court. The writ is a request for a judge to reconsider a matter that has already been decided because the initial decision was based on a factual error or omission, which, if known at the time, could've changed the outcome. Cheeks told the Associated Press, "Our contention is that Brett had a First Amendment defense that he was not allowed to go forward with because the government withheld this particular document."

A magistrate held a hearing and denied the writ in October 2008. Lewis wrote about the hearing, "Michael did a superb job, but this magistrate was eyebrow deep in South Carolina Republican politics and simply never going to rule against the power structure with all the Bush administration backing. What a shame, and once again showing how politicized the legal system has always been." Bursey recalled, "We ultimately lost in court, but won the hearts and minds of citizens of all political persuasions by raising high the notion that 'America is a Free Speech Zone.'"

Lewis and Bursey's friendship has spanned six decades. Each year, Lewis joins him in Columbia to train activists at the Modjeska Simkins School for Human Rights, which Bursey cofounded. Bursey's description of their 2019 session read, "This [session] features Lewis Pitts and Brett Bursey rambling down memory lane with personal stories of the dangers of being raised well in Amerika. . . . Lawyer Pitts defended Bursey and hundreds of other civilly disobedient citizens. . . . Not only are Pitts and Bursey deadly serious about making revolution, they are funny. They both have kept true to the 1968 radical paean, 'And remember kids, when you're smashing the state, keep a smile on your lips and a song in your heart.' The event is free and open to the open-minded concerned about the plight of civilization."

Bursey shared, "Lewis is one of the rare and treasured attorneys who not only understands that the defense of liberty sometimes necessitates being civilly disobedient, he acts on this principle with humility and the selfless commitment of a true patriot."

CHAPTER 17

Personal and Professional Transitions

From 2003 to 2014, Lewis experienced a series of significant personal and professional transitions. In 2003, he saw his son, Stephen, off to college and separated from his wife, Katie Greene. Four years later, he remarried. The following year, his mother passed away. Then, in 2014, he retired from LANC and began the process of becoming the first person to ever resign from the North Carolina State Bar.

Stephen Pitts and Katie Greene

As a father, Lewis was determined to follow his parents' positive examples and to practice what he preached as a child advocate. He was an engaged and loving father. He cooked breakfast for Stephen most mornings. Before eating, they'd recite a blessing Lewis made up: "Bless this food to the nourishment of our bodies so that we may pursue love, knowledge, and justice worldwide." Then, they'd read a daily passage from a book by Eknath Easwaran, a spiritual teacher. At night, he'd read to Stephen before bed. Lewis reminisced, "We read all the classics, but eventually I began to make up stories where he was the 'good guy.' For example, in a story, there would be a 'poor' kid on the playground, and Stephen would bring the kid home and offer food and friendship; or Stephen would defend his Black friends when someone picked on them."

Lewis was Stephen's basketball coach and Cub Scouts' den leader. He also brought Stephen to marches, rallies, and other activist events. For example, in January 1991—ten days before George H. W. Bush announced the start of "Operation Desert Storm"—the *Herald-Sun* published a photo of Lewis and Stephen at an antiwar protest. Stephen, age six, held a sign that read, "WAR IS BAD FOR KIDS."

Stephen fondly remembered Lewis pulling him in a red wagon, wrestling with him, and playing catch and basketball with him. Stephen's happiest childhood memories include traveling with his parents to go camping, enjoying the beach each summer, and visiting family in South Carolina and New York.

Stephen shared that he has never resented Lewis for working long hours or traveling often. Greene shared similar sentiments: "Though there were stretches of time when he was away, . . . Lewis was an engaged father who actively participated in Stephen's care and upbringing. He delighted in teaching Stephen anything, in taking him on trips or adventures, in attending Field Day and PTA-sponsored events, in playing with Stephen and his friends. . . . Lewis was an avid supporter of Stephen's athletic talents. He loved his son's sensitivity, his sense of fairness, . . . that he was kind and smart."

In 2003, Stephen graduated from Riverside High School in Durham and matriculated at the University of North Carolina at Greensboro (UNCG). Lewis wrote in 2018, "Stephen has so many admirable traits. Being his 'pops' is something I'm very proud of, and the memories of his childhood are treasures forever embedded in my heart."

Lewis and Greene met in 1978, married in 1982, and had Stephen in 1985. They shared a deep love for each other and their son, a commitment to social justice, and plenty of good times. However, shortly after Stephen graduated high school, Lewis and Greene separated. Their divorce was finalized in October 2004. Greene wrote, "Sharing a common understanding of the world and commitment to work for the public good brought us together but, in the end, it was not enough to keep us together. The love and history we had shared, and our deep, take-your-breath-away love for our son, motivated and compelled us to work on our issues over the years. But when all was said and done, we could not bridge the widening gap in our understanding of and approach to day-to-day issues or challenges. . . . Our differences had become incompatibilities. Though difficult, . . . splitting up was the right and necessary thing to do." Lewis agreed with Greene's assessment, noting that they ultimately "couldn't meet each other's emotional needs."

Spoma Jovanovic

A couple of months after separating from Greene, Lewis met his third wife, Spoma Jovanovic, who had also recently separated from her spouse. She was a professor of Communication Studies at UNCG. In July 2003, Lewis presented about the Greensboro Massacre at the BCC. Afterward, Jovanovic asked Lewis questions, invited him to present to her UNCG class, and gave him her business card. She wrote, "My initial impression of Lewis was that he was incredibly smart and passionate. . . . I hung onto his every word as he expertly brought new information to us in terms we could both understand and fully appreciate. . . . Lewis' passion for justice and his attention to detail energized me." Lewis shared about meeting Jovanovic for the first time, "I felt something very special about her. Her questions were intelligent and probing. She was very attractive. . . . It was a magically happen-stance encounter."

Their first date, in August 2003, involved going to the Greensboro Massacre site, eating and drinking wine outside a local restaurant, and talking late into the night. Subsequently, Lewis and Jovanovic began spending as much time together as possible, despite living sixty miles apart. They quickly fell in love. She explained her attraction to him: "I found Lewis endearing in so many ways. More specifically, it was his overflowing sense of joy, commitment to justice in everything he did and saw, his sharp mind, and his playful spirit that were so attractive to me. . . . But there was much more. Lewis adored his son, his family, his friends, and everyone he met on the street. I saw then . . . Lewis' unlimited capacity to care for people. That defining feature of Lewis is his best." Lewis described Jovanovic as "brilliant, beautiful, feisty, giving, hard-working, and wonderfully stubborn and outspoken," "a great mother," and "so very thoughtful."

Lewis and Jovanovic were an unlikely duo for reasons beyond just their decade gap in age—he was fifty-five; she was forty-five. His family had lived in South Carolina for generations; she's the child of Serbian immigrants. He's a southern boy; she's a west coast girl. He was a "radical," movement lawyer with little money to his name, living in an apartment in Durham; she'd gone from the business world to academia, and had a beautiful, spacious home in Greensboro and financial stability. He was a sporting event, honky-tonk bar, whiskey kind of guy; she was an art gallery, dinner party, wine kind of gal. Their differences, however, enhanced the attraction for Lewis.

Jovanovic's three teenage children accepted Lewis from the beginning of his relationship with their mother. Her daughter, Lena Mattson, wrote, "I think Lewis is one of the best people I have ever had the honor of meeting and how incredibly cool that he gets to be in my life all the time. I am so proud of his activism. . . . He's truly inspiring to be around."

After dating for a year or so, and finalizing their divorces, Lewis moved from Durham to an apartment down the street from Jovanovic's house. He'd spend the next decade commuting nearly two hours round trip between Greensboro and his office in Durham.

Lewis and Jovanovic began linking their respective work. First, they were both involved in the Greensboro truth and reconciliation process, and Jovanovic wrote a book, *Democracy, Dialogue, and Community Action: Truth and Reconciliation in Greensboro*, with Lewis's fact-checking assistance. Additionally, in January 2007, Lewis, Jovanovic, and thirty of her students collaborated with a local church and Habitat for Humanity to help Lewis's client, John, fix up his house. Lewis also joined Jovanovic, and her students and colleagues, to oppose a proposed $9.2 million UNCG recreation center, which they called the "wreck center." They were concerned about gentrification, costs amid rising student debt and declining state education funding, and the company hired to study building a center being the same company awarded the contract to build it. Finally, Lewis had been a regular speaker at Jovanovic's classes and campus events. She wrote, "What's very helpful to me, and others, is his ability to connect larger issues together . . . so others and I can situate our work as not simply a specified project, but instead as work designed to advance a deeper agenda that recognizes the importance of self-governance and equity."

In 2005, Lewis proposed to, and moved in with, Jovanovic. Since marrying in July 2007, the couple has had two dogs (John Henry and Bernie) and four chickens (Baba Lou, Emmy Lou, Fannie Lou, and Dixie Chick); bought a cabin in the Blue Ridge Mountains; and traveled to eighteen US states and Austria, Cuba, England, France, Germany, Italy, Jamaica, the Netherlands, and South Korea. Most days, they work out, cook, read, and rant about current events together.

Lewis and Jovanovic believe they've changed each other for the better. She said he "catapulted her shift from public service and charity toward justice." He shared that she has helped him "temper" his "radicalism and moral outrage" without making him feel "tamed," "chill out for the sake of [his] health and general well-being," and "realize not every dollar spent is a victory for capitalism, and it's okay to have nice things."

Jovanovic wrote, "I am unbelievably proud to be married to Lewis. Every single day he makes my heart jump. I look at him and wonder how I ever got so lucky to meet him and further to marry him. I love him more every single day. . . . He has invested his entire life and soul to pursuing what is right, all the while taking care of those in his closest circle of family and friends."

Lewis's Parents

Lewis remained close with his parents throughout their lives. Initially, they tolerated his activism; however, over time, his mother and, to a lesser extent, his father came to understand, and even appreciate, Lewis's work. Deep down, they believed good works transcend whatever one professes as his faith. In their eyes, Lewis practiced Christianity through his deeds, even though he was a nondenominational hippie. They even attended some of his court appearances in the 1980s. In 1991, they wrote to him, "We support you and feel pride in your efforts to be a modern-day Amos, crying for justice in the streets."

At his parents' fiftieth wedding anniversary party—just a few years before his father died suddenly from an infection in his lungs caused by a burst stomach ulcer in 1999—Lewis delivered the following remarks:

> Years ago I concluded that the most important lesson my Mom and Dad taught me was to treat other people as I would want to be treated. They taught me the core values of integrity and right living. . . . At times over my twenty plus years as a public interest lawyer attempting to fight for the "little people" of the country, folks have asked how I came to make those life choices. It did not take much reflection to answer: My parents get the blame or the credit because they showed me by word and deed the supremacy of the human dignity of every individual.

Lewis Pitts Sr. and Martha Pitts planted a seed in Lewis that grew into the person and advocate he became. In his words, they "modeled empathy for others, albeit within city limits"; showed him the meaning of "to love thy neighbor"; instilled in him that "an injury to one is an injury to all"; and taught him that "red and yellow, black and white, they are all precious in His sight." Lewis lost his mother to colon cancer in 2009. Her obituary read, "She lived her life radiating Christian love."

Retirement

After practicing law for forty years, Lewis stepped down as managing attorney of ACS and retired from LANC in January 2014. He believed the time was right for a handful of reasons.

First, Lewis was, in his words, fed up with lawyers "spewing empty rhetoric about access to justice" and failing to live up to his ideals for the legal profession. For four decades—in courtrooms, at conferences, and elsewhere—Lewis promoted the notion of the lawyer as "a public citizen having special responsibility for the quality of justice," as stated in the first sentence of the ABA's "Model Rules of Professional Conduct" and in many states' rules. Time and again, he was disappointed by attorneys who viewed their profession as an "industry" and their jobs as money grabs. Moreover, he was disgusted by most lawyers' willful ignorance, or passive acceptance, of the rapidly deteriorating rule of law, exemplified by rendition, indefinite detention, torture, drone strikes, and unregulated and unaccountable corporations bestowed with personhood by the US Supreme Court.

Second, Lewis was perpetually frustrated by LSC restrictions. He'd often say that LSC-funded organizations, such as LANC, were forced to advocate "with one hand tied behind their backs." Susan Epstein, his colleague in the MHU, said, "His everlasting frustration was making legal aid work consciousness raising political activism. It was really a fine line to walk." In June 2012, LANC was forced to endure a grueling "Program Quality Visit" from an LSC "Review Team," which was one of the last straws for Lewis.

Third, Lewis was annoyed by what he viewed as LANC's "pessimistic career bureaucrats who lacked creativity and energy" and "made decisions based on funding fears." These fears intensified in 2011, after cuts to LANC's federal funding forced the closures of four regional offices and layoffs of about thirty attorneys. More budget cuts were on the horizon when Lewis retired. He believed LANC's leadership should've more publicly and vociferously articulated how the cuts made a mockery of "equal justice under the law" and chilled zealous advocacy and explained that legal services funding was on the chopping block because of austerity and lawmakers' desire to limit legal accountability for banks, agri-business, landlords, and other moneyed interests. Lewis recognized, however, that critiquing LANC's leadership was easy for him because he didn't have to manage backlash. He also acknowledged that being publicly critical and confrontational, instead of "playing the game," could've led to retaliatory additional cuts.

Fourth, Lewis was tired of commuting two hours roundtrip between Greensboro and Durham, where ACS's offices were located. The drive was physically exhausting and he preferred to spend the time working or with Jovanovic, engaged in local campaigns, reading, or exercising.

Finally, Lewis was financially positioned to retire. He'd saved money during his twenty years in legal aid and turned sixty-six in December 2013, entitling him to one hundred percent of his Social Security benefit. Additionally, Jovanovic had a good salary and benefits from UNCG, with at least another eight years before retirement.

Despite Lewis's frustrations throughout his nearly two decades in legal aid organizations, he retired without regrets. He had joined legal services believing he'd exhausted all available options to continue full-time, North Carolina-based, grassroots movement lawyering. At LANC, Lewis had the income, benefits, and work-life balance he needed for himself and his family, while still positively impacting the lives of North Carolinians living in poverty and remaining active in movements outside of work.

In 2017, LANC's then executive director, George Hausen, wrote about Lewis:

> From our first meeting, it was readily apparent that his passion for our work was outsized and sincere—traits that never altered or faltered in the fifteen or so years that we worked together. And he could be relied upon to call us out if he felt that our zeal or our courage was either lacking or flagging in the face of the many resource and compliance obstacles with which we were, and are, daily confronted. . . . Lewis was always consistent in his principles and unashamed to pronounce them. The very same remarks would thrill and inspire many of us and also the many groups of undergraduates or law students with whom he spoke who were searching for meaning and for a way to make a difference. . . .
>
> Lewis believed that lawyers, particularly poverty lawyers, were morally obligated and, more to the point, specifically licensed to equalize the (capitalist) system by engaging the plunderers and their alienating forces whenever and wherever the battle could be waged. . . . Lewis's radicalism on civil rights and his espoused social justice principles were firmly rooted in liberal democracy and equally in our own history and our own Constitution. Lewis was extremely well-read and well-versed in both.
>
> Lewis was courageous in the extreme and unafraid to lose. . . . Along with being fearless and ready to make a case, he was a skilled and meticulous craftsman and professional. . . . His pleadings and his claims always had a solid foundation. . . .

His most important legacy may well be the lawyers he inspired and trained and the advocacy unit, Advocates for Children's Services, that he nurtured and built. The development and the lives of countless children have been changed and improved through the work of Lewis and the brilliant colleagues that he has recruited to ACS. . . .

He continues to be a model lawyer as well as a hero to me.

Indeed, during Lewis's nearly fourteen years as ACS's managing attorney, he exponentially increased the number of lives he positively impacted by teaching, mentoring, encouraging, and inspiring those he supervised. The appreciation and admiration of Lewis from former staff is effusive.

Chaya Rao, ACS's paralegal from 2002 to 2007, described Lewis as "a man of conviction and courage," "consumed by doing right," and "an exemplary role model who not only talked the talk but walked the walk."

Keith Howard, an ACS attorney from 2005 to 2011, viewed Lewis as a father figure who taught him about recognizing the humanity of clients and fueled his passion for civil and human rights.

Erwin Byrd, an ACS attorney from 2005 to 2012, shared, "One of the first times I went to district court with him, a juvenile defender in another case was doggedly, passionately and ably defending her client, and Lewis quietly said something along the lines of 'hell yes,' with great admiration. He made sure to find her and cheer her on afterwards. Years later, I was in the middle of a closing argument in Superior Court and Lewis, sitting next to me, said under his breath, 'Shit yeah.' That was probably my proudest moment as a lawyer."

David Sapp, an ACS attorney from 2006 to 2008, recalled that Lewis taught him about "being fearless and tireless in advocating for clients."

Cary Brege, an ACS attorney from 2008 to 2010, wrote:

Lewis helped me see all people with compassion and care for them without having to analyze whether their suffering was "worth" the effort or better/worse than someone else's. Lewis never missed the humanity in any situation of injustice. . . .

I cannot imagine having lived through and seen all that Lewis has and not ending up hardened, cynical and jaded. . . . Lewis' unrelenting optimism is the most attractive and distinctive thing about him. It draws others to him and motivates them to keep going, even in David and Goliath size fights. Lewis has seen the darkest parts of humanity . . . but chooses—defiantly!—to hope and to believe that change and justice are possible. Defiant hope—that is what I think of when I think about Lewis Pitts.

Peggy Nicholson, an ACS attorney from 2011 to 2016, remembered Lewis's "natural gift for working with clients." "He serves as the example of the lawyer I want to become," Nicholson added.

Finally, Jennifer Story, an ACS (now called the Right to Education Project) attorney since 2013, described Lewis as "an amazing civil rights activist" because he treated "everyone with the same unfailing respect and dignity" and possessed an "innate, genuine ability to make people feel important and valued."

While ACS's managing attorney, Lewis was awarded the *Indy Week*'s Citizen Award, Wake County ACLU's Finlator Award, North Carolina Academy of Trial Lawyers' service award, and North Carolina State Bar Association's Deborah Greenblatt Outstanding Legal Services Attorney Award. A 2003 profile of Lewis in *Indy Week* read:

> Pitts is . . . a self-described country boy who . . . 25 years ago . . . was standing with rural folks against the power of the nuclear industry and the policies of the federal government. He's been on the underdogs' side, using the law and his own activism, ever since.
>
> As a lawyer, Pitts has had his ups and his downs, in cases big and small. But he's never faltered in his cause: "Helping people get engaged in making choices to run their own lives—'We, the people,' remember?" . . .
>
> Not surprisingly, of course, Pitts has been branded a radical. "Boy," Pitts shrugs at that. "I think what I believe is totally balanced and therefore moderate. I think the essential political unit is the individual, and not corporations. So in that sense I guess I'm a populist." . . .
>
> He's become one of the state's top advocates for children. . . .

A month after he retired, Lewis was given the North Carolina ACLU's Frank Porter Graham Award—the organization's "highest honor awarded for longstanding and significant contributions to the fight for individual freedom and civil liberties in North Carolina." In his speech at the awards banquet, Lewis railed against "corporate rule," "racist plutocracy," the "stench of inequality," "capitalism as organized crime," and "institutional immorality." He pleaded with the hundreds in attendance to have "transformational vision and leadership" and to fight "for fundamental change of our culture and institutions."

Resignation from the North Carolina State Bar

A few months after retiring, and twenty years after fighting to become a member in the first place, Lewis began an unprecedented battle to resign from the North Carolina State Bar. At the time, the bar had only two options for members—active and inactive; resigning wasn't an option. In April 2014, Lewis wrote to the bar's president, Ronald Baker Sr., and staff to notify them that he wished to resign, rather than transferring from active to inactive status:

> My resignation is because I see an overall breach by the Bar as a whole of the most basic notions of professional conduct and ethics such that I do not want to be associated with the Bar. . . .
>
> I take no pleasure in my resignation and the assertions below. I do not wish to be mean or flippant. The ministry of law has been a powerful force in my life and I have had the pleasure of working with many terrific people in pursuit of justice—lawyers and non-lawyers. I want these parting words to stir your minds and hearts into reflection, boldness, and transformational action. . . .
>
> From my earliest days as a lawyer I have been concerned that the role of our profession has been to serve and protect the political and business Establishment and not to uphold Rule of Law; not to adhere to the Preamble to the Rules of Professional Conduct mandate of being "a public citizen having a special responsibility for the quality of justice;" not to seriously fight for justice and equality for all. . . .
>
> I hope the reasons for my resignation will generate meaningful discussion and debate . . . about how the legal profession can better serve, not business and finance, but the public good. . . .

Baker informed Lewis that voluntary resignation wasn't an option, and therefore, the bar would treat Lewis's letter as a petition for "inactive status." Shortly thereafter, the bar's membership director, Tammy Jackson, notified

Lewis that his petition for inactive status had been granted, pending payment of $350 for his 2014 membership fees.

Lewis told Jackson that he never submitted such a petition. His letter back to her read, "I remain firmly committed to my deeply held views stated in my April 23rd letter and wish no such affiliation. I have resigned from the NC State Bar."

Jackson sent Lewis a thoughtful and complimentary response; however, she also reiterated that "inactive" was his only option and would cost him $350. Lewis replied, "It is simply unfathomable that a lawyer cannot exercise personal choice based on protected First Amendment political dissenting views and voluntarily elect to resign from the Bar. . . . The Bar is certainly an arm of the State and as such is bound by the Federal and State Constitutions to protect the rights to freedom of speech, association, and dissent."

In November 2014, the state bar issued a "notice to show cause" to Lewis for failing to pay annual membership dues. Lewis filed a response, alleging the bar's refusal to accept his resignation was an unconstitutional violation of his rights to freedom of speech and association, as well as retaliation intended to discredit his criticism of the bar. However, he didn't want delinquent dues to interfere with making broader points about the legal profession or permanently resigning. So, he paid the $350, transferred to inactive status, and continued fighting to be the first person ever to resign from the state bar.

In September 2015, the North Carolina Supreme Court adopted a rule allowing bar members to petition the bar council "to enter an order of relinquishment." The rule directed the council to grant the petition as long as the petitioner had no unresolved complaints of misconduct or financial obligations to the state bar and had properly "completed the wind down of his or her law practice."

Lewis immediately filed a "Petition for Relinquishment of State Bar Membership." In October 2015, the council ordered "that P. Lewis Pitts is no longer a member of the North Carolina State Bar." The *News and Observer* read:

> When asked why he did not stay in the profession and try to make it better by working within his field, Pitts responded: "I did for 43 years."
>
> There was no "hair trigger" that made Pitts decide to step away when he did. "It was like the hypocrisy was eating me physically

and psychologically," Pitts said. "There are individual lawyers that have a conscience, but they're trampled by the system."

Pitts called his appeal "a desperate plea" in "some explosive times when the rule of law really needs to mean something."

"I guess it's time for our profession to undergo a moral checkup," Pitts concluded.

Roch Smith Jr., a freelance reporter and advocate, wrote on his website, Greensboro 101, "Genteel and articulate with a disarming, syrupy voice, Lewis Pitts' sharp observations go down easy. He would be played by Matthew Mc-Conaughey in the movie. Except this wouldn't be yet another lawyer role. Pitts isn't a lawyer—not anymore."

Lewis was an adjunct professor at Elon Law School for three semesters between 2012 and 2015. He taught a course titled, "Influence and Responsibility of The Lawyer as Public Citizen." One of his former law students wrote—in a paper titled, "Cause Lawyer: The Legal Profession's Outsider"—"For cause lawyers like Mr. Pitts, it was not so much that he quit the 'club' but that he never really became part of it."

Although Lewis retired in 2014, and resigned from the state bar in 2015, he has continued fighting for justice, especially around police reform and racial justice in Greensboro. Most of his advocacy has been about complainant processes, body-worn cameras, excessive force, and government transparency and accountability. He has authored op-eds, model policies, and resolutions; spoken at community forums, rallies, press conferences, and city council meetings; and helped with community organizing and legal advocacy. Throughout it all, Lewis has fought side-by-side with Nelson Johnson, cofounder and codirector of the BCC, and Lewis's friend, comrade, and mentor for over four decades. In 2021, Johnson wrote, "In the long journey of life . . . we encounter a few people whose work, substance and quality of life are indelibly engraved in our memory. For me, Lewis Pitts is one such person. . . . If I were asked to nominate a person who epitomized the characteristics of an outstanding citizen—an individual who models being informed, being strategically wise, being tactically smart, and being courageous—then Lewis Pitts would definitely be my nominee."

In 2017, Lewis shared that, some days, he feels like he's "out to pasture" and compelled to "wind things down." He wonders whether he should spend less time engaged in activism and more time playing his guitar and riding his motorcycle. However, he added, "Most days, something happens, and I feel like I don't have a choice." In his words, he lies awake at night worrying about "corrosion of the human soul," "fulfillment of human potential," and "liberation"; and is pulled back in by an "innate, compelling desire to fight against that which hurts people." He often reminds himself of the words of Black playwright Lorraine Hansberry: "The acceptance of our present condition is the only form of extremism which discredits us before our children." Lewis commented, "All I know to do is keep shaking a fist as much as my energy allows and not give up. I sure as shit wanna go out with my boots on."

Conclusion

For more than a half century, Lewis has advocated for environmental and racial justice, participatory democracy, children's rights, and a variety of other progressive causes; and he's done so at extreme personal sacrifice. He spent significant time broke, unemployed, and sleeping in his car. His law firm was insolvent and then the organization he created and dedicated his life to for a decade went bust. Work often took him away from his family. Also, he faced threats to his physical safety. He was arrested, jailed, and prosecuted multiple times. Moreover, Lewis encountered fierce opposition from powerful foes, including corporations, government agencies, silk-stocking law firms, white supremacists, police, prosecutors, judges, and politicians. Enemies in high places have attacked his reputation, defamed his character, retaliated against his clients, thrice subjected him sanctions, and attempted to have him disciplined by, and excluded from, state bars.

Nevertheless, Lewis successfully defended antinuclear protesters, Native American criminal justice activists, and Black public housing tenants, voting rights advocates, elected officials, and advocates for other causes. Through litigation, he changed laws related to prison escapes and jury pool selection in South Carolina; secured one of the first verdicts finding law enforcement jointly liable with the KKK; established the right for abused and neglected children to bring termination of parental rights proceedings in Florida; and in North Carolina, stopped social services from stealing money from foster children and secured medical, mental health, and educational services for countless children. Lewis played significant roles in movements to oppose construction of nuclear plants, reactivate the government of a predominantly Black rural town and hold its first elections in fifty-five years, protect Gullah culture and African burial grounds, and end police brutality and corruption. Along the way, he also won cases on behalf of hundreds of individual clients from oppressed and marginalized communities, including criminal defendants, civil plaintiffs, mental hospital patients, children with disabilities, and students in the school-to-prison pipeline.

Still, Lewis's most lasting impact will be how he has made people feel. He naturally feels others' pain and absorbs their suffering to his core. Lewis told a writer in 1989, "I squirm and wiggle and can't hardly stand it when people are hurting. I think that's good." He then envelops them in heartfelt warmth and compassion. His deep love for and faith in people make them feel more fully human.

Those around Lewis can't help but absorb some of his subversive joy, limitless energy, and fighting spirit. He has been spiritual Gatorade for countless clients, activists, students, coworkers, friends, other allies, and strangers. He doesn't allow the people around him to become apathetic, acculturated to the way things are, or tolerant of suffering. Lewis makes them want to proclaim both "get the bastards!" and "ain't life rich!"—as he often does.

Perhaps Lewis's most contagious quality is his genuine and unwavering hopefulness. He embodies one of his favorite quotes, from Václav Havel: "Hope is not prognostication. It is an orientation of the spirit, an orientation of the heart; it transcends the world that is immediately experienced, and is anchored somewhere beyond its horizons." The hope in Lewis's spirit and heart is anchored in an inspiring vision of a more humane and just world. He compels others to join him in rejecting pessimism and in keeping hope alive. He chooses to "transform the suffering into a creative force" instead of "react[ing] with bitterness," in the words of Martin Luther King Jr. Howard Zinn wrote, "What we choose to emphasize in this complex history will determine our lives. If we see only the worst, it destroys our capacity to do something. If we remember those times and places—and there are so many—where people have behaved magnificently, this gives us the energy to act, and at least the possibility of sending this spinning top of a world in a different direction." Lewis's emphasis on optimism and his courageous pursuit of justice generate energy for others to act.

Unfortunately, the United States continues to be plagued by many of the same issues Lewis battled, including environmental degradation, voter suppression, poverty and inequality, police corruption and violence, discrimination, and other injustices. The diseases that produced Donald Trump and his ilk—racism and xenophobia, patriarchy and sexism, homophobia and transphobia, greed and capitalism, and egoism and individualism—are as palpable as ever. Our antiquated two-party system is dominated by fascistic elements on the right and conservative Democrats beholden to corporate, moneyed interests on the other side. Meanwhile, nearly half of Americans are poor or low income; the top one percent of US households holds fifteen times more wealth than the bottom fifty percent combined; with more than 2,300,000 people behind bars, America leads the world in incarceration; every day, more than one hundred Americans are killed with guns and more than 230 are shot and wounded; and a climate catastrophe is well underway. The recitation of crises could go on and on.

As Lewis recently voiced, "We gotta keep our foot on the gas." And as "we" do, his mentality and approach are instructive for "staying sane in an insane world"—another one of his common sayings.

He has never viewed himself as a single-issue person or technocrat. He knows the law isn't a silver bullet or cure-all. He hasn't navigated life on a rigid career path; instead, he's always followed his heart and moral compass. He doesn't think of himself in terms of narrow labels, like Democrat, manager, or attorney. Finally, he recognizes his own privileges and appreciates intersectionalities. To borrow from Malcolm X, Lewis is "a human being, first and foremost," and as such is "for whoever and whatever benefits humanity as a whole." And like Angela Davis, Lewis views himself "not as a single individual who may have achieved whatever, but . . . part of an ongoing historical movement." This mindset has enabled Lewis to connect with a broader range of people—morally, across issue areas, and in terms of tactics and theories of change; to avoid vainglory, a savior complex, or resting on his laurels; and to ward off pitting oppressions against each other and movement cannibalism.

Moreover, Lewis doesn't view service and activism as his career; instead, for him, it's a state of being—something he's naturally compelled to do. In 2020, he said, "Injustice is a breach, a tearing of the solidarity and oneness that we all should be feeling. And fighting, I don't know, it's just what has to be done." He believes, like labor leader and civil rights activist Dolores Huerta, that "every moment is an organizing opportunity, every person a potential activist, every minute a chance to change the world." When asked why he continues fighting—even after witnessing so much suffering and disappointment, experiencing so many heartbreaks and hardships, and understanding that the moral arc of the US is still terribly long—Lewis answered simply, "What's the alternative?" He has had his "foot on the gas" no matter how much money he has made or the dearth of resources at his disposal; regardless of ideological shifts among powerholders and institutions; and despite the cyclical nature of social progress. This approach has enabled Lewis to endure after losses and suppress complacency after victories, to practice self-care without worry about "work-life balance," to always be available and reliable, and to avoid burnout. His bulldog mentality, hopefulness, and idealism have coexisted across ten presidencies, national tragedies and triumphs, recessions and recoveries, and a variety of social justice moments that have largely come and gone.

An introduction of Lewis for UNCG's "Unsung Heroes of the Civil Rights Movement" oral history project, written in 2020, reads, "He is a tireless fighter who at age 72 still breathes the fire of commitment, based on a deep faith that justice can prevail, no matter the odds." Lewis told the project, "And you maybe can tell, I hope, at 72-years-old, I'm still burning and alive with that. I can't do as much, and I'm trying not to do as much, but that's a fire that if . . . we want the future generations to have life in any way that is decent, we'd better . . . engage and realize that democracy is not something you have. It's something you do." Lewis's life is an example of that doing. He is a light for countless people and causes—just as we all can be.

Acknowledgments

This book wouldn't have been possible without everyone who shared their memories and feelings about Lewis, including: Mavis Belisle, Paul Bermanzohn, Loretta Beyer, Ashaki Binta, Jerri Blair, John Bonifaz, Candace Bothwell (formerly Losey and Grissom), Helen Bradley, Czerny Brasuell, Cary Brege, Pat Bryant, Brett Bursey, Erwin Byrd, Willena Cannon, Eddie Carthan, Shirley Carthan, Bennie Copeland, Julie Dews, Ann Marie Dooley, John England, Susan Epstein, Gaston Fairey, Tammy Figueroa, Sonny Garner, Jim Garrison, Charles Gill, Katie Greene, Alan Gregory, Emma Gresham, Rob Hager, Bob Hallman, Harry Harkins, George Hausen, Graham Holt, Keith Howard, Brian Hunt, Marcus Hyde, Eleanor Jacobs, Timothy Jacobs, Joyce Johnson, Nelson Johnson, Susan Johnson, Earl Jones, Paul Jones, Spoma Jovanovic, Jeanne Lenzer, Rachel Losey, Hazel Mack, Roger Manus, Lorraine Manzella, Lena Mattson, Doug Mays, Carolyn McAllaster, Louise McKigney, Jenny Miller, Tom Mills, Janice Mink, Marcia Morey, John Mungo, Marty Nathan, Sara Nelson, Elaine Nichols, Jerry Palmer, Margaret Parker, Travis Payne, Hester Petty, Paul Pitts, Stephen Pitts, Costa Pleicones, Rosemary Pomeroy, Jim Primdahl, Mia Prior (formerly Kirsh), Chaya Rao, Alan Rosenthal, Charles Sackrey, Jim Schermbeck, Danny Sheehan, Lanny Sinkin, Mary Smith, Roch Smith Jr., Jennifer Story, Steve Swearingen, Mark Tanenbaum, Flint Taylor, Michael Tigar, Earle Tockman, Michael Trinkley, Signe Waller Foxworth, Bob Warren, Jim Warren, Beverly Weidner, Deborah Weissman, Kim West, Carlos Williams, Yvonne Wilson, Barbara Bennett Woodhouse, and "John" (name redacted to protect identity).

I am grateful to the individuals who taught and inspired Lewis, but who, due to illness or death, were unable to share their perspectives, including, but certainly not limited to: Anne Braden, W. Haywood Burns, Fred Carter, John Hope Franklin, Arthur Kinoy, William Kunstler, Lee Faye Mack, Gwendolyn Patton, Martha Pitts, Pascal Lewis Pitts Sr., David Purpel, Leonard Schroeter, Gayle Shepherd (formerly Korotkin), H. John Taylor, Jon Thames, Johnnie Walls Jr., Bobby Ward, Leonard Weinglass, and Cozelle Wilson.

I appreciate professors Mark Dorosin (Florida A&M University College of Law), Barbara Fedders (University of North Carolina School of Law), Alexi Freeman (University of Denver Sturm College of Law), Jeff Jones (University of North Carolina at Greensboro), and Spoma Jovanovic (formerly University of North Carolina at Greensboro) for their feedback.

This book benefited greatly from the extensive research assistance and feedback from my brother, Sean Langberg, a social justice lawyer himself. My partner, Rachel Langberg, and our son, Everett Langberg, provided me with much-needed encouragement and love throughout the seven years this book was in the works.

Aran Shetterly, author of *Morningside*, a forthcoming book about the Greensboro Massacre, and Emily Mann, author of *Greensboro: A Requiem*, provided me with helpful guidance about writing and marketing this book.

Thank you to social justice lawyers Mark Trustin and Sarah Morris, and other friends, who supported this book.

Critical research assistance was provided by Peggy Nicholson, Cynthia Vela-Wash, and staffs of various libraries, including the: Duke University, David M. Rubenstein Rare Book and Manuscript Library; Indiana University–Purdue University Indianapolis Library, Ruth Lilly Special Collections and Archives; Marshall University Libraries, Special Collections Department; New York Public Library, Schomburg Center for Research in Black Culture, Manuscripts, Archives and Rare Books Division; University of Louisville Libraries, Archives and Special Collections Department; University of North Carolina at Chapel Hill Libraries, Wilson Special Collections Library; and University of South Carolina Law Library.

I appreciate Cary Brege, Julie Dews, Jerry Markatos, Sayaka Matsuoka/ *Triad City Beat*, Lena Mattson, the *Texas Observer*, and Jim Warren/NC WARN for their permission to use photographs; and Olimatta Taal for assistance in identifying individuals in photographs from Selma, Alabama.

Finally, my gratitude goes to Dr. Ehren Foley and the University of South Carolina Press for believing in me and the positive impacts of sharing Lewis's life story.

Source Notes

Incorporated into each chapter is information from newspapers, court cases, and interviews and correspondence with more than a hundred individuals, including Lewis and his family members, friends, clients, coworkers, cocounsels, and comrades. Case-related records that I used included complaints, replies, answers, affidavits, indictments, memoranda, exhibits, motions, briefs, docket sheets, transcripts, orders, and opinions.

Chapter 1–3

For Lewis's time living in South Carolina—including his childhood in Clinton and Bethune, education at Wofford College and the University of South Carolina School of Law, and work at the Richland County Public Defender's Office and The Law Offices of Warren and Pitts—I relied heavily on family histories, obituaries, and Lewis's personal records and possessions. I consulted sources such as his birth certificate, yearbooks, report cards, academic transcripts, military records, state bar records, letters, and diary. I interviewed Lewis' siblings, childhood friends, college and law school classmates, and coworkers. Bob Warren shared useful records and entertaining stories.

Court opinions provided additional details about some of Lewis's cases during the first six years of his legal career—e.g., *State v. Callahan*, 263 S.C. 35, 208 S.E.2d 284 (1974); *State v. Thomas*, 264 S.C. 159, 213 S.E.2d 452 (1975); *State v. Worley*, 265 S.C. 551, 220 S.E.2d 242 (1975); *State v. Lee*, 269 S.C. 421, 237 S.E.2d 768 (1977); *State v. Parker*, 271 S.C. 159, 245 S.E.2d 904 (1978); *State v. Goodson*, 273 S.C. 264, 255 S.E.2d 679 (1979); *State v. Warren*, 273 S.C. 159, 255 S.E.2d 668 (1979); *State v. Newton*, 274 S.C. 287, 262 S.E.2d 906 (1980); and *Simkins v. Gressette*, 631 F.2d 287 (4th Cir. 1980).

Chapter 4

Interviews were especially useful for learning about Lewis's time in the antinuclear movement. Conversations with his fellow activists—including Mavis Belisle, Brett Bursey, Jim Garrison, Jerry Palmer, Jim Primdahl, Jim Schermbeck, and others—were informative and delightful.

Christic Institute records and Daniel Sheehan's autobiography, *The People's Advocate: The Life and Legal History of America's Most Fearless Public Interest Lawyer*

(Berkeley, CA: Counterpoint, 2013), provided insights about Lewis's work on the Karen Silkwood campaign in Oklahoma.

Carrie Barefoot Dickerson's book, *Aunt Carrie's War Against Black Fox Nuclear Power Plant* (Tulsa, OK: Council Oak Books, 1995), was a helpful source, especially for learning more about the Sunbelt Alliance's advocacy and the relationships among the various antinuclear organizations in the area.

The Texas Legacy Project, an oral history archive about efforts to protect the natural resources and public health of Texas, and the *Texas Observer*, a progressive nonprofit news outlet and print magazine, were key sources of information about opposition to the Comanche Peak Nuclear Power Plant. So was a book that Jerry Palmer wrote, *Buttons, Bolt Cutters & Barricades: Texas Anti-Nuke Actions* (Rock Hill, MS: Gerald Palmer, 2022).

Chapters 5–12

In researching Lewis's other work from 1982 to 1994, I made extensive use of Christic Institute South and Southern Justice Institute records, including correspondence, brochures, flyers, fact sheets, booklets, newsletters, bylaws, articles of incorporation, resolutions, meeting notes, memoranda, petitions, press releases, speeches, budgets, and funding proposals. More than fourteen thousand items from the organizations are in the Southern Historical Collection at the Louis Round Wilson Library at the University of North Carolina at Chapel Hill.

I also utilized records from the John Taylor Collection in the Special Collections Department at Marshall University Libraries; the Anne McCarty Braden Papers in the Archives and Special Collections Department at the University of Louisville Libraries; the Haywood Burns Papers in the Schomburg Center for Research in Black Culture, Manuscripts, Archives and Rare Books Division at the New York Public Library; and the John Hope Franklin Papers in the David M. Rubenstein Rare Book and Manuscript Library at Duke University. Lewis cocounseled with Taylor on Fred Carter's case in West Virginia, and Braden, Burns, and Franklin were CIS/SJI board members. Additionally, I used other organizations' records, including Black Workers for Justice, the Daufuskie Island Historical Foundation, the Gulf Coast Tenant Leadership Development Project, Keysville Concerned Citizens, the Rural Justice Center, and the Southern Organizing Committee for Economic and Social Justice. *Southern Exposure*, a print journal published by the Institute for Southern Studies from 1973 until 2011, was another key source. Lewis's former CIS/SJI colleagues—Ashaki Binta, Czerny Brasuell, Alan Gregory, and Mia Prior (formerly Kirsh)—were hugely helpful sources.

Numerous books have been written about the Greensboro Massacre. Two of the most useful for this book were written by survivors Sally Bermanzohn (*Through a Survivors' Eyes: From the Sixties to the Greensboro Massacre*, Nashville, TN: Vanderbilt

University Press, 2003) and Signe Waller (*Love and Revolution: A Political Memoir*, Lanham, MD: Rowman & Littlefield, 2002). Extensive information about the Greensboro Massacre is available in the Greensboro Massacre Collection at the University of North Carolina at Greensboro University Libraries, and in the Greensboro Civil Rights Fund Records in the Southern Historical Collection at the Louis Round Wilson Library at the University of North Carolina at Chapel Hill. William H. Chafe's *Civilities and Civil Rights: Greensboro, North Carolina and the Black Struggle for Freedom* (Oxford, UK: Oxford University Press, 1980) provides important historical context for the massacre. The Greensboro Truth and Reconciliation Commission's final report (May 2006) was especially useful.

Christic Institute records and Sheehan's autobiography also provided details about Lewis's work on the National Campaign to Free Mayor Eddie James Carthan and the Tchula Seven and to Preserve Black Political Rights in Mississippi. Professor Minion K. C. Morrison's scholarship provided useful information related to Lewis's work in Mississippi—e.g., "Federal Aid and Afro-American Political Power in Three Mississippi Towns." *Publius* 17, no. 4 (Autumn 1987): 97–111; and "Intragroup Conflict in African-American Leadership: The Case of Tchula, Mississippi." *Comparative Studies in Society and History* 32, no. 4 (October 1990): 701–17. *Beyond Boundaries: The Manning Marable Reader* (Boulder, CO: Paradigm, 2011) by Manning Marable includes an illuminating chapter titled, "The Tchula 7: Harvest of Hate in the Mississippi Delta." Lewis worked with Marable on Carthan's case. John Kincaid's article "Beyond the Voting Rights Act: White Responses to Black Political Power in Tchula, Mississippi" (*Publius* 16, no. 4 [Autumn 1986]: 155–72) was also instructive.

For Lewis's work on the Greene County Five campaign in Alabama, *Rumor, Repression, and Racial Politics: How the Harassment of Black Elected Officials Shaped Post-Civil Rights America* (Athens: University of Georgia Press, 2012) by George Derek Musgrove was a useful resource, as was *Black in Selma: The Uncommon Life of J.L. Chestnut, Jr.* (New York: Farrar, Straus and Giroux, 1999) by J. L. Chestnut and Julia Cass. John England, Kim West, Carlos Williams, and other lawyers who worked on the campaign helped me fill the gaps.

In the movement to reestablish local government in Keysville, Georgia, Lewis worked closely with Laughlin McDonald, former director of the ACLU's Voting Rights Project. McDonald later authored *A Voting Rights Odyssey: Black Enfranchisement in Georgia* (Cambridge, UK: Cambridge University Press, 2003) and coauthored, with Daniel Levitas, "Voting Rights Litigation, 1982-2006: A Report of the Voting Rights Project of the American Civil Liberties Union" (March 2006), both of which benefited this book. Binny Miller's article, "Who Shall Rule and Govern? Local Legislative Delegations, Racial Politics, and the Voting Rights Act" (*Yale Law Journal* 102, no. 1 [October 1992]: 105–203), includes helpful information about the "compelling tale of racial strife" in Keysville. Two documentaries about Keysville, both of which were produced in 1989 and included Lewis, were tremendously valuable: "Justice for

Keysville, Now," a video produced by CIS, in tandem with Keysville Concerned Citizens and Sally Alvarez, a union organizer and communications specialist; and "Keysville, Georgia: Old Dreams in the New South," an audio recording produced by Long Haul Productions for public radio.

Liberalism, Black Power, and the Making of American Politics, 1965–1980 (Athens: University of Georgia Press, 2009) by Devin Fergus provided context for Lewis's work with Lee Faye Mack, Larry Little, and other Black Panthers in Winston-Salem, North Carolina. FBI files on the North Carolina Black Panther Party demonstrate the scrutiny they were under by law enforcement.

Media coverage, Christic Institute records, and Sheehan's autobiography were valuable in writing about Lewis's work to expose the Iran-Contra Affair and those behind a bombing in Nicaragua. Congressional records and books, such as *Iran Contra-Connection: Secret Teams and Covert Operations in the Reagan Era* (Montreal, Quebec: Black Rose Books, 1987) by Jonathan Marshall, Peter Dale Scott, and Jane Hunter, and *Cocaine Politics: Drugs, Armies, and the CIA in Central America* (Berkeley: University of California Press, updated 1998) by Peter Dale Scott and Jonathan Marshall, were also enlightening.

Mab Segrest's *Memoir of a Race Traitor* (Boston, MA: South End Press, 1994) includes a chapter titled, "Robeson, Bloody Robeson," which provided useful details about how Lewis became involved in the Robeson Defense Committee. *The Lumbee Indians: An American Struggle* (Chapel Hill: University of North Carolina Press, 2018) by Malinda Maynor Lowery tells the history of the Lumbee Tribe of North Carolina and includes a section about corruption in Robeson County and the hostage taking by Hatcher and Jacobs. The Southern Oral History Project Collection at the Louis Round Wilson Special Collections Library at the University of North Carolina at Chapel Hill has recorded interviews about Robeson County with Lewis, his client, Timothy Jacobs, and one of his cocounsels, Barry Nakell.

Interviews with Lewis's former clients were not only informative but also a privilege for me. Among those with whom I spoke or corresponded were Pat Bryant, Eddie Carthan, Emma Gresham, Timothy Jacobs, Nelson Johnson, Marty Nathan, Signe Waller, and Yvonne Wilson.

Chapter 13

In exploring Lewis's time advocating for children's rights, I relied on interviews and correspondence, newspapers and magazines, briefs and court opinions, organizational records (including from the National Committee for the Rights of the Child and its Legal Action Project), journal articles, and books.

The cases included *In re A.C.*, 415 N.W.2d 609 (Iowa 1987); *In re Clausen*, 502 N.W.2d 649 (Mich. 1993); *Kingsley v. Kingsley*, 623 So. 2d 780 (Fla. Dist. Ct. App.

1993); *Grissom v. Grissom*, 886 S.W.2d 47 (Mo. Ct. App. 1994); *In re J.J.B.*, 894 P.2d 994 (N.M. 1995); and *Petrosky v. Keene*, 898 S.W.2d 726 (Tenn. 1995).

Some of the publications were authored by Lewis, including: "A State Court Remedy for the Keffeler Problem: A Call to Action." *Clearinghouse REVIEW Journal of Poverty Law and Policy* 42, nos. 1–2 (May–June 2008): 81–85; "Fighting for Children's Rights: Lessons from the Civil Rights Movement." *University of Florida Journal of Law and Public Policy* 16, no. 2 (2005): 337–60; "The Bar's Ethical Responsibility to Children." *Children's Rights* 5, no. 2 (Spring 2003): 1–3; "The Right to Be Heard: The Child as a Legal Person." In *Children as Equals: Exploring the Rights of the Child.* Alaimo, Kathleen, and Brian Klung eds., 165–81. Lanham, MD: University Press of America, 2002; "Beyond Rhetoric to Due Process Protective Rights for Children: A Civil Rights Approach is Imperative." In Robinson, Marcia Lowry, ed. *Perspectives in Child Advocacy Law in the Early 21st Century*, 31–51. Chicago, IL: American Bar Association Fund for Justice and Education, June 2000; and "Samantha Frazer—A Child Trailblazer." *ABA Child Law Practice* 17, no. 6 (August 1998): 89–90.

Among other helpful publications were Reardon, Kathleen K., and Christopher T. Noblet. *Childhood Denied: Ending the Nightmare of Child Abuse and Neglect* (SAFE, 2009); Woodhouse, Barbara Bennett. *Hidden in Plain Sight: The Tragedy of Children's Rights from Ben Franklin to Lionel Tate.* Princeton, NJ: Princeton University Press, 2008; Woodhouse, Barbara B., and Sarah R. Katz. "Martyrs, the Media and the Web: Examining a Grassroots Children's Rights Movement Through the Lens of Social Movement History." *Whittier Journal of Child and Family Advocacy* 5, no. 1 (Fall 2005): 121–63; Scarnecchia, Suellyn. "Imagining Children's Rights." *Thomas M. Cooley Law Review* 12, no. 1 (1995): 1–20; Jost, Kenneth. "Children's Legal Rights: Should the Legal Rights of Children Be Expanded?" *CQ Researcher* 3, no. 15 (April 23, 1993): 337–60.

Chapter 14

Law review articles were essential to understanding the increased use of Rule 11 to attack civil rights lawyers like Lewis—e.g., Tobias, Carl. "Civil Rights Conundrum." *Georgia Law Review* 26, no. 4 (Summer 1992): 901–58; Cochran, George. "The Reality of a Last Victim and Abuse of the Sanctioning Power." *Loyola Los Angeles Law Review* 37, no. 3 (2004): 691–726; and Hart, Danielle Kie. "Still Chilling after All These Years: Federal Rule of Civil Procedure 11 and its Impact on Federal Civil Rights Plaintiffs after the 1993 Amendments." *Valparaiso University Law Review* 37, no. 1 (2002): 1–160.

I obtained much of the information about Lewis's fight to be admitted to, and then to resign from, the North Carolina State Bar from his state bar records and his "Character and Fitness" hearing attorney, Harry Harkins Jr. Those state bar records include applications, notices, subpoenas, letters, affidavits, stipulations, reports, and orders.

Chapter 15

The Encyclopedia of North Carolina (Chapel Hill: University of North Carolina Press, 2006), edited by William S. Powell, covers a wide variety of topics, including a history of psychiatric hospitals in the state.

I learned a lot about the history of legal aid in the US from the Center for Law and Social Policy's report, "Securing Equal Justice for All: A Brief History of Civil Legal Assistance in the United States" (Alan W. Houseman and Linda E. Perle, January 2007).

Susan Epstein, Lewis's colleague in the Mental Health Unit, was a valuable resource.

As Lewis's coworker at Advocates for Children's Services from 2009 to 2014, I witnessed firsthand some of his work that's described in this book.

Chapters 16–17

I relied heavily on interviews with Lewis's family, former coworkers at Legal Aid of North Carolina, and campaign comrades, including John Bonifaz, Brett Bursey, Janice Mink, Jim Warren, and Nelson Johnson.

The ACLU's report, "Freedom Under Fire: Dissent in Post-9/11 America" (2003), and accompanying fact sheet (2003) are essential resources for understanding attacks on First Amendment rights during the George W. Bush administration. The White House's *Presidential Advance Manual* (October 2002) demonstrates how the attacks were coordinated and targeted.

An archive of public hearing statements and other resources are available on the Greensboro Truth and Community Reconciliation Commission website (https:// greensborotrc.org). More information about the commission and its significance can be found in *Democracy, Dialogue, and Community Action: Truth and Reconciliation in Greensboro* (Fayetteville: University of Arkansas Press, 2012) by Spoma Jovanovic, Lewis's wife.

Further Reading

Books

Kinoy, Arthur. *Rights on Trial: The Odyssey of a People's Lawyer.* Larchmont, NY: Bernel Books, 1993.

Lopez, Gerald P. *Rebellious Lawyering: One Chicano's Vision of Progressive Law Practice.* Boulder, CO: Westview, 1992.

Sarat, Austin, and Stuart A. Sheingold, eds. *Cause Lawyering and Social Movements.* Redwood City, CA: Stanford University Press, 2006.

Journal Articles

Alexander, Amanda. "Nurturing Freedom Dreams: An Approach to Movement Lawyering in the Black Lives Matter Era." *Howard Human and Civil Rights Law Review* 5, no. 2 (2020–2021): 101–39.

Ancheta, Angelo. "Community Lawyering." *Community Law Review* 81, no. 5 (October 1993): 1363–99.

Ashar, Sameer M. "Movement Lawyers in the Fight for Immigrant Rights." *UCLA Law Review* 64, no. 6 (December 2017): 1464–1507.

Cummings, Scott L. "Movement Lawyering." *University of Illinois Law Review* 2017, no. 5 (2017): 1645–1732.

Cummings, Scott L. "Rethinking the Foundational Critiques of Lawyers in Social Movements." *Fordham Law Review* 85, no. 5 (2017): 1987–2015.

Cummings, Scott L., and Ingrid V. Eagly. "A Critical Reflection on Law and Organizing." *UCLA Law Review* 48, no. 3 (2001): 443–517.

Elsesser, Charles. "Community Lawyering—The Role of Lawyers in the Social Justice Movement." *Loyola Journal of Public Interest Law* 14, no. 2 (Spring 2013): 45–74.

Freeman, Alexi, and Jim Freeman. "It's about Power, Not Policy: Movement Lawyering for Large-Scale Social Change." *Clinical Law Review* 23, no. 1 (Fall 2016): 147–66.

Freeman, Jim. "Supporting Social Movements: A Brief Guide for Lawyers and Law Students." *Hastings Race and Poverty Law Journal* 12, no. 2 (Summer 2015): 191–204.

Gordon, Jennifer. "The Lawyer Is Not the Protagonist: Community Campaigns, Law, and Social Change." *California Law Review* 95, no. 5 (2007): 2133–46.

Hing, Bill Ong. "Coolies, James Yen, and Rebellious Advocacy." UC Davis Legal Studies Research Paper No. 107. *Asian American Law Journal* 14, no. 1 (2007): 1–44.

Hung, Betty. "Essay—Law and Organizing from the Perspective of Organizers: Finding a Shared Theory of Social Change." *Los Angeles Public Interest Law Journal* 1, no. 1 (Spring 2009): 4–30.

Hung, Betty. "Movement Lawyering as Rebellious Lawyering: Advocating with Humility, Love and Courage." *Clinical Law Review* 23, no. 2 (Spring 2017): 663–69.

Kim, E. Tammy. "Lawyers as Resource Allies in Workers' Struggles for Social Change." *City University of New York Law Review* 13, no. 1 (Winter 2009): 213–32.

Lobel, Jules. "Courts as Forums for Protest." *UCLA Law Review* 52, no. 2 (December 2004): 477–562.

Marshall, Shauna. "Mission Impossible? Ethical Community Lawyering." *Clinical Law Review* 7, no. 1 (Fall 2000): 147–226.

Narro, Victor. "Finding the Synergy between Law and Organizing: Experiences from the Streets of Los Angeles." *Fordham Urban Law Journal* 35, no. 2 (2008): 339–72.

Pow, Veryl. "Grassroots Movement Lawyering: Insights from the George Floyd Rebellion." *U.C.L.A. Law Review* 69, no. 1 (2022): 80–163.

Piomelli, Ascanio. "The Democratic Roots of Collaborative Lawyering." *Clinical Law Review* 12, no. 2 (2006): 541–614.

Quigley, William P. "Letter to a Law Student Interested in Social Justice." *DePaul Journal for Social Justice* 1, no. 1 (Fall 2007): 7–28.

Quigley, William P. "Reflections of Community Organizers: Lawyering for Empowerment of Community Organizations." *Ohio Northern University Law Review* 21, no. 2 (1994): 455–79.

Quigley, William P. "Revolutionary Lawyering: Addressing the Root Causes of Poverty and Wealth." *Washington University Journal of Law and Policy* 20 (2006): 101–66.

Quigley, William P. "Ten Questions for Social Change Lawyers." *Public Interest Law Reporter* 17, no. 3 (Summer 2012): 204–11.

Quigley, William P. "Ten Ways of Looking at Movement Lawyering." *Howard Human and Civil Rights Law Review* 5, no. 1 (2020): 23–43.

Ressl-Moyer, Tifanei, Pilar Gonzalez Morales, and Jaqueline Aranda Osorno. "Movement Lawyering During a Crisis: How the Legal System Exploits the Labor of Activists and Undermines Movements." *City University of New York Law Review* 24, no. 1 (Winter 2021): 91–121.

Shah, Purvi. "Movement Lawyering Reading Guide." *Hofstra Law Review* 47, no. 1 (2018): 99–116.

Shahshahani, Azadeh. "Movement Lawyering: A Case Study in the U.S. South." *Howard Human and Civil Rights Law Review* 5, no. 1 (Fall 2020): 45–54.

White, Lucie E. "Mobilization on the Margins of the Lawsuit: Making Space for Clients to Speak." *NYU Review of Law and Social Change* 16, no. 4 (1987–1988): 535–64.

White, Lucie E. "To Learn and Teach: Lessons from Driefontein on Lawyering and Power." *Wisconsin Law Review* 1988, no. 5 (1988): 699–770.

Organizations

Advancement Project, https://advancementproject.org.

Community Justice Project, http://communityjusticeproject.com/.

Law for Black Lives, http://www.law4blacklives.org/.

Movement Law Lab, https://movementlawlab.org/.

Index

Page numbers in *italics* refer to photographs.